LOUISA S. McCORD

Selected Writings

THE PUBLICATIONS OF THE
SOUTHERN TEXTS SOCIETY

Michael O'Brien, Editor

LOUISA S. McCORD

Selected Writings

EDITED BY RICHARD C. LOUNSBURY

University Press of Virginia
Charlottesville and London

Publication of this book has been supported by grants from the Women's Research Institute, the College of Humanities, and the Department of Humanities, Classics, and Comparative Literature, Brigham Young University.

THE UNIVERSITY PRESS OF VIRGINIA
© 1997 by the Southern Texts Society
All rights reserved

First published 1997

∞The paper used in this publication meets the minimum requirements of the American National Standard for Information Sciences—Permanence of Paper for Printed Library Materials, ANSI Z39.48-1984.

Library of Congress Cataloging-in-Publication Data
McCord, Louisa Susanna Cheves, 1810–1879.
  [Selections. 1997]
  Louisa S. McCord : selected writings / edited by Richard C. Lounsbury.
      p.   cm. — (The publications of the Southern Texts Society)
  Includes bibliographical references and index.
  ISBN 0-8139-1760-3 (alk. paper)
  1. McCord, Louisa Susanna Cheves, 1810–1879—Correspondence.
2. Women authors, American—19th century—Correspondence.
3. Gracchus, Gaius Sempronius, 154–121 B.C.—Drama. 4. Rome—History—Servile Wars, 135–71 B.C.—Drama. 5. Women—Southern States—Correspondence. 6. Women—Southern States—Poetry.
7. Slavery—Southern States. I. Lounsbury, Richard Cecil.
II. Title. III. Series.
PS2355.M6A6   1997
818'.309—dc21   97-8829
                                                                                  CIP

Contents

List of Illustrations	vi
Abbreviations	vii
Introduction	1
Chronology	16

Part I

1. The Right to Labor	21
2. Separate Secession	28
3. Negro-mania	47
4. Woman and Her Needs	52
5. *Uncle Tom's Cabin*	83
6. A Letter to the Duchess of Sutherland from a Lady of South Carolina	119
7. Slavery and Political Economy	130
8. The Burning of Columbia	149

Part II

9. Poems	165
10. *Caius Gracchus*	181

Part III

11. Letters	255
Bibliography	297
Index	299

Illustrations

Following page 153

Louisa Susanna McCord

Langdon Cheves, by Clark Mills

Mary Elizabeth Dulles, by Edward Greene Malbone

David James McCord

Langdon Cheves McCord

Louisa Rebecca Hayne McCord, Charlotte Reynolds, Hannah Cheves McCord, Elizabeth Horner Dulles

Louisa Susanna McCord to Langdon Cheves, Jr., March 5 [1856]

Indian Rock, Narragansett, by William Stanley Haseltine

The British and North American Royal Mail Steamship *Persia*

The McCord House in Columbia

Gravestone of Louisa Susanna McCord

Louisa Susanna McCord, by Hiram Powers

Abbreviations

Chesnut	C. Vann Woodward, ed., *Mary Chesnut's Civil War* (New Haven, 1981)
De Bow	*De Bow's Review*
LSM	Louisa Susanna McCord
PDBL	Richard C. Lounsbury, ed., *Louisa S. McCord: Poems, Drama, Biography, Letters* (Charlottesville, Va., 1996)
PSE	Richard C. Lounsbury, ed., *Louisa S. McCord: Political and Social Essays* (Charlottesville, Va., 1995)
SCHS	South Carolina Historical Society, Charleston
SHC	Southern Historical Collection, University of North Carolina, Chapel Hill
Smythe	Louisa McCord Smythe, "Recollections of Louisa Rebecca Hayne McCord (Mrs. Augustine T. Smythe)" (typescript), South Caroliniana Library, University of South Carolina, Columbia
SQR	*Southern Quarterly Review*

LOUISA S. McCORD

Selected Writings

Introduction

Soon to be invited to lob the first shot at Fort Sumter, Edmund Ruffin chose to be in Columbia in the days after Abraham Lincoln's election to the presidency on November 6, 1860. Unlike Ruffin's own state of Virginia, South Carolina had threatened immediate secession should Lincoln be elected; November 10 saw a bill introduced in the legislature calling for a convention to meditate separation from the Union. On November 12, the day scheduled for final reading of the bill, Ruffin "visited Mrs. McCord, the widow of Col. David McCord, and the daughter of Langdon Cheves. To her and to her husband, at their residence and elsewhere, and also to her distinguished father, I had been indebted for much kind attention. It was but by accident, and lately, that I learned that Mrs. McCord resides here. She is a lady of fine mind and manners, and of no small note as an author. She received me with much cordiality and apparent gratification. Her carriage was ready to convey her to the State House, to hear the debates, in which I accompanied her, with her daughter and another young lady." Wife of an important man, daughter of an eminent man, as Ruffin observed, Mrs. McCord was also—what he did not say—a secessionist as fiery as himself. "Of no small note as an author," Louisa S. McCord was, moreover, as a contemporary reviewer had said of her most ambitious work, "a brilliant anomaly in our literature."[1]

Her grandfather Alexander Cheves had emigrated from Scotland to Charleston in 1762. He traded in the Carolina backcountry as an agent of Charleston merchants, until by 1772 he had the means to buy a farm near Long Canes and in 1774 to wed Mary Langdon, daughter of a neighboring farmer and physician. Their only child, Langdon Cheves, was born September 17, 1776. After his mother's death three years later, Langdon was placed in the care of a Cheves aunt. When the British captured Charleston in May 1780 and established control over the state, Alexander Cheves enrolled in the local Loyalist militia; but soon Revolutionary victories compelled

---

1. Ruffin, "Diary," entry of Nov. 12, 1860, Library of Congress; "Mrs. M'Cord's Caius Gracchus," *De Bow*, n.s., 1 (Oct. 1852): 427–29; 428.

Cheves, with other Loyalists, to flee to British-held territory on the coast, thence to Nova Scotia and to England, where in September 1784 he appealed unsuccessfully to a commission set up to hear Loyalist claims for recompense of losses suffered in the war. Cheves returned to South Carolina and collected his son.

Langdon Cheves was a remarkable man. He did not get on with the stepmother whom his father had brought back from Scotland and very soon became independent. Although apparently with few resources, he had the golden touch: everything prospered to which he turned his hand, whether law, politics, or rice and cotton planting. In 1806 he married accordingly. Mary Elizabeth Dulles (born May 27, 1789) was the daughter of a wealthy merchant in Charleston; her mother was a daughter of a planter with extensive holdings in St. Matthews Parish, about fifty miles north of Charleston. When Louisa was born on December 3, 1810, Langdon Cheves was a successful lawyer, former attorney general of South Carolina, and lately elected to the United States Congress. The family spent the next years in Washington, joining the refugees when the British attacked and burned the city, and in South Carolina, where Cheves was appointed to the state bench in 1816. In 1819, having been made president of the Bank of the United States by President James Monroe, Cheves moved his family to Philadelphia, where Louisa and her elder sister Sophia attended school and studied French with an émigré from France, and where Northern hostility toward slavery, as Louisa later recorded in a rare bit of autobiography, proved to be "one of our earliest trials in life."[2]

The Cheves family returned to South Carolina in December 1829. Langdon Cheves took up rice and cotton planting. Sophia was married in 1830, and because Mary Cheves was weakened by her numerous pregnancies Louisa assumed much of the responsibility of running the Cheves household. From family correspondence we catch glimpses of her at this time, instructing her younger brother Charles and younger sister Anna in English, French, writing, and arithmetic, earning her mother's praise by making clothes for the domestic staff, having charge of the illness of a servant whose mother had just died. "L[ouisa] is," her grandmother observed, "an uncommon Girl[;] I dont know how the [family] would make out without her." In 1835 Louisa joined friends for a summer tour to New York City, Newport, and Ballston Spa, near Saratoga Springs. A purpose of the journey may have been marriage. If so, no suitor seems to have presented himself; and the following spring Mary Cheves planned a second trip north, with "Louisa as my companion," to seek medical advice for herself in Philadelphia but also

---

2. Chap. 5, "*Uncle Tom's Cabin*," pp. 87–88.

to visit "the Falls, the Lakes, Canadas, etc. etc. . . . and thus dispose of the summer as much to [Louisa's] gratification as possible, for she did not reap much last summer."[3] The plans were cut short when Mary Cheves died on April 5, 1836. Louisa now found herself in sole charge of the household's management and of the younger Cheves children.

In 1834 Langdon Cheves had inherited large properties from an aunt of his wife, among them the plantation Home Place in Orangeburg County near Fort Motte, about thirty-five miles south of Columbia. Cheves renamed this plantation Lang Syne, intending it for his eventual retirement. It was at Lang Syne that his wife died and, on May 20, 1840, that Louisa Cheves was married to David James McCord. Recently a widower, his wife having died the previous August, McCord (born January 13, 1797), a former newspaper editor and member of the state legislature, was a lawyer and president of the Bank of the State of South Carolina in Columbia. In December his eldest daughter, Charlotte, had been married to Louisa Cheves' younger brother Langdon. Anna Cheves, hopeful of another great occasion at which to meet beaux, was disappointed. "As I suppose like most other people you are anxious to hear all about a wedding," she wrote to a cousin, "I must exert my powers of description to acquaint you with all the proceedings of Sister's wedding; but I fear, if I endeavour to do so, I will be obliged to put into play those of imagination also, for as to the bare facts, it would be a difficult matter to find many of those, for the scene was not near as animated a one as at Charlotte's wedding. It was about as quiet an affair as could well take place. . . . We thought of getting up a picnic or something of the kind, but our plans here were also frustrated, for Mr. McCord was obliged to return to Columbia the day after he was married on business."[4]

In 1841 Louisa McCord received Lang Syne from her father. Visitors recorded their impressions. Edmund Ruffin stopped at Lang Syne in May 1843 while conducting an agricultural survey of South Carolina. David James McCord, whom Ruffin had met in Charleston and found to be "an intelligent and agreeable companion," escorted his guest about the nearby plantations and delighted him with his collection of fossil shells. "Among the most beautiful and delicate" of all the shells that Ruffin saw during his survey were two specimens, each of a hitherto unknown species, which Mrs. McCord "found and presented to me." Ruffin named one of these *Cytherea maccordia* in her honor. In November 1845 Edward Dagge Worthington, a young physician

---

3. Sophia Dulles to Joseph Heatly Dulles, June 21, 1834, and Mary Cheves to her son Alexander Cheves, Feb. 26, 1836, Langdon Cheves I Papers, SCHS.

4. Anna Cheves to Anna Dulles, May 24, 1840, Dulles-Cheves-McCord-Lovell Papers, SCHS.

from Quebec traveling for his health, came to Lang Syne and stayed for two months. When pneumonia broke out he accompanied Mrs. McCord during her regular morning inspections of the slaves' quarters. "Then she would take me off for a gallop through the open to some high point commanding a view of the country. . . . She was a tall *queenly* woman, and a very queen at heart; motherly and kind. She treated me as though I were an over grown boy." Sally Baxter of Boston and New York, visiting Lang Syne in April 1855, regretted in a letter home that "write as I may I can never say all I would to furnish you with an idea of the beauty of this place. . . . This Plantation is considered rather a model place even in South Carolina where there are so many fine ones."[5]

In October 1850 James Burrill Angell, later president of the University of Michigan but now recently graduated from Brown University in Providence, set out with a friend on a tour of the Southern states. Angell had probably met the McCords, vacationing at Narragansett Bay, that summer. The travelers were entertained to tea by Mrs. McCord in Columbia, who, although "extremely cordial," told her young guests, "We ought to fight you of the North." They then spent the Christmas holidays at Lang Syne. Angell recalled its meticulous management, elegant mansion, and splendid grounds, the hospitality and "dinner parties and hunting parties on the plantations in the neighbourhood." All was not merriment. "Our visit corrected our impression that the life of the planter and his wife was one free from care." Although he believed that they had more leisure than Northern farmers enjoyed, Angell was made aware that profits depended on alert supervision. "Our hostess, during our visit, was up all night caring for a sick negro baby. . . . She had given much attention to the economics of plantation life. She told us that she would prefer to have $25,000 in good bank stock rather than $100,000 in negroes and plantations."[6] Lang Syne was no pastoral haven. It was a business and her livelihood.

Its library provided a respite, though a respite no less industrious than the management of her estate. Commending Louisa McCord's review of *Uncle Tom's Cabin,* Sally Baxter explained: "The Chives and McCord family is as much the stronghold of the slavery party as the Adams faction is of the Aboli-

---

5. William M. Mathew, ed., *Agriculture, Geology, and Society in Antebellum South Carolina: The Private Diary of Edmund Ruffin, 1843* (Athens, Ga., 1992), p. 82 (entry of Feb. 11, 1843), and Ruffin, *Report of the Commencement and Progress of the Agricultural Survey of South Carolina, for 1843* (Columbia, S.C., 1843), pp. 44, 47; Worthington to David Ross McCord, 1894, in Smythe, *For Old Lang Syne,* pp. 4–5; Sally Baxter to George Baxter, April 15, 1855, in A. F. Hampton, ed., *A Divided Heart: Letters of Sally Baxter Hampton, 1853–1862* (Spartanburg, S.C., 1980), p. 21.

6. *The Reminiscences of James Burrill Angell* (New York, 1912), pp. 56, 58–61.

tionists. Mrs. McCord is hotly engaged in the strife and almost all her feeling and intellect seem to be expended on that one topic, and she and her husband warmly espouse the cause in every paper and periodical to which they can get admission."[7] Much of this work, and much other literary work, was done in the library at Lang Syne. There was also the academic life in Columbia, where in 1849 the McCords built a house across the street from South Carolina College, of which David James McCord had served three four-year terms as a trustee (1829–40). But the McCords were often restless in Columbia as at Lang Syne. It was worst in the summers. The heat was oppressive (and did not suit her son's uncertain health), the campus nearly deserted, the town emptied of most of its society. "I am glad to hear," she wrote to her cousin Mary Dulles, "that you are all enjoying yourselves so well at Nar[r]agansett. What would I not give for a walk on the beach . . . with my brats tumbling along before me[?] I am almost sick of this horrid little place Columbia. I hope that Mr. McC. will get his fill of it some day. For surely I cannot see where the society he dreams of is. For myself, I do not care a fig for the society, but I long for a climate where a family can keep healthy and grow strong." Her husband "certainly does not look well, but I cannot see what is the matter with him. I verily believe he is just sick, for want of company and a little excitement of some kind or another. He will have it that this is a charming place; but apparently it is charming for me to stay in, and for him to go away."[8] Vacations were therefore welcome, such as that to the spas in Virginia in 1851. But these were unsettled, too—by politics.

At White Sulphur Springs the author of *Swallow Barn*, John Pendleton Kennedy, reported encountering "several South Carolinians . . . ridiculously distempered with nullification and Disunion." David James McCord, predicting civil war, "is the most moderate of them—though I am told his wife, who has lately written a tragedy called 'Gracchus,' is not." At Red Sweet Springs, Louisa McCord met diarist Jane Caroline North. "Mrs. McCord paid us a visit this afternoon. Aunt Harrie did not see her as she was lying down, with a headache—She made me quite a long visit—she is a masculine clever person, with the most mannish attitudes and gestures, but interesting and very entertaining. Mrs. [Langdon] Cheves[, Jr.,] is her step daughter and sister in law—her children are made to call her Aunt, Mrs. McCord not believing in the relationship of half sister—so I was told at least." Carey North elaborated to her sister: "Mrs. McCord has just paid me quite a long visit. . . . She was very pleasant—of course very talkative. What a strong

---

7. Sally Baxter to George Baxter, April 15, 1855, in Hampton, *A Divided Heart*, p. 23.
8. LSM to Mary Cheves Dulles, Aug. 25, 1852, in *PDBL*, pp. 291–92.

masculine person she is! . . . She told me that when 'Mr. [Benjamin Franklin] Perry and others of the submissionists were on one occasion being abused, as all the party are you know, when the person who was speaking mentioned your Uncle Mr. [James Louis] Petigru, he paused, Oh!—Petigru is a fine fellow, a very fine fellow, but—he's queer.' She laughed heartily then and said 'it was all covered with that—he's queer.' Tell Aunt May, I did not give in, but to her question said, 'yes, I was staunch on the same side.'"[9]

Domestic troubles overcast the political separation that Louisa McCord foresaw and desired. On May 15, 1855, David James McCord died. His wife owning Lang Syne in her own right, his will left nothing to her or to his three children by her. There was gossip that Mrs. McCord would contest the will, would rob her stepchildren. In the autumn her brother Charles died suddenly and unexpectedly at the age of thirty, "a sad shock to us all and a fearful blow to my dear old Father," who suffered a stroke upon hearing the news. He was removed from his retirement home in the Sandhills outside Columbia to his daughter's house in the city. It was at once plain that his mind was failing irretrievably. The ordeal of caring for him was made even more grim because Langdon Cheves had been the single most important fact in his daughter's life—her "Idol through childhood and womanhood," as she put it in her memoir of him. "My feelings towards my Father, have through life been almost those of worship, rather than simply of affection."[10] Cheves lingered until June 26, 1857. His death was followed by a quarrel over the legacies left in his will to his youngest son, Robert Hayne Cheves, who had died during his father's senility. There was a lawsuit in 1858, which caused Louisa much distress lest it injure her father's name. Even in 1860 the business had not yet been settled. While she was disposed to acquiesce in whatever settlement of her father's estate her brothers and sisters and brothers-in-law might finally decide upon, yet "as regards negroes I cannot consent to receive any more, for I am almost out of my senses with those that I have, and with my now permanently established defective vision, am entirely unfit for learning anything about planting concerns. Those that I have now, I must keep, only till Cheves is ready (which with *his* drawbacks of vision etc. will

---

9. Kennedy, Journal, 7 (July 14, 1851–June 1, 1852): entry of July 29, 1851, John Pendleton Kennedy Papers, Peabody Institute, Baltimore; North, "Journal of an Excursion to the Virginia Springs, No. 2," entry of Sept. 12, 1851, in Michael O'Brien, ed., *An Evening When Alone: Four Journals of Single Women in the South, 1827–67* (Charlottesville, Va., 1993), p. 174; North to Mary Charlotte North, Sept. 11 and 12, 1851, Pettigrew Family Papers, SHC.

10. LSM to Mary Cheves Dulles, December 1855, in *PDBL*, p. 301; ibid., "Memoir of Langdon Cheves," p. 259; LSM to Langdon Cheves III, April 6, 1876, ibid., p. 397.

not be for years) to take them. To embarrass myself with more would be wretchedness to them and death to me."[11]

Her "now permanently established defective vision" was the outcome of eyestrain that had begun to develop after her husband's death. Visits to resorts in 1856 and 1857 gave no relief. "Her health is not good," her sister Sophia reported to a friend, "and her eyes are so much affected in some way, that she is entirely prohibited the use of them; not even to expose them to a strong light, night or day. It is a great trial, but the danger is so great, that she submits I believe in great measure to these directions." Besides, her son Cheves began to show symptoms of cataract. Finally, in July 1858 she sought medical advice in Europe. "I have nothing that will interest you," she wrote to her brother Langdon, "for I travel as usual with all my shyness and want of knowing how to push, about me. . . . I have been a month in Paris and have not gone into ecstacies with it yet. On the contrary have a stupid longing all the time for my own chimney corner. I am in *apartemens meublés* [on the Champs Elysées] and have my two servants with a carriage and driver which I found myself obliged to hire. I spend money (because I don't know how to manage) until it frightens me, make no acquaintances, get very tired, etc. etc. My eyes, face light better than they did, but I do not think mean ever to let me use them as I wish and have been accustomed to do."[12] This gloomy estimation did not forbid her to accomplish, with her son and daughter Louisa, an enterprising tour in Europe. There was also an item of business: the commission of a bust of her father from the sculptor Hiram Powers. Coming in April 1859 to his studio in Florence, she found that the casts and other materials which her brother Langdon had promised to send before her had not yet been received—had not, as it transpired, been sent at all. Rather than waste the appointment, she sat to Powers herself. The result was pronounced by her daughter Louisa in the 1890s to be the best likeness surviving of Louisa McCord.

Disembarking in New York on October 26, 1859, the McCord family was greeted by news of John Brown's raid on Harpers Ferry, Virginia. Her daughter recalled: "My mother said, 'There goes then this glorious Union.' . . . I remember the shock it gave me and the way my brother looked as he said 'Oh no, don't say that.' . . . She answered him, 'Yes, you will see—this is not the end of it, we will be forced to assert ourselves.'" To the war that followed, Louisa McCord owed much of her immediate fame. Having ar-

---

11. LSM to Langdon Cheves, Jr., Jan. 18, 1860, ibid., p. 353.
12. Sophia Cheves Haskell to Eleuthera Du Pont, March 24, 1857, Langdon Cheves III Papers, SCHS; LSM to Langdon Cheves, Jr., Oct. 30, 1858, in *PDBL*, pp. 346–47.

rived in jubilant Charleston in time for the surrender of Fort Sumter, she dined that evening with the diarist Mary Chesnut. It was fitting that the two saw in the war together. Mrs. Chesnut was there to record the deeds, what many thought the heroic deeds, of her friend. Mrs. McCord expected the conflict to be long. She set promptly to work. She turned over Lang Syne to the cultivation of provisions, outfitted at her own expense a company of Columbia Zouaves under her son's command, managed the hospital established in buildings of South Carolina College and a ward in her own house. She became the first president of the Soldiers' Relief Association (later resigning the office when pressed by nursing duties) and of the Soldiers' Clothing Association in Columbia. She derided profiteers, blockade-runners, fashionable ladies who supposed nursing to be an opportunity for capturing admirers, and the "drill sergeants or military old maids" masquerading as generals of the Confederacy. Such blunt speaking was characteristic of her. "Mrs. Preston and I whisper," said Mary Chesnut. "Mrs. McCord scorns whispers."[13]

Amid a dispute over the naming of a new Confederate gunboat, she impatiently proposed: "Let it be 'she-devil,' for it is the devil's own work it is built to do." The cause, the war, was just; it was not romance. On December 11–12, 1861, from the roof of a kinsman's house in Charleston where she had taken refuge with her daughters when their hotel was threatened, she watched fire destroy much of the center of her birthplace and the birthplace of secession. The omen was manifest. In 1862 a nephew lost an arm to the fighting; the wife of another nephew died in childbirth; the only son of her brother John was killed. On August 29 Cheves McCord was wounded at Second Manassas. His mother brought him home. The serious wounds in his body were mended, and a surgeon removed a bullet from his skull—it seemed a lesser injury—and pronounced him ready for service. His mother was not so sure, tried to persuade him to delay, pointed out that his wife would soon be delivered of their first child. But Cheves felt that he must go, if declared fit to go. Back in Virginia, either during a skirmish or at a dress parade—the family never learned for sure which it was—he collapsed. As his sister recollected many years later, "Mamma was at the hospital—Lottie was with her mother—I was taking a music lesson from little Miss Garnett while Hannah was sitting chatting with Annie Hampton. I remember it all so well and yet I don't remember it for I cannot tell who brought the dispatch. I know that the boy who had it was searching for Mamma over at the hospital and in some way Lottie got it first—then it was brought to us and Mamma

13. Smythe, p. 37; *Chesnut*, p. 361.

got it last of all—it was from Cousin William Miles and said that Cheves was dying. . . . All seemed blackness and confusion after that—the next thing I remember was a carriage at the door and Alex Haskell who had been at home wounded was putting her into the carriage and about to step in after her as he was to go on with her when someone handed her another dispatch. Cheves was dead."[14]

Louisa Smythe wished it to be remembered of her mother "that [her] son's death and the failure of the cause she loved so well ended her life. After that she only waited patiently for the welcome release." In the years immediately after the war Louisa McCord lived intermittently at Lang Syne, which her son-in-law Augustine Smythe was attempting to run at a profit. The attempt failed; the plantation was leased, then sold. South Carolina under Reconstruction had become intolerable to her. "By the sad results of our War, and our crushed out Liberties, now with no settled home, and much a wanderer," after 1870 Louisa McCord chose exile, briefly in Virginia and North Carolina, less impermanently in Canada.[15] But she did not neglect the South that she had relinquished. In 1867 she had made a sworn affidavit to a committee of Columbia citizens investigating the causes of the burning of Columbia. After the Treaty of Washington between Great Britain and the United States appointed an international commission to adjudicate claims for damages incurred during the war, in May 1873 Louisa McCord was in Charleston, where before the British consul she deposed an account of her experiences while the Federal general commanding in Columbia made his headquarters in her house. Her last piety, however, she saved for her father. In 1875 she contracted for an obelisk to adorn the Cheves tomb in Magnolia Cemetery, Charleston. In 1876, at the request of her nephew Langdon Cheves III, she wrote a memoir of her father carried down through his early career as a lawyer and meditated a more ambitious memorial in verse and prose. In 1878, after retiring to Charleston where she made her home with her daughter Louisa and her husband, she resumed the plan for a bust of Langdon Cheves. Hiram Powers had died in 1873, having never completed the commission. This had stipulated a colossal bust, intended to stand as the focus of a funerary monument, and a life-size copy of that bust for herself. Now reduced circumstances compelled her to be content with a life-size bust only, ordered from Hiram's son Preston Powers. The task was complicated, as before, by the want of reliable images to guide the sculptor. "When I sat

---

14. *Chesnut,* p. 329; Smythe, p. 53.

15. Louisa McCord Smythe to William Porcher Miles, Feb. 26, 1880, in *PSE,* p. 484; LSM, "Last Will and Testament," Feb. 12, 1876, in *PDBL,* p. 393.

to your Father, I indulged the faint hope, that he might retain from the family likeness, (which was said to be considerable in me, such as Woman may bear to Man) some far off glimmer of the grand head."[16]

In January 1879 Louisa McCord purchased a house adjacent to the Smythes in Charleston, and by early November she was planning extensive renovations with a contractor. She had been troubled for some months by an ailment diagnosed as "gout in the stomach," which seemed to have left her by late September. It recurred abruptly. After five days of suffering great pain, finally in agony, she died. When the physician had lost hope that she would survive, her daughter had asked her if she was willing to meet death. "Willing, my child? *Glad*—glad to rest."[17] She was buried in Magnolia Cemetery. The Charleston *News and Courier* of November 27 offered an obituary: "Died, at her home in Charleston, S.C., on the 23d day of November, 1879, after a brief illness, in the 69th year of her age, Mrs. Louisa S. McCord, widow of Col. D. J. McCord and daughter of Hon. Langdon Cheves." Of her defense of the South and her service to the Confederacy, and of her writings, there was nothing.

Among the many genres essayed by Louisa S. McCord, her contributions to periodicals were the most frequent and have become the most familiar. These, after the fashion of her time, used recent books and articles as hooks upon which to hang discussion and polemic about political and social issues. For a woman to write for publications like the *Southern Quarterly Review* and *De Bow's Review* was unusual enough; even more unusual was Mrs. McCord's first choice of subject: political economy.[18] The choice may be explained in part by her unconventional education. According to family tradition, as a

---

16. LSM to Preston Powers, April 21, 1878, in *PDBL*, p. 406.
17. Louisa McCord Smythe to Sophia Cheves Haskell, Dec. 4, 1879, in *PSE*, p. 480. See also "Forms of Prayer to Be Used at Sea," *The Book of Common Prayer* (New York, 1992), p. 361 (Ps. 107:23–30): "They that go down to the sea in ships: and occupy their business in great waters; These men see the works of the Lord: and his wonders in the deep. For at his word the stormy wind ariseth: which lifteth up the waves thereof. . . . So when they cry unto the Lord in their trouble: he delivereth them out of their distress. For he maketh the storm to cease: so that the waves thereof are still. Then are they glad, because they are at rest: and so he bringeth them unto the haven where they would be."
18. John Seely Hart in his anthology *The Female Prose Writers of America* (Philadelphia, 1852) observed that Louisa McCord's first essays, "Justice and Fraternity" and "The Right to Labor," "characterized by masculine vigour and an enlarged acquaintance with the subject," were written by "one of the few women who have undertaken to write on the difficult subject of political economy" (p. 187). More generally, Sarah Josepha Hale's *Woman's Record,* 2d ed. (New York, 1855), noted that Louisa McCord "has distinguished herself in what may be styled political literature, a species of writing seldom attempted by woman" (p. 894).

girl about ten years old she had been detected hiding behind a door, taking notes and working problems, while her brothers were being tutored in mathematics in the next room; her father therefore decided that henceforth she should be instructed also in subjects taught more usually to boys. In 1848 she had published *Sophisms of the Protective Policy,* her translation of the *Sophismes économiques* of the French political economist Frédéric Bastiat. But she had dared no more than to translate: the book's foreword was written by her husband and the introduction by family friend Francis Lieber, professor of history and political economy at South Carolina College. By the following year she was more venturesome. Her first periodical contribution, "Justice and Fraternity," translating in large part an article by Bastiat in the *Journal des économistes,* included also commentary of her own; the next, "The Right to Labor," covering several articles by Bastiat and other economists published in the same journal, provided less translation, more her own opinion. For her interest in political economy was not only, or even primarily, theoretical. Rather, in political economy she sought protection from the pernicious nostrums of socialism and communism, already being imported from France into the United States. "They are even beginning to show themselves in our own State, in that South Carolina whose principles, we had fondly persuaded ourselves, were among the most conservative in all the country.... Believe it, the levelling system of socialism gives no equality but that which is found in one general ruin. It is the system of anarchy, disorder, misery, and death—death political, moral, and physical. Our existence as a State, our existence as men, depend equally upon the maintenance of order and unanimity in our councils."[19] The interests of her beleaguered state soon expanded to comprise those of her beleaguered region: published in October 1851, "Separate Secession" adopted her father's premise that South Carolina must find salvation along with the South as a whole; it could not stand alone.

Turning to confront other enemies besides socialism—women's rights advocates, abolitionists, the multifarious apparatus of Northern tyranny— Louisa McCord retained her conviction that order and unanimity must be the aim of all right thinking. Right thinking was what her opponents lacked. They thought badly, they wrote badly. They were all of a piece. It was not merely that slavery and woman's role were at bottom the same subject, that "the positions of women and children are in truth as essentially states of bondage as any other, the differences being in degree, not kind." Behind the fulminations of abolitionists and feminists alike, as she diagnosed them, lurked an intellectual arrogance, a contempt for evidence and argument.

---

19. *PSE,* "Justice and Fraternity," pp. 77–78.

"Documents here—documents there. White, they are; presto, black. True, they are; presto, false. Pretty jugglery! and worthy of all admiration!" From "Mrs. Stowe, Lucretia Mott, Gerritt Smith, and all the other old women, breeched and unbreeched, who go into hysterics of agony over the evils of a system of which they know absolutely and literally nothing," what need or expectation of evidence? "False assertions cannot be argued against. If a man insists, as a fact in his experience, that the rainbow is black, what argument can be advanced to the contrary? We may talk of decomposed light, refracted rays, etc., etc. It does no good; he still swears that he saw it. You may call him fool and liar if it will comfort you, but that is the mere enjoyment of personal luxury, and in no degree advances your argument."[20]

This ignorant pride paraded by her adversaries offended, furthermore, her religious opinions. She was not herself devout. "Were I a pious Christian," she wrote of her brother John, who was inclined to contest the terms of their father's will, "I would say 'God forgive him!' As it is I can but *try* to forgive him myself." But her own beliefs did not matter. "To the philosopher and the philanthropist, independent of personal belief, christianity is equally sacred. With it modern civilization walks hand in hand; from it proceed all those softening influences which make us feel, spite of the *chefs d'oeuvres* of ancient art, now inimitable, that the world is better and wiser than it has been. It stands, after a trial of eighteen centuries, the purest code of philosophy and morals that the history of man has ever developed." Therefore, that Mrs. Stowe and her British allies drew a screen of Christian charity across their callousness and hypocrisy was doubly detestable. Louisa McCord had in addition the deist's horror of those who would pervert the workings of Providence, as revealed in nature and by reason. "There is evil in God's blessed world (why, God only knows), but there is also good—deep, earnest good—for those who will seek it deeply and earnestly. Below the nauseous froth-scum of sickly philanthropy and new-light Christianity, runs, quiet but clear, the pure stream of God-given reason and common-sense humanity. Ladies and reviewers, *God is God,* but *ye* are *not* his prophets."[21]

Louisa McCord prodded at "the nauseous froth-scum of sickly philanthropy and new-light Christianity"; one by one, she detected and demolished the falsehoods and subterfuges of "that most crushing of all tyrannies, the tyranny of dominant and bigot opinion."[22] She reviewed the arguments for

20. Chap. 7, "Slavery and Political Economy," p. 138; *PSE,* "British Philanthropy and American Slavery," p. 300, and "Carey on the Slave Trade," pp. 394, 386.
21. LSM to Langdon Cheves, Jr., April 3, 1858, in *PDBL,* p. 339; *PSE,* "Diversity of the Races; Its Bearing upon Negro Slavery," p. 164, and "British Philanthropy and American Slavery," p. 283.
22. *PSE,* "Justice and Fraternity," p. 74.

and against polygenesis of the human species, the latter often being improperly motivated, in her view, by a desire to discredit racial slavery. The opportunity of English novelist Charles Kingsley's muckraking *Alton Locke* allowed her to ridicule the hypocrisy of British abolitionists, anxious for foreign happiness while ignoring the squalor and suffering endured by the poor within their own country. The Northern political economist Henry C. Carey forsook his commitment to free trade and exacerbated sectional strife simultaneously. But Mrs. McCord's fiercest scorn was reserved for the most astonishingly successful of abolitionist tracts, Harriet Beecher Stowe's *Uncle Tom's Cabin,* "that abominable woman's abominable book. . . . It is one mass of fanatical bitterness and foul misrepresentation wrapped in the garb of Christian Charity."[23] Louisa McCord reviewed the novel at the invitation of William Gilmore Simms, editor of the *Southern Quarterly Review*, then assessed approbatory responses to Mrs. Stowe's triumph as they appeared in the dangerously influential British quarterlies. Even more insupportable than these was an address to the women of America, urging the abolition of slavery. Ghostwritten by the relentlessly reforming earl of Shaftesbury, it was signed by a majestic register of noblewomen, at the head of whom was the foremost of Mrs. Stowe's British patrons, the duchess of Sutherland. At first according to custom, in "British Philanthropy and American Slavery" (March 1853) Louisa McCord dealt with the address alongside an abolitionist article published in the *North British Review*. Some months later, she decided that the address required more ingenious treatment. After the example of Edmund Burke's *Letter to a Noble Lord,* her "Letter to the Duchess of Sutherland from a Lady of South Carolina" deployed irony and sarcasm modifying, while yet quickening, the vigor and ferocity typical of her periodical essays.[24]

She had much experience in thus playing with form and genre. Having treated of women's rights in two periodical essays, "Enfranchisement of Woman" and "Woman and Her Needs," she summarized her arguments in a poem written in blank verse, "Woman's Progress."[25] Even the lyric poems assembled in *My Dreams,* although a genre deemed suitable to women, demonstrated unconventional choices, whether in subject matter like "Poor Nannie"'s hints of autobiography or in complicated meters both within and among poems. Most remarkable of all was her verse tragedy *Caius Gracchus*,

23. LSM to Mary Cheves Dulles, Oct. 9, 1852, in chap. 11 below.

24. The letter was "deservedly admired for its dignified tone," according to Hale, *Woman's Record,* p. 894. See also William J. Grayson, *The Hireling and the Slave, Chicora, and Other Poems* (Charleston, S.C., 1856), p. xiii.

25. "Enfranchisement of Woman," *SQR,* n. s., 5 (April 1852) = *PSE,* pp. 105–24, is reprinted in O'Brien, *All Clever Men* , pp. 337–56; David A. Hollinger and Charles Capper, eds., *The American Intellectual Tradition,* 3d ed., 2 vols. (New York, 1997), 1:403–15.

modeled upon Shakespeare (*Coriolanus* chiefly) and adopting its subject from the tumultuous history of the Roman republic in the second century B.C. Few wrote tragedies on classical themes any more, and women never. "South Carolina has produced," wrote a contemporary reviewer, "the only American poet whose productions may be said to belong to the elder school; which appeal to the intellect more than the fancy, and are marked by such sinewy strength of thought and expression as to be stamped at once with a character of originality. . . . She is wholly unlike any of her sisters of the lyre, and writes with a terseness, vigor, earnestness, and masculine energy, which show her to be altogether of a different order."[26]

We may speculate about Louisa McCord's reasons for choosing her subject. Two letters to her husband's cousin William Porcher Miles suggest that the play's hero, enjoying fame as an orator, supplied occasions for her to demonstrate the love of eloquence which, as a woman, she could not put to public use. Cornelia, proverbial mother of the Gracchi, daughter of one of Rome's greatest heroes, conferred the authority whereby the proper role of woman might be dramatized; Cornelia's world, torn by civil unrest, represented Mrs. McCord's own world, a male world of violence that could be tamed only by woman's civilizing power. Or could it be tamed? For in *Caius Gracchus* Cornelia fails to persuade others to prudence or, when her persuasions prevail, they are either too late or powerless to guide events. Her son is killed. Yet Cornelia remains so forceful a character in the tragedy that Mary Chesnut got the title wrong (she called it *The Mother of the Gracchi*) when she introduced Louisa McCord into her diaries. Indeed, contemporaries assumed that Louisa McCord had made a portrait of herself. A tutor of the McCord children remembered that, having a mind "Roman in its cast, and heroic in its energy, . . . in person Mrs. McCord might personate Cornelia herself." In her diary Mrs. Chesnut recorded a visit to Cheves McCord at his mother's house in Columbia.

He had been badly wounded at Second Manassas, in both the head and the leg.

Mrs. McCord went at once to Richmond and found he was still at or near Manassas Junction. She went to Mr. Miles to get her a passport to go down for him. He said the thing was impossible. Government had seized all trains, and no passports were given. "I let him talk," said Mrs. McCord, "for he does it beautifully. That very night I chartered a special train. We ran down to

---

26. "Mrs. M'Cord's Caius Gracchus," *De Bow*, n.s., 1 (Oct. 1852): 428–29. The review was reprinted in the New York *Knickerbocker* 41 (Jan. 1853): 69–72.

Manassas and I brought back Cheves in triumph. You see he is nearly well, with our home nursing."

"Mother of the Gracchi," we cried.[27]

The Texts

The texts selected for this book are (with occasional and slight correction) those established in Richard C. Lounsbury, ed., *Louisa S. McCord: Political and Social Essays* (Charlottesville, Va., 1995) and *Louisa S. McCord: Poems, Drama, Biography, Letters* (Charlottesville, Va., 1996). For identification of Louisa McCord's writings, most of them anonymous, and for editorial policy, the reader is referred to the Note on the Texts in each volume.

Louisa McCord frequently quotes other writers. Differences between her quotation and the original of the text which she quotes are indicated thus: (1) words or letters omitted by her are restored within square brackets; (2) words changed by her are inserted back into her text within angle brackets (<>) immediately following the place where change was made; (3) if such a change is found to have been greater than of one or a few words, the change is indicated in a note. Of her two favorite sources of quotation, Shakespeare is cited by act, scene, and line number as given in the New Arden Shakespeare, and the Bible in the Authorized (King James) Version.

A note written by Louisa McCord is designated by [LSM] at its conclusion.

27. J. W. Davidson, *Living Writers of the South*, pp. 351, 357; *Chesnut*, p. 428.

Chronology

1810   Born Louisa Susanna Cheves in Charleston, South Carolina (December 3), second daughter and fourth of the fourteen children of Langdon and Mary Elizabeth Dulles Cheves.

1819   After her father is appointed president of the Bank of the United States, the Cheves family moves to Philadelphia.

1829   The Cheves family returns to South Carolina (December).

1833   Receives from her father 1,530 acres adjacent to the plantation of her sister Sophia and husband Charles Haskell near Abbeville.

1836   Mother dies (April).

1839   With her father, older brother Alexander, and younger sister Anna, spends the summer at resorts in western Virginia.

1840   Is married to David James McCord (May).

1841   Birth of Langdon Cheves McCord (April). Langdon Cheves divides his property among his children (November). LSM, ceding the land given to her in 1833, receives Lang Syne plantation.

1843   Birth of Hannah Cheves McCord (September).

1845   Birth of Louisa Rebecca Hayne McCord (August).

1848   Publication of a book of poems, *My Dreams,* and a translation of Frédéric Bastiat's *Sophismes économiques.*

1849–56   Publishes articles on political economy, women's rights, and slavery in the *Southern Quarterly Review, De Bow's Review,* and *Southern Literary Messenger;* also fugitive poems in the *Southern Literary Gazette.*

1850   Spends summer with family and younger brother Hayne at Narragansett Bay, Rhode Island.

1851   Publication of *Caius Gracchus,* a tragedy in five acts. Spends summer at resorts in western Virginia.

1855   Death of David James McCord (May). LSM's health becomes cause for worry: in particular, symptoms of severe eyestrain grow more troublesome. Death of brother Charles.

1856   Incapacitated by a stroke, father moves into LSM's house in Columbia. For reasons of health, LSM takes her children to spend the summer at Narragansett Bay, then to the White Mountains in New Hampshire. Brother Hayne dies of tuberculosis in Florence (August).

1857   Father dies (June). Again in search of health, with her children LSM visits the Virginia springs.

1858   Quarrels and lawsuit over father's will. LSM sails for Europe on the paddle steamship *Persia* (July), accompanied by son Cheves and daughter Louisa. Tours Britain and Ireland. In Paris, consults ophthalmologists.

1859   Travels to Italy. In Florence, sits to sculptor Hiram Powers (late April–May). Further travels in France, England, the

	Netherlands, Germany, Switzerland. Returns to the United States (October).
1861	Son Cheves marries Charlotte Reynolds, daughter of a professor at South Carolina College (October).
1862	Cheves McCord is wounded at Second Manassas (August).
1863	Death of Cheves McCord (January); his only child, a daughter, is born less than two weeks later. In July, LSM's brother Langdon and her nephew Charles Haskell are killed at siege of Battery Wagner in Charleston Harbor, a second nephew, Charles' brother William, at Gettysburg.
1865	LSM's house, made headquarters of the Federal forces having captured Columbia, survives the burning of the city but is looted twice; also looted is Lang Syne (February). Daughter Louisa is married to Charlestonian Augustine T. Smythe (June).
1869	Daughter Hannah is married to John Taylor Rhett (March). LSM becomes first president of the South Carolina Monument Association, formed to build a memorial to the state's soldiers lost in the war.
1870	In March, sends to Hiram Powers in Florence to inquire after a bust of Langdon Cheves commissioned before the war. Responds indignantly (April) to a character of her father published in a Charleston newspaper. In June, resigns the presidency of the South Carolina Monument Association. Lang Syne is sold (December).
1871–75	Lives away from South Carolina, mostly at various places in Canada.
1872	Daughter Hannah dies after the birth of her second child (November).
1876/77	Retires to Charleston.
1879	Dies in Charleston (November 23).

Part I

1.

The Right to Labor

Within this specious formula—"the right to labor"—lie concentrated the greater number of those terrible fallacies which now threaten to overrun and devastate civilized society. The hydra of communism holds struggling in its deadly folds the Hercules of truth. That the latter conquers, who can doubt? Man's nature, his soul, and instinct, alike lead him to the light. The world is progressive. The past shows, the present hopes for, and the future promises this; but fearful are the doubts, the despondencies, and the agonies, through which society must pass to attain its highest tone! Around each great truth is gathered a crowd of errors—deceitful reflections of its beauty—giving to the mischievous a pretext for ill, and often, with *ignis fatuus* light, misleading even the true-hearted and the good.

There are crises in the world's course, when, rousing from temporary lethargy, reason seems more than usually wide awake to the influence of truth and light. But, in this very waking, is she also more subject to the misleading influence of error. The craving heart—the longing, seeking, hungering for truth—is roused; and, in its eager search, how often, alas! is the will-o'-the-wisp mistaken for the star-beam! Through one of these crises are we now struggling. The world is in labor of a great truth, but its sick fancy is cheated with the bewildering dazzle of its own delirious dreams.

One of society's closest guards—a kind of shepherd's dog, as it were, of the flock—stands political economy. Watching, barking, wrangling at every intruder, suspicious of outward show, nor satisfied with skin-deep inspection, it examines, before admitting all pretenders as true prophets, and strips many a wolf of his sheep's clothing. The evil-inclined, thus, naturally, hoot and revile it. The ignorant mistrust it. What do we, its advocates, ask in its defence? Simply nothing, but that the world should learn to know it. We wish no law for its imposition—no tax for its protection. Let truth be but heard: there is in the heart of man an instinct to know and to seize it. Error is simply negative; like shadow, it is only want of light. Heaven's sunbeam on the material world—reason's effulgence on the thinking soul—alone suffice to work *God's* purposes. Man, his humble instrument, cannot *make* the light; he can but strive to remove the obstacles which intercept its abundant flow.

We ask, then, only to be heard. Let the world know us. Let the *people* know us. Let political economy be the science of *the crowd*. It is neither incomprehensible nor abstruse. It requires but that each individual man should think—think, not imagine, not dream, not utopianize—but think, study, and understand for himself. Where the masses are ignorant, what more natural than that they stumble into wrong? Mind must act; and more and more, as the world advances, does it call for the right of exerting and developing its power. In earlier ages, learning, information, thought being limited to the few, the masses took the word from these high-priests of reason, whose veiled holy of holies was sacred from the intrusion of the crowd. But, now, the veil is rent asunder. Not you, nor we, nor he—nor any chosen one—nor ten, nor twenty—but *man*—now claims the right to think for himself. He claims it; he will have it; he ought to have it. Let but those who are ahead in the race of knowledge give to those who need; guide those who stumble in the dark; and each, thus putting in his mite of well-doing in the cause, ward off, as much as possible, the calamities which necessarily hover round the great and progressive change through which the world is passing. Great changes are oftenest wrought out only through great convulsions. It is a man's work, and man's heart is in it, when the humblest individual, with shoulder to the wheel, stands boldly and honestly forth, to raise his hand in warding off the avalanche of evil.

France, which now stands before the world, in the agonies of her struggles—great alike in truth and in error—France has experimented, and written for us, in her sufferings, a mighty lesson. May we but read and learn it! Revelling in the madness of newly-gained freedom, her people not knowing the use of what they had seized, for them it became the synonyme of license. Rushing from extreme to extreme, they forgot that liberty was but enfranchisement, and, with "democracy" for their watchword, exercised a despotism much more fearful than that of the single tyrant, because its power, like its name, was "legion."[1]

And what is the result? Credit dead; industry paralyzed; commerce annihilated; her starving people now sinking despondent under their difficulties—now driven to the madness of revolt, against they know not whom—asking, they know not what. France, terrified at her own acts, calls out for succor, and on every side resound the answers of her best and wisest citizens: "Step back from your errors; give truth its way"—*laissez passer—laissez faire.*

Amidst the throng of confused theories, each of which burns into the very vitals of the suffering state its brand of crime and folly, while

> lean-look'd prophets whisper fearful change,[2]

political economy alone, with its great and simple truths, seems to hold forth some hope of a real regeneration. It alone enjoins upon its disciples to follow, step by step—to sift to the bottom its theories and their remotest effects—before launching the world upon untried experiments. It alone gropes patiently its way, grappling with doubts and difficulties, making sure and clear its footing, before calling upon society to follow. Its opponents—socialists of every grade—leaping blindfold to their conclusions, and taking impulse for inspiration, recklessly drag on their devotees from one wild dream to another, until

> contention, like a horse
> Full of high feeding, madly doth break loose,
> And bears down all before him.[3]

They do not mean the evil which they do. Very possibly, their hearts are of the purest—but their ideas, unfortunately, not of the clearest. Without examining into the practicability of their own schemes, they give way to a misty vision of goodness—a kind of foggy virtue—which, often but the rushlight of their own unregulated fancy—too indolent or too cowardly to probe to its source, and follow to its end—they imagine an inward light, a transmitted beam of heaven, and so dream on!

Many, too, who would shrink from the broad notions of communism and forced fraternity, most unwittingly often assist in scattering the poison through society. Something they find out of joint: the world might be better certainly; and, forthwith, they set about preaching the vague ideas of fraternity, equality! Heaven knows the while (for they themselves do not) what it

---

1. Mark 5:9.
2. *Richard II* 2.4.11.
3. *2 Henry IV* 1.1.9–11, reading "hath broke" for "doth break."

is all aiming at! Such a writer as Carlyle, for instance, popular and plausible, forever holds up to view the wretchedness of the masses, with threats of undefined evil to the better classes, if this is not remedied, scoffing bitterly, the while, at the *laissez faire* system. His heart, we believe, is good, his intentions pure; but does he himself know—has he ever put the question to his own heart, and answered it fairly?—where he is leading? We mistake much, if Carlyle would not shrink from forced legalized fraternity, from communism, or from Owenism;[4] and yet to such do his vague generalities drag us. Working up discontented, and even well-intentioned minds, to a restless feeling of the need of something better, he does not sufficiently impress upon them that if, in his own beautiful words, "always there is a black spot in our sunshine, it is even the shadow of ourselves,"[5] and that "he who seeks *out of himself* what is found *in* himself, will seek forever and find nothing"— (Zchokke).[6] Many, to save themselves the trouble of thinking (and do not ninety-nine in the hundred shirk this when they can?), take it for granted that *he has* his idea—that *he has* his plan; and, as it seems to be philanthropic, well rounded with groans and appeals for suffering humanity, they range themselves under his banner. But to what does all this complaining lead? There is sorrow—ay, and wretchedness and suffering, oppression and injustice, trampled misery and heartless power, enough, too much—in this world of ours; we see this as well as he—but where is *his remedy*? While he is continually telling us that the *laissez faire* of political economy is treason against the rights of the poor, and that something must be done; *that something* he never indicates, never hints at. The crowd, having taken his dictum so far—"something is wrong, it must be righted"—when he comes to a halt, for which they are totally unprepared, are almost forced to rush on a little farther, into the arms of some better revolutionizer—Cabet, Proudhon, etc.[7]

    4. Robert Owen (1771–1858), Welsh socialist, proposed a completely environmental basis for human character; cooperative communities based on his ideas were established in Britain and the United States.

    5. Thomas Carlyle (1795–1881), *Sartor Resartus* 2.9 ("The Everlasting Yea"), in *Works*, Ashburton ed., 17 vols. (London and Philadelphia, 1885–88), 3:130: "Always there is a black spot in our sunshine: it is even, as I said, the *Shadow of Ourselves*."

    6. Johann Heinrich Daniel Zschokke (1771–1848), born in Magdeburg; settled in Switzerland in 1796; playwright, novelist, journalist, historian.

    7. Etienne Cabet (1788–1856), French socialist, wrote the utopian novel *Voyage en Icarie* (1840); in 1849, under the influence of Robert Owen, founded a community called Icaria in Nauvoo, Ill. Active in the 1848 revolution in France, anarchist Pierre-Joseph Proudhon (1809–65) remains celebrated for his aphorism "Property is theft," enunciated in *Qu'est-ce que la propriété?* (1840).

It might be well for this energetic writer to con over more frequently his own humorous fable:

> Once upon a time, a man, somewhat in drink belike, raised a dreadful outcry at the corner of the market-place, that the world was turning all <all turned> topsy-turvy; that the men and cattle were all walking with their feet uppermost; that the houses and earth at large (if they did not mind it) would fall into the sky; in short, that unless prompt means were taken, things in general were on the high road to the devil. As the people only laughed at him, he cried the louder and more vehemently; nay, at last, began objuring, foaming, imprecating, when a good-natured auditor, going up, took the orator by his haunches, and, softly inverting his <his> position, set him down upon <on> his feet. The which upon perceiving, his mind was staggered not a little. "Ha! deuce take it," cried he, rubbing his eyes; "so it was not the world that was hanging by its feet, then, but I that was standing on my head!" Censor, *castigator morum*,[8] radical reformer, by whatever name thou art called, have a care—especially if thou art getting loud!⁹

And how correct this habit of half way thinking? this grasping at superficialities? By teaching the masses to think rightly. *Popularize* (allow us the word) popularize political economy. Most truly and beautifully does the distinguished writer whom we have just ventured to animadvert upon remark: "All misery is but faculty misdirected, strength that has not yet found its way. [. . .] No *smoke*, in any sense, but can become flame and radiance."¹⁰ All the confusion and turmoil which we now see bubbling up in restless discontent upon the troubled surface of society, has its mission, has its result. There is much of great, much of good under it. Let but now the true thinker, he who thought

> Till thought is standing thick upon the brain
> As dew upon the brow——for thought is brain-sweat,

let him not grudge the fruit of his study, but *popularize* it for the crowd. . . .

"Nothing," says Guizot, "has a more certain tendency to ruin a people than a habit of accepting words and appearances as realities."¹¹ The fashion

---

8. "Chastiser of morals" (Latin).

9. Thomas Carlyle, "Four Fables," in *Critical and Miscellaneous Essays*, vol. 1, in *Works* 15:627.

10. Thomas Carlyle, "The Gifted," *Past and Present*, in ibid., 2:244.

11. François Guizot, *Democracy in France. January, 1849* [trans. of *De la démocratie en France*] (London, 1849; rpt. New York, 1974), p. 15. François-Pierre-Guillaume Guizot (1787–1874), French historian, foreign minister (1840–47) and first minister (1847–48) to Louis Philippe, forced from public life by the Revolution of 1848.

of our age is *cant,* a whining pretension to goodness. Ultra in every thing, it condemns and tosses aside, as scarcely worth the hearing, each sober thinker, who without "ahs!" or "ohs!", without groaning over the heavy and unparalleled suffering, and exulting in the great and unexampled enlightenment, of his time, sees the world, in steady progress, advancing by almighty behest, through its destined changes, to its appointed might of developed reason and civilization. This man is too cold, exclaims the one side; he has no heart for sympathy, or he would join with us in revolutionizing this world where crime and vice play so dominant a part. He is dull, says the other; he cannot see the glorious progress of the age, and keeps plodding along at his old jog-trot, instead of leaping at once to perfection. And then both extremes, meeting, join in their loud "hallelujahs" for fraternity and equality. But a little of the old jog-trot prudence might be useful here. Would our improvers but pause and think, nor trust quite so much to the inspiration of impulse, perhaps they might find that they are foisting up "words and appearances" instead of "realities." "Life has one virtue," beautifully remarks George Sand, *"the eternal sacrifice of self."*[12] Pure and chaste thought!—which we quote from Mme. Dudevant, but which beamed upon the world in the softening influence of christianity, eighteen centuries before her birth! "Give to him that asketh of thee, and from him that would borrow of thee, turn not thou away." But he who preached this lesson to man, taught him also, to "render unto Caesar the things which are Caesar's."[13] Far from the tone of charity and benevolence thus inculcated, is the wide-spread spirit of tyranny and spoliation which now usurps its place; and Mme. Dudevant has learned but half her lesson. Charity can only go hand-in-hand with justice, and he who robs to give is scarcely less culpable than he who robs to enjoy. In the volume under review (page 56) we find Mr. Proudhon exclaiming before the French assembly; "Why talk about property? Property does not exist; it is abrogated; the provisional government in recognizing *the right to labor* has annulled it. If lodgers now pay their rent, farmers their leases, or debtors their creditors, it is simply because it is agreeable to them to do so."[14] And this is fraternity! This the right to labor! Take, keep, borrow, and do not return, is the lesson of these ultra-sympathizers, who thus crush all morality in their wild interpretation of the gentle maxim, "Love ye one another."[15]

Even so well intentioned a man as Lamartine (and after his famous free-

---

12. Amandine-Aurore-Lucile Dupin Dudevant (1804–76), French novelist under the pen name of George Sand.
13. Matt. 5:42; Mark 12:17.
14. "Chronique," *Journal des économistes* 21 (Aug. 1848): 50–56; 56.
15. John 13:34, 15:12, 17.

trade speech at Marseilles) declared (p. 219): "If in such questions as these [Politico-Economical] we find our limits, it would be necessary to efface from our constitution the three sublime words, liberty! equality! fraternity! to replace them by the two low, filthy [*immondes*] substitutes, *buying and selling*."[16] Ah! M. Lamartine, if you would live in the clouds, keep to poetizing and let alone legislating! Fancy delights, but sober reason must rule the world. Buying and selling—service and compensation—are at the basis of the world's law of action, its great foundation stone. We must possess before we can give. Property must precede charity and individual superiority exists before the very idea of benevolence can have birth. Your fanciful equality, may, in truth, drag all down to one level of starvation and beggary; but although this may the better suit the poetic fancy of M. de Lamartine, for this work-day world of ours, perhaps the old plan may be the best. At least as M. Amédée Gratiot says to his compeers (p. 162), "Workmen, let us go to our work, our spinning machines, our presses, and our forges; let us leave our friends, the socialists, to make up their minds, and experiment upon systems among themselves; next year perhaps they will have determined how to make us all happy."[17] For *God's* sake, gentlemen, you, our socialists of America, Mr. Horace Greely, Albert Brisbane, etc.,[18] make up your minds—in the words of M. Gratiot, "une solution s'il vous plaît," before you plunge us deeper into this quagmire of unexplored utopias. Leave us to our old vulgar practices of "buying and selling" until at least you shall have invented some feasible substitutes for them.

16. "Chronique," *Journal des économistes* 21 (Sept. 1848): 219–24; 219 (LSM's interpolations and italics). Alphonse-Marie-Louis de Prat de Lamartine (1790–1869), French poet, minister of foreign affairs in the Provisional Government set up after the abdication of Louis Philippe.

17. *Messieurs les socialistes, une solution, s'il vous plaît* (Paris, 1848), cited in "Bibliographie," *Journal des économistes* 21 (Sept. 1848): 162–63; 162. LSM condenses the original text. Amédée Gratiot (1812–80), printer and poet; secretary of the Chamber of Printers; judge on the Tribunal of Commerce (1850).

18. Horace Greeley (1811–72), journalist and reformer, founded the New York *Tribune* in 1841 and promoted, among other causes, the Free Soil movement and abolitionism. Albert Brisbane (1809–90), author of *Social Destiny of Man* (1840) and *Association* (1843), established in 1843 a Fourierist phalanx at Red Bank, N.J.

2.

Separate Secession

SEPARATE SECESSION! Terror thrills us at the thought. Ay, though fiery and rampant valour may hiss disgrace at a word so inconsistent with the fashion and spirit of the day, yet must we confess, terror thrills us at the idea of a course so suited, we solemnly believe, to crush our dearest hopes for liberty, and plunge into anarchy, ruin, and slavish bondage all that is nearest and dearest to us. If any step be well calculated to retard the hopes of the South, making us the patient hewers of wood and drawers of water for our Northern aggressors, we believe it to be this well-meant, but mistaken expedient.[1] We have no love for the Union; we have no fear of its dissolution. Welcome as summer shower to the sun-parched earth—welcome as heaven's free air to the heart-sick tenant of a dungeon—would come to us the voice of freedom, the word, the deed, which would tend to burst our bonds and, in earnest faith, contribute to the disruption of this proud fabric (once beautiful, but now rotten to the core) which, under the name of Union, threatens

SQR, n.s., 4 (Oct. 1851) = PSE, pp. 203–21. Publication reviewed: *Proceedings of the Meeting of Delegates from the Southern Rights Associations of South Carolina* [subheading: "held at Charleston, May, 1851"] (Columbia, S.C.: Johnston and Cavis, 1851). A convention of the Southern Rights Associations of South Carolina met on May 5, 1851, in Charleston's Military Hall and on May 8 voted its approval of proposals to the effect that South Carolina should secede from the Union "whether with or without the co-operation of other Southern States" (ibid., p. 20).

1. Josh. 9:23: "Now therefore ye are cursed, and there shall none of you be freed from being bondmen, and hewers of wood and drawers of water for the house of my God."

to crush us beneath its unholy power. As *God* is true, we believe that we speak truth when we say that there is no risk of life or property that we would shrink from, in the accomplishment of so desirable an end; for, albeit most certainly a noncombatant, in every legal and customary application of the word, we believe that we, too, could be roused, if need were, to give our mite of strength, in a struggle for hearth and home. Our little mockbird (Carolina's nightingale) will, at the risk and sacrifice of life, fight for its nest, against odds the most fearful! Is there a heart in Carolina less bold than that of our poor fluttering song bird? But where hearth and home, child and country, are to be heedlessly thrown into the balance, against a vaunting spirit, a headlong rashness, which mocks the counsels of our wisest and our best, methinks the *God* of battles is against us, and terror is not too strong a word, when we contemplate the countless woes, the fathomless abyss of ills, which may ensue.

In all revolutions, impulse is undoubtedly the motive cause, with the masses; but thinking men, who act by reason, and well-weighed, long-considered, deeply-studied motives, must—unless *God* has marked out a people for destruction—sway and direct that impulse to its proper course. If, then, the voice of the convention of delegates held in Charleston, in the beginning of May last, were indeed the voice of the State, it would present a fearful crisis in our history. *Quem Deus vult perdere, prius dementat.*[2] Has *God* made us cast aside all the counsels of wisdom, that he may thus crush us under the weight of our own madness? We trust not; we believe not. The voice of the convention of May was *not* the voice of the State; its members were *not* the delegates of the State; they were the delegates of certain associations of the State, useful in their way, no doubt, but who have gone a step too far, who have assumed too much, in the course which they have pursued. Violent, enthusiastic (we speak, of course, of the majority, whose voice has alone been heard), actuated by the best motives, but misled by impulse—impatient and sore under insufferable oppression, but excited by the heat of unripe counsels—they have thought, by this display of passion, to bind the State to a course which *they* believe the safest for her interests, and to thus influence the action of her proposed State convention.[3] This unauthorized

---

2. "Whom God wishes to destroy, he first makes mad." Unattributed Latin motto.

3. A convention was called (June 3–12 and Nov. 11–18, 1850) at Nashville, Tenn., to discuss Southern grievances arising, for the most part, from Northern attempts to prohibit slavery in the territories acquired after the Mexican War (1846–48). At the end of the Nashville Convention's meeting in November a call was issued for a congress of slaveholding states to be held, at which resistance and possible independence might be considered. On Dec. 20, 1850, the legislature of South Carolina passed a bill endorsing a Southern congress, setting Oct. 13 and 14, 1851, as dates for the election of delegates to this congress, and

step is calculated to do much harm. Efforts to have it accredited, as an act of the State, have, to a considerable extent, been but too successful, both at home and abroad. Our object is, before going farther, to show the fallacy of such an impression.

The intrinsic nature of the elective bodies to this convention ought, perhaps, to be sufficient to convince us of such a fallacy. District associations, got up by individuals, are, necessarily, from their very qualities of being, most regularly attended by their more active and violent members. Sober and orderly men, however patriotic, are apt to tire of such meetings, which, although they may be occasionally useful in keeping up the flagging spirit of the people, or bringing the doubtful to the mark, will be found too often to degenerate in their tendency (like the revolutionary clubs of France) into a factious disposition to mob-rule.

We mean no slur upon the high-spirited people of our gallant and noble State;[4] but such is the general tendency of all similar associations. They fall, necessarily, into the hands, and under the management, of the restless and violent, and are thus, even in a good cause, liable to rush into dangerous extremes. Not only, then, were the elections, in each district, made by this portion, alone, of its citizens; but from the very irregular numbers of the delegates we easily perceive that each district, or rather, each district association, was represented without regard to the population, property, or representative force of such respective districts. Lancaster, with a legislative representation of *two,* and a population of 5,794 free, and 5,014 slave, sent *nineteen* delegates; while Laurens, with a similar legislative representation, and a population of 11,453 free, and 11,953 slave, sent *seven.* Georgetown (comprised in parishes of All Saints and Prince George, Winyah) and Greenville, with each a legislative representation of *four,* sent, respectively, *eight* and *nine* delegates; while Richland and Barnwell, with each a similar legislative representation, sent, respectively, *twenty-seven* and *thirty-three.* Marion, Orangeburgh, and Fairfield have each a legislative representation of *three.* The population of Marion is 9,888 free and 7,720 slave; of Orangeburgh, 8,199 free and 15,425 slave; of Fairfield, 7,164 free and 14,246 slave. The delegates of Marion to the convention of May were *three,* from Orangeburgh, *twenty-one,* and from Fairfield, *thirty-five*!! Pickens had *one* delegate, for a population of 13,228 free and 3,679 slave. Besides sundry of the

---

providing for a constituent convention (to which LSM here refers) in South Carolina; the legislature also elected four delegates-at-large to the proposed congress, among them Langdon Cheves.

4. The nature of our article compels us to write, more than is desirable for a *Southern Quarterly,* in the limited view of South Carolinian rather than under the wider designation of Southron. [LSM]

parishes, as St. James, Goose Creek, St. James, Santee, St. Thomas and St. Denis, St. George, Dorchester, St. Pauls and St. Lukes, we find not only the whole district of Horry, with a population of 5,824 free and 2,082 slave, entirely unrepresented, but the populous district of Spartanburgh, whose inhabitants number 18,358 free and 8,038 slave, entitled to a legislative representation of *five* (almost double that of Fairfield, which sent *thirty-five* delegates), stands in the same category—not one voice from Spartanburgh. Will any man who can add two and two together contend, for one instant, that such an assembly has the shadow of a right to speak for the State, or can, in the smallest degree, bind or compromise her by the expression of its opinions? On the contrary, ought not its bold action and spirit of dictation to startle us into prudent watchfulness? These men mean well, perhaps. The majority of them, no doubt, do. But so, we are told by veracious historians, did Robespierre. A good man was Robespierre, a kind-hearted man, say these, and *he thought* he was doing the best for his country, when he was bringing upon her a "desolation of desolations," for there was death, "and hell followed with him."[5] He was her guide and protector. *God* shield us from such self-constituted guides and protectors!

But permit us here to ask, what was the power of a Robespierre or a Danton, other than the gift of such clubs as these very associations which formed the convention we are discussing?[6] They were but the agents of a similar power, pushed to a further extreme. Let us here, once for all, disclaim any wish to cast the taint or shadow of a doubt upon the sincerity of men whose zeal, alone, we regard as their stumbling-block. They love their State, but *qui amat non semper amicus est.*[7] Their love is death. Robespierre and Couthon, at the height of their assumed power, *thought themselves right,* and acted for the weal of their country.[8] It is somewhat startling to find that our convention intends not to resign the power (whatever it may be) that it swayed in May last. Its members have declared themselves a permanent body, "*preserving its organization, under the same officers.*" We have seen how, and

---

5. Rev. 6:8.
6. Maximilien-François-Marie-Isadore de Robespierre (1758–94), French revolutionary politician; a leader of the Jacobin Club; member of the second Committee of Public Safety (1793), instituted Reign of Terror as instrument of policy; guillotined. Georges-Jacques Danton (1759–94), French revolutionary politician; president of the Jacobin Club; member of the Committee of Public Safety; arrested by his rival Robespierre; guillotined.
7. Seneca *Epistulae morales* (*Moral Letters*) 35.1: "Qui amicus est amat; qui amat non utique amicus est." "Who is a friend, loves; who loves, is not always a friend."
8. Georges Couthon (1755–94), French revolutionary politician; member of the Committee of Public Safety; supplied legal foundation to the Reign of Terror; guillotined with Robespierre.

by whom, these officers have been elected. They have appointed a "Central Committee," to "promote the [common] cause," and thus govern the State; and they have pronounced that all future members shall be elected—not by the people—but by district associations, and by *district associations* ALONE![9]

Carolinians, are you awake? Will you sanction the proceedings of such a body, as the *proceedings of the State*? Will you take the voice of unruly faction for the voice of the people? Heaven save us from ourselves, if *this* be Southern patriotism! But it cannot be. When faction speaks, let it speak in its own name, nor pass its dictates for the fiat of a people.

We are glad to believe that the convention, formed and elected as we have above shown, was, even under such circumstances, by no means so unanimous as we are led to suppose from printed accounts. Five and six dissentient voices, even to the most objectionable of its resolutions, is the report we receive; but, in the triumph expressed concerning this most astonishing unanimity, we are not told, but are left, from accident, to gather the fact, that many of the more moderate members, who were members elect to the State convention, abstained, upon principle, from a vote, which was calculated to compromise them, and to shackle their action, as servants of the State.[10] Hon. Mr. Butler, in his speech before the convention, remarks: "The measures intimated in the draft of the address, and in some of the resolutions, will not allow many of this convention to vote upon them. All who are members of the constitutional convention of the people cannot give a vote to control their future judgment. They ought not to be required to do so. I have conversed with several of them, and they have come to a common conclusion: to give no vote upon any matter upon which they will have to deliberate when there shall be a real occasion for their officially responsible judgment."[11]

Here, then, we are brought to a stand. We see the graver men, even of this meeting, not only shrinking from the violence of its course, but advising, imploring, headstrong valour, to check itself by prudence, and heed "the pauser, Reason."[12] Alas!

> But older men are monitors too dull
> For passionate youth.

---

9. *Proceedings of the Southern Rights Associations*, p. 21 (LSM's italics).

10. We are informed, upon the best authority, that this meeting refused to allow the yeas and nays to be called. [LSM]

11. Andrew Pickens Butler (1796–1857), U.S. senator from South Carolina (1846–57), spoke at the morning session on May 7. His speech is printed in the Charleston *Mercury*, May 17, 1851.

12. *Macbeth* 2.3.109.

And in

> That season when the fancy is a god,
> Hope a conviction,

wild work may be made upon unwary faith by the spirit of party, faction, and demagoguism. Cassandra-like rise the warnings of our long-tried counsellors. *Young* Carolina heeds them not. The opinions of men whom the State delighted to honour are trampled upon, as not worth the hearing. The eloquent appeals, the labored reasonings, of a Barnwell[13] or a Butler are cast aside, for the passionate declamations of some new Camille Desmoulins.[14] The opinion of the venerable Cheves, in whom

> old experience doth attain
> To something like prophetic strain;[15]

whose voice, at Nashville, startled the country, and half roused the South from its lethargy,[16] meets with less respect than that of the noisiest gabbler of "drawn swords and bloody bones" whom the convention could produce.[17]

Scarcely had his last words of warning been spoken (we will not say listened to),[18] when the chairman "from the Select Committee of Twenty-one"

---

13. Robert Woodward Barnwell (1801–82), born in Beaufort, S.C.; president of South Carolina College (1835–41); delegate to the Nashville Convention, where he advocated cooperative secession; a commissioner sent to negotiate with President James Buchanan after South Carolina's secession in December 1860; member of the Confederate Senate. Barnwell spoke at the afternoon session on May 7. His speech is printed in the Charleston *Mercury,* May 27, 1851.

14. Camille Desmoulins (1760–94), French revolutionary politician, pamphleteer, and journalist; Danton's secretary in ministry of justice; guillotined with him.

15. John Milton, *Il Penseroso,* ll. 173–74.

16. Langdon Cheves was chosen as delegate to the Nashville Convention by a caucus of the legislature of South Carolina. At the November session he delivered a speech of nearly three hours, recommending the secession of a united South; the speech was immediately published as a pamphlet, a second edition in 1851. Andrew Pickens Butler, in the speech from which LSM quotes above, also referred to her father as "the venerable Cheves."

17. Samuel Butler, *Hudibras* 3.2.677–82: "For Zeal's a dreadful Termagant, / That teaches Saints to Tear, and Rant; / And Independents, to profess / The Doctrine, of Dependences; / Turns meek and sneaking Secret ones, / To Raw-heads fierce, and Bloody Bones." Raw-head and Bloody Bones were bugbears used by nurses to frighten children.

18. We know that an afterthought sought to cover the appearance of want of respect, and that the letter, to which a reading was first refused, was afterwards voted to be printed; but the facts are as we state them. [LSM] Cheves, although elected a delegate from Charleston to the May meeting of South Carolina's Southern Rights Associations, did not attend but sent a letter containing his views opposing separate secession; the letter, which was read out to the convention at its afternoon session on May 6, is printed in *Proceedings of the Southern Rights Associations,* pp. 8–12; also in the Charleston *Mercury,* May 7, 1851.

submitted *his* resolutions and address, evidently cut and dried for the occasion.[19] There was little intention to make the meeting a deliberative assembly, for it is scarcely possible to suppose that the committee of twenty-one, whatever the genius and talent of its members, had taken sufficient time, since its nomination, to compose so important an address, and mature such momentous resolutions, when we remember that its nomination had only been on the morning of the same day. The committee, or at least the acting portion of it, had very evidently decided itself a committee, and determined its measures, before the assemblage even of the convention. Such is universally the action of clubs and club-meetings. They are never governed but by caucus and demagoguism. Let, then, the action of this convention be taken for what it is worth, i.e., for the action of certain associations, who have most undoubtedly a right to the expression of their own opinions; but none, whatever, to endeavour to give to those opinions the impression of State action. Few as there are of submissionists and Union men in our State, still there is, even of these Yankeeized Southrons, some small sprinkling to be found. These men might, with equal propriety as the convention to which we refer, gather themselves together, as district delegates, pass their resolutions, write their addresses, and claim to be exponents of the spirit of South Carolina. Difference of numbers would make no difference in legality of action. Both of these meetings are, or rather would be, the representatives only of party, and both would be, we regret to say, in our opinion, equally mischievous, could they succeed in giving to their voice the impress of State sovereignty. When the State speaks, let it be through her proper authorities, and with the due solemnity of legalized assemblies, not the party violence of club-meetings. We think it will be a question worth the consideration of our approaching legislature, whether men who have prematurely committed themselves to any decisive mode of action, independently of future events, have not thus incapacitated themselves as members of a grave deliberative body such as our State convention, should it ever assemble, ought to be; and whether it might not be the wisest course of such legislature to abstain from calling the meeting of so important a body, under circumstances which would so much shackle, and contribute to prevent, its discreet and sober action. Faction and party-spirit have worked hard, and done much, since the elections to the proposed convention have been made.[20] To such a meeting, its members ought to come with clean hands and clear heads.

---

19. *Proceedings of the Southern Rights Associations*, pp. 12–17.

20. Elections for South Carolina's constituent convention were held on Feb. 10 and 11, 1851. Langdon Cheves was head of the Charleston delegation. The Charleston *Mercury* calculated 127 of the 169 delegates elected to be in favor of separate secession. By the time of

The present is a crisis of vital importance, not to South Carolina alone, but to the South generally. Indissolubly are we united, for weal or for woe, with our Southern sisters. As Ruth clave unto Naomi, so we to them.[21] Surely, their people should be our people, and their *God* our *God*. One we are in interests, one in hopes, and one in dangers; and one we *must be*—unless the Almighty has frowned upon us his darkest measure of reprobation—one we must be in effort. Surely, so important a consummation is worth years of patience and of striving. Shall we, then, throw away our last chance, in the violent excitement of party dispute, and to maintain the honour of inconsiderate heroism?

We have talked enough—more than enough—of "Palmetto banners," "bleaching bones," and "Southern chivalry." Such boasts have become a byeword, and a taunt, in the mouths of our opponents. It were well to let them sleep. When a man talks much of his own valour, we are aptest to doubt it, and the truly brave and great need not trumpet their own merits. There is a self-respect to be exercised, as well by communities as individuals; and is there not, in this continual vaunting, an implied disgrace—a doubt, at least, of the spirit of our people, which would thus appear to need such a system, to keep it to the point of action? This "blood and ashes" style of oratory suits only the schoolboy, or the vaunting Bobadil.[22] The continual exercise of it has placed us somewhat in the position of the champion in the Eastern tale who, having it in aim to conquer some magic spell of evil, is suddenly introduced into a capacious and mysterious abode, where are suspended before him a sword and a horn, with an accompanying inscription, importing that victory will fall to him who chooses rightly between these implements. The rash, nervous, and, if we may so express ourselves, *timorous valour* of the would-be hero, induces him to seize the horn; but, as he blows, troops of armed knights rush upon the unfortunate and defenceless wight, felling him to the ground, and leaving the victory to be gained by the wiser and braver

---

elections in October for delegates to the proposed Southern congress, however, the opponents of separate secession had rallied; they won decisive victories in twenty of the state's twenty-nine judicial districts and by an aggregate vote of about 25,062 to 17,617. When the constituent convention met, after numerous postponements, on April 26, 1852, Langdon Cheves moved that a Committee of Twenty-One be appointed to oversee the convention's business and to draft its report; Cheves was appointed its chairman. The convention approved the committee's two measures, which together asserted South Carolina's right to secede from the Union; no further action was taken. The proposed Southern congress never met.

21. Ruth 1:14.
22. John Milton, "Sonnet 18: On the Late Massacre in Piedmont," l. 10. Captain Bobadill is the boastful soldier in Ben Jonson's *Every Man in His Humour*.

champion, whose cool courage and deliberate reason prompt him to *draw the sword* before he blows the horn.

We have boasted too much—quite too much—already. An act of separate secession would be but a continued boasting—a farther blowing of the horn. Every reasoning man feels that it would be so, and if he, for a moment, sincerely maintains the contrary, it will be found, we think, to be because he has not fairly weighed and sifted his own words. He advocates separate secession, not because he believes in the efficacy of separate secession *per se,* but only so far (in his own mind, at least) as he regards it as a means of precipitating the course of our sister States, and dragging them into action. The talk about San Marino republics,[23] English alliance, and so forth, is merely a glittering bait, to amuse the crowd—a new way of blowing the horn. We speak of thinking men, for no doubt there are thousands of unfledged lads, whose green reason exudes in boiling wrath and illogical conclusions, who would contend, and believe too, in the sincerity of their enthusiasm, that South Carolina can live and flourish by the mere chivalry of her sons, a Lilliput empire, with the spirit of the world against her and her institutions. But this can never do. As we love the South, as we love our State, as we cherish her institutions, her honour, her very existence, let us cease this trumpeting, nor again blow the horn before we draw the sword—ay, even before we have the sword to draw! Is it the part of valour, or of prudence, thus weaponless to give the taunt, hoping that others may be roused to redeem our pledge?

And will they thus be roused? This is a fearful throw, and the advocates of separate secession are playing a game of brag, too alarming to contemplate with composure. Desperate gamesters, they cast into the stake not only property and life, but children and country—and for what? *"Because the State cannot recede, without dishonour."* Ay, say they so, these men of valour? Truly, we love our State as devoutly, and shrink from her shame with as nice a sense of honour, as they; but we deny that our honour is engaged, to the breaking of our own necks, by this worse than Curtius-like leap.[24] There has been no oracle, to promise us that this self-devotion shall save our country. On the contrary, the voice of wisdom calls a halt. The State, thank heaven! is *not* pledged to separate action and, we trust in *God,* will not be driven to a measure so suicidal. The State has declared that the South ought to act, and

---

23. San Marino, a tiny (24 sq. mi.) independent republic, southwest of Rimini, twelve miles from the Adriatic coast, traced its existence back to the fourth century.

24. In his account of the year 362 B.C. the Roman historian Livy records (7.6.1–5) that, a chasm having opened in the Roman Forum, a young soldier named Marcus Curtius, commanded by an oracle, rode fully armed, his horse likewise, into the gulf as a sacrifice to secure the safety of the republic.

holds herself in readiness to act, according to the pledge given by her best and boldest sons, at Nashville and elsewhere, so soon as she sees opportunity for doing so, without breaking her own neck by a desperate plunge and, at the same time, stabbing to the heart, in her blind struggles, the last hope for liberty of her Southern sisters. The State is ready to redeem every pledge she has ever given, and will only fail to do so if driven on by party, which thus coolly assumes her dictatorship. She would prove false to the cause by committing herself to a move so treasonable, as is separate State secession, to Southern interests. By pausing with dignity, in an effort to unite, instead of alienating the South, South Carolina is *not receding;* she takes no step backward but, on the contrary, firmly stands precisely where she did when, at the last session of her legislature, she stood, proud of the counsels of him, her "old man eloquent,"[25] who, confident alike in her boldness and her prudence, brought to her legislative halls the pledge which, in *her* name, he had just given at Nashville, and received the only reward suited to his merit, the hearty "well done, thou good and faithful servant,"[26] echoed by the true representatives of his native State. Has the State changed, since this period? and, while South Carolina holds such a position, resolute and unflinching, has she the traitor-son who will dare accuse her of receding from her pledges? If such there be, let the mother who bore him shrink from his kiss, for would the Judas who defames his country spare even his mother's blush?

"Faithful and true,"[27] South Carolina stands to her pledges. We pause, but we do not recede. The South bids us pause, and she has *a right* so to do. Each and every Southern State has a right to deliberate and investigate, before taking a step so momentous in our history as a disruption of this Union, foul and rotten though it be. We are convinced that disunion is the only remedy for our ills. Gladly would we persuade our Southern sisters to the same belief; but, pending their decision, they have a right to bid us pause. We pause, not to yield, but to maintain our position, while our hosts are gathering. They have never told us that they will desert us; they have never surrendered their arms; and we will win their confidence by admitting that they will not prove recreant to their duty—that they are not slavishly apathetic to their rights. We differ from them in time and expediency of action, but must allow something to their judgment, nor endeavour to gag them with our ideas of right. We will never make a man our friend by calling him a rascal,

---

25. John Milton, "Sonnet X: To the Lady Margaret Ley," ll. 6–8. This quotation, referring to the Athenian orator Isocrates (436–338 B.C.), appears also in LSM's defense of her father, *PDBL,* "Langdon Cheves: Review of 'Reminiscences of Public Men,'" p. 236.
26. Matt. 25:21.
27. Rev. 22:6.

and giving him a kick to prove it; nor, we believe, will the plan be likely to prove at all more effectual with States than with individuals. The former, like the latter, may feel that they have a right to the guardianship of their own honour, and be rather revolted than convinced by the dictatorial *ipse dixit* of another.

One of the arguments of the separate secessionists is, that the State is now ready for action, and it is doubtful whether it will bear delay. They think it necessary to keep up an eternal puffing and blowing, for fear the fire will burn out, and the glowing iron cool. Fie upon it! Is it so hard to keep "our courage to the sticking point"?[28] and cannot we be trusted to keep our honour's truth, but we must, like some poor coward, dragged up to the lists, be held there at the bayonet's point, lest we may turn and run? If such were the spirit of our State, then indeed were it time to bow ourselves in the dust— then indeed is "the glory departed from Israel."[29] Such courage is fear, such fire but cowardice! If our spirit of resistance has not strength to survive prudent delay, it is but a mocking semblance of firmness, and failure becomes certain. But we have a higher opinion of our people. We need not fight today, for fear that, ere tomorrow, our bottled up courage will evaporate, and leave the trembling slave to crouch to the yoke. The firm spirit can "bide its time," and the truly brave among Carolina's statesmen do not fear to trust Carolina's sons.[30] They feel that these are ready for duty when the fitting time shall come, and will not need to be whipped up to the cannon's mouth, as an alternative to a regular *stampede*.

Let us give up the "Hercules' vein,"[31] and confess—for there is no shame in it—that we are not strong enough, we of South Carolina alone, to maintain our cause. We can die! ay, and bury our children beneath the ruins of our hearthstones, that our enemies may triumph and our names be forgotten. But it would be desperation, not courage, which would prompt us to this. True courage can bear and forbear, can wait and watch, and strive and endure. It is impatience, not courage—it is coward shrinking, not resolution—which casts itself upon the sword point to terminate its struggles. The ancient Roman was half a barbarian, when he sought death as a cure for

---

28. *Macbeth* 1.7.60–62 (the speaker is Lady Macbeth): "We fail? / But screw your courage to the sticking-place, / And we'll not fail."

29. 1 Sam. 4:21–22.

30. George Croly, "The Woe upon Israel," in *Scenes from Scripture, with Other Poems* (London, 1851), ll. 35–40: "Israel, where are now thy wise? / Woe to those who live by lies, / Calling (all their souls deceit) / Evil good, and bitter sweet, / Selling justice, pampering crime, / But revenge shall bide its time!"

31. *Midsummer Night's Dream* 1.2.36–37: "This is Ercles' vein, a tyrant's vein: a lover is more condoling."

life's evils; a higher civilization—a nobler philosophy—teaches us to *bear* and *conquer* them.

Because we are weak, our enemies have trampled us. Because we are weak, yet a little longer must we endure their insult. But because we are weak, not therefore are we cowards. Rather is the sense of our wrongs keener, from the sense of our weakness, and, if we pause, we pause that our strength may grow with our endurance. The South *must* unite, and our spring will be the more vigorous and resistless from the gathered might of our temporary crouch. We have much faith in our legislature. We cannot believe that this body, upon the eve of so momentous a step, will move without due consideration. When great events require great minds to work them out to their conclusions, such minds are generally found to rise, as it were, heaven-inspired from the chaotic mass which surrounds them. We trust in *God,* that He has not so shut us out from all hope of mercy that our every beacon-light is to be dashed aside and extinguished by the roar of passion which environs us. We trust in *God,* that the legislature, upon the prudence of whose action so much depends, will (although a majority of its members may be young in years) act like grave men, upon whose decision the destinies of a nation hang, and not like some rabble-rout of school-boys, impatient to rid themselves of the supervision of their preceptors, and who fancy that noisy bragging can be mistaken for heroism. The members of such a body have assumed to themselves, on entering it, heavy duties and responsibilities, well calculated to make men pause in the acting. All their boldness they will need; but should it not be purged from the very shadow of rashness? Men upon whom a nation's fate depends have no longer the right to be young. Deep thought, which sits like dew upon the brow—"for thought is brain-sweat"—should

> From the table of their memory
> All trivial records wipe,
> Leaving the book and volume of the brain
> Unmixed with baser matter.[32]

There is, in the question which we discuss, and the decision of which must virtually fall upon our legislature, matter

> To make the brow to ache, the eye turn dim,
> And resolution search itself for rashness,
> Or ere it dares to plunge.

---

32. *Hamlet* 1.5.98–99, 102–4: "Yea, from the table of my memory / I'll wipe away all trivial fond records, . . . / And thy commandment all alone shall live / Within the book and volume of my brain, / Unmix'd with baser matter."

We have faith in our legislature, and *God* grant that we be not deceived.

The *right* of secession we are not inclined to discuss—we consider it too well established to need argument. The *risk* of it, to life, limb, and property, not one who deserves the name of man will shrink from. The *mischievous folly* of separate secession, acting as an alienating medium between ourselves and our true and natural allies, is alone what we fear. If the step be taken, our life for it, you have no truer soldiers than those who now warn you from action. "Our country, right or wrong,"[33] will be the watchword of our State. (Alas! alas! that our own blind precipitancy should oblige us to limit this certainty to *our State*, rather than extend it to *our country*, our *Southern Union*, our home of hope!) If there is to be any "bleaching of bones" upon our battle-fields, the names and families of such men as Cheves, Barnwell, and Butler will have as full a share in the anticipated sacrifice as those of any other more fiery heroes of all the State rights associations in the country. "These men are cautious, fearful; we will not listen to their arguments; this is a time to act, and not to reason," say our hot-headed and unripe counsellors. These men, we answer, *are* cautious, fearful; but of what? Cautious of *self*? Fearful of *personal* risk? If there be tongue of slander vile enough to utter, if there be ear of folly senseless enough to listen to, so vapid a charge, we will not disgrace our pen by referring to it. They are cautious for their country; fearful of *her* perils; and, while their blood boils beneath oppression, they have the courage and self-possession to plead with us: patience, prudence, even for the sake of that cherished country. They have the courage to raise their voices against the stormy cry of faction, to warn that faction against its own rashness. They have the courage of that Aemilius who, at Cannae, after vainly striving to check the hot zeal of an imprudent colleague, when that colleague had, in spite of all remonstrances, made such a disposition of his troops as completely to place himself in the power of the enemy, was yet ready to die nobly, in the desperate struggle, brought on by the headlong rashness of another. While the boastful Varro fled from the slaughter consequent upon his own obstinate folly, Aemilius died upon the field. "My part is chosen," exclaimed the expiring hero when urged to flight. "My part is chosen. Go and tell the Senate, from me, to fortify Rome against the approach of the conqueror."[34] If the State needs victims, she will find, perchance, the firmest not among her noisiest politicians.

33. From a toast given at Norfolk, in April 1816, by Marylander naval hero Stephen Decatur (1779–1820).

34. Lucius Aemilius Paullus and Gaius Terentius Varro, the consuls of 216 B.C., were in personal command of the Roman army when it met the Carthaginian forces, under the command of Hannibal, near the town of Cannae in Apulia. Tradition held that Varro rashly committed his troops to battle without consulting his colleague, who was compelled by

We were at first inclined to believe that the expression of opinions made by the "meeting of delegates of Southern Rights Associations," of May last, was calculated not only to do much, but unmitigated, evil. The rashness and dogmatic assumption of its course (we begin, however, to hope) is bringing its own antidote. Men are startled at the idea of being thus over-ridden; and the warning, we hope, will prove salutary. Leaders of clubs are seldom the best leaders for nations; and a revolution effected by mere animal excitement is inevitably a failure. Revolutions ought not to be made too easily: they are fierce remedies, for fiercer ills, and, when rashly applied, they become, like the knife of the surgeon in the hands of the quack, instruments, not of healing, but of death. Revolutions, to be efficient, must be the work of intense thought, grave effort, systematized action, and, consequently, of time. They ought not, we repeat, to be made too easily. Witness France, where revolutions have become the bloody toy of the multitude; who fight for they know not what; spurning today the idol of yesterday, and calling for revolution as they would for a parade or "un spectacle." Hasty revolution (and it were folly to deny that we are on the eve of revolution, for, however legalized, still it is revolution at which we aim) must always be inefficient, if not mischievous. Give us time: time to arrange our forces; time to bring our people to the point of action (by people we mean our Southern people, not simply Carolinians); time to show them the necessity and the right of that action; time to accustom themselves to the idea of severing old ties— for, even when such ties are chains, the habit of wearing them is to be conquered. No people roused by a fit of momentary passion (and years are but moments, in the history of nations) has ever accomplished great deeds. Oh! you, our too hasty brethren, to whom, in our heart of hearts, we cling— for one aim, one thought is ours—pause yet, ere the Rubicon be passed, which is to sever us not only from foes but from friends; pause, ere we throw down the gauntlet of defiance, not to our oppressors alone, but to those, our sisters in endurance, who (give them but the time) must yet be with us in our struggle. Pause, were it but for unanimity in our own State, at a crisis when division were death. Give us time!— time!

"Time," you answer, "we have had time enough! This storm has been brewing for a quarter of a century." Most truly, and in very deed, it hath! The seeds of it were planted even with the forming of that constitution to which we have vainly clung, and looked for aid, and fain would have called sacred, while our opponents have sneered at our credulity, and trampled it in the dust. This storm has, of a truth, been brewing long; but who among

---

events to come to his aid; Paullus, with most of the Roman army, was killed, Varro being among the survivors. LSM follows Livy 22.45–49 and Plutarch *Fabius Maximus* 14–16.

us have been fully awake to the muttering wrath of its insidious approach? awake to the consciousness of danger? awake to the point of resistance? It is but of very recent date that the word "disunion" has ceased to be (even in South Carolina) a word almost of treason. Has there been, until within the last three or four years, more than one voice in the country which dared to boldly predict, and warn us of the possible necessity of, such a measure. Mr. Cheves, we know, as far back as the year 1830, publicly expressed the opinion that joint resistance of the Southern States was the only hope for the preservation of the Union in its integrity, and, that hope failing, disunion, if not our choice, might be "our necessity."[35] But did not Mr. Cheves stand alone? Did not even the nullifiers, of that date, against whose expedient he argued as a partial and inefficient measure, shrink from the word "disunion"? We have ourselves heard a Hayne and a Hamilton,[36] then among the most active resistants to governmental oppression, and personal intimates of Mr. Cheves, answer the arguments of the latter by the avowal that they were not prepared to go so far. They believed his remedy to be more severe than was needful. Time, alas! has proved but too fully the correctness of Mr. Cheves's position; and the same voice which, in 1830, exclaimed, "Submit? Why, the question is, whether we shall <will> bear oppression or not!"—the same voice which counselled us then that "any measure, by one of the suffering states alone, will be a measure of feebleness, subject to many hazards; any union, among the same states, will be a measure of strength, almost of certain success"—twenty years after echoed itself at Nashville, "Submit? Submit? The very sound curdles the blood in my veins! But O! great God, unite us, and a tale of submission shall never be told!"[37]

Mr. Cheves, then, foresaw the necessity which has fallen upon our times, but stood alone in so doing. How long is it (three or four years, we think) since Mr. Calhoun, decidedly the most popular man in the State of South

35. Langdon Cheves to John Taylor et al., Charleston, Sept. 15, 1830, reprinted from the Columbia *Times and Gazette* in *Niles' Register* 39 (Oct. 1830): 129–32; 131–32: "Disunion will not be her [South Carolina's] choice, but her necessity." At a States' Rights Dinner given in Charleston on July 1, 1830, at which prominent nullifiers were the speakers, Langdon Cheves had spoken in opposition to nullification, favoring instead united action by all Southern states. This opposition he reiterated in the letter cited above, replying to an invitation to attend another States' Rights Dinner, to be held in Columbia on Sept. 20, 1830.

36. On Robert Young Hayne, Cheves' law partner and close friend, see LSM to Langdon Cheves, Jr., Oct. 7, 1839, in chap. 11 below. James Hamilton (1786–1857), governor of South Carolina (1830–32); president of its convention adopting an Ordinance of Nullification (November 1832).

37. Cheves to Taylor et al., p. 130; *Speech of the Hon. Langdon Cheves in the Southern Convention at Nashville, Tennessee, November 14, 1850* ([Nashville?]: Southern Rights Association, 1850), p. 30.

Carolina, declared that, if there were any man in the Union sincerely attached to it, that man *was himself.* We cannot doubt the perfect sincerity of Mr. Calhoun, in this declaration, and certainly there was, at that time, no single voice in the State so potential, or so well calculated to speak the spirit of the majority, as his. Progress is never found in rapid change, and the sudden and fierce desire of a large portion (we will not believe it the majority of the State) to throw itself "o' the other side"[38] speaks impulse rather than reason. We must not attempt (time and space—our editor being stringent against long articles—forbid it) to sum up our authorities in favour of waiting upon a Southern Union, as opposed to hurried separate State action; neither have we space to dwell upon the inevitable evils, the bitter feuds, the heart-burnings and jealousies, which the opposite measure entails upon us, terminating in long if not permanent estrangement among States whose prosperity, whose very existence, depends upon union among themselves; neither can we dwell upon the crushed hopes, the bitter remorse, the angry revilings which must ensue, even among the now united advocates of this hasty measure, to make our State a very hell of discord, and passion, violence, and rancour the rulers of its fate. Such thoughts would swell our article into a volume. They have been profoundly discussed and, we hope, will be as profoundly studied. But, having mentioned the popular name of Calhoun, and as our violent party have made large use of it, delighting in rhetorical flourishes about his "guardian spirit," which they suppose to be looking down sympathizingly upon their course, we must be allowed to quote the authority of this distinguished statesman himself against these worshippers and desecrators of his name. In a letter addressed to Mr. Foote in August, 1849, and recently published in the New Orleans *Delta,* Mr. Calhoun, after stating his desire, which he presumes to be that "of every true hearted Southern man, [. . .] to save, if possible, the Union, as well as ourselves; but, if both cannot be, then to save ourselves at all events," remarks,

> *Without concert of action, on the part of the South, neither can be saved;* by it, if it be not too long delayed, it is possible *both yet may be.* Without it, we cannot satisfy the North that the South is in earnest, and will, if forced, choose resistance; and, until she is satisfied of this,[39] the causes which have brought the question between the two sections to its present dangerous stage from a small beginning, will continue to operate, until it will be too late to save the Union, and nothing will be left us but *to dissolve the connection. To do that,*

38. *Macbeth* 1.7.25–28: "I have no spur / To prick the sides of my intent, but only / Vaulting ambition, which o'erleaps itself, / And falls on the other."
39. "Of this" added by LSM.

concert of action would be necessary, not to save the Union, for it would be too late; but *to save ourselves.* Thus, in my <any> view, *concert is the one thing needful.*[40]

From the above extract we may draw two conclusions, most important to our argument. First, that Mr. Calhoun had, at this period, become entirely concurrent in the opinions of Mr. Cheves, expressed nearly twenty years before, concerning the necessity of a *concert of action* among the Southern States, which, as we see, he here pronounces to be *"the one thing needful"*; and, secondly, that, at so late a period as August, 1849, but a few months before his death,[41] he had by no means abandoned the hope of seeing the Union preserved in its integrity. In favour of this hope we are not inclined to argue. The measure of our sufferings has long been full, and new injuries have heaped it to overflowing. We feel, with Mr. Cheves, that "the Union is already dissolved," and the constitution a "*caput mortuum*"—a "shape of dead formalities," wherein we have no farther interest than had "free Rome" in that constitution by which "Caligula made his horse a Roman consul."[42] We argue not for the Union—"the glorious Union"—at whose chariot-wheels we have long been dragged, the victims of its triumphal progress; but we notice the above-quoted opinion of Mr. Calhoun, as showing how rapid a change has come over the spirit of our State—for we presume there is no man to dispute that Mr. Calhoun was, from his extreme popularity, as much as any one man could be, the exponent of that spirit. Certainly South Carolina was not, at the date of this letter, prepared for disunion—still less for separate secession. Two short years have since passed over us. And are two years enough to so entirely change the sentiments of her people as to authorize not only the great and momentous revolution which we contemplate (and which may heaven speed!), but such an eagerness for forcing on that revolution that we, in our hot haste, must throw overboard all hope of uniting our sister States and, calling them traitor and recreant because they think as we did two years ago, rush headlong upon separate secession? True, we have suffered new injuries since that time; but does the tumultuous and unregulated action by which it is proposed to right these injuries not better

---

40. John C. Calhoun to Henry Stuart Foote, Fort Hill, Aug. 3, 1849, in the New Orleans *Daily Delta,* May 29, 1851; reprinted from the *Delta* in the Charleston *Mercury,* June 4, 1851 (LSM's italics). Henry Stuart Foote (1804–80), senator (1847–52), then governor (1852–54), of Mississippi.

41. John C. Calhoun died in Washington, D.C., on March 31, 1850.

42. *Speech of the Hon. Langdon Cheves in the Southern Convention at Nashville, Tennessee, November 14, 1850,* p. 17. The Roman biographer Suetonius records only that the emperor Caligula (A.D. 12–41) was reported to have intended to confer the consulship upon his favorite racehorse Incitatus (*Gaius Caligula* 55.3).

suit a schoolboy rebellion, and barring out (in which the actors, as a matter of course, are not only destined, but expect, to be punished and whipped back into submission), than the grave action of grave men, legislating for the most important crisis which the history of their country could present?

It cannot be that this disgrace has come upon our time.

Our *true leaders,* resolute in resistance, are opposed to violent and separate action. Among the party in favour of such action, there is scarcely a single man to whom the State has hitherto been accustomed to look for advice. All whom South Carolina has hitherto held dear and venerable in authority are opposed to this movement. She will, she must, be guided by the kindly, calm, and rational counsels of her long-tried advisers. We will not believe otherwise of the State we love so well!

The question is not, with us, one between resistance and submission. We are unanimous for resistance—resistance to the death—and the wariest of our counsellors, when the struggle comes, will be found shoulder to shoulder with the warmest. The doubt is not *whether,* but *how* shall we resist? and our leading men plead with us, even as a father pleadeth with his children,[43] to use wisely those means which God and nature have given us, rather than throw them away in weak, futile, and misguided effort. If there is, as we have suggested, a hope in the spirit of reaction caused by the dictatorial tone of the May convention and its evident desire to force the State into premature action, there is also, we cannot deny to ourselves, the fear of a result much to be dreaded and, should it occur, never too deeply to be deplored. This reaction may become too extreme. There is, in every country, and amidst the most enlightened population, a large proportion whose natural instinct leads them, in difficult political questions, to submit the guidance of their judgments to stronger minds, whose power and truth experience has taught them to venerate. There is danger that such men, misled by the opprobrium which the violent party endeavours to cast upon the more prudent, may become, to a certain extent, embarrassed between the submissionist and the *bona fide* resistance party. The principles, the faith, and the men of these parties are, indeed, wide as the poles asunder; but an error or a slander, constantly and emphatically repeated, obtains finally, in the ears of unthinking men, a familiarity which stamps it with a semblance of truth. There are many men who will have sufficient diffidence of their own judgments, and sufficient respect for such names and opinions as we have cited, to induce them, very much, to regulate their course by these opinions. If, then, the vituperation of party violence can succeed in convincing such individuals that the almost dying words of a Calhoun, that the earnest and

43. Job 16:21.

prophet-like appeals of a Cheves, that the advice of a Barnwell, a Butler, besides a host of true and noble men, fire-tried in our political struggles, are in favour of submission, is there not danger that such vituperation is doing much to the manufacture of submissionists?

As we believe that there are many, very many, true and earnest hearts among those against whom we argue, those our only too zealous brethren, we would beg them, in God's name, to beware of such a result. Then, indeed, might South Carolina be in danger of receding from her pledges; then, indeed, might there be fear that she would hold out her hands to the shackles; and then, when trampled under the heel of the oppressor, would the sin and the shame be upon those who have deceived her people into believing that this was the voice, this the advice, of her wise men, her seers and her prophets! Hush the voice of passion and of slander; let the people judge for themselves, rather than through the dictation of party associations; and we have no fear that they will be misled by the opinions of those very men whose trumpet-call to freedom has been the first to rouse them to the consciousness and defence of their rights. We have no fear that they will be deceived, by *ignis fatuus* lights, from the flame of those altars, where the fire of their patriotism has first been lighted! *Pro patria! Fide et Fiducia.*[44]

44. "For our country! With loyalty and confidence." The collocation of *fides* and *fiducia* is very old, dating at least from Plautus (d. c. 184 B.C.).

3.

Negro-mania

The highest capacity of man, and its noblest use, is the discovery and execution of the Almighty behests, thus enabling him to second instead of opposing the beautiful order of God's developed thought in creation. If the negro be an inferior man, the struggle against God's will, which aims at putting him upon the same footing as the superior, is only not an impious work in so far as it is a blind and a foolish one. Folly, unfortunately, often leads to consequences fatal as vice, and there is nothing more mischievous than active ignorance. In the fanaticism which now actually desolates some of the most favored and beautiful parts of our globe, threatening others even at the risk of dragging to earth the high-reared monuments of man's civilization, we find vicious malevolence and ignorance combining their power to raise some higher law than any which God has sanctioned; and because the black man cannot reach the level of the white, they would even drag down and degrade the white to *his* capacities.

Can it be that in an age when science walks abroad, astonishing the world by a progress hitherto unequaled in her annals—when no longer, with snail-like advance, she labors the ascent to knowledge, but rather leaps forward to her magnificent conclusions—when she girdles the world with steam, and flashes her lightning thought, even with lightning speed, through the expanse of a continent—when we see her votaries (in the eloquent language

---

De Bow 12 (May 1852) = *PSE*, pp. 222–44; this excerpt at pp. 224–29. Publication reviewed: John Campbell, *Negro-mania: Being an Examination of the Falsely Assumed Equality of the Various Races of Men* . . . (Philadelphia: Campbell and Power, 1851).

of Professor Lieber), "like priests of nature, revealing [some of] her great <greatest> mysteries and showing thought, one thought, the thought of God, pervading the universe and its phases"[1]—oh! can it be that this is to be swept aside, or rather crushed down to the level of a Haytien civilization? Can it be, that the great *one thought*, that *thought of God*, so beautifully pictured out even in the lowest, as in the highest, of his works, is to be tinkered at and defaced, patched and plastered, by a set of madmen, whose one idea seems to be built upon some whining, Wilberforcian, Clarksonized wail of "black brethren" and "negro improvement"?[2] Verily, nature "suffereth long and is kind,"[3] or, ere this, had her curse fallen upon us. We struggle against her, we fiercely resist her teachings, and fancy that these poor heads of ours—to say nothing of black Sambo's and Cuffee's—can regulate matters by a higher law than hers. But the time cometh when our probation can last no longer. Then, and in "rather a terrible manner,"[4] it is to be feared, we will receive our lesson! Is it not even now, alas, beginning? What is this cry over Europe, echoing even to our own shores? What means this darkly-shadowed caricature of good—this horrible disfigurement of Christian charity—which, but that it stalks in terrible reality before us, would seem like the mockery of some fearful dream? The angel form which we have gazed upon and worshiped as Christian charity and brotherly love, now suddenly starts forth, grinning upon us in hideous deformity of vice, and gibbering out its horrible obscenities of "socialism" and "communism," drags along upon its track the shouting mob, who, in their ravings for "negro abolition" and "universal equality," trample under foot at once God's law and man's law—virtue and decency. The demon is unchained. This widespread and wider-spreading evil figures forth, not badly, the beast of the Apocalypse, unto whom "was given a mouth speaking great things and blasphemies; . . . and he opened his mouth in blasphemy against God, to blaspheme his name, . . . and power was given him over all kindreds, and tongues, and nations."[5]

---

1. Francis Lieber, *The Necessity of Continued Self-Education: An Address to the Graduating Class of S.C. College, at Commencement, on the First of December, 1851* (Columbia, S.C., 1851), p. 10. Francis Lieber (1800–1872), German-born political economist; professor at South Carolina College (1835–56); at Columbia College in New York City (1857–65) and Columbia Law School (1865–72).

2. William Wilberforce (1759–1833), English politician (member of Parliament from 1780 to 1825), evangelical Christian, and a leader of the antislavery crusade. Thomas Clarkson (1760–1846), English abolitionist; associate of Wilberforce; author, among other works, of *History of the Abolition of the African Slave-Trade* (1808).

3. 1 Cor. 13:4.

4. Campbell, *Negro-mania*, p. 514 = [Thomas Carlyle], "Occasional Discourse on the Negro Question," *Fraser's Magazine* 40 (Dec. 1849): 670–79; 675.

5. Rev. 13:5–7.

The strength of this hideous power is now interesting itself largely in the negro cause; and because the innovators find the impossibility of putting into execution their crude theories among their white brethren, and more nearly equalized population, they, in their agony for action, look about for something tangible, something less impossible, and fancy that it is found in the abolition of negro slavery. Alas! for the mistaken folly of those who, in thus acting, act sincerely. Their well-meaning and officious ignorance is pushed on by the powerful lever of fanaticism to ends from which they would shrink in affright could they see them in full development, but which, in half-way execution, they rejoice over, as the poor idiot gazes in delighted wonder and warms his fingers by the blaze which is demolishing his dwelling, fancying the while that he has done a wise thing in the application of the spark which has lighted to their destruction his own and his neighbors' homes.

Alas for their folly! But wo! wo! a wo of darkness and of death! a wo of hell and of perdition to those who, better knowing, goad folly on to such an extreme! This is indeed the sin not to be forgiven, the sin against the Holy Ghost and against the spirit of God.[6] The beautiful order of Creation, breathed down from Almighty intelligence, is to be moulded and wrought by fanatic intelligence! until dragged down at last to negro intelligence!!

The Almighty has thought well to place certain of his creatures in certain fixed positions in this world of ours, for what cause he has not seen fit to make quite clear to our limited capacities; and why an ass is not a man, or a man an ass, will probably forever remain a mystery to our limited intellects. One thing, however, he has in his mercy made clear enough, viz., that by no manner of education; no stocks, braces, nor regimental drillings; no problems, theories, nor definitions; neither by steam nor by telegraph, neither by mesmerism nor by chloroform, can our unfortunate brother ass, whether mentally or corporeally, be induced to consider himself as a gentleman, and act accordingly. *He,* at least, is not capable of attaining the *white* civilization of this our nineteenth century. We hope that our philanthropic friends will allow us this. We would fain have some sure ground to stand upon, but do not feel quite certain that they may not come with some new-fangled theory of communism to knock this platform also from under our feet. Believing, however, that (until the spirit of improvement rises a step or two higher) they will allow us our position, we would beg them to instruct us upon what principle of justice this unfortunate brother ass—this hirsute relative—should be so bedeviled and trampled upon. Why should he not lie amidst feathers and velvet, as well as the best in the land? And why, above all, must

---

6. Ezek. 16:23: "Woe, woe unto thee! saith the Lord God"; Matt. 12:31: "All manner of sin and blasphemy shall be forgiven unto men: but the blasphemy against the Holy Ghost shall not be forgiven unto men."

he help work to make such feathers and velvet comfortable lodgings for his so-called betters? God-given intellect and power to attain count for nothing in this modern system of arguing. The ass has as good a right to the possession of intellect as the man; and if God has not given it to him, we must remedy the injustice by some patent "free-and-equal" system. The process is easy enough. If the ass cannot stand on two legs, knock the man down to all fours (nothing is simpler), and *vive la fraternité!* Why did not the Almighty save us all this trouble, and make the ass a man, or the man an ass, from the beginning? Truly, 'tis a problem hard to solve, and poor donkey, with his lamentable braying, comes as near an explanation as all our philosophizing can do. God made the world—God gave thee there thy place, my hirsute brother; and according to all earthly probabilities and possibilities, it is thy destiny therein to remain, bray as thou wilt. From the same great power have our sable friends, Messrs. Sambo, Cuffee, and Co., received their position also; with which position, allow us to remark, the worthy ancestors of Messrs. Sambo, Cuffee, and Co. have continued perfectly satisfied for some four thousand years (longer, perchance, but records go no farther), and their descendants would, most undoubtedly, have so continued; but behold, Satan, as when

> Squat like a toad, close at the ear of Eve,
> Assaying by his devilish arts to reach
> The organs of her fancy,[7]

comes now in the likeness of an "all men are born free and equal" advocate, to raise "vain hopes, vain aims, inordinate desires"[8] in poor Cuffee's hitherto quiet brain!

Alas, "my poor black brother!" thou, like the hirsute, must do thy braying in vain. Where God has placed thee, there must thou stay. "You, Quashee, my pumpkin—not a bad fellow either, this poor Quashee, when tolerably guided!—idle Quashee, I say you must get the devil *sent away* from your elbow, my poor dark friend! In this world there will be no existence for you otherwise."[9] To the immortals, perchance, this tempest in a teapot, this little hubbub on our little globe, may look trifling enough, they seeing very certainly that at the end of some score of centuries all things will go right again. Quashee will either have gone back to his quiet corner in this world's civilization or, perchance, have vacated it forever in favor of some higher claimant. It matters little in all likelihood to the supreme spectators of this world's

---

7. John Milton, *Paradise Lost* 4.800–802.
8. Ibid., 4.808.
9. Thomas Carlyle, "Model Prisons," *Latter-Day Pamphlets,* in *Works* 5:58.

game, what confusion of checking and checkmating may be going on in our little ant-hill. The thought of God must conquer finally,[10] and the score or so of centuries more or less would be but a moment in its development. But to us, my brothers, and our children, these twenty centuries, what are they? White and black, were it not well to think on this a little? Truly to us, my biped brethren of all complexions, this abolitionist Satan is preparing (if so be we chain him not in time) a sorry chase through this world's existence. Only the hirsute can flourish then: ranging at will through beauteous regions, cast back again to wildness and the desert. There nature's bounty may furnish grass to the hirsute, but, truly, no bread to the biped. Black Quashee cannot understand this; God has not given him the intellect for it; and if we teach him to bray out for liberty, i.e., for idleness, verily it is as easy for him to bray to that tune as to any other. But the white man! Of what is he dreaming, when he listens even for a moment to such cant? To him God *has* given intellect (would he but use it!) to see the truth. Brother (for if acting conscientiously, and no devil's firebrand sent by Satan to our undoing, even as a brother, although differing, we hail thee), brother, thou speakest, perchance, in ignorance. Hast thou ever lived along side of Quashee? noticed his habits, his mind, his character, his tastes, his virtues, and his vices? clothed him in health, and nursed him in sickness? cheered him in merriment, and comforted him in sorrow? rejoiced with him, and suffered with him? laughed with him, and wept with him? Thou *hast not;* but there be those who have. "Go thou and do likewise,"[11] and when (if ever) thou dost, *thou wilt cease to be an abolitionist.* The white man, whose heart truly warms to the fate of the negro, would cease to agitate this question in that moment that he would become well acquainted with him, for thus would he learn its utter impracticability. At the hideous thought of amalgamation, even the abolitionist white-blood shudders. The white and the black race can only exist together in their present relations. Abolition is the extinction of the one or the other.

> *I* to herd with narrow foreheads, vacant of our glorious gains,
> Like a beast with lower pleasures, like a beast with lower pains!
> Mated with a squalid savage—what to me were sun or clime?
> *I* the heir of all the ages, in the foremost files of time![12]

The civilized man must retain his position, or perish.

10. See chap. 10 below, *Caius Gracchus* 2.4.22–28.
11. Luke 10:37.
12. Tennyson, "Locksley Hall," ll. 175–78.

4.

Woman and Her Needs

Myriads on myriads of men, before the time of Isaac Newton, must have sat under apple-trees; and vast numbers of them, too, undoubtedly, had apples to drop upon their heads; while not a few, it is likely, puzzled themselves to know why the apple should fall plumb down (thereby entailing upon them the evils of a headache) instead of flying off at a tangent, a right angle, or a curve. Many a one of these myriads might, perchance, just as well as the great philosopher, have guessed out the wonderful law of gravitation; only— not one of them did it. Why was this? Not want of intellect, surely. No doubt there were many men, before as well as since Sir Isaac Newton, quite his equals in mental power. But they did not solve the riddle, and *he* did. The time for the solving of it being come, even then came the man to solve it. Perhaps the day may yet arrive, when all puzzling questions in physics and metaphysics, in morals and in ethics, may be as clearly disposed of; but in the meantime we must be content, like the non-Newtons of the past world when the apples came tumbling about their ears, to scratch our heads and bear the penalty of our ignorance. To be sure, we will still, in the midst of this head-thumping process, look up inquiringly and ask, "Why?" Why are some things hard and other things soft? some things square and other things

De Bow 13 (Sept. 1852) = *PSE*, pp. 125–55. Publication reviewed: E. Oakes Smith, *Woman and Her Needs* (New York: Fowler and Wells, 1851). Elizabeth Oakes Prince Smith (1806– 93) first published as a series in Horace Greeley's New York *Tribune* the papers later collected into *Woman and Her Needs*.

round? Man has a great propensity for asking "Why?" and, upon the whole, it is a fortunate tendency. By perpetual knocking at a closed door, sometimes a hand comes to open it.

Why, then, among the darkest of life's problems, constantly recurs to us the question: Why is there evil in this world? and how is it to be remedied? "Why?" "why?" "why?"—has the weary thought of man constantly interrogated of Nature, appealed to Reason, and searched Revelation to discover. But ever there has come back to him only the dull echo of his own inquirings: "Why?" What is Evil? Can any man put his hand upon it? Can any man explain it in its nature, its birth, or its causes? Is it truly a Lucifer breath, a blast from hell, sent to poison our world, that God's mercy may find scope to redeem us from it? Is it the inspiration of some great Satanic creation, which strides our earth in mystic significancy of unimagined mysteries? Is it an active power, or a passive one? an existence, or only a deficiency? a something that is? or rather, a something that is not? a virtue left imperfect? a good not filled up? even as darkness, ignorance, and error are in themselves nothing—only deficiencies, *minus* quantities of light, knowledge, and truth? These are the questions—and such as these—over which, age after age, the wise and the good have thought themselves weary; while the imaginative and the weak have sought among the stars, and thought to read their destinies from leaves and flowers; and listened to their dreams, and believed that it was God who called them. But all have passed away, and, one after another, they have resigned their gray hairs and wearied hearts to the dust, while still upon their expiring lips quivered the great, unanswered, "Why?"

Today, in this great age of "new lights," we have solutions numberless offered to this our world-wide problem. Every "*ism*" upon earth has got its explanation of, and its remedy for, this monster Evil, which the poor, ignorant world has so long imagined inexplicable and incurable. What is this bugbear of the world? this sin—this pain—this suffering? Nothing, forsooth, it would now appear—nothing but a nightmare dream; a kind of world dyspepsia; at worst, a species of toothache, which, by some socialistic, communistic, feministic, Mormonistic, or any other such application of chloroform to the suffering patient, may be made to pass away in a sweet dream of perfection. If we will only believe our doctors and open our mouths wide, we are cured at once. Down goes their nostrum, as glibly as the new-fashioned *capsule,* by help of which the lucky individual to whom a nauseous dose of castor-oil is prescribed may (so declareth to us the immaculate truth of advertisements) luxuriate in a dainty something, resembling a luscious piece of turtle-fat; one luxurious gulp, and, lo! the deed is done.

Startled by the loud-mouthed Eurekas of each new sect as it starts into being, we turn to investigate their discoveries—but alas! like the fabled fruit of the Dead Sea, these are but dust and ashes to the taste.[1] Their great discoveries, forsooth, end in the tautologous declaration that the world is evil, simply because it is not perfect. They write books, and they make speeches; they plan and they counterplan; they fancy they have found a perfect mine of thought, and they dig away at it valorously. But, behold! the fancied jewels which they dive at prove to be but cast-off glass—the refuse offal of those great laborers who have preceded them; while still, in its fullest development, the same great mystery of evil, for which neither man nor woman has yet found a cause or a cure, looms out, not only in spite of, but even in bolder prominence from, their ignorant meddling. Quacks they are, whose salve fires the wound, whose potion poisons the blood, and the sick world writhes under their ill-judged medicaments. Back, fools! to what ye were made for!—your plow and your loom, your spindle and your shears; these, and these only, are the tools Heaven destined for you. *Ne sutor ultra crepidam.*[2] Wo to the world which seeks its rulers where it should but find its drudges! Wo to the drudge who would exalt himself into the ruler! Nature is vigilant of her laws, and has no pardon for the breakers of them. The sentenced wretch appeals in vain; and the hair-brained Phaeton, who would guide the chariot of the sun, must perish amidst the suffering he has caused.[3]

The world has supped full of horrors under such false guides. Blind leaders of the blind, they have led us through dirty slough and miry way, until filth and corruption seem almost our natural element. But we are about to touch upon womanhood, and must, in courtesy, somewhat soften our language, though we are by no means sure that the feminine reform corps may not take our deference, thus offered, as an invidious distinction, maliciously bestowed upon their sex. Strong, however, in the purity of our intentions, the defender, not the libeler of the sex, we must, while we will do our "spiriting" as gently as the circumstances of the case allow, endeavor to show the false position in which the innovators have placed themselves, as well as the slanderous assertions which their course is calculated to throw over the true cause of womanhood.

The reforming ladies have not yet got an "ism" for their move; but have nevertheless come forward scarcely less boldly than their masculine coad-

---

1. Byron, *Childe Harold's Pilgrimage* 3.301–4: "But Life will suit / Itself to Sorrow's most detested fruit, / Like to the apples on the Dead Sea's shore, / All ashes to the taste."

2. Pliny *Natural History* 35.85: "ne supra crepidam sutor iudicaret" ("the cobbler should make no judgments away from his last").

3. When his father, the Sun, promised any gift he should ask, Phaethon begged to be allowed to drive his father's chariot; insisting despite the Sun's advice, Phaethon was unable to manage the horses, which dragged the chariot out of control, scorching the earth, until Phaethon was hurled to his death.

jutors—or, perhaps, we should rather say competitors—in the world-doctoring system. We have had some curiosity to see their arguments; and being, we confess, both unable and unwilling to plow through the mass of declamation with which they favor the world, have endeavored to limit our studies, in this line, to selections. Following this course, our attention has happened to fall upon Mrs. E. O. Smith, who is, we are informed, among the most moderate of the feminist reformers! Tolerably fair specimens of the other extreme have been made public in the sundry women-convention reports which have appeared, and also in a very remarkable article which graced, or rather disgraced, the pages of the last July number of the *Westminster Quarterly*.[4] We have not, with a superficial view of criticism, limited ourselves to a glance over title-page and final flourish, with a hurried glimpse or two at the intervening pages of the little work we have undertaken to review, but, with a sober spirit of inquiry, have set about finding whatever we could find in it of true or of false, marking and remarking everything noteworthy in our progress, and are, we think, ready to give the authoress credit for any merit of thought or style which she may have exhibited.

We will say little of the last—simply remarking, that if the lady is not a very careless writer, she has to complain of a very careless printer, her thoughts (or vacancies of thought, we cannot quite determine which) being not unfrequently given in a form which fairly puzzles our grammar as well as our logic. How many of these discrepancies belong to the printer, we will not undertake to say, having ourselves suffered enough from the impish fraternity of the printing-office to learn a most sympathizing fellow-feeling towards our co-sufferers in that line. We take it, moreover, for granted, that many worse literary delinquencies must be frequent among the reformist sisterhood (the lady in question ranking, we are informed, among their literati), and we have cause to thank our stars that we have not, in the boldness of our exploring expedition through these unknown regions, fallen into worse hands. If we are, as we frankly confess ourselves, somewhat mystified even now, by the irregular currents and the confusion of words and ideas around us, what might have been our fate had we become entangled midst the overwhelming icebergs of female-convention polemics? Would the world have immortalized in us a second Sir John Franklin?[5] Upon the whole, we have laid down our little volume with a most sympathizing consciousness

---

4. [John Stuart Mill and Harriet Taylor Mill], "Enfranchisement of Women," *Westminster Review* 55 (July 1851): 289–311; reviewed by LSM in *PSE*, "Enfranchisement of Woman."

5. Sir John Franklin (1786–1847), English explorer, led several expeditions into the Arctic in search of the Northwest Passage; in the last (1847–48) was lost with his entire company.

of the truth of a remark we encountered in a recent number of *Blackwood*. The reviewer there observes, that the fashion of the day, among a certain class of writers, is to dwell with great emphasis and a kind of inspired frenzy upon the word "infinite," which they have appropriated to their use in a peculiar, mystified, indefinite, indefinable signification. "They have made the discovery that this poet or that painter talks or paints the 'infinite.' They find in every obscurity of thought, in every violence of passion, the 'infinite.' There is no such thing as 'sound and fury signifying nothing.' They always signify the 'infinite.'"[6] Very decidedly Mrs. Smith deals largely in the "infinite"; and we confess ourselves matter of fact enough to wish that she had, instead, confined herself to the much more distinct, as well as more succinct, explanation of a certain Mrs. Mehitable Haskell, who, rising to make a speech at the first Worcester Convention, frankly acknowledges that "she does not know what are woman's rights, but for forty, nay, fifty years, she has known what woman's wrongs are, for she has felt them."[7] Now there is something right hearty—something earnest and downright—in the declaration of this good lady. We feel that *she, at least,* did not frequent the conventions for the purpose of displaying her graces, whether of person or rhetoric. We fancy we can see the good Mrs. Mehitable before us: broad, square-shouldered; somewhat raw-boned; sharp gray eyes; teeth deficient (she would disdain to mend her oratory or her looks by false ones); a bony hand which hath shown service over the washtub, and well calculated, in its mere appearance, to excite admonitory twinges in the flagellatable parts of luckless youth, said hand being used with some vehemence of gesticulation. All her motions angular; all her forms angular. Worthy Mrs. Mehitable, vastly rather would we shake hands with thee in all amicable companionship, than stand a few of those angular motions, energetically applied about our ears. In very truth, too, we confess to something of sympathy with thee. Evidently, thou art an earnest soul. Earnest, doubtless, in thy washtub, as in thy flagellatory duties; and earnestly, too, frequentest thou these conventions, hoping that some good may be hatched out of them. Alas! good Mrs. Mehitable, take home that earnest soul of thine. There is work for it elsewhere, but none here. Here is Babel-confusion, brawling presumption, restless vanity; no room for truth. Thy woman's wrongs, borne for fifty long years,

6. [William Henry Smith], "Miss Mitford's *Recollections*," *Blackwood's Edinburgh Magazine* 71 (March 1852): 259–72; 263, citing *Macbeth* 5.5.27–28.

7. *The Proceedings of the Woman's Rights Convention, Held at Worcester, October 15th and 16th, 1851* (New York, 1852)—reviewed by LSM in *PSE*, "Enfranchisement of Woman"—pp. 95–96, reports in direct speech the words of "Mehitable Haskell, of Gloucester." The Woman's Rights Convention of October 1851 was the second held at Worcester, Mass.

canst thou not bear yet a little longer? Let suffering teach thee patience. Let patience teach thee love. Let love teach thee gentleness, charity, forbearance; and although we will not warrant thee a disfranchisement from woman's wrongs—for our world is far from perfect, and ever the strong hand must abuse its power—credit us, worthy Mrs. Mehitable, thus thou hast done more to put down the abuse of that strong hand—more in the true cause of woman—than scores of conventionists can accomplish. Thus all that one woman can do, thou hast done. For hast thou not shown that gentleness can master passion? Bowing before the strong hand, hast thou not shamed it? And doth not thus thine earnest soul teach to all within the circle of its influence, the true lesson of Christian charity and philosophical forbearance?

But let us return to Mrs. Smith, who, being a literary lady, a "woman of genius" [44, 88], as we understand her occasionally to intimate, would in all probability spurn the idea of comparison with so humble a sister reformer as this most excellent Mrs. Mehitable, the charm of whose name and eloquence has drawn us off from our more immediate subject of discussion. We have confessed that Mrs. S. is too high in "the infinite" for our clouded intellects to penetrate her dream-land. We have done our best, but cannot exactly find out what she would be after. We even doubt whether, in the full flow of inspiration, her genius could condescend to settle so trifling a point in her own mind. When folks are in "the infinite," they are of course, and ought to be, incomprehensible to other people; very likely, also, to themselves. She, too, preaches love and gentleness; but it is with a reservation: a resistance reservation, a conventionist reservation, a right-of-voting reservation, a spontaneity reservation, an intuition reservation. In short, her argument, rushing to and fro on every varying gale, from communism to socialism, from Christianity to free-thinking, from real woman-thought to conventionist woman-thought, is as impossible to follow as an *ignis fatuus*. We can only say that it has, in all its veerings, a most distressing tendency to the "higher law" fallacies, and our authoress has, much more than she is herself probably aware of, exhibited to us the undeveloped Louis Blanc in petticoats.[8] We must however here do the ladies the justice to remark, that the feminine move has at least this advantage over the various masculine ones, that, more than any theory yet advanced, it logically carries principles to their climax. Granted that A is B, and B is C, inevitably then A must be

---

8. Socialist politician and author of *L'Organisation du travail* (1840), Jean-Joseph-Charles-Louis Blanc (1811–82) as a member of the Provisional Government in France (1848) secured a guarantee of employment to workers, until forced into exile in England (1848–70).

C. The ladies jump to their conclusion boldly, while men stand higgling with the relics of old prejudice. Given the premises that "all men[9] are born free and equal"; that "intuition is God's law," and that "aptitude is no argument of use," they are right, and have the merit of bringing out their principles in unadulterated perfection. A strange *pot pouri* of a world must indeed result from such premises!

Our authoress complains of the degradation of woman in society: that she is out of her place, unappreciated, having her talents and powers not only hidden under a bushel, but absolutely thrown away, while she becomes either the slave or the toy of man. Now this is all true of some women—many women—perhaps, we must even confess, of a majority of women. (We are not quite ready to concede this position in its full force, but for the sake of argument will give our antagonists the furthest point to which they can possibly lay claim.) Yet we will not allow the universality nor the necessity of such an effect, from the operation of the actual laws of existing society. It is not woman, as a class, who is thus degraded, but only so many individual women, each one of whom is separately, and from causes quite extraneous from her position as woman, so degraded. Many, noble (and we believe increasing in proportionate numbers with the advance of civilization) are the examples of high, self-relying, heaven-depending, duty-fulfilling women in every position of life, who, by a noble self-abnegation, and a faithful adherence to the laws of God and nature, are daily showing that woman is not inherently, either in her nature or her position, what our authoress would wish to prove her. Many women (we have already said we will even grant an unfortunately large proportion of women) are degraded, not because they have submitted themselves to the position which nature assigns them, but because, like Mrs. Smith, they cannot be content with the exercise of the duties and virtues called forth by that, and in that, position. They forget the woman's duty-fulfilling ambition, to covet man's fame-grasping ambition. Woman was made for *duty,* not for *fame;* and so soon as she forgets this great law of her being, which consigns her to a life of heroism if she will—but quiet, unobtrusive heroism—she throws herself from her position, and thus, of necessity, degrades herself. This mistaken hungering for the forbidden fruit, this grasping at the notoriety belonging (if indeed it

---

9. It would be, as the ladies have justly remarked, mere quibbling, to contend that the word "men" in this oft quoted sentence does not mean (if it means anything) human beings, and includes them as well as Cuffee. [LSM] The ladies had justly remarked this in [Mill and Mill], "Enfranchisement of Women," pp. 291–92, and *Proceedings of the Woman's Rights Convention,* p. 12.

properly belongs to any) by nature to man, is at the root of all her debasement.

Look at the ballroom belle for instance. Why is she a flirt, a coquette, a heartless trifler with hearts? Not because there is harm in the ballroom enjoyment of youth; in the joy-waking music, or the spirit-rousing dance; but because she would be *talked* of, and forgets duty, conscience, and heart, in the love of notoriety. Why does the young mother forget the sick baby in its cradle, to listen to the whispered inanities of those bewhiskered fops who surround her? Why, but because she cannot resign to duty that petty fame to which she degrades herself. Why does the gray and wrinkled matron, whom nature and duty would keep at her fireside corner to wake the young hearts round her to the love of God, nature, and virtue, rush out with her be-rouged cheek and stained locks, to try and play the belle a little longer? Still she grasps at her shame. It is her ambition that degrades her. Why does the literary lady leave too often her infant to the hireling, her sick and her poor to chance charity? What is it that stocks the world with Harriet Martineaus, George Sands, and Lady Bulwers?[10] Is it not the same hungering love for notoriety, the same misdirected ambition; misdirected still, though in another track? There is nothing unwomanish in the fullest exercise by woman of the thought and mind, which, if God has given, he has given for use. There is nothing unwomanish in the writing of such thoughts; nothing unwomanish even, we think, in the publishing of them. Society has accordingly permitted, and does permit, unblamed and unchecked, woman's fullest liberty in the exercise of her literary powers in every line; and she has, equally with the man, as far as she is able to use it, this theatre of effort open to her. If she has not, equally with the man, distinguished herself in it, it is because her talents and disposition do not indicate this as the career best suited to the fullest exercise of her faculties and virtues. It is *not her highest destiny*. It is *not her noblest life*.[11] Nevertheless many women, with great and

---

10. Harriet Martineau (1802–76), English political economist, abolitionist, and women's rights advocate; author (among other works) of *Illustrations of Political Economy* (1832–34) and *Society in America* (1837). Rosina Doyle Wheeler Bulwer-Lytton (1802–82), having been legally separated (April 1836) from her husband, the novelist Edward George Earle Lytton Bulwer-Lytton—her children were removed from her two years later—turned novelist herself with *Cheveley, or the Man of Honour* (1839), containing a hostile portrait of her husband, whom she continued to pursue with recriminations until his death in 1873.

11. "In the field of literature, how many women have enjoyed all the advantages which men can command, and yet how very few have distinguished themselves; and how far behind are even those few from the great and burning lights of letters! Who ever hopes to see a woman Shakspeare? And yet a greater than Shakspeare may she be. It may be doubtful whether the brilliant intellect which, inspiring noble thoughts, leaves still the great thinker

true woman-minds, have written, have published, and have done good, by so expanding the brighter developments of woman-thought. But so soon as woman strives with man's ambition, so soon as she forgets the ruling thought of duty, letting its throne be usurped by the illegitimate hungering for fame and notoriety which so fatally misleads her, her writings, as her nature, become corrupted in the struggle. She has resigned herself to an *ignis fatuus* guide, which fails never to plunge her into the mire of degradation. Man, like woman, may fall, and does fall, through similar causes, to similar degradation. But as the woman's fall is from a higher and a purer elevation, even so grovels she lower in her debasement, and closer and heavier clings to her its consequent soil. Because women have thus sinned, we behold their punishment. Degraded they are, even in that proportion wherein they have erred. The ballroom coquette, in the midst of her triumph, is degraded in her heart and in her being. The brilliant George Sand, bold in her impudence and her talent, is degraded to the dust before the blushing mother, who watches that her innocent child shall not lay its hand upon the foul productions wherein France's brilliant novelist often competes in obscenity with the nauseous filth spewed forth, as though in devilish scorn, by her compatriots, a Sue and a Dumas, upon a community sufficiently degraded to admire them.[12] In a steady pursuit of duty such names would be perhaps entirely unknown. But dares any one say that they are better for being thus known? or is there anything but a sickly appetite for notoriety which could make such a position to be coveted? Is a Ninon de l'Enclos, a duchess of Pompadour,[13] or a George Sand (indisputably celebrated women all of them) so good, so pure, or so noble in the eye of God, as the unknown mother who strokes to sleep the weary eye of her baby, and whispers to its waking thought her never-to-be-forgotten lessons of duty and of truth. Brilliant fallen ones the world have seen; but nature turns from them in sorrow. She glories not, but weeps for her fallen children.

It is this same misguided love for notoriety which now misleads women

---

grovelling in the lowest vices and slave of his passions, without the self-command to keep them in sway, is superior to that which, knowing good and evil, grasps almost instinctively at the first. Such, in its uncorrupted nature, is woman's intellect—such her inspiration." *PSE,* "Enfranchisement of Woman," pp. 121–22.

12. Eugène Sue (1804–57), French writer, some of whose novels, set in the Parisian underworld, promote socialism; Alexandre Dumas father and son (1802–70 and 1824–95), French novelists and playwrights, of whom LSM elsewhere (chap. 5 below, "Uncle Tom's Cabin," p. 85) singles out for blame the former's *Le Comte de Monte Cristo* (1844) and may have in mind also the latter's *La Dame aux camélias* (1848) and *Diane de Lys* (1851).

13. Anne, called Ninon, de Lenclos (1620–1705), French courtesan; Jeanne-Antoinette Poisson, marquise de Pompadour (1721–64), made duchess (1752), mistress of Louis XV of France, exerting strong political influence.

to insist upon political rights, as they word their demand—that is to say, admission to the struggle for political distinction. And what is this that they ask? What, but that like the half-barbarous, half-heroic Spartan maid they may be permitted to strip themselves to the strife, and wrestle in the public arena? Can civilized, Christianized woman covet such a right? They pretend, or they mislead themselves to the belief, that they are actuated by a pure desire to ennoble the sex. Let them look honestly and calmly to the bottom of the question, and they will see that it is but notoriety, not elevation, which they seek. In all derelictions from the right, the just, the holy, and the true, woman is responsible for her own degradation, inasmuch as it entirely proceeds from her own act, in casting herself out from her true position. She is herself, we repeat, the sole cause of it; and we wish to lay a stress upon this, because we maintain her to be a responsible, reasoning being, and not man's puppet. It is no excuse for her that man tempts her into folly. Man is unfortunately ready enough to tempt woman to err, and does not always stop to calculate the possible evil resulting from his pleasures and amusements. It amuses him to see the performances of the circus-clown or the monkey-man. It pleases him to have woman for his toy. He will pay the former with his money, the latter with his flattery, and thus tempt to degradation, but he cannot degrade. The degradation can be accomplished only by the consent of the degraded. The accessory to murder cannot be held guiltless because tempted by his principal. No reasoning being can be made an accessory but by his own consent. We may pity the weakness that falls by temptation, but cannot receive it as exculpation from the crime, except by acknowledging, in so far as it is thus received (as in the cases of infants or maniacs), a defect or inferiority in the reasoning powers of the person misled. We allow no such defect or inferiority to woman, and therefore hold her fully responsible for her own course. Seeking notoriety and applause, if (as too often she does) she stoops to conquer, she stoops with her own free will.[14] Man's wishes cannot degrade her. She degrades herself to man's wishes. Let her feel her duty as a woman, avoiding alike an undue valuation of man's applause, and an unworthy grappling with him for notoriety, and there is no shadow of degradation in her position. There may be no publicity, no far-spread reputation, no fame; but certainly there is no degradation in the holy, full, conscientious, and unguerdoned fulfilment of duty.

There are, undoubtedly, many false positions in which woman may be placed, where the fault is not so entirely her own as in the classes above noticed. But none of these are of the same vital importance, for by none of them is the woman-nature so entirely neutralized and destroyed. Our au-

---

14. Oliver Goldsmith, *She Stoops to Conquer* (1773).

thoress attacks the established laws of society as defective, as not sufficiently protecting woman in the right of holding property; not sufficiently upholding her in the right of laboring for its acquisition; and, last and greatest, not sufficiently checking her in the right of getting married before she has the sense to know what she is about. We are far from maintaining that our laws are perfect in the varied system of checks and balances required, or that they may not exhibit some ill-jointed legislation upon these and many other subjects; but strongly suspect, from the legal instinct (intuition) displayed by Mrs. Smith, that, if she and her compeers were set to put the laws to rights, we should have a strong compound of the Draconian and the barn-burner systems.[15] Tyranny here, license there—lock doors and bolt windows on this side of the street, but over the way throw all open, pray for "the good time coming,"[16] and trust to "the law of our own intuitions." We should like to see Mrs. S. at the head of a family of some half-dozen young ladies of sixteen and there about, who had made up their minds to get married with or without permission. What system of restrictions and legal checks she could devise to keep her unruly little community in order, we think would be a vast puzzle to her genius, requiring a higher exercise of mind, of Christian charity, of philosophy, and of every noblest intellectual characteristic, than the writings of some scores of such volumes as that wherewith she has now seen fit to edify the public. We strongly suspect that much more could be effected in such a case by one sensible, matronly, gentle, and judicious mother or aunt, kindly watching and counseling from that throne of woman, her own chair, by her own fireside, than by troops of voting and speech-making conventionist lawgivers.

"If," says Mrs. Smith,

> any woman of genius is so untrue to herself as to say she should have been happier as an in-door, painstaking, fireside woman; careful for the small savings of a household, holding the rod *in terrorem* over unruly urchins, and up in the morning early to scold the servants, her nature satisfied with this ordinary manifestation of sex, she is from some cause disqualified for the holding of God's beautiful and abundant gifts in reverent stewardship—she is the Jew, better pleased with the worship of Apis than the sublime mysteries

---

15. Draco (fl. 7th century B.C.), Athenian lawgiver, famous for his severity. Given their name (about 1843) from the fabled farmer who burned down his barn to rid it of rats, the Barnburners were the radical, antislavery faction of the Democratic party in New York State.

16. Smith, *Woman and Her Needs*, p. 34; Charles Mackay, "The Good Time Coming," st. 1: "There's a good time coming, boys! / A good time coming." Charles Mackay (1814–89), Scottish songwriter, poet, and journalist.

of Jehovah, looking to the flesh-pots of Egypt, and turning from the heavenly manna.[17]

Mrs. S., we presume, considers it a mark of *genius* to make oneself as happy as convenient, leaving duty to knock, unheeded, outside the door. We can only say, that the highest and most intellectual specimens of womanhood we have ever seen, scorning not the duty of managing children and servants, took into their hands and hearts the task which nature gave them, and fulfilled it, with the fullest powers of a God-given, soul-beaming intellect. If these were Jews worshiping Apis, Heaven preserve us from the *sublime mysteries* with which Mrs. S. would replace such worship!

>　We must and will feel the stirrings of a great nature if it be great, and we are happy only as we obey its monitions. We are not happy in a half life, a half utterance; for the wealth struggles for its power; the smothered fire burns and consumes till it finds <find> room for its healthful glow. A thousand women are ill-natured and miserable, not from positive ills about them, but from compression; they have that within, demanding space and indulgence, and they pine for its freedom—the laws of their life are not comprehended, and they sink into <to> imbecile complaints, only because there is no voice to call them forth to freedom and light. [89–90]

Still the question seems, not "what ought I to do," but "what would I like to do?" It is, apparently, in the opinion of our authoress, sufficient excuse for a woman to be *ill-natured* and *miserable,* that she suffers *from compression.* A man, too, may, we suppose, suffer from compression as well as a woman. He may be as ill suited to the plow or the counting-house, as she is to the spindle or the nursery; but has he, therefore, the right to be "ill-natured and miserable"? Has he the right to say, "I am a genius, and it is an unjust fate that places me here"? Men, as well as women, certainly do follow such a course not unfrequently, grumbling very unnecessarily and very uselessly at the defects of this God-made world, which they would have made so much better. But we, until enlightened by these recent new-light developments, have always supposed that the old fable of the child crying for the moon, was the most usual, as well as most reasonable, mode of answering such complaints against the orderings of life and destiny. Human cravings soar high. Perhaps there is no human being, not born in a state of imbecility almost as cramped as that of the oyster in his shell, who does not suffer, or fancy that he suffers, from

---

17. *Woman and Her Needs,* p. 88. Cf. Exod. 16:3, 14–35, 32:4–6.

compression. Shall we all begin to pout for the moon? to be ill-tempered and miserable over our state of compression? Such are they, who

> By the road-side fall and perish,
> Weary with the march of life.[18]

Such are they who wantonly waste the talent which God has given them. The true soul, the strong soul, with shoulder to the wheel, asks not, "How shall I be happy?" but "How shall I do right?" and, choosing its course, strives forward bravely, cheerily, and God-fearingly, to its goal.

Sorrow and silence are strong, and patient endurance is God-like.[19]

Sisters, is it we who preach unto you degradation? Is it we who point you from the "heavenly manna" to "the flesh pots of Egypt"?

In the little book before us, we find many a glimmering of the true consciousness of what woman ought to be—glimpses of genuine woman-nature, showing how difficult it is, even embroiled among such sophistries, to entirely corrupt it. But every where comes the adjunct, the unlucky reservation which spoils everything that is good and truthful in the thought. For good and truth there are, even here, struggling, as ever they do struggle, at the groundwork of every error. Good and truth there are in the thought which says that woman is not what she should be; but falsehood and mischief in the cry which hounds her on to these most unwomanish proceedings, by way of bettering a condition which needs not *change*, but *cure;* not *reform*, but *perfection*. Never spake prophet truer words than these of Mrs. Smith:

> There is a Woman's sphere—harmonious, holy, soul-imparting; it has its grades, its laws from the nature of things. [28]
>
> There is <I know of> nothing more holy, more God-serving, ay, and more beautiful, than the steady, self-denying labor of the large class of women in the middle ranks of life, who, with woman-like dignity and solid sense, pursue a calling humble and painstaking to earn an honest subsistence for their families. The lives of these women are often truly heroic, are silent, beautiful epics, breathing the best aspirations of poetry and romance. [39]
>
> I see no way in which harmony can result in the world without entire recognition of differences, for surely nothing is gained upon either side by antagonism *merely*. [28; LSM's italics]

---

18. Henry Wadsworth Longfellow, "Footsteps of Angels," st. 4: "He, the young and strong, who cherished / Noble longings for the strife, / By the roadside fell and perished, / Weary with the march of life."

19. Longfellow, *Evangeline* 2.59.

Alas! for that unlucky little word "*merely.*" Therein lies snugly hid away the mischievous devil who is whispering his reservations to the ear of our modern Eves.[20] Antagonism is all right, we may suppose, though not *antagonism merely.* Happy would we be, however, did the reservation of our authoress end here; for, unfortunately, the mass of her little volume is one succession of bitter antagonism, illogical reasoning, romantic dreaming, and half-understood truths. We regret this the more, as she is evidently not one of the deepest-dyed reformers; and if (as we think not at all unlikely) she sports the "Bloomer," we will wager our newest gold pen that she "wears it with a difference."[21] She is not "perfectly certain" of the efficacy of woman's rights conventions; but she rejoices in the fact, that this "stirring of woman-thought originates in our own country,"[22] and sees no reason why women should not "associate, as do our compeers of the other sex, for the purpose of evolving better views, and of confirming some degree of power" [14]; nor why "those [of ours] who have a fancy to tinker a constitution, canvass a county, or preach the Gospel, should not be permitted to do so, provided they feel this to be the best use of their faculties" [27].

> Hereafter, in the progress of events, I see no reason why the influence of woman should not be acknowledged at the ballot-box. [90]
> I do not know that I am prepared to say, as has been said, that women have a right to our halls of legislation, our courts of justice, our military posts, and each and all spheres where men "most do congregate."[23]

She doubts; but why? Not because woman is there entirely out of her place, but because (here the lady takes a plunge into the *infinite*) she thinks that a "pure state of society" is approaching wherein "these needs will pass away" [45]. "But," she continues, "but till 'the good time coming' arrive, let her be free to her own intuitions" [45].

> Merrily swim we; the moon shines bright.[24]

Verily, at this rate, we will soon be in the deep of the waters.

A step or two further we will venture, under the guidance of Mrs. Smith's

---

20. John Milton, *Paradise Lost* 4.799–809.

21. *Hamlet* 4.5.180–81 (Ophelia to Claudius): "You must wear your rue with a difference." Amelia Jenks Bloomer (1818–94), woman's rights advocate; founder and editor of the journal *Lily* (1849–55); promoted the item of apparel named for her.

22. *Woman and Her Needs*, p. 31: "I am glad this peculiar stirring of womanly thought upon womanly requirements originated in our own country."

23. Ibid., p. 45; *Merchant of Venice* 1.3.44.

24. Sir Walter Scott, "Fording the River," l. 1 and later refrains; the song, perhaps deriving "the moon shines bright" from *Merchant of Venice*, 5.1.1, appears in chapter 5 of *The Monastery* (1820).

moonlight; warily, however, lest we find ourselves over head and ears in the bog, before we are ready for the plunge. The lady's own mind, as our readers may have perceived, does not appear to be quite determined on many of the most important points of her subject. She "sees no reason"; she is "not perfectly certain," etc., etc. What guide then does she propose to herself and us, through these labyrinthian mazes? *"Our intuitions are to be trusted"* [9; LSM's italics]. Here we are, then. Behold it: the mystery of mysteries!—the inspiration!—the intuition! In a word (although she does not just give it the fashionable name, perhaps because her mind is not quite made up), the higher law! "Emancipate from external bondage, and the internal law written upon every human heart makes itself audible. Thus the most free are the most bound" [34], e.g., the Mormon governor, with his score or threescore (we really forget which it is) of wives.[25] Verily, *he is bound,* being most free.

Our authoress continues: "A woman is better when she acts *out of* her own spontaneity, tenfold, than when she attempts to conform to any theory" [111]. This somewhat dubious expression, we take it, would be more clear if the "out of" we have italicized were replaced by "from"; and as to the merit of the sentiment, let it be judged of by what follows. Referring to the *duty* of a wife, she exclaims:

> Duty! why it is the spontaneous, the natural action and privilege of her soul, not her cold duty; she, the true wife, does not say "it is my duty"; the law of God in her heart teaches a nicer view than this, a more intimate and sacred relation. [111–12]

Good! if such be her spontaneity. But what if the spontaneity lean on the other side? Wo, then, to the household over which she presides. Duty has gone to the dogs; the husband may go to the devil; and should there be any unlucky brats of things called children, which the feminine individual's spontaneity leaneth not kindly towards, let them also betake themselves to Old Nick, or wherever luck may send them, while the lady spontaneously turns herself to the constructing of some woman's rights constitution in readiness for "the good time coming."

> Can they not, will they never learn, that the Good Father is wise in the bestowal of his gifts; that he does not impart a superfluous intelligence; that he does not create a desire <need> without its appropriate, safe, and harmonizing medium of gratification? [36]

---

25. Brigham Young (1801–77), head of the Mormon church from 1844, its president from 1847; led Mormon migration to Great Salt Lake valley in Utah; first governor of the territory of Utah (1849–57).

Have we then no desires which we have not the right to gratify? This is a dangerous doctrine, which the most run-mad reformer of the day will, we think, scarcely undertake to carry to its extreme, without consigning the actor of it either to the gallows or the madhouse. Besides, we must remember that there are male spontaneities and intuitions as well as female ones; the former possessing the indisputable advantage of being backed by physical force, which will secure, as it always has secured, male supremacy, in case of a clash between contending spontaneities. Man's "higher law" must certainly override woman's. What then is the necessary result to woman of such a combat of intuitions? What but the most fearful oppression exercised by an exasperated tyrant over a conquered foe; or, at best, the degrading kindness of the master-husband with his threescore wives? EXCELSIOR![26] Is this the height of Mrs. Smith's vision of perfected civilization? Why, the world is but just emerging from such a rule; and even the Grand Turk[27] throws not the handkerchief so boldly as did his fathers. Let the weak cling to the law. For him or for her, the worst legislation is better than none. The rule of intuitions is the rule of brute force. What doth it benefit, that my intuition is clearer, brighter, truer than his? What matters it that my impulses are good while his are evil? If the evil be strong, if the dark be mighty, even evil will sweep away good; even darkness will conquer the light. Cling therefore to the law; for the law, however faulty, is still the feeble effort of right to embody itself into a rule which time and experience may perfect. It is the struggling forward of the spirit of good. It is the concession of the powerful evil to the weaker good. Ye who are feeble, ye who are oppressed! cling to the law, even although that very law may oppress you. That it does oppress you, is proof in itself that the strong were the makers of it. How then can you wrest it from them? How then can your feebleness better it? The law is a concession from the strong to the weak; and because the concession is but a lame one—is but a half-accorded justice—will the weak gain by its rejection? Will he not act more wisely to nurse and cherish it, if possible, to a nobler growth. Woman! thou whom Nature hath made to persuade and not to combat—to entreat but not to force—cling thou then to the written law. Ay, e'en as to thine ark of safety, amid the surging billows, the deluge of brute force—cling even to its very letter.[28] Better it, if thine influence may; but as thou valuest the rule of reason and of God, abolish it not to make way for intuitions and spontaneities.

26. Longfellow, "Excelsior!" (1841).
27. The Ottoman sultan.
28. Cf. Byron, *Heaven and Earth* 1.3.272–73: "God hath proclaimed the destiny of earth; / My father's ark of safety hath announced it."

Our lady reformers will answer, that they do not reject, that they would only reform, the law. But stumbling in their darkness, they talk of they know not what. What becomes of written law, when such impertinent twaddle as the following is listened to?

> In our Integrity we stand poised in our own Unity, a Law, a Life. [117]
>
> Yes, the sin about which so much is vaguely preached, is the violation of this great light within us. It is the putting out of the light in God's temple, that we may not see the requirements of his laws, all violations of which shall be revealed, as from the house-tops of our being. We must look within to learn these laws, and go forth in holy obedience. [119–20]

Such was the law of a Robespierre, who looked within himself, and went forth in holy obedience to slaughter and to drown his country in blood. Such is the law of the Mormon, who, in holy obedience, takes to himself his threescore wives; such the law of the communist, the socialist, the Fourierist;[29] and such finally of this new sect, as yet but limitedly known, which is, we learn, springing up in the interior of the State of New York, and proving itself, even more than all these, grossly ready to follow "intuitions," in "holy obedience" to which its members speak and act in a way to make common decency veil her eyes.[30]

However, the ladies are aggrieved; let us return to them, and examine how they propose to right themselves. "When our Fathers," says Mrs. Smith, "planted themselves upon the firm base of human freedom, claimed the inalienable rights of life, liberty, and the pursuit of happiness, they might have foreseen that at some day their daughters would sift thoroughly their opinions and their consequences, and daringly challenge the same rights" [10]. Warlike this, rather. Again, elsewhere, in advocating marriage reforms, and woman's right to hold property, she remarks: "Allow woman the rights of property, open to her the avenues to wealth, permit her not only to hold property, but to enter into commerce, or into the professions, if she is fit for them. In that case she would assuredly take the stand that her forefathers <fathers> took, that taxation without representation is oppressive," etc.

---

29. François-Marie-Charles Fourier (1772–1837), French social theorist, in his *Théorie des quatres mouvements et des destinées générales* (1808) advocated a division of society into self-reliant phalanxes; settlements, called phalansteries, were founded upon his ideas in France and the United States.

30. In 1852 the New York *Observer* and other religious newspapers preached a crusade against the Oneida Community and its leader, John Humphrey Noyes (1811–86), on account of the practice of "complex" (i.e., communal) marriage, which relied on *coitus reservatus* (male continence) to permit sexual relations without procreation and, thus, a sexual freedom designed to copy that of the angels.

[75] And of course, we presume, fight for that stand as her fathers did. The *voie de fait*[31] is, after all, the only way of defending disputed rights in this world; and at this rate, ladies, it is time to throw aside your kid gloves, and accustom yourselves to something even more manlike than your satin and muslin Bloomer equipments.[32] Your fair hands must harden themselves to the management of Colt's revolvers, of bombs, grenades, and whatnot. But, ladies, room, if you please, for one little thought. You know we had *mothers* as well as *fathers*—pilgrim mothers and patriot fathers. Women, true women they were; women of the home and of the hearth; women of true hearts and earnest faiths; of bold councils—ay, and when need was—of bold actions, too. And yet these, disdaining neither their duties nor their petticoats, had nothing to do with votings and conventions, nor ever claimed the right "to our halls of legislation, our courts of justice, and our military posts." *Quaere,*[33] whether our fathers or our mothers, with all due reverence for both, were the truest models for their daughters' imitation.

A glimmering of common sense seems to come over our authoress when she remarks that "the 'proud stomach' of the manish Bess had something to command respect, at least; and unless we can do, as well as talk, it were better to be silent."[34] Here has an evident little truth, plain enough for the

31. Assault and battery.

32. One word *en passant* of "the Bloomer." We really mean nothing disrespectful of the dress, which, as far as we know anything about it, is not only entirely unobjectionable, but we decidedly think, from description (we have never ourselves been so happy as to encounter a real live Bloomer), a great improvement upon the dirty length of skirt wherewith our fashionables sweep the pavements and clear off the ejected tobacco of our railroad cars. The *dress* is not only convenient, but entirely modest; and could the same be said of its *wearers,* we would decidedly be of the number of its advocates. We object to it, not as intrinsically wrong in itself, but only in so far as it is used for wrong purposes. The Bloomer dress has been adopted as a kind of flag of rebellion against established usage, and when some good-tempered peacemakers, endeavoring to excuse it on the score of health and neatness, ventured to advance the plea that it was nothing new, inasmuch as a similar garb had been worn for centuries by eastern womanhood, forthwith a meeting of the Bloomers inform these ignorant meddlers, that they do not know what they are talking about; that the Bloomer is no eastern dress, but the chosen garb of such ladies, who consider themselves as having a full right to consult their own sense of propriety, and to indulge the freedom of their nature in the pursuit of health, happiness, and humbug! It is the rallying standard of woman's rights advocates, and as such unfit for a modest female. Had it been but the invention of some Parisian *modiste,* or some country, field-tripping milk-maid, or of any other womanish thing, imagined womanishly and worn womanishly, we would not have hesitated to recommend it to our daughters. But indifferent things become vicious entirely by their uses; and the uses to which the Bloomer dress has been applied condemn it *in toto.* [LSM]

33. "Query" (Latin).

34. Smith, *Woman and Her Needs,* p. 106. Prov. 16:18: "After a proude stomake there foloweth a fall" (trans. Miles Coverdale). "Bess" is Elizabeth I of England (1533–1603).

comprehension of the simplest dairy-woman or cook-maid, escaped the pen of our reformist lady. But surely her mind, used to higher speculations, cannot stoop to comprehend it clearly, or she would cease to talk of woman's *daringly challenging her rights.* These ladies forget, when they cite their favorite exemplifications of woman's abilities in such characters as Shakspeare's Portia [41, 91], and wise or warlike queens, that the first class are so entirely poetic as to require all Shakspeare's genius to cause them to be tolerated even on the stage; the simple truth, quoted above, that it is necessary to *do* as well as to *talk,* being sufficient to prevent their appearance in real life. Imagine Mrs. Smith, or any other real Bloomer or non-Bloomer, attempting the role of a Portia at the New York bar. Does it need an argument to prove the certainty of her most egregious failure? The hissings of the street boys would soon settle the question in spite of her fancied logic. She may argue that the street boys are thus exhibiting a great want of decorum; that such a course is contrary to the philosophy of things and the higher law; and that she being the *equal* ("all men are born free and equal") of the street boys, she has as good a right to hiss as they. Verily, the philosophy of things and the higher law must cede to the nature of things and the divine law. We deny that Mrs. Smith is the *equal* of the street boys. If she consent to degrade herself by the comparison, she sinks far below them; for while *they* are in their place, acting more or less perfectly in accordance with their being, *she,* in aiming to reverse the laws of nature, becomes an inferior in a position for which nature unfits her; a crawling counterfeit of man, instead of that noble, pure, and exalted being which Nature intended when, bestowing upon her woman's being and woman's instincts, she gifted her also with perhaps somewhat more than ordinary woman's intellect. Examples from poetry are no proofs of fact; and if ladies will borrow arguments from imaginary characters, why not take at once the powerful Minerva springing full-armed from the brow of Jove, and contend that the world is not, cannot, and shall not be considered as properly managed, until all the female sex shall have reached that point of perfection?

As regards the position of governing queens, who with the "manish Bess have something to command respect," whence, we would ask, get they that something? Does their case show any power in the woman, whether different in its nature or differently exercised, at all deviating from that exhibited by the ordinary individuals of her sex in the ordinary duties of life? Have they anything inherent in their characters which enables them to conquer and maintain their position? or does their so maintaining it simply show, that when men are *willing* to be ruled, when they have *established laws for their own government,* they will submit to be reined even by the hand of a woman?— ay, and frequently the feeblest of women. Surely no one will contend that

Queen Victoria, for instance, keeps her place either through talent, energy, or any other characteristic of her own, whether natural or acquired. If a woman becomes anywhere man's inferior, it is in such a position; which, being by nature unsuited to her faculties, makes her, in so far as she is the tool of the active and acting man, simply his puppet—a dressed-up doll, if you please, a worshiped statue; but still, only a doll and a statue. There is perhaps no woman in the world whose natural expansion of true woman-intellect and woman-nature is more shackled by circumstance and cramped by position than that of England's Queen. Her limited faculties are of a kind which are crushed rather than developed by her position. As a *queen* she receives the homage of her place, but as a *woman* she is certainly neither exalted nor perfected by it. Like all inefficient monarchs, who form but the centre points of acting governments, she stands a mere figure-head, which men have chosen to place at the head of the vessel of state, having no more agency in her own position than the literal wooden block from which we draw our figure. "The manish Bess," and others of her stamp, have, we grant, been something different. But besides the impossibility, which even they would have found, to retain their positions, had not the *prestige* accorded by man to their place separated them from the rest of their sex, the very epithet *manish* shows how far nature had isolated such from the mass. God forbid that we should look upon such isolation as a merit or a source of admiration! Rather do we regard it as a kind of moral monstrosity which may suit the queen, but not the woman. A hive thrives under its one queen-bee; but a community of such could never exist. A single queen Elizabeth might be tolerated, and, if suited to the taste of the nation over which she ruled, even admired; but a race of such monster-women could only exist as a race of Amazons. *Men* must disappear from a world where *men-women* should gain the ascendancy.

    This may be a very faulty arrangement, and perhaps the world would have been improved by some difference in the relative position of the sexes. Thus, no doubt, think our lady-champions. For our part, we have never allowed ourselves to speculate upon the propriety or impropriety of an arrangement, so evidently marked by the Almighty hand that we have resigned ourselves to it as a fixed necessity, taking it for granted that here, as elsewhere, he has made all things good. When God created man, "male and female created he them."[35] Male and female nature requires that they remain, not only in body and form, but in act and deed. We are sorry to be obliged so to offend the delicate sensitiveness of Mrs. Smith as to use, and repeatedly use, the "obnoxious word *female*" [84], which she considers so objectionable as to

35. Gen. 1:27.

deem it necessary on one occasion to make an apology for its use, even when introduced in a quotation [91], and in another remarks, "The persistent use of the obnoxious word *female* in our vocabulary is proof of the light in which we are regarded" [84]. Now, we confess to the existence in ourselves of more blunted sensibilities. We—even we, the reviewer—must acknowledge ourselves of the feminine gender, of the female sex—woman; and can, in the fullest exercise of any intellect with which God has gifted us, feel, see, or discover no possible reason why we should find anything "obnoxious" in any of the above epithets. They can only become a reproach, they can only become obnoxious, by being applied where they ought not to be merited. They are insulting to men, because the characteristics which accompany them are generally unsuited to man; and their application implies that he has failed to bring himself up to the character which nature intended men generally to fulfil. They are becoming—they are suited—they are fitting to the woman (be she true woman), and the shame is not when she suits herself to, but when she avoids, them. An epithet is objectionable only when the nature that it indicates is objectionable; and therefore the word "female," as indicating woman-nature, can only be obnoxious to the woman who mistakenly aims to rank herself in a position antagonistic to her nature. There is something out of joint in her reasoning, when she can come to the conclusion that "female" is an obnoxious epithet, or "manish" a flattering one. It is the high duty of every reasoning mortal to aim at the perfecting of his kind by the perfecting of his individual humanity. Woman's task is, to make herself the perfected woman, not the counterfeit man.

We have been obliged to confess ourself woman, because only as woman can we take the defensive in this question. Man is excluded from the discussion as a party interested against this female move, and the question is assumed to be one in which the sexes are placed in antagonism. Only as woman, therefore, can we attempt the defence of woman against a move calculated in every step of its progress to lower her from the position which nature has accorded to her. Only as woman can we efficiently enter our protest against the folly and madness of ideas of which, we do their woman-advocates the justice to believe, that there is not one in a thousand degraded enough to maintain them, could she logically deduce the inference from her own premises. There is enough of pure, enough of holy in the God-created and heaven-endowed woman-nature, to make it shrink from contact with the foul chaos which such a deduction would develop. In their ignorance they have done this.[36]

---

36. Acts 3:13–17: "His son Jesus . . . ye delivered up, and denied him in the presence of Pilate, when he was determined to let him go. But ye denied the Holy One and the Just,

Mrs. Smith (of whom, once for all, we know nothing personally, and only in so far as she has published her theories feel at liberty to take her as the exponent of the more quiet class of reformers) has in advance considered not only the antagonistic animal, man, as opposed to her theories, but also deprecates the admission of a large portion of her own sex to this argument. She divides womankind into three classes; and as we have confessed our womanhood, we will endeavor to satisfy ourselves, and let our readers judge, to which of these categories we shall be consigned, or whether we have the right, in the name of the female sex, to claim a different classification:

> There is a large class of our sex so well cared for, "whom the winds of heaven are not allowed to visit too roughly,"[37] who are hemmed in by conventional forms, and by the appliances of wealth, till they can form no estimate of the sufferings of their less fortunate sisters . . . a class [. . .] delicate, amiable, lovely even; but limited and superficial. These follow the bent of their masculine friends and admirers, and lisp pretty ridicule about the folly of "Woman's Rights" and "Woman's Movements." These see no need of reform or change of any kind; indeed, they are denied that comprehensiveness of thought by which they could hold the several parts of a subject in the mind, and see its bearings. Society is a sort of grown-up mystery which they pretend not to comprehend, supposing it to have gradually developed to its present size and shape from Adam and Eve, by *natural gradation,* like Church Bishops. [11–12; LSM's italics][38]

Need we enter our disclaimer against being included in this category? We believe, if our readers have followed us thus far, that they will need no argument to convince them that we are not of the above class of pretty lispers,

---

and desired a murderer to be granted unto you; and killed the Prince of life, whom God hath raised from the dead. . . . And now, brethren, I wot that through ignorance ye did it, as did also your rulers."

37. *Hamlet* 1.2.139–42: "So excellent a king . . . / . . . so loving to my mother / That he might not beteem the winds of heaven / Visit her face too roughly."

38. Our thanks, by the way, to Mrs. S. for this piece of information, quite new to us, with regard to the Bishops. We did not know that these Rev. gentlemen were *gradually developed* by *natural gradation.* We shall, in future, study with a double zest the beautiful developments of natural history, in hopes of further enlightening ourselves upon so interesting a question. The great Agassiz must hide his diminished head before this wonderful discovery of Mrs. Smith. What are his fish and his polypi to her Bishops? [LSM] Jean Louis Rodolphe Agassiz (1807–73), Swiss-born American naturalist, whose "Diversity of Origin of the Human Races," *Christian Examiner* 49 (July 1850): 110–45, LSM reviewed in *PSE,* "Diversity of the Races; Its Bearing upon Negro Slavery." Milton, *Paradise Lost* 4.34–35: the sun "at whose sight all the stars / Hide their diminished heads."

and will credit our assertion when we claim to have lived long enough, and to have suffered enough, to learn that life is an earnest duty, and woman's share in it one of deep and soul-searching responsibility.

> Then there is another class doomed to debasement, vice, labor of body and soul, in all their terrible manifestations. Daughters of suffering without its ennobling influence; too weak in thought, it may be, to discern the best good; or, it may be, too strong in passion to resist the allurements of the immediate; or, it may be, ignorant only, they wake to the sad realities of life too late to find redress for its evils. These are the kind over whom infinite Pity would weep, as it were, drops of blood. These may scoff at reform, but it is the scoffing of a lost spirit, or that of despair. It is the blind utterance of regions denied the light of infinite love, and condemned to the Fata Morganas of depraved vision. [12–13]

Again we beg leave to plead "not guilty." Among these "lost spirits," condemned to "blind utterances" and "Fata Morganas," believe us, gentle reader, we are not. The affections, as well as the duties of life, have laid upon us their guiding hand, teaching us to love, to suffer, and to hope. When our feet stumble in the path, as in all humility we confess right often they do, truly it is by human weakness, and no "Fata Morganas," that we are misled. Let us pass now to class No. 3, the elect of the sex, according to reformist creeds.

> Then come the class of our sex capable of thought, of impulse, of responsibility—the worthy to be called Woman. Not free from faults any more than the strong of the other sex, but of that full humanity which may sometimes err, but yet which loves and seeks for the true and the good. These include all who are identified with suffering, in whatever shape, and from whatever cause; for these, when suffering proceeds from their own acts even, have that fund of greatness or goodness left, that they perceive and acknowledge the opposite of what they are. These are the ones who are victims to the falseness of society, and who see and feel that something may and will be done to redeem it. They are not content to be the creatures of luxury, the toys of the drawing-room, however well they may grace it—they are too true, too earnest in life, to trifle with its realities. They are capable of thinking, it may be far more capable of it than those of their own household who help to sway the destinies of the country through the ballot-box. They are capable of feeling, and analyzing too, the evils that surround themselves and others—they have individuality, resource, and that antagonism which weak men ridicule, because it shames their own imbecility; which makes them

obnoxious to those of less earnestness of character, and helps them to an eclectic power, at once their crown of glory. [13–14]

We quote literally, that our readers may, should they possess sufficient profundity of intellect, seize the whole mysterious beauty of this sublime extract. For ourselves, credit us, O most indulgent reader—so little are we, in our humility, akin to this class of elect who sit crowned in eclectic power—that we really cannot even feebly comprehend the mystic signification of the "eclectic power, at once their crown of glory," here so mystically sketched. These reformist saints, as well as their sinners, are, we are free to confess, entirely beyond our matter-of-fact comprehension; and if we were more than bothered to grasp the idea of blind utterance and Fata Morgana ladies, we are now doubly mystified in our attempt to catch even the faintest outline signification of these beatific and inspired eclectics. Behold us, therefore, according to Mrs. Smith's classification, as we belong to none of her categories, fairly ousted, not only from our womanhood, but in no little danger of finding ourselves ultimately pushed altogether out of our humanity; for of the bearded species (Heaven help us!) we are, if we may trust our looking-glass, certainly not. Under penalty, therefore, of being classed among apes and elephants, or being picked up as a specimen of some new and undefined family of the vertebratae, it will, we trust, be permitted us to enter our humble protest in favor of such of the female sex as, without having reached the sublime height of the eclectic crown of glory, may yet feel that they are neither "lost spirits," nor yet "toys of the drawing-room."

There certainly are, unless this world has been to us a dream, true women, of every grade of intellect, who belong to none of Mrs. Smith's categories. We find them varying, of every type, from the simple, confiding woman-heart, which, knowing little but the instinct of its nature, feels only that such instinct is to lean, and that its being is dependent, up through every nicely changing shade of individual loveliness and intellectuality, to the less happy, perhaps, but nobler existence, the highest model of womanhood—the woman of thought, of mind, of genius, and yet filled with deep-brooding woman-love and woman-nature. She, the earnest striver, wrestling with life's cares, but contemning not its duties, feels so sensibly her noble nature, that she scorns to degrade it by placing it in an unnatural antagonism with man's, and presents in her pure woman-existence, we truly think, the highest model to which humanity is capable of attaining.[39] But, spirits of eclectic

39. "There is with us of the Southern United States a strong *corps de reserve* of sober, quiet women, who, satisfied to find out duties at home (not for want of thought, but because thought teaches us that therein lies woman's highest task, and the fulfillment of her noblest

womandom! most certainly such a woman is not of *you;* for while she speaks neither in "blind utterances" nor pretty lispings, yet is she innocent of ballot-boxes and conventions. Such a woman needs not to make any man feel "shame of his imbecility"; nor to place herself in antagonism with any, whether weak or strong. Her mission is one of love and charity to all. It is the very essence of her being to raise and to purify wherever she touches. Where man's harder nature crushes, her's exalts. Where he wounds, she heals. The lowest intellect, be it but combined with a sincere nature, shrinks not from her, for in her it perceives, reflected and ennobled, its own virtues; the highest, worships, for it understands her. In every grade, then, between these two extremes, there are women—and we are proud to believe, in spite of the world's vices and its follies, the majority of women—whose very existence Mrs. Smith has, in her classification, entirely ignored; and these are the women in defence of whose true womanhood we now venture to enter our disclaimer in opposition to the assumed position of our lady-reformers, that, as the world is, woman "must use mean weapons because the nobler are denied her; she cannot assert her distinctive individuality, and she resorts to cunning, and this cunning takes the form of cajolery, deception, or antagonism in its many shapes, each and all as humiliating to herself as it is unjust to man" [35]. No true woman feels that the nobler weapons of life are denied her, because she cannot tinker at constitutions and try her hand at law-making. Her's are the noble weapons of philosophy and Christianity. She may find it difficult to wield them, and, in her human weakness, sometimes murmur at the hardness of that lot by which a mysterious Providence has assigned a task so difficult to her feeble frame; but she cannot, she dare not, call degrading a task which, executed in its perfection, would make her the truest personification of our great Christian law. One advantage, at least, to cheer her in her path, she has over man. Her duty is always clear, while *his* may be doubtful. Her's is the Christian law of love and charity, to which (however passion may tempt) unvarying points the finger of duty. His is too often a divided struggle. She has but to strive and to pray; while he has to strive and to fight. She *knows* that to soothe, to comfort and to heal, is her highest duty. He *doubts* whether to wrangle, to strike and to wound, be not his. God, man, and nature alike call upon her to subdue her passions, to suffer, to bear, to be meek and lowly of heart; while man,

---

mission), can nevertheless start up with the true feeling of womanhood in defence of right and property, hearth and home. *Ora et labora*—strive and pray. Such is the lesson of our life, ladies, and it were hard to find a better. With us woman finds her noblest rule, her highest privilege, a privilege which, in the aggregate, her sex has never abused." *PSE*, "British Philanthropy and American Slavery," p. 319.

summoned by nature, and often by duty, to the whirl of strife, blinded in the struggle, forgets too often where wrath should cease and mercy rule. What, then, more beautiful than woman's task to arrest the up-lifted arm, and, in the name of an all-pardoning Heaven, to whisper to his angry passions—"Peace, be still!"[40]

"I long," says Mrs. Smith, "to see my own sex side by side with man in every great work, and free to see the light, when his vision is dimmed with the dust of his chariot-wheels in the mighty race in which he is engaged" [101]. And how will she do this, if she throws herself even in the thick of the dust beside him? Let her stay where she is, out of the blinding cloud of struggling passion, where, from the beautiful eminence on which nature has placed her, she looks down like some pitying saint, some angel of mercy, some ray of God's own sunlight glancing over a bloody battlefield, to soften, to cheer, and to bless. God forbid that ever she should sink to wallow in dust and blood beside him whom it is her duty and her privilege to rescue from the soil to which his nature clings! Woman the civilizer! woman the soother! how is your holy mission forgotten, striving thus to degrade itself!

"If," says our authoress, "if she be a simple, genial, household divinity, she will bind garlands around the altar of the Penates, and worship in content. If more largely endowed, I see no reason why she should not be received cordially into the school of Arts, or Science, or Politics, or Theology, in the same manner as the individual capacities of the other sex are recognized." [26–27] And this, in Mrs. Smith's opinion, would be *raising* her condition. Too *largely endowed* for a household divinity, she casts aside that divinity, and who dares contemplate the struggle into which her feeble ignorance precipitates her? These reforming ladies have pushed forward in their move from the instigations of a most egregious vanity, which has induced them to consider themselves as so superior to the rest of their sex, that they have finally (as our quotations a few pages back may show) come to the conclusion, and quietly assumed the ground, that they alone—they, the throned in "eclectic power" [14]—are the thinkers of their sex. Our effort, through this article, has been to prove to them that they may perhaps be mistaken. We would now entreat them to look a little forward into the practicability and operation of their system. Allowing, for a moment, the fulfilment of their demands to be desirable, how do they propose enforcing it? Why have men always legislated, but because they have the power? and by what process is this power to be wrenched or coaxed from them? We presume our authoress, when the point of action should come, would hardly advise the sisterhood to so far imitate the deeds of their fathers, as to shoulder muskets in

---

40. Mark 4:39.

the cause. What then can they do, but ask the proposed reform through men, their legislators? Here then we have woman, by her own voluntary act, as seeking to graft man's nature upon her own, reduced to the degrading position so much deprecated by Mrs. Smith, wherein she "must receive happiness not as the gift of her Maker, careful for the well-being of the creature he had made, but as a boon from Man—who had the *right* to make her miserable, but forebore the exercise of his prerogative" [33]. Herself, grasping at rights not naturally belonging to her, places herself in the position of receiving, as a "boon from man," what her Maker has in his wisdom seen fit not to gift her with. Mrs. Smith vainly may answer that her improved system would make woman her own legislator. This is impossible. Power exercised through the tolerance of another is never a free power, but only in fact the delegated authority of him who tolerates. Woman legislators could thus act only under the influence and authority of men, because men would at any moment have the power, the might, to depose them. As we cannot fight, so we cannot enforce our claims—so we cannot insist. We can but entreat, we can but sway, we can but receive as a boon. If woman is to be admitted as co-legislator with man, it can only be through man's prior legislation. He must *give* the right, which she has not the power to *take*. Is this condition of things wrong? Go then, if it be, and cavil with the God who hath thus dictated it. *He* gave to the man the right, even as He gave him the power. *He* laid upon his strong right arm those folds of muscle by whose might he can rule, must rule—ay, and in all physical right ought to rule—all that God in his wisdom hath made weaker. Ought to rule, we say; because whatever God has made ought to be. Where *He* has seen fit to give checks and balances to the various powers of various beings, there we see Nature forces such checks and balances into action. To the man, for instance, pitted against the corporeally stronger beast, has been given the governing reason which forces the brute to crouch before him; and here, as elsewhere, *power* is the stamp and seal of God to indicate His will—the only real right of His creature. Man has then the corporeal, physical right to rule the woman, and she combats God's eternal law of order when she opposes it; combats it to her own undoing; for who can strive against God? Physically, then, she must be ruled, and submit her "proud stomach," be it her curse to bear one, to the necessities of her case.

Morally, physically, let us next consider, what is woman's destiny? We believe, the highest. The beautifully developed soul is hers; and truly has Mrs. Smith said that woman is man's "superior in the elements that most harmonize life" [26]; and only in her self-wrought debasement (a debasement brought about by her forgetfulness of her own individuality and her natural position) has she been forced to beg "for tolerance where she before had a right to homage—pleaded her weakness as a motive for protection, because she had laid aside her own distinctive powers, and become imbecile and subservient. Women must recognize their unlikeness; and then, understanding what needs grow out of this unlikeness, some great truth must be evolved." [26] This is as wisely said, as if the spirit of the great Solomon himself had placed itself at the lady's elbow, and made her his medium to knock out this spiritual truth for our benefit. But, alas! the spirit of wisdom is wearied soon of its work of charity, for even in the same paragraph follows the sentence we quoted above. Woman, she says, must seek her sphere; "if she be a simple, genial, household divinity, she will bind garlands around the altar of [the] Penates, and worship in content. If more largely endowed, I see no reason why she should not," etc. [26–27]

Now, *we* contend that to be a divinity, a genial, household divinity—not in that character, at least, to *worship* (which by some confusion of thought Mrs. Smith has assigned as the occupation of a household divinity), but to *be worshiped* at that holiest altar of the Penates, the home hearth; to be the soul of that home, even as our great Father-God is the soul of creation; to be the breath, the life, the love-law of that home; the mother, the wife, the sister, the daughter—such is woman's holiest sphere, such her largest endowment. This is the natural position from which she has stepped; this the individuality which she has forgotten; these the distinctive powers which she has laid aside, to become imbecile and subservient in the exercise of others unsuited to her nature. This beautiful recognition of her unlikeness to man, is the sole mystery of her existence; the one great truth which must be evolved to make woman no longer the weak plaything of a tyrannic master, no longer the trampled thing, pleading for tolerance at the foot of her conqueror, but the life, the soul, the vital heart of society; while in her and through her thus circulates the every throb of this great living world. She does not rule, she cannot rule, by stump-speech, convention, or ballot-box; but she can rule, and she does rule, by the great quiet soul-power, which, silent as the blood through the arteries of life, throbs on forever, ceasing but with the existence of the body which it vivifies.

Such is woman's noble task. Can any be nobler? What disgrace and degradation have ever fallen upon her, whether individually or in the mass, have been the result of, and in proportion to, her neglect or contempt of this her God-marked mission. "If more largely endowed!" [26]—Is it from largeness of endowment, or is it from the cramping guidance of an ill-ordered intellect, that she is induced to throw herself out of such a position, to become a suppliant and an inferior in one whose duties are inconsistent with her nature? If woman will fulfil her destiny, let her put away from her head and heart the idea that she is man. Let her abandon the thought of an equality or superiority, or inferiority, between the sexes, which exists neither in nature or fact, but simply in the mistaken views which men and women have both taken of the subject. Each is inferior, when attempting to fulfil a part destined to the other. A horse or an ass is certainly not the superior of man; and yet let man, or woman either, attempt to fulfil the duties of the poor brute, and how immeasurably inferior is he to the quadruped he rivals. We assure our conventionist sisters, that they are as ill qualified to perform the part of the man as the ass, and would advise them to attempt neither. The celebrated monkey-man, whose wonderful performances attract roars of applause from delighted audiences, is still far behind the veritable baboon whom he apes. Woman, in emulating man in his own sphere—and consequently out of hers, even though she succeed to the height attained by "the manish queen Bess," with "her proud stomach," so often quoted as proof of the powers of woman—holds still to man the second rate, inferior, and imitative position, which the poor actor does towards the baboon; the belittling ambition of the monkey-man and the man-woman being equally but a sad model for the general imitation of society. Woman's sphere is higher, purer, nobler. She ought *not* "to be received [cordially] into the schools <school> of Arts, or Science, or Politics, or Theology, in the same manner as the individual capacities of the other sex are recognized" [27].[41] She ought not to be so received, because her individual capacities are different. We do not bid her be ignorant of these matters. We do not say that her mind is incapable of grasping them. On the contrary, we believe that her capacities are fully suited to them, and that it is not only her right, but her duty, as it is that of every intelligent being, to forward the world's progress by the accumulative impulse of individual progress. Every mind has a thought which may be of benefit in the circle of its influence, and we sin in cramping that thought. Woman's mind is made for improvement, and her duty would lead her to seek that improvement, according to the inclination and capacities of her intellect. But that improvement must be gained and used in a manner consistent and in harmony with her nature. Her arts and science are *not* for the public schools. Her theology is not for the pulpit; nor are her politics for those arenas of strife where rougher man is soiled by the polluting struggle, and shrinks often in disgust from the stifling contamination. She may counsel, she may teach, she may uphold the weary arm of manhood—of the husband, the brother, or the son—and rouse him to the struggle for which nature never designed her; but she may not (without foregoing her nature) rush into the

---

41. Our readers, we trust, do not hold us responsible for the halting grammar of our authoress (or her printers), which has, we confess, puzzled us in more sentences than the remarkable eclectic glorification one, though we have not always stopped to note it. [LSM]

combat of blood, shouting man's war-cry and the victim's death. Side by side she may stand with man, to guide, to strengthen, to check, or to soothe; but let her keep clear of the blinding "dust of his chariot wheels" [101], that her eye may see and her tongue may counsel, by the clear dictates of her unstained soul, while *his* eye and spirit are alike dimmed in the strife. Woman, we believe, is designed, by nature, the conservative power of the world. Not surely, therefore, useless, because comparatively inactive in the tumultuous rush and turmoil of life, she checks oftener than she impels. The lock-chain which arrests the downward rushing and precipitously destructive course of the ever forwardly impelled vehicle, is not useless because temporarily allowed to rest in the uphill tug. Life and limb are saved by the proper use of that which, injudiciously applied, would be in itself destruction.

That "good time coming," the political millennium towards which Mrs. S. looks forward, when "the lion will lie down with the lamb, and the sting shall be taken from whatever is noxious, and the dragon of restrictive and retributive law loosen its folds upon human society" [100], will certainly never be brought about by woman's conventions, woman's speeches, nor woman's votes. Rather, if the world shall ever see it, will it be perfected by the home divinity of woman, whispering her truths to the heart of man, wrapping his soul in the inspiration of a revealed duty, and bearing him upward and onward to the fulfilment of that duty. Is it a degradation to *her,* if, while thus ennobling man by her all-pervading influence, he fail, as much as he might, to profit by it, and sometimes in his error may even scoff and sneer at her? No; only when that scoff and sneer rouse her to unfeminine resistance, or still more unfeminine imitation, is the evil done. Then, indeed, are both degraded in the sin of both. Thus woman's weakness in its human imperfection truly often errs; but, again, nobly often, spite of scoff and sneer, does woman's strength soar almost above humanity, whilst, bending beneath ills too great for man's endurance, she humbly joins in that Godlike prayer of resignation, "Father, if it be thy will, let this cup pass from me; nevertheless, not as I will, but as thou wilt."[42] Can there be degradation in bearing the cross of patient endurance midst rebuff and wrong, even to the great Calvary of self-abnegation and triumphant love? Woman! if man forgets his duty, what nobler lesson than to recall him to it, by remembering yours? What more degrading, at once to yourself and to him, than to fight and squabble like hungry dogs over a bone, for a something which, even could its acquisition be proved desirable to your sex, you are still called to, not by duty, but simply by wish and appetite. We are no enemy of woman,

---

42. Matt. 26:39.

but rather have ventured, as her champion, upon this her defence; believing that the recent demonstration, among certain members of her own sex, is at once the most degrading, the most insulting to her, and the most dangerous attack that can be made upon her true liberty. Liberty is never license. It is the freedom to fulfil, in their highest perfection, the duties of our God-given being. The true defender, therefore, of woman's rights and woman's liberty, asks only that she may be permitted to perfect, not to alter, her nature.

In conclusion, let us remark, for those of the masculine gender who (if there be any such) may perchance think our authority worth quoting against womandom, that we beg not to be misunderstood. Our argument being solely against the female move, our effort has been to show its false assumptions and ludicrous inefficacy; but we have not, therefore, intended to signify that man is sinless towards woman. Far from it. If we have endeavored to lay upon woman the burden of her own sin, as a reasonable, responsible being, and to prove to her how necessary is the exercise of her own inward strength for the performance of life's duties, and how doubly necessary it becomes to her, through physical weakness, that she should guard herself in the position where God and nature have placed her—we have endeavored to be the more forcible in so doing, because we consider her danger doubled through man's constant thoughtless and often heartless oppression. She must guard not only against her own folly and her own weakness, but also against his. If we have pointed out her aberrations from duty, and blamed or ridiculed her short-comings, it is not that we would make her the butt of man's ridicule, who has sinned both with her and against her, but because we consider her as more than him disinterested, more than him swayable by the purer instincts, and more than him exalted above the passions of our common nature. If woman has erred, to man, clamorous in her accusation, we would say—"He that is without sin among you, let him first cast a stone at her."[43] Man the oppressor, man the tempter, will he dare to strike? or rather, checked by the holy word of reproof spoken to the repentant Magdalene, will he not take to his bosom the lesson intended for her? Happy would it indeed be for both, could each, in the holy fulfilment of the duties of their differing spheres, "*go, and sin no more.*"[44]

43. John 8:7.
44. John 8:11.

5.

Uncle Tom's Cabin

Truly it would seem that the labour of Sisyphus is laid upon us, the slaveholders of these southern United States. Again and again have we, with all the power and talent of our clearest heads and strongest intellects, forced aside the foul load of slander and villainous aspersion so often hurled against us, and still, again and again, the unsightly mass rolls back, and, heavily as ever, fall the old refuted libels, vamped, remodelled, and lumbering down upon us with all the force, or at least impudent assumption, of new argument. We anticipate here the answer and application of our charitable opponents. We, too, have studied our mythology, and remember well, that the aforesaid Sisyphus was condemned to his torment for the sins of injustice, oppression, and tyranny.[1] Like punishment to like sin will, no doubt, be their corollary.

SQR, n.s., 7 (Jan. 1853) = PSE, pp. 245–80. Publications reviewed: Harriet Beecher Stowe, *Uncle Tom's Cabin or, Life among the Lowly*, 2 vols. (Boston: J. P. Jewett, 1852); [Rufus W. Griswold?], "Contemporary Literature of America," *Westminster Review* 58 (July 1852): 272–87. Page references to *Uncle Tom's Cabin* given below are those of the Library of America edition of Harriet Beecher Stowe, ed. Kathryn K. Sklar (1982), which reprints the first American book edition of *Uncle Tom's Cabin*.

1. More precisely, Sisyphus, king of Corinth, suffered for insulting the gods (*hubris*). Sentenced to die for betraying one of Zeus' love affairs, Sisyphus instructed his wife Merope to refuse his body proper burial. In the Underworld he persuaded Hades to permit him to visit earth, so that he might punish Merope for her impiety before returning to the Underworld. Hades agreed; Sisyphus then was careful never to punish Merope. But when he came

Boldly, however, before God and man, we dare hold up our hand and plead "not guilty." Clearly enough do we see through the juggle of this game. It is no hand of destiny, no fiat of Jove, which rolls back upon us the labouring bulk. There is an agent behind the curtain, vulnerable at least as ourselves; and the day may yet come when, if this unlucky game cease not, the destructive mass shall find another impetus, and crush beneath its unexpected weight the hand which now directs it, we scarce know whether in idle wantonness or diabolic malice.

Among the revelations of this passing year, stand prominent the volumes we are about to review. In the midst of political turmoil, Mrs. Harriet Beecher Stowe has determined to put *her* finger in the pot, and has, it would seem, made quite a successful dip. Wordy philanthropy—which blows the bellows for discontent, and sends poor fools wandering through the clouds upon its treacherous breezes, yet finds no crumb of bread for one hungry stomach—is at a high premium nowadays. Ten thousand dollars (the amount, it is said, of the sales of her work) was, we presume, in the lady's opinion, worth risking a little scalding for. We wish her joy of her ten thousand thus easily gained, but would be loath to take with it the foul imagination which could invent such scenes, and the malignant bitterness (we had almost said ferocity) which, under the veil of christian charity, could find the conscience to publish them. Over this, their new-laid egg, the abolitionists, of all colours—black, white, and yellow—foreign and domestic—have set up so astounding a cackle, it is very evident, that (labouring, perhaps, under some mesmeric biologic influence) they think the goose has laid its golden egg at last. They must wake up from their dream, to the sad disappointment of finding their fancied treasure an old addle thing, whose touch contaminates with its filth.

There is nothing new in these volumes. They are, as we have said, only the old Sisyphus rock, which we have so often tumbled over, tinkered up, with considerable talent and cunning, into a new shape, and rolled back upon us. One step, indeed, we do seem to have gained. One accusation at least, which, in bygone times, used to have its changes rung among the charges brought against us, is here forgotten. We see no reference to the old habit, so generally (according to some veracious travellers) indulged in these Southern States, of fattening negro babies for the use of the soup-pot. This, it would appear, is a species of black broth which cannot be swallowed any longer. If, however, Mrs. Stowe has spared us the story of this delectable soup, with the small *nigger paws* floating in it by way of garnish, truly it is all

---

to die of old age, Hades had not forgotten the trick and sentenced Sisyphus eternally to roll up a hill a boulder which, at the summit, eternally rolls back down again.

that she *has* spared us. Libels almost as shocking to humanity she not only indulges herself in detailing, but dwells upon with a gusto and a relish quite edifying to us benighted heathen, who, constantly surrounded (as according to her statements we are) by such moving scenes and crying iniquities, yet, having ears, hear not, and having eyes, see not[2] those horrors whose stench become[s] an offence to the nostrils of our sensitive and self-constituted directors.

Most painful it is to us to comment upon a work of this kind. What though "our withers be unwrung"?[3] Does slander cease to be painful because it is gross? Is it enough for us to know that these obscene and degrading scenes are false as the spirit of mischief which dictated them? and can we, therefore, indifferently see these loathsome rakings of a foul fancy passed as current coin upon the world, which receives them as sketches of American life by an American citizen? We cannot; and loathsome as is the task; little as we hope to be heard in any community where such a work can be received and accredited, and where the very fact of such reception proves at once that our case is prejudged; yet will we speak and sift the argument of this fair lady, who so protests against vice that we might think her, like that "noble sister of Publicola," that "moon of Rome,"

> chaste as the icicle
> That's curdied by the frost from purest snow
> And hangs on Dian's temple,[4]

were it not that her too vivid imagination, going so far ahead of facts, shows too clearly that not now, for the first time, does it travel the muddy road. Some hints from the unfortunately fashionable reading of the day, some flashes from the French school of romance, some inspirations from the Sues and the Dumas', have evidently suggested the tenor of her pages.

The literary taste of our day (i.e., the second-rate literary taste, the fashionable novel-reading taste) demands excitement. Nothing can be spiced too high. Incident, incident, and that of the vilest kind, crowds the pages of those novels which are now unfortunately all the vogue. *The Mysteries of Paris, Monte Cristo, The Wandering Jew,*[5] *et id genus omne,*[6] leave the diseased taste of the reader, who has long subsisted on such fare, sick, sick and palled as it is with the nauseous diet, still with a constant craving, like that of the diseased

---

2. Ps. 115:5–6; Jer. 5:21.
3. *Hamlet* 3.2.237–38: "Let the galled jade wince, our withers are unwrung."
4. *Coriolanus* 5.3.64–67.
5. *Les Mystères de Paris* (1842–43) and *Le Juif errant* (1844–45) by Eugène Sue; *Le Comte de Monte Cristo* (1844) by Alexandre Dumas the elder.
6. "And all that sort" (Latin).

palate of the opium eater, for its accustomed drug. For such tastes, Mrs. Stowe has catered well. Her facts are remarkable facts—very. Let us see on what authority she bases them. This is a question worth examining, as she here assumes to have given us an exhibition of slavery in its "*living dramatic reality*" [513; Stowe's italics]. In her "concluding remarks," appended to the second volume of the edition (seventh thousand) which we have, she says:

> The writer has often been enquired of, by correspondents from different parts of the country, whether this narrative is a true one; and to these enquiries she will give one general answer.
>
> The separate incidents which <that> compose her <the> narrative are, to a very great extent, authentic, occurring, many of them, [either] under her own observation, or that of her personal friends. She or her friends have observed characters the counterpart of almost all that are here introduced; and many of the sayings are word for word as heard herself, or reported to her. [510]

We can only say, in answer to this, that "she and her friends" are far from being, in our minds, decisive authority. If she says "it is," just as emphatically do we answer "it is not." What vender of falsehood but vouches for the truth of his own fabrications? She tells us, "Some of the most deeply tragic and romantic, some of the most terrible incidents, have also their parallel in reality" [510]. And again, of one of her most horrible inventions, she remarks: "That this scene <the tragical fate of Tom, also,> has too many times had its parallel, there are living witnesses, all over our land, to testify" [510]. Living witnesses all over our land are such intangible antagonists that it would be a worse combat than that of Don Quixote against the windmills for us to undertake them, and therefore we must let them pass. One stray sheep, however, she does introduce; and as we cannot be cheated, by the clouds of dust she has kicked up, to mistake him for a giant, we will not need, to encounter him, the courage exhibited by the celebrated Don in his attack upon a flock of the same animals. She says, with reference to a story of brutal persecution and slow murder:

> The story of "old Prue," in the second volume, was an incident that fell under the personal observation of a brother of the writer, then collecting-clerk to a large mercantile house, in New Orleans. From the same source was derived the character of the planter Legree. Of him her brother thus wrote, speaking of visiting his plantation on a collecting tour: "He actually made me feel of his fist, which was like a blacksmith's hammer, or a nodule of iron, telling me that it was 'calloused with knocking down niggers.' When I left the plantation, I drew a long breath, and felt as if I had escaped from an ogre's den." [510]

The testimony of this brother is the only one which she cites, except in the general "all over the land" style which we have noticed; and we think any one who has spent six months of his life in a southern city will recognize the type of this her solitary authority. Who has not seen the green Yankee youth opening his eyes and mouth for every piece of stray intelligence; eager for horrors; gulping the wildest tales, and exaggerating even as he swallows them? Why, this fellow is to be met with in every shipload of candidates for clerkships who come out like bees to suck our honey; but so choke-full the while of all they have heard of the horrors and dangers incident to these latitudes, that they wink their eyes and dodge a fancied pistol or bowie-knife whenever a man but raises his hand to touch his hat to the stranger. Having made up their minds that Southerners are all brutes, what earthly power can cure the moral near-sight? Not reason, certainly, nor fact either. Their school dame taught it to them with their catechism; and surely those green eyes could never be expected to see across the catechism and the school-dame's teachings far enough to learn the truth. Pity that this gentle Balaam of a brother had not possessed a little of the cunning and courage of those favourite heroes of our childish days, "Puss in Boots," and "Jack the Giant Killer," that he might have decisively disposed of this redoubtable ogre with nodules of iron hands, instead of sneaking out of his den and leaving him there, like a great "Giant Despair," to devour all unfortunate pilgrims who fell in his way.[7] How poor Balaam summoned courage to feel *of* that fist, "calloused with knocking down niggers," we cannot imagine. Verily, there are trials by land, and trials by water, and poor Balaam, apparently, cared not to put his delicate person in danger from any of them. Seriously, is it not easy here to perceive that a raw, suspicious Yankee youth, having "happened" (as he would say) in contact with a rough overseer, a species of the *genus homo* evidently quite new to him, has been half gulled by the talk of the fellow who has plainly intended to quiz him, and has half gulled himself with his own fears while in the vicinity of this novel character, whom he, poor gentle specimen of Yankee humanity, has absolutely mistaken for an ogre because his hand is hard? That the fellow himself made the speech quoted by Balaam, viz., that his fist was *"calloused* by knocking down niggers," we more than doubt—that elegant word "calloused" being one entirely new to our dictionary, and savouring, we think, much more of Yankee clerk origin and Noah Webster, than of Southern birth.

Upon the whole, the authorities of our authoress put us in mind of one

---

7. On Balaam see Num. 22–24. In John Bunyan's *Pilgrim's Progress* (Harmondsworth, Eng., 1965), pp. 151–57, Giant Despair imprisons Christian and Hopeful in Doubting Castle.

of our earliest trials in life. Our first entrance upon school being made in one of our Northern cities, we found ourselves, before the first week of probation was over, the object of some comment among the younger members of the establishment, and were finally accused, by the leader of the little faction, of coming from the land of negrodom. To this charge, we, of course, could but plead guilty, wondering, in our little mind, what sin there could be in the association. A portion of our iniquities we soon had revealed to us. "Father's cousin's wife's sister was at the South once, and she knows all about how you treat your negroes! She knows that you feed them with cotton-seed, and put padlocks on their mouths to keep them from eating corn while they are in the field." Vainly we protested; as vainly reasoned. Authority was against us, and the padlock story vouched by "father's cousin's wife's sister, a very nice lady, that always told the truth," was swallowed by the majority, and received in our Lilliput community with as undisputed credence as Mrs. Stowe's brother's account of the fist "calloused by knocking down niggers" will be gulped down by her admirers. A lady-friend of ours, travelling northward a summer or two since, was similarly enlightened as to some of the iniquities constantly practiced round us, but which, blinded creatures that we are, we have to leave home to discover. Miss C., she was informed, had a cousin who had gone school-keeping to Georgia, and that cousin told Miss C., on her word, as a lady, that she had often and often seen baskets full of ears and noses cut and pulled from the negroes by way of punishment and torture. Miss C. couldn't say whether they were big baskets or little ones; she supposed they were not very big ones, because the supply of ears and noses would be exhausted, and she did not suppose it was a case to call for miraculous increase. She could not account for it all exactly, but she knew that it was true—she did. Her cousin was a lady, and had seen it herself. Pity it is that Mrs. Stowe had not made acquaintance with Miss C.'s cousin; the ears and noses would have made a fine picturesque point, graphically introduced among her "dramatic realities." The Balaam brother, however, seems to answer her purpose pretty well, and upon his testimony about the nodule-fisted gentleman, and some enlightenments from a speech of the freesoil Massachusetts senator, Horace Mann, she has manufactured a character which would shame the Caliban of Shakspeare.[8] That great master of the human mind, when he imagined a being devoid of all human feeling and yet possessed of something like human form, remembered that, in the

---

8. *Uncle Tom's Cabin*, pp. 511–12. Horace Mann (1796–1859), lawyer and educator; member of the Massachusetts legislature (1827–33), and senate (1833–37); of U.S. House of Representatives (1848–53); Free Soil candidate for governor in 1852. Caliban is the bestial servant of the magician Prospero in *The Tempest*.

wildest flights of imagination, there must still be kept up a semblance of probability, and painted him, therefore, free also from human parentage. Shakspeare's Caliban was a monster of devilish origin, to whom Sycorax, his dam, bequeathed but little of humanity. Mrs. Harriet Beecher Stowe, however, gives to *her* Caliban a human mother; a gentle, fair-haired, loving mother, and does not shame to pass upon us as a man this beast, this brute, without conscience and without heart, devoid equally of common sense and common feeling.

The *Westminster Review,* in noticing, with high approbation, these volumes of Mrs. Stowe, takes upon itself to pronounce that she has therein exhibited the "concealed realities" of the system of slavery, "without falling either into vulgarity or exaggeration." The opportunities of the writers of the *Westminster* to judge of our habits and manners must, we should suppose, be small; and whence they may have received the capacity for so dogmatically determining the point at issue, we cannot well guess.[9] Simple assertion is easily answered by counter-assertion. *We* assert that there is in this dramatic sample of abolitionism not only vulgarity and exaggeration, but gross vulgarity and absolute falsehood. The *Westminster* goes on to remark of this infamous libel upon our people, that the "darkest part of it is *possible within the law,*" that "the slave-code *authorizes these very enormities,*" and, therefore, whether these things be true or not, it is the "privilege of the artist" so to represent them.[10] We answer, that such transactions are *not possible within the law,* that murder of the slave is equally punishable with murder of the free man; that the slave-code does *not authorize these enormities;* that our laws protect, as far as legislation can, the very beast from cruelty and barbarous treatment. How much more the slave! Cruelty cannot always be prevented. The parent may ill-treat his child, the man his wife, without giving tangible cause for prosecution. But where such cause can be found, an individual may with us, precisely as in any other well-governed country, be indicted for unjust oppression of any kind, whether of beast, of child, or of slave. The public feeling with us is, we believe, as delicate, and as much on the alert upon such points, as in any part of the world. Indeed, the existence of a system of slavery rather tends to increase than diminish this feeling, as, leaving a larger portion of society in a state of tutelage, naturally and necessarily greater attention is turned to the subject. If, therefore, the shadow of such enormi-

---

9. "Contemporary Literature of America," pp. 282–83. If Rufus W. Griswold (1815–57)—born in Vermont, Baptist clergyman, editor and critic in New York, and notorious libeler of Edgar Allan Poe—is the author of "Contemporary Literature of America," his opportunities to judge of Southern "habits and manners" were not so small, or at least not so remote, as LSM supposes from their publication in an English journal.

10. "Contemporary Literature of America," p. 283; italics in original.

ties as these volumes describe may sometimes be, we deny that it is "the artist's privilege" to cull out the most horrible exceptional cases, and to represent them as forming the manners and habits of a whole people, vouching for them as *fac simile* representations of real life. What would the *Westminster* say if one should take the celebrated murderer Burke (whose notorious name has given a new word to our language), with some half dozen other such desperadoes easy to imagine, and write a novel thereon, to depict English manners of the nineteenth century, only using so far "the privilege of the artist" as to represent Mr. Burke as an accomplished gentleman, circulating freely in English society, and his satellites as tolerated and everyday frequenters of the same?[11] What would Mrs. Stowe herself say should we take the Parkman tragedy (a much better foundation, by the way, than anything she has raked up in her Southern investigations), and represent such gentlemen as of daily frequency in the pure New England society, the morals of which she would contrast with our own.[12] If the lowest vices of the lowest men, if the darkest crimes of the darkest villains—actions which the vilest of mankind, only in their moments of blackest passion, can perpetrate—are to be culled out with care, and piled upon each other, to form a monster disgusting to humanity, let the creator of so unnatural a conception give to his Frankenstein the name as well as the character of the monsters of fable. Let the creature stalk before us as some ghoul or afrite, and we shudder at the supernatural might of evil, which does not strike us as unnatural because it does not claim to be of the nature of anything with which we are acquainted. But let the same creature be represented to us as a man—above all, as one of many men, forming an integral part of a community of civilized men—and the effect becomes simply ridiculous where it is not disgusting.[13] God made man in his own image; Mrs. Stowe has very decidedly set up a rival manufacture in the devil's image.

The *Westminster* says that this work "cannot be accused of presenting a one-sided view <picture>"; that "it is rather remarkable <remarkable

---

11. William Burke (1792–1829), with accomplice William Hare, killed at least fifteen people in Edinburgh in order to sell the cadavers to anatomy schools; executed.

12. The physician George Parkman (uncle of the historian Francis Parkman) disappeared in Boston on Nov. 23, 1849. Remains identified to be his were found in the laboratory of John White Webster, Erving Professor of Chemistry and Mineralogy at Harvard and lecturer at Massachusetts Medical College, who owed Parkman money. Convicted of murdering Parkman, Webster was hanged on Aug. 30, 1850.

13. LSM echoes the diplomat Robert Moylan Walsh (whose dispatch to Secretary of State Daniel Webster on conditions in Haiti, dated April 10, 1851, is quoted in *PSE*, "British Philanthropy and American Slavery," pp. 313–15): "Nothing saves these people from being infinitely ridiculous but the circumstance of their being often supremely disgusting by their fearful atrocities." See also ibid., "Carey on the Slave Trade," p. 415.

rather> for its breadth of view, . . . its genial charity." There are some good men and women, it thinks, among the characters represented. "St. Clare is a humane and cultivated gentleman."[14] We must make our readers acquainted with this model Southern gentleman before answering this observation.

In the meantime, permit us to ask whether, in the results of governmental systems, as in all else, it is not a fair criterion to judge the tree by its fruit?[15] Shall we cut down the fruitful and flourishing tree because, theoretically, it was ill-planted, or because its roots do not grow by rule as A., B., or C., or even as whole communities of A's, B's and C's, judge most decorous and most productive? If there is any community whose system of government works better for *all classes* than our own, we are willing to abandon the defence of ours. But if, after all honest investigation, it has to be conceded— as, in spite of travellers' slanders, is conceded, has been proved by many an able essay, and can easily be proved again, whenever space and time are allowed for the subject—if, we say, it be acknowledged that no where are the higher classes more elevated—no where are the lower more comfortable— no where do both and all work together in their several positions with less of bitterness or more of the genial spirit of christian love and charity—that no where is there less misery and less vice exhibited than under the working of our system; if cases of wrong and oppression (which exist in every system, and must exist so long as man is not perfect) are, as in all good governments they must be, exceptional cases, and not cases in rule; if all this is, as we contend it is, proved and conceded, what matters it if Mrs. Stowe's theory, or Mr. Horace Mann's, or Mr. Giddings's, or Mrs. Stowe's store-clerk brother's theory points it out as iniquitous?[16] It is *not* enough to condemn such a system, even were it true, as the *Westminster* falsely states, that the horrors imagined by Mrs. Stowe are "possible within the law." Evils, to be felt, must be tangible and not theoretic evils. It is not enough that a master *might* do this, and *might* do that. The question is, what *does* he, in the majority of cases, do? How does the system work? not how *ought* it to work, according to my theory, or your theory, or his theory? Theory has done, and is doing, wild work in our world, of late years. The French universal equality and fraternity theory, for instance, after inundating the country in blood, and trying its wing in every variety of communistic and socialistic flight, has fi-

14. "Contemporary Literature of America," p. 283.
15. Matt. 12:33: "Either make the tree good, and his fruit good; or else make the tree corrupt, and his fruit corrupt: for the tree is known by his fruit."
16. Joshua Reed Giddings (1795–1864), Ohio member of the U.S. House of Representatives (1838–42, 1842–59), was censured by the House in 1842 for violent antislavery activities; opposed the Compromise of 1850.

nally theorized itself away into as hard a despotism as tyrant could desire. The Mormon theory has introduced regular and legally established polygamy into these United States. The woman's rights theory is putting the ladies into their husbands' pantaloons; and Mrs. Stowe's theory would lead them, Heaven knows where! All spirit of joking leaves us as we look shudderingly forward to *her* results. Amalga[ma]tion is evidently no bugbear to this lady.

But let us look a little into the drama of our romance. The book opens with the introduction of "*two gentlemen,*" seated at a table in a house, of which the general style "indicated easy, and even opulent circumstances." The master of the house is one of the "gentlemen." The other, "when *critically* examined, did not seem, *strictly* speaking, to come under the species." [11; LSM's italics] This gentleman, who proves to be a slave-trader, but who must be so *critically* examined to discover that he is not *strictly a gentleman,* seems, however, quite at his ease, and rattles his watch-seals like a man of consequence, hale fellow well met with the opulent signor, whom he constantly and familiarly terms Shelby (leaving off the form of Mr.) and occasionally slaps on the back, to make his conversation more impressive. Into what society can Mrs. Stowe have been admitted, to see slave-traders so much at their ease in gentlemen's houses? We have lived at the South, in the very heart of a slave country, for thirty years out of forty of our lives, and have never seen a slave-trader set foot in a gentleman's house. Such a début argues somewhat queerly for the society with which madame and her clerk-brother have associated, and prepares us for some singular scenes in the elegant circles to which she introduces us.[17]

To give some idea of the style of these volumes, we will presently quote a page from the conversation of these two *gentlemen.* Mr. Shelby, the opulent owner of the house, is, it appears, in debt to an amount not stated, but, as he proposes paying his debt by the transfer of *one* negro, we are to presume that it does not exceed a thousand dollars. Strange to say, this opulent Kentucky gentleman has no resource in so pressing a difficulty but the sale of a favourite negro, the manager of his farm and his companion from childhood. There are, apparently, neither banks nor friends who could loan so enormous a sum as one thousand dollars to rescue the opulent gentleman from this difficulty, or Mr. Shelby is of the same opinion, perhaps, as our little girl

---

17. "In no State in the Union is a negro-trader less respected, than in South Carolina. It has always been so within the recollection of the writer, which extends to more than half a century. Familiar with most of the Southern States, he believes the same feeling of dislike exists everywhere in the slaveholding country. They are always contemptuously called by the negroes, 'speculators'; and it would astonish Cuffee to see 'a speculator' at a gentleman's table, no less than to see a black face like his own taking wine with 'mauser.'" David James McCord, "Life of a Negro Slave," *SQR,* n.s., 7 (Jan. 1853): 206–27; 209.

of six years old, who shakes her head gravely and exclaims, "One thousand dollars! Why, there is not so much money in this world, I think." At any rate it is so insurmountable a difficulty that, for this one thousand dollars, our opulent gentleman forgets that he is a gentleman—forgets that he is a man—forgets honour, principle, gratitude, and common sense, and offers his old black friend, his father's slave, his childhood's companion and guardian, the manager of his farm, the husband and father of a whole family of attached servants, to this brute of a slave-dealer, with decidedly more coolness than we could command in ordering the whipping of a thievish cur. To heighten the value of the commodity offered, this gentleman is praising his wares in rather singular language, by the way, for an educated man: "Tom is a good, steady, sensible, pious fellow. He *got religion* at a camp-meeting, four years ago" [12; LSM's italics]. To which remark the gentleman negro trader, who must be so *critically* examined to discover that he is not *strictly* of the first stamp, responds (we beg our readers to notice the elegant familiarity of his style):

> Some folks don't believe there is pious niggers, Shelby, [. . .] but *I do*. I had a fellow, now, in this yer last lot I took to Orleans—'twas as good as a meetin', now, really, to hear that critter pray; and he was quite gentle and quiet like. He fetched me a good sum, too, for I bought him cheap of a man that was 'bliged to sell out; so I realized six hundred on him. Yes, I consider religion a valeyable thing in a nigger, when it's the genuine article, and no mistake. [12]

To this, instead of kicking the scoundrel out of doors, our opulent gentleman answers, politely falling into the tone of his companion:

> "Well, Tom's got the real article, if ever fellow had, [. . .] You ought to let him cover the whole balance of the debt; and you would, Haley, if you had any conscience."

> "Well, I've got just as much conscience as any man in business can afford to keep— just a little, you know, to swear by, as 'twere," said the trader, jocularly; "and, then, I'm ready to do anything in reason to 'blige friends; but this yer, you see, is a leetle too hard on a fellow—a leetle too hard." [12]

O tempora! O mores! This is a *leetle* too hard to swallow. But let us go on. After a little more conversation of the same kind, "a small quadroon boy, four or five <between four and five> years of age," makes his appearance. Evidently this "small quadroon" is a gentleman at large, and a pet in the family, for he enters unsummoned, is patted on his "curly head," and "chucked [. . .] under the chin" by his master, who receives him in whistling and "*snapping* a bunch of raisins at <towards> him." The gentleman master then, for the amusement of his gentleman visitor, causes his "small quadroon" to go through sundry funny exhibitions, such as imitating "Uncle Cudjoe when he has the rheumatism," showing "how old Elder Robbins leads the psalm," etc., during which exhibitions "both the gentlemen laughed *uproariously.*" [13–14; LSM's italics] On their termination, the gentleman visitor bursts out anew:

> "Hurrah! bravo! what a young 'un! [. . .] that chap's a case, I'll promise. Tell you what," said he, suddenly clapping his hand on Mr. Shelby's shoulder, "fling in that chap, and I'll settle the business—I will. Come, now, if that ain't doing the thing up about the rightest!" [14]

The mother of the child, at that moment making her appearance, carries him off; and as soon as she leaves the room, our facetious and gentlemanly trader, struck with *her* saleable qualities, takes a new start.

> "By Jupiter! [. . .] there's an article now! You might make your fortune on that ar gal in Orleans, any day. I've seen over a thousand, in my day, paid down for gals not a bit handsomer." [14]

The *Westminster* finds no vulgarity nor exaggeration in these volumes! In answer to this vulgar insolence, the master of the house can apparently find no better way of showing his disapprobation than by uncorking a fresh bottle of wine, of which he politely asks the opinion of his polished guest.

> "Capital, sir—first chop!" said the trader; then turning, and slapping his hand familiarly on Shelby's shoulder, he added: "Come, how will you trade about the gal?" [14–15]

But enough of this disgusting vulgarity. Need we say to any reader who has ever associated with decent society anywhere, that Mrs. Stowe evidently does not know what "a gentleman" is. We will pass over the one who, upon *critical* examination, shows that he is somewhat deficient; but what will any gentleman or lady say to Mr. Shelby? Mrs. Stowe has associated much, it would appear, with negroes, mulattoes, and abolitionists; possibly, in her exalted dreams for the perfection of the race, she has forgotten the small punctilios of what, in the ordinary parlance of the world, is called decent society. She will, therefore, perhaps, excuse a hint from us, that her next dramatic sketch would be much improved by a somewhat increased decency of deportment in her performers. Whatever may be the faults, the vices, or the crimes of any man holding the position of gentleman (at least we vouch for a southern community), he would be above such coarse vulgarity. We would suggest, too—as she, no doubt taken up with her glorious aspirations and high and *uncommon* feelings, has forgotten what portion of *common* ones more ordinary creatures have—that it would be well to allow the appearance of the shadow of such even to us wretched slaveholders. If we are brutes, we usually try to appear a little more like human beings; and it would decidedly look more "nateral like" so to represent us. She describes this Mr. Shelby as "a fair average kind of man, good-natured and kindly" [19]; and yet, after the above scene, and a great deal more of discussion as to how a mother bears to have her children taken from her, in which the negro-trading gentleman, Haley, edifies the opulent gentleman, Shelby, with sundry descriptions in the taste and tone of the following:

> "I've seen 'em as would pull a woman's child out of her arms, and set him up to sell, and she screechin' like mad all the time—very bad policy—damages the article—makes 'em quite unfit for service sometimes. I knew a real handsome gal once, in Orleans, as was entirely ruined by this sort o' handling. The fellow that was tradin' <trading> for her didn't want her baby; and she was one of your real high sort, when her blood was up. I tell you, she squeezed up her child in her arms, and talked, and went on real awful. It kinder makes my blood [run] cold to think on't; and when they carried off the child, and locked her up, she jest went ravin' mad, and died in a week. Clear waste, sir, of a thousand dollars, just for want of management." [15–16]

After this, we say, the "good-natured and kindly" Mr. Shelby determines to sell the child in a quiet way, to avoid the *screechin'*, by stealing it away from its mother. Upon this very probable and natural incident, as Mrs. Stowe and the *Westminster* pronounce it, turns the principal romance of the story. The woman runs away with her child, and after adventures infinite, finally arrives among the Quakers and in Canada, etc.

In the next scene, the authoress introduces us to one of her high and noble characters, one of those whose hearts, uncontaminated by the debasing effects of our system, rise above it. We will see whether she understands this class better than the gentlemanly, "good-natured and kindly": "Mrs. Shelby was a woman of a high class, both intellectually and morally," with "magnanimity and generosity of mind, . . . high moral and religious sensibility and principles, carried out with [great] energy and ability into practical results" [20–21]. This very sensible, moral, and religious lady, when made acquainted with her husband's brutal conduct, is very naturally distressed at it. But what remedy does she find? Does she consult with him as a wife should consult? Does she advise as a woman can advise? Does she suggest means and remedies for avoiding such a crisis? Does she endeavour to show her husband the folly and madness, as well as the wickedness, of his course? No. After a few remonstrances, feebly advanced, she, too (the high intellectual woman!), seems to be struck dumb with the insurmountability of that terrible debt which is to be paid by the sale of *one elderly man and a little child;* she, too, seems to think there is no imaginable way for a comfortable farmer or planter to get round that enormous sum of the one thousand dollars or thereabouts; and neither she nor her good-natured and kindly husband seem[s] to imagine or to care whether it might not be possible—quite as easy, perhaps—should they be forced to part with a negro or two, to dispose of them in families to some humane neighbour (such servants as these are described to be seldom go begging for owners), instead of tearing them apart and selling to a brutal slave-dealer, whom Mr. Shelby himself describes as "cool and unhesitating, and unrelenting as death and the grave" [49]. No; she thinks she fulfills her Christian duty much better by letting the "faithful, confiding, excellent creature, Tom," who is willing "to lay down his life" for his master, "be torn in a moment" from all he holds dear,[18] the petted and delicate child from its petted and delicate mother, while she, the magnanimous woman, who carries out her high principles with energy into practical results, bursts out into a tirade which, if anything could, might excuse the cold brutality of her husband, by the supposition that the poor man had gone crazy under similar lectures:

> "This is God's curse on slavery!—a bitter, bitter, most accursed thing!—a curse to the master and a curse to the slave! I was a fool to think I could make anything good out of such a deadly evil. It is a sin to hold a slave under laws like ours—I always felt it was. . . . Abolitionist! If they knew all I know about slavery, they *might* talk!" etc., etc., etc. [48]

Poor Mr. Shelby! Perhaps we have blamed him too soon. It would not have been astonishing if, with so inspiring a sample of femininity about him, he should have gone raving mad, and after cutting, selling, and slashing, wound up in a lunatic asylum. This worthy couple, however, go quietly to bed; and such was their philosophical equanimity of mind, that "they slept somewhat later than usual the ensuing morning." And so little is Mrs. Shelby troubled by the impending evil (having, we presume, set her conscience at ease by the cursing steam-burst of the preceding evening) that, on waking up somewhat later than usual, she quietly lies in bed, ringing her bell to summon Eliza (the unfortunate mother of the "small quadroon," who is this morning to see her son transferred to Mr. Haley's tender mercies); and "after giving repeated pulls of her bell <giving her bell repeated pulls> to no purpose,"

---

18. Stowe, *Uncle Tom's Cabin*, p. 47, reading: "I do believe, Mr. Shelby, that if he were put to it, he would lay down his life for you. . . . How can I ever hold up my head again among them [the servants], if, for the sake of a little paltry gain, we sell such a faithful, excellent, confiding creature as poor Tom, and tear from him in a moment all we have taught him to love and value?"

coolly exclaims: "I wonder what keeps Eliza!" [57] Oh! blessed composure amidst life's whirl! *She* has apparently no sins upon *her* mind, nor cares either, dear, virtuous lady! She cursed them all off upon her husband and slavery last night!

But enough of this incomprehensible family. This Mrs. Shelby is one of Mrs. Stowe's "first chop" ladies. Let us now look a little into the *model* gentleman slaveholder of the work, Mr. St. Clare, who is pronounced by the *Westminster* to be a "humane and cultivated gentleman." He is first introduced to us joking familiarly with the fascinating Mr. Haley (who seems to have a wonderful facility in making his vulgarity acceptable to real gentlemen) concerning the purchase of Uncle Tom, of whom having taken possession, "soul and body" (to use a favourite expression of Mrs. Stowe, to the propriety of which we are far from prepared to accede), we follow him into the home of an elegant New Orleans family. The household consists of the master, who, having been partly educated in New England, cannot be entirely corrupted by the system of things round him; a New England cousin, with some prejudices, but very sensible of course, and

<blockquote>e'en her failings lean to virtue's side;[19]</blockquote>

a wife, of whom more anon; and a very angelic little daughter, who, being destined to die early, is, according to approved rule in such cases, represented as a terrible piece of precocity, and a kind of ministering, guiding angel to the whole family.

The wife had been, "from her infancy, [. . .] surrounded with servants, who lived only to study her caprices; the idea that they had either feelings or rights [had] never dawned upon her, even in distant perspective" [185–86]. Heartless, selfish, foolish, and entirely corrupted by "the system," this strangely obtuse person still appears before us as an elegant woman of fortune. She seems to have no object in life but by continued fretfulness to torment her husband, servants, and household generally, just as much as one person can well manage. Yet, as she is at the head of a princely establishment, and has been all her life accustomed to the elegances, indulgences, and luxuries of the highest style of living, we must, it is to be presumed, take it for granted that she has the manners of a lady, whatever inherent defects of character, selfish or even cruel, might exist. Indeed, the authoress seems anxious to impress upon us a high opinion of the elegant ease and grace of this voluptuously educated lady, whom she describes as "so graceful <slender>, so elegant, so airy and undulating in all her motions" [213], who has

---

19. Oliver Goldsmith, *The Deserted Village*, l. 164: "And even his failings leaned to virtue's side."

been cradled and grown up in such luxurious elegance as would become some Eastern sultana.

Such a woman, it may be well imagined, might be selfish in the extreme. Spoiled and indulged from her birth, she might snub her husband, neglect her child, be peevish and exacting with her servants; but she *could not* be the vulgar virago. We do not deny that our Southern character has its faults—faults, too, which take their stamp, in part, from our institutions and our climate, as do those of our Northern neighbours from theirs; but we do deny that any Southern woman, educated as a lady, could sit for such a portrait as Mrs. Stowe has drawn. Shrinking timidity, and an almost prudish delicacy, is perhaps a fault of our Southern women—at least, it is certainly a characteristic, which, in the opinion of many, is a fault, and which, whatever merits it may possess at a home fireside, makes them necessarily less prominent to the public gaze, less remarkable to public inspection, and gives a quietness of manner which, when compared to the much more free and easy ways of our Northern sisters, sometimes amounts to insipidity. Such, at least, are the faults which we have heard found by Northern critics. With its disadvantages, however, this manner retains also its advantages; and a Southern lady, even in her faults—aye, term them, if you will, her vices—retains still the shadow of that delicacy which is inherent in her education, if not in her nature.

With what Southern society Mrs. Stowe and her clerk-brother have associated, we leave to be guessed by any Southern lady or gentleman who reads her description of Mrs. St. Clare. To judge from a variety of New England idiomatic expressions, such as: She asked him "to smell *of* hartshorn" [185]; "I can't sleep nights"; "She offered to take care of me nights"; "I don't see *as* any thing ails the child" [320]; etc., etc., we should have a shrewd suspicion that she had found her character somewhat nearer home than New Orleans. These are expressions which are almost as foreign to the idioms of our Southern tongue as Greek or Hebrew. And again, when speaking of an incorrigible servant, this lady is made to say (vol. ii, p. 99):

> "She has been talked to and preached to, and every earthly thing done that any body could do, and she's just as *ugly as always*."[20]

We doubt if one Southern person in a hundred, who has not taken an enlightening journey to New England, would imagine the meaning of the expression. The word ugly, with us, is applied entirely to physical, never to moral,

---

20. Stowe, *Uncle Tom's Cabin*, p. 335, reading: "If she hasn't been talked to, and preached to, and every earthly thing done that anybody could do—and she's just so ugly, and always will be."

deformity. However trifling these verbal faults may appear, we deem them worthy of note, as showing that Mrs. Stowe does not even know the language of the society she undertakes to depict.

The spirit of it is still farther beyond her. *Vide* Mrs. St. Clare's elegant discussion (vol. ii, p. 81), as to whether she or her daughter *sweats* most:

> "Very often, night after night, my clothes will be wringing wet. There won't be a dry thread in my night clothes, and the sheets will be so that Mammy has to hang them up to dry! Eva doesn't sweat any thing like that!" [321]

And again, to a negro girl (vol. ii, p. 97):

> "What now, you *baggage!*—what new piece of mischief! You've been picking the flowers, hey?" and then Eva <and Eva> heard the sound of a *smart slap.*
>
> "Law, Missis! they's for Miss Eva." [. . .]
>
> "Miss Eva! A pretty excuse! You suppose she wants your <your> flowers, you *good-for-nothing* nigger! Get along off with you." [334; LSM's italics]

Elegant Southern gentleman, however curtain-lectured or hen-pecked, will you acknowledge this as a picture of your wife? *You baggage! You good for nothing nigger!* Southern language in select society! Mrs. Stowe, by way of showing the effect of "the system," endeavours to make the maids and their mistresses speak as much alike as possible. Her mulatto ladies are at times as unnaturally elegant as their mistresses are vulgar. We have no time for them, however, but must exhibit Mrs. St. Clare a little farther. The coarse indifference which this elegant lady constantly expresses for the feelings of her dependents, and particularly for those of "Mammy," an old family servant, who has tended her from childhood, and whom she has separated from husband and children, can find its parallel in no rank of society. *Never,* we contend, was there the Southern woman, brought up in decent associations, at once so heartless and so foolish that, supposing it possible for her to feel nothing in such a case, would not, for mere fashion and gentility sake, imitate those feelings of which she would know it to be her shame to be devoid. It is not the *fashion* with us to hang out the flag of hard-heartedness. If *"the system"* necessitates in us that short-coming from virtue (as the omniscient Mrs. Stowe most dogmatically asserts that it does, has done, must and ever will do), at least we have learned the hypocrisy to conceal the calamitous deficiency under which we labour. No woman but would, by the tacit moral sense of any Southern community, be excluded from all decent society, did she dare to talk as this lady, the spoiled child of elegance and luxury, is represented as doing.

"Just as if Mammy could love her little dirty babies as I love Eva! Yet St. Clare once really and soberly tried to persuade me that it was my duty, with my weak health, and all I suffer, to let Mammy go back, and take somebody else in her place. That was a little too much even for *me* to bear. [. . .] I did break out that time." [207]

This is bad enough—ridiculous enough; but we did not break out till some half page farther, at which point we did break out into most uncontrollable laughter when this elegant, spoiled, lounging Southern lady remarks:

"I keep my cowhide about, and sometimes I do lay it on (!!!); but the exertion is always too much for me. If St. Clare would only have this thing done as others do, . . . send them to the calaboose, or some of the other places, to be flogged. That's the only way." [207; LSM's exclamation points]

Ye gods! we do not believe that there is a lady's maid south of the Potomac who would not blush through her black or yellow skin, at hearing her mistress use such language, however much she might think it her right to occasionally indulge in it herself. An elegant Southern lady keeping a *cowhide,* and *laying it on sometimes!*

Mon Dieu! Mein Gott! We feel like a little one we have known, who, learning the French and German languages simultaneously with the English, used the several tongues indifferently, until she got into a passion, and then, the French and German sounding, we presume, more *cursing-like* to her ear, she whipped out those in high style. We could use French, German, Hebrew, or Cherokee—anything, *mein Gott!* except our own native tongue, which this lady (?) has so defiled.

We wish Mrs. Stowe would undertake an English high-life novel, and give the *Westminster* a home sample of the "privilege of the artist" for which it contends. Should she carry through her characters with a consistency similar to that exhibited in the present work, we might perchance be introduced to Queen Victoria and her ladies drinking beer or gin and water at the first convenient "exchange" (as dram shops are elegantly termed out West), and, when they should get a little tipsy, royalty might amuse herself by boxing the ears of her satellites. Prince Albert, the while, should stand by with a gentlemanly simper, or perhaps offer the "cowskin" to royalty, that she might assert her prerogative *à l'Américaine.* All this, if we mistake not (we humbly defer, however, to the judgment of the *Westminster*), is "*possible within the law,*" and if it be the "privilege of the artist" to consult only possibilities, and leave probabilities out of the question, Mrs. Stowe, with her vivid imagination, might revel in such a subject.

If our readers have a fancy for another scene in the same style, we refer them to vol[ume] two (p[p]. 146–7), where our same elegant lady, become a widow, after *slapping the face* of her maid writes an order in her "delicate Italian hand, to the master of a whipping-establishment, to give the bearer fifteen lashes" [373], the bearer being a sensitive, delicate, and beautiful quadroon girl, as white as her mistress, whom the lady declares it her intention to have whipped until she "brings her down." "I'll teach her, with all her airs, that she's no better than the raggedest black wench that walks the streets" [374]. Reader, we gasp for breath, and are happy, once and forever, to take leave of this elegant Southern lady. We confess to being almost as much frightened as was the clerk-brother in the "ogre's den."

We must return to the gentleman specimen, from whom we have been drawn off by his wife. Mr. St. Clare's New England education, we should say, had marked, whether or not his virtues, certainly his English, very decidedly—unless, indeed, as Mrs. Stowe has put a similar phraseology in the mouth of his wife, she intends to pass upon us such expressions as the following for the English of educated Southern society: "Isn't it dreadful tiresome." "They arn't." "That isn't my affair *as* I know of." "I don't know *as* I am." "I've travelled in England some," etc., etc. This (according to the *Westminster*) humane and cultivated gentleman, besides an occasional habit of being "helped home [. . .] in a condition when the physical had decidedly attained the upper hand of the intellectual" [241], seems to do very nearly nothing but lie upon sofas, read newspapers, and indulge himself in occasional abuse of a system by which he holds a property the possession of which he considers as iniquitous in the extreme, and yet never takes one step to correct this iniquity. The whole tenor of Mrs. Stowe's book implies that all benevolent slave owners are benevolent only because they feel that they have no right to be slave owners at all, and, therefore, endeavour, by kindness and indulgence, to, in some sort, pay the slave for that of which, in their own opinions, they are habitually defrauding him. Verily, this is a sickly kind of goodness enough, and one of which, we are happy to state, we have met with but few instances. To rob a man and pay him back a moderate percentage on the spoils of his own pocket, is not Southern honour.

We are not such votaries of the convenient and the expedient that it has become the habitual life of our "humane and cultivated gentlemen" to daily and hourly continue in the commission of a flagrant act of injustice, because it suits their convenience so to do. If such be the Stowe and *Westminster* idea of a gentleman, we are unfortunate enough to have less convenient consciences; and, singular as the fact may appear to this knowing fraternity, we are willing to state upon oath, or in any other, the most veracious manner possible, our fixed belief and certain opinion, that there *really are* a good many among our Southern inhabitants, men and women, who do what they think right, and are not living with a constant lie on their lips and in their hearts; who own slaves because they believe "the system" to be the best possible for black and white, for slave and master; and who can, on their knees, gratefully worship the all-gracious providence of an Almighty God, who has seen fit, so beautifully, to suit every being to the place to which its nature calls it. Ay, Mrs. Stowe, there are pious slaveholders; there are christian slaveholders; there are gentlemanly slaveholders; there are slaveholders whose philosophic research has looked into nature and read God in his works, as well as in his Bible, and who own slaves because they think it, not expedient only, but right, holy, and just so to do, for the good of the slave—for the good of the master—for the good of the world. It is not only a New England "Miss Ophelia" who "would cut off her right hand, sooner than keep on from day to day doing what she thinks wrong."[21] There are men, and women too, slave-owners and slaveholders, who need no teachings to act, as closely as human weakness can, to such a rule. Southern hearts and Southern souls can beat high, and look heavenward, with noble and pure aspirations, blessing God for his mercies, blessing "the system" through which His wisdom obviates what to man's little intellect might seem insurmountable evils, and blessing that beautiful order of creation which ignorant bigotry, vainly, as yet, has striven to cast back into chaos. We believe that there is not, in the whole of these United States, one solitary instance of a Southern gentleman owning slaves and using or even *thinking* such language as the following:

> "The short of the matter is, cousin, [. . .] on this abstract question of slavery there can, [as] I think, be but one opinion. Planters, who have money to make by it—clergymen, who have planters to please—politicians, who want to rule by it—may warp and bend language and ethics to a degree that shall astonish the world at their ingenuity; they can press nature and the Bible, and nobody knows what else, into the service; but, after all, neither they nor the world believe in it one particle the more. It comes from the devil, that's the short of it; and, to my mind, it's a pretty respectable specimen of what he can do in his own line." [261]

Was there ever a more impudent, wholesale accusation, at once of bold iniquity and crouching meanness, than is here coolly put forward by this humane gentleman in this work so "remarkable for its breadth of view" and "its genial charity." A whole population, not cheating themselves but, with open eyes, living in iniquity, educating their children to it, praying to their God

---

21. Ibid., p. 260, reading: "It seems to me I would cut off my right hand sooner than keep on, from day to day, doing what I thought was wrong."

for it, and not one prophet rising in the midst of this glaring, this heinous offence, to cry "Wo! wo!"[22] Why, this is worse than heathendom. The idol-worshipper, crouching before his gods of clay and of wood, believes at least in the Mumbo Jumbo whom he worships, and seeks to make his adoration agreeable to it. Covered with blood and bathed in crime, he still brings to his deity a sincere sacrifice. But *we* dare to kneel before a christian God, mocking him with prayers of which we know the hollowness, and, boasting of the sin which we pray him not even to pardon, content ourselves with claiming Omnipotence as a kind of partner in the concern! "The short of it is," then, to sum up the gentleman's words a little more concisely, that slaveholders are, without exception, the greatest set of, at once, bold rascals and sneaking fools that ever lived. No exception, we presume, can be claimed in favour of such characters as Mr. Augustine St. Clare himself, for, surely, there are few who, entertaining such liberal views as the *Westminster*, would set him down as a humane and intelligent gentleman.

As concerns his humanity, let us examine a little farther. Constantly repeating such opinions as we have just quoted, and adding thereto, frequently, the most vituperative abuse of every thing connected with "this monstrous system of injustice," hoping that there yet "may be found among us <among us may be found> generous spirits, who do not estimate honour and justice by dollars and cents" [365–66], he yet continues to hold the iniquitous possession and, without the courage of a Pilate to wash his hands clean of the sin,[23] he continues to receive the price of blood, and idly luxuriates in the income of his slave-labour, in as matter-of-course a manner as Queen Victoria does in hers, and finally dies suddenly without having ever taken the trouble to secure his dependents from the unlimited control of their supremely elegant and brutal mistress. It is singular enough, too, that this conscientious gentleman, who, converted to religious views very much through the instrumentality of the faithful Tom, dies a true christian death; holding in his own the hand of this devoted black friend; conscious of his situation; knowing Tom perfectly; entreating him to pray for his parting spirit; joining in those earnest prayers sent for him to Heaven's throne from the very depths of this generous, devoted, self-forgetting heart, yet dies forgetting his duty, his solemn promise of liberation to this humble friend, and leaves him hopelessly separated from all that he has dear upon earth, in the power of the worst of owners, under this (according to his own statement) "monstrous system of injustice." Strange conduct, to say the least, for an intelligent, humane, christian gentleman.

22. Ezek. 16:23: "Woe, woe unto thee! saith the Lord God."
23. Matt. 27:24.

Apropos of Tom's liberation, what does our authoress mean by talking as she does, at sundry different times, about his master "commencing the legal steps necessary to Tom's emancipation" [356]? Is it so hard to get rid of a negro in New Orleans, that one cannot tell the fellow in three words, or by a stroke of the pen give him a permit to be off? In some of our Southern States there is, we know, a law forbidding liberation within the precincts of the State; but, besides that this is not the case in Louisiana, even in the States where such a law does prevail there is no difficulty whatever in letting the individual take himself off, as Tom desired to do, to "Kentuck," or any where under Heaven, where he could be admitted; and we are quite mystified by these incomprehensible "legal formalities for his enfranchisement" [356] which were the root and cause of all Tom's subsequent difficulties. Do they tattoo negroes in New Orleans when they want to liberate them? Or is there a kind of Freemason ceremony to go through? Or what was the difficulty, that Tom could not take himself off to Kentucky in half an hour, after his master chose to permit him to do so? *We,* in our ignorance, should have supposed that, not only could it have been done at any hour within the many weeks during which the subject was in agitation, but that, even if previously neglected, one word from the master to the physician or any other reliable witness, as he lay upon his death-bed, soothed by the negro's devoted care, would have been quite sufficient to secure the execution of his desires on this point. But the *Westminster* determines that all the horrors and difficulties of the actors in Mrs. Stowe's *dramatic realities* are strictly and entirely according to the laws of the divers States wherein they are stated to have occurred. *Westminster Review* contributors must, of course, be well versed in Southern United States laws. So high an authority cannot be disputed by poor folks, who have not been enlightened on the subject of their own laws and customs by having "travelled in England some," as Mr. St. Clare would say.

We have laboured through the painful task we have given ourselves, to the middle of the second volume of Mrs. Stowe's dramatics, and are heartily sick of our task; yet the most disgusting part of the work is left untouched. We confess, our courage fails us. Not that there is a single argument to answer or a single fact proved against us. But what argument avails against broad, flat, impudent assertion? The greatest villain may swear down an honest man: and the greatest falsehoods are oftenest those which it is impossible to disprove. Mrs. Stowe, among those of her accusations which are the most revolting at once to decency, truth, and probability, puts constantly and nauseously forward, the object for which *she* chooses to assert, that mulatto and quadroon women are particularly valued at the New Orleans market. If, as the only way of answering it, we give this charge the lie, the *Westminster* responds it is "possible within the law";[24] and it would seem, according to *Westminsterian* logic, for an author who professes to give the dramatic realities of life, a legal possibility is fair material, and human nature's probabilities and possibilities not worth considering. If we answer that there is no more moral population in the world than that of our Slave States (few, indeed, equally so), we are answered with a sneer of derision. We, who live at home in the midst of it, cannot know as well as Mrs. Stowe, who gets her intelligence from "personal friends," and "collecting clerks," or as the *Westminster* reviewer, who know[s] all about it from Mrs. Stowe. We can but meet false evidence by counter evidence; we can but meet false assertion by counter assertion. If Mrs. Stowe, the *Westminster,* and their followers, are willing to listen, we will give them as much of that as would satisfy any reasonable human being. But no. They have had a vision of the truth. It is possible within the law to sell babies and to ill-treat women; therefore it is done, is their sapient conclusion.

So let us, also, imagine a novel of legal possibilities. Here we suppose is a father, his wife, and some half dozen children under age, consequently subjected to his authority. The poor wife, broken down by cruelty, privation, exposure, and hard labour (throw in here much pathetic reading about fascinating beauty, female delicacy, etc.), falls into a consumption, and is dying of want in a wretched cellar. A skeleton infant, hanging on her withered breast, sucks up disease instead of nourishment; while a child of some two summers old, whose emaciated limbs, projecting cheek bones, and eager, ravenous eye, show too plainly that starvation is the disease of which it is dying, as it lies moaning by the bundle of rags which forms its mother's pillow (not even a handful of straw has she to keep her from the cold, damp ground), gnaws, eagerly as its prostrate strength will permit, a mouldy crust which an elder brother has raked from the filth in the street. Other spectres of famine move languidly about the apartment, while the brutal father amuses himself by mocking their staggering steps, and then, pausing by his dying wife, rattles in his pocket some certain amount of cash which he has this instant received from a burly, comfortable looking citizen, who stands coolly looking on at the agonies of the dying woman as her husband, with a diabolical sneer, informs her that not one penny of the contents of his pocket shall she or her brats ever touch. She points to the starving child, which her husband only pushes aside contemptuously with his foot and then, snatching from it the mouldy crust, flings it back into the street, as he exclaims, "Let the little devil die! The sooner the better. I can't kill it, for the laws would catch me; but damn it if I won't be glad to see the whole set of you in your

24. "Contemporary Literature of America," p. 283.

graves." The burly citizen seems too much amused with the progress of events to think of interrupting them by calling in assistance to the sufferers. One of the wretched boys starts up as though he would do something; but the father, striking him back, asks him what he means by his insolence, and the almost idiotic creature (brutalized as he is, and stupified by long suffering) creeps back to the corner where he has heretofore crouched. The dying struggles now come upon the woman, and both the men amuse themselves by mimicking the contortions of her agony, as she lies upon the cold ground. The husband, kicking away from her head the bundle of rags which has hitherto supported it, tells her the sooner she goes to the devil the better, and then carries on in her hearing an infamous bargain with the other brute, for the sale of his second daughter (beautiful girl, shrinking innocence, etc.— these may be much expatiated upon), with the understanding that, should the law by chance enquire into the affair, the assumed ground is, that the child is sent for benefit of education, etc.; and in case of resistance or attempt to escape insanity can be easily sworn to. The mother, who has already seen her elder daughter torn from her by a similar bargain of infamy, now, vainly endeavouring to utter a remonstrance, groans her last; and, as her dying words are checked by the death-rattle, the husband, pushing aside the almost corpse, tears the terrified girl from that last embrace, which seems as though it would drag her away from the hell that hangs over her young and innocent life, and, turning to the citizen, bids him count out his cash. He comments on the beauties of the child, tells how it is a young, fresh thing, and should pay well; while the other looks—

But *God* forgive us! It is too horrible thus to follow out imaginations whose only aim is to blacken *God's* creatures, and

> Little knowing how to value right
> The good before us, thus pervert best things
> To worst abuse, or to their meanest use.[25]

Shall we abolish the relations of husband and wife, of parent and child, because they are sometimes abused, and because some foul imagination delights in painting them as ten-fold worse perverted than ever truth has shown them? Shall we abolish every tie that can by possibility be abused? Shall we take such a scene as the above, and because it is possible, as the *Westminster* might say, "within the law," or rather, to speak more correctly, by *evasion* of the law (and just as possible and just as natural it is, as Mrs. Stowe's dis-

---

25. John Milton, *Paradise Lost* 4.201–4: "So little knows / Any, but God alone, to value right / The good before him, but perverts best things / To worst abuse, or to their meanest use."

gusting dramatics), because such things might, by an imaginary possibility, come to pass in England or any other civilized country, under existing laws, shall we, therefore, declare that they *do* exist in fact, and exist not as exceptional cases merely, but as the daily habit and general custom of such countries, and that, therefore, every system of government shall be reversed and "chaos come again"?[26]

It is the habit of a certain class of Gospel-quoting writers, so to quote those beautiful maxims that they are turned to wrath rather than charity. The scriptures may be quoted, as we once heard it remarked by a venerable divine, to sound very much like cursing. Such persons seem to themselves to rise in virtue, just in such proportion as they can degrade their fellows. They do not mount the ladder of righteousness; but, fixing themselves sturdily on a certain round, they do their best to keep off all competitors, quite sure of being saints, so soon as they can transform their brethren into devils. They discover, imagine, invent blots on the robes of others, that they may boast their own saintly purity, and thank God that they are not as other men. And lest the Omniscient hear them not, then do they cry aloud in remonstrance: "Cry aloud, for He is a God; either he is talking, or he is pursuing, or he is in a journey, or peradventure he sleepeth, and must be awaked." Thus has Mrs. Stowe lifted up her voice, and with a furious onslaught on the mote of her brother's eye noteth not, perchance, the beam in her own.[27]

To disprove slanders thus impudently uttered, and obstinately persevered in, is impossible, unless those who are to judge the question had some little insight into the facts of the case and could know something of our habits and our laws, thus being enabled to judge of the respective worth of the testimony brought before them. So far from this being the case in the present question, not only is our cause prejudged, but our very accusers assume to be our judges. They make the assertion; they swear to its truth; they pronounce sentence; and then, at once judge, jury, witness, and plaintiff, they set up the most lamentable wailings over the horrible creations of their own fancy. To those who are determined to credit such assertions, in spite of all testimony, no argument can be of avail. To such as are willing to hear both sides, we have endeavoured to invalidate Mrs. Stowe's testimony by proving that, so far from being well acquainted with our habits and manners, she has probably never even set foot in our country, and is ignorant alike of our

---

26. Shakespeare, *Venus and Adonis*, l. 1020; *Othello* 3.3.93.
27. Luke 18:11: "The Pharisee stood and prayed thus with himself, God, I thank thee, that I am not as other men are"; 1 Kings 18:27; Matt. 7:3: "And why beholdest thou the mote that is in thy brother's eye, but considerest not the beam that is in thine own eye?"

manners, feelings, and even habits of language. She makes her Southern ladies and gentlemen talk rather vulgar Yankee-English. Her Louisiana negroes all talk "Kentuck." She is probably not aware that the negro dialect varies even more than the white, in accordance with the local bringing up of the speaker. No negro, we believe, except a Virginia or Kentucky one, uses "thar," for there; "har," for hair; "that ar," for that; "hev," for have, etc. They have a *patois,* much more unintelligible frequently, but not the Kentucky lingo which she puts into their mouths. We doubt if Mrs. Stowe has ever crossed the line of a slave state at all. If she has, it has evidently not been further south than the mere crossing of the Kentucky border. There, with all her prejudices wide awake, she has seen slavery (if, indeed, she has seen it anywhere), in the worst condition in which it can exist. In a border state, constantly open to the attacks of meddling fanaticism, every man feels that his property (while the legal institutions of his state, formed for its protection, are staggering) stands but by a very doubtful tenure, and he naturally looks forward to parting with it in some way or other. Peaceably or forcibly, at a loss or a profit, in some way or the other the thing must come. By this habit of mind, a severance of old ties and affection soon springs up. The child is no longer educated to think that the slave is almost a part of himself, a dependant to live and die with. The idea is constantly held forward of some necessary change; and how to make that change, at the least loss to himself, will, of course, be a frequent question with the property holder. Then comes the clash between interest and humanity, and, the old link of mutual affection broken, too often the sick and weak negro becomes a burden, the strong one simply a property. *This* is no longer the slavery we love to defend. This bastard growth of abolitionism grafted on selfishness, is *not* Southern United States Slavery. It is border state slavery, from which, thanks to abolitionism, have sprung *some* (thank God! only *some,* only a few) of those horrors which abolition writers delight to depict. Here, more than elsewhere, may exceptional cases be seen, that abuse of power which occurs when affection is blotted out, humanity weak, and selfishness strong.

These cases are still comparatively rare; but they are a melancholy proof of what may be effected, when man opposes himself to his God. God directs and man perverts. Make a law perverting nature by which (as our woman's rights reformers would have it) woman and man are equal, and created with similar rights; and what ensues but bloody barbarity and tyrannic force, trampling to earth the beneficent, though often abused, relations which now exist between them? Make a law by which (because the parent sometimes abuses his authority) the child shall become the free and equal competitor for that parent's privileges, to aim at a general home democracy and, on true free soil principle, to take what suits him of house or land; and what again follows but the extinction of all affection, the early murder of infants, the reign of blood and brute force, instead of charity, affection, beautiful dependance, and christian love? Make your laws to interfere with the God-established system of slavery, which our Southern States are beautifully developing to perfection, daily improving the condition of the slave, daily waking more and more the master to his high and responsible position; make your laws, we say, to pervert this God-directed course, and the world has yet to see the horrors which might ensue from it. The natural order of things perverted, ill must follow. The magnitude of that ill, may heaven protect us from witnessing! Mrs. Stowe has seen, on the border lands, where something of a clash has arisen between the rival powers of abolitionism and slavery, a shadow of those evils which would result to the slave when, the natural boundaries of the system being broken down, the master would retain the powers without the affections belonging to his position. These evils her imagination has multiplied an hundred fold; but yet are to be depicted those scenes when the slave, struggling with his destiny, shall force into opposition the rival might of civilization and barbarism, of brute force and intellectual power. Imagination has not yet depicted *those*. She threatens us with a second Haytien tragedy. Hayti! She knows not of what she talks. As the ocean to the wave—as the rill to the torrent—as the zephyr to the whirlwind—would any such scenes, if possible among us, be to those of Hayti, fearful as they were; and as ocean's gulf to a rain-puddle, would be the ensuing barbarism. Mrs. Stowe has a fertile imagination, and has got up quite a respectable collection of "tales of wonder," which would rival in horrors those of Monk Lewis;[28] yet, though she should go on, and on, and on, till even *her* thought should quail, and even *her* heart sink at the fearful picture, yet will she not have touched, yet can she not have begun to imagine, the fearful penalties which indulgent nature would attach to her so outraged laws.

"Thus far shalt thou go, and no farther,"[29] hath God said, not to the great ocean only, when he chained it within its bed, but equally to every creature within the limits of its uses and its intelligence. To the white man, he has given *his* place; to the negro, *his*. The white man who abuses his God-given power, is indeed criminal, both to God and to man. Hitchings there are, and disorders numberless, in the great world-system of machinery, which Omniscience has not seen fit to make perfect; but what are these, compared to the general crash which would follow, should man, with his tinkering, upset the whole fabric that he may rectify its errors by his puny wisdom?

---

28. Matthew Gregory Lewis (1775–1818), famous for his Gothic novel *The Monk* (1796), was editor of, and largest contributor to, *Tales of Wonder* (London, 1801).

29. Job 38:11.

The civilized world must totter to its foundations, when, if ever, African slavery in America ceases to exist.

As Mrs. Stowe seems to forget, or rather to deny, the possibility of all human feeling in slaveholders, we will not pretend to argue against her grossest imaginations on that ground, but will base what further we have to say upon the moral impossibility of her facts, and their improbability as connected with the one question of "dollars and cents," which she represents as the all-absorbing one of the system. This consideration would, certainly, be alone sufficient to prevent a man from whipping to death a property, a chattel, an ox, or an ass, for which he had paid, and for which he could obtain a large equivalent by a simple transfer of the property to other hands. By Mrs. Stowe's own argument, the slave, being a chattel and a property, would, in the natural law of things, fall under the same rule. But her ingenious malignity, cleverly as it generally works, sometimes, in the zeal of argument, forgets its logic. While her effort is, constantly, to represent the slave as a mere chattel in the eye of the master, occasionally, in order to exhibit the action of some demoniac cruelty, she suddenly forgets her own reasoning and argues upon the supposition of a rivality of feeling; a hatred, not simply as of man to man, even in the indifferent positions of life, but such a hatred, such a rivality, as could only exist among individuals whose clashing ambitions and contending interests should have cast them struggling together in the closest juxtaposition, in one arena, with similar aims, similar hazards, similar hopes, and similar jealousies. In the ordinary relations of master and slave, such feelings are not only impossible, but the mere supposition of them becomes ludicrous, to any one who has looked into the institution as it exists in the United States, between the white man and the African. Such human links as exist between the races under this system are, necessarily, all of a softening character. The natural antipathies of race are checked, and almost obliterated, by the peculiar relation which, at once, unites and separates the races, acting in social life like the disjunctive conjunction in grammar, linking, yet severing so distinctly, that there is no possibility of confusion among the objects thus connected. The master gives protection; the slave looks for it. Interest combines with humanity to tighten these bonds, and it would be impossible for the most satanic malignity of disposition to imagine laws which, under this system, could sever these two great incentives to action. Occasional acts of cruelty, of maiming, or of murder, when they do occur (as undoubtedly, in all relations of life, the nearest, the dearest, they do and must occur), are always, when exercised from master to slave, the result of violent passion and impulsive anger. A man will, perhaps, in a fit of rage, shoot the horse which has thrown him; but can it be imagined that he would subject to a long course of torture, with the purpose of disabling or subjecting to a lingering death, in cold-blooded revenge, the animal which, if he have taken a dislike to it, he can more easily rid himself of, by sale of transfer, with pecuniary profit to himself? Mrs. Stowe forgets that even the vices of men are so arranged by an Omniscient Providence, that they are frequently found to balance one another, and even were the slave-owner the devil she imagines him, his malignity must be checked by his avarice.

We have not room for the story of George Harris, a remarkably intelligent mulatto, perfectly orderly, submissive, and obedient, who is, by his ingenuity and talent, making immense profits for his master at a neighbouring factory. The master, without the slightest provocation on the part of his slave, suddenly becomes jealous of his extraordinary capacity, and determines to put him down. Purposely, therefore, to *force him to be good-for-nothing,* he withdraws him from the only kind of service to which he is adapted, and puts him to the most degrading drudgery, expressly with the intention of destroying the value of his labour. Not satisfied with this, he uses every means that "tyrannical ingenuity can <could> devise," to render his condition "more bitter by every [little] smarting vexation and indignity"; and what reason, forsooth, does this reasonable master give for such a course? "The man is <man's> *mine,* and I do what I please with him—that's it!" [25]

Let us imagine similar conduct towards a horse, an ox, an ass, and what would be the universal comment? That the man is cruel—hard-hearted—brutal? No—that he is fit for Bedlam. Did ever a man in his senses ruin his property, because he is jealous of it? "Dollars and cents! dollars and cents!" Mrs. Stowe, you have rung the changes upon these so often, you should have surely remembered them still. What sends men to the California diggings? What sends them to Australia? What sends them to the devil? Dollars and cents; dollars and cents; dollars and cents. We argue nothing for the conscience, the humanity, the charity, the decency of these abominable slave-owners, given up, as they are, to Satan and his devices; but—dollars and cents, Mrs. Stowe; there is no getting around that difficulty. George Harris's master, if he had taken a dislike to George Harris, would have sold him for as many dollars as he could bring, and not by a slow process of torture have undertaken to ruin and make thoroughly valueless the animal which he held in such fine saleable order. We have here adopted Mrs. Stowe's own manner of reasoning, and in her own style, and following up her own arguments, prove, we think, her conclusions somewhat illogical. No man will, in cold blood, burn down his house, because he has got out of temper with its manner of construction; no man will torment to death, or uselessness, whether his beast or his slave, simply because he has taken a prejudice against the structure of body, or turn of mind, of the article. In either case, however much as he may dislike the concern, he will very much prefer handing it over to the first purchaser for a reasonable equivalent in dollars and cents. The malignity of jealous spite can only arise in cases where rivality has existed. The deadly venom of smothered hatred may rise in the bosom of rival against rival; of friend against friend; of brother against brother; but not—of master against slave.

But our argument is becoming so prolix, that we must cut it short. We could run on for fifty pages, showing our author's blunders and inconsequences. Let any one look at the strange system of management she attributes to her Caliban, Legree; and say how long it would be, with such a system of mingled brutality and familiarity, before a man would be murdered by his own negroes. It would be wonderful if his very horses and oxen, similarly treated, should not learn to gore and kick him to death. Look at her brutal slave-trader, who, after enlightening the reader with sundry horrible tales of mothers driven to suicide or insanity, by having their infants torn from them, finally, by way, apparently, of illustrating his lectures, sells a child of *ten months* old, from a woman whom he has just purchased, and has the pleasure, accordingly, a few hours after, of hearing that she has (as, we are to presume, he, of course, intended, from his experience in former cases) drowned herself. This man must, we should presume, have been some disguised student of the anatomy of the human feelings, who experimented thereon, much as young surgeons do upon the agonies of their cats and dogs. Surely, he was no simple negro-trader, carrying on his barbarous traffic for its accruing gains, or he would have better learned how to cast up his balance of profit and loss. Look again at the wonderful accumulation of instances she offers of *quadroons* and *mulattoes,* so fair as to be almost mistaken—frequently, quite mistaken—for white; with glossy brown curls, fair soft hands, etc., etc. Indeed, seeming to forget that her principal task is the defence of the negro, decidedly the majority of the persecuted individuals brought forward for our sympathy are represented as whites, of slightly negro descent, not negroes. We cannot forbear copying a page to illustrate her manner of exhibiting such characters. Cassy, one of these unfortunates who has made her escape from hellish bondage, appears in a steamboat under the protection of Mr. George Shelby, a young Kentucky gentleman:

> She sat upon the guards, came to [the] table, and was remarked upon in the boat as a lady that must have been very handsome. [. . .]
>
> The next [state-]room to Cassy's was occupied by a French lady, named De Thoux, who was accompanied by a fine little daughter, a child of some twelve summers.
>
> This lady, having gathered, from George's conversation, that he was from

Kentucky, seemed evidently disposed to cultivate his acquaintance; in which design she was seconded by the graces of her little girl, who was about as pretty a plaything as ever diverted the weariness of a fortnight's trip on a steamboat.

George's chair was often placed at her state-room door; [. . .]

"Do you know," said Madame de Thoux to him, one day, "of any man, in your neighbourhood, of the name of Harris?"

"There is an old fellow, of that name, lives not far from my father's place," said George, "We never [have] had much intercourse with him, though."

"He is a large slave-owner, I believe," said Madame de Thoux, with a manner which seemed to betray more interest than she was exactly willing to show.

"He is," said George, looking rather surprised at her manner.

"Did you ever know of his having—perhaps you may have heard of his having—a mulatto boy, named George?"

"Oh certainly, George Harris, I know him well; he married a servant of my mother's, but has escaped, now, to Canada."

"He has?" said Madame de Thoux, quickly. "Thank God!"

George looked a surprised enquiry, but said nothing.

Madame de Thoux leaned her head on her hand, and burst into tears.

"He is my brother," she said.

"Madame!" said George, with a strong accent of surprise.

"Yes," said Madame de Thoux, lifting her head, proudly, and wiping her tears; "Mr. Shelby, George Harris is my brother!"

"I am perfectly astonished," said George, pushing back his chair a pace or two, and looking at Madame de Thoux.

"I was sold to the South when he was a boy," said she. "I was bought by a good and generous man. He took me with him to the West Indies, set me free, and married me. It is but lately that he died; and I am <was> coming up to Kentucky, to see if I can <could> find and redeem my brother." (2d vol., p. 291 [493–95])

Some further conversation shows that the wife of this brother is the daughter of the quadroon lady, Mrs. Cassy, who is passing herself off for a Spanish lady of rank and who, thereupon, falls insensible upon the floor. Forthwith, the cabin is crowded with ladies, and all proper bustle, and other accompaniments of fainting-fits, occur; but, strange to say, nobody on this Southern steamboat ever seems to divine that the mulatto ladies are anything but the French and Spanish dames for which they pass themselves off. Verily, we can inform the *Westminster* that whether such scenes be possible, or impossible, "within the law" according to *Westminster* readings, they are most certainly impossible within the law of nature; and if we of the South had wished to pass a good hoax upon our northern or transatlantic brethren, we could not easily have imagined a more ridiculously improbable scene than that of the woolly-headed and yellow-skinned mulatto, Madame de Thoux (for the woolly-head and yellow skin must have been there, in spite of Mrs. Stowe and the *Westminster*), established as, and passing for, a lady in the cabin of a Southern steamboat.

Earlier in the work, this same "mulatto boy named George" is represented as boldly entering into a hotel in Kentucky, within a few miles of his master's residence (from which he has just made his escape), as a "well-dressed, gentlemanly man," who drives up in his buggy, escorted by his negro servant, having assumed no other disguise than the *dyeing* of his hair and face, to pass himself for a Spanish complexioned gentleman.

> He was very tall, with a dark, Spanish complexion, fine, expressive black eyes, and close-curling hair, also of a glossy blackness. His well-formed aquiline nose, straight thin lips, and the admirable contour of his finely-turned limbs, impressed the whole company instantly with the idea of something uncommon. He walked easily in among the company, and with a nod indicated to his waiter where to place his trunk, bowed to the company, and, with his hat in his hand, walked up leisurely to the bar, and gave in his name, etc., etc.

In the meanwhile, although "the whole party examined the newcomer with the interest with which a set of loafers in a rainy day usually examine every newcomer," this elegant gentleman seems to pass muster, as true white blood.

> The landlord was all obsequious, and a relay of about seven negroes, old and young, male and female, little and big, were soon whizzing about, like a covey of partridges, bustling, hurrying, treading on each other's toes, and tumbling over each other in their zeal to get massa's <Mas'r's> room ready, while he seated himself easily in <on> a chair in the middle of the room, and entered into conversation with the man who sat next to him. (vol. 1, p.160 [131–32])

These quotations are so delightfully racy, that we find it difficult to abridge them. But we are fast nearing the utmost limits of our article, and must stop. The readers of these volumes will find in them one mass of gross misrepresentation and ridiculous blundering. The authoress is so ignorant of Southern life and slave institutions, that she does not know how very far she leaves behind her the track of probability, and her vouchers of the *Westminster* might, perhaps, if induced to reconsider the matter, be gracious enough to acknowledge that there are some things quite "possible within the law," and yet impossible in nature. We know of no human law forbidding the moon to be green cheese, and the inhabitants of this globe from establishing a balloon communication and furnishing the universal market with the commodity, thereby seriously conducing to the detriment of all future generations, who would thus, by our greedy avarice, be seriously curtailed in their due allowance of moonshine. And yet it will hardly be contended that it is the "privilege of the artist" to make such the material of anything but a "Mother Goose" fairy tale. Mrs. Stowe has wandered almost as far from the possible. If she has not given us moons of green cheese, she has given what is just as far from God's creation: a nation of men without heart, without soul, without intellect; a nation, too (strange incongruity!), of cultivated human beings, so ignorant of right and wrong, so dead to all morality, that it were an insult to Deity to believe in their existence. So anomalous a creation was never sent by God upon this earth, and Satan or Mrs. Stowe must claim the honour of the invention.

We thought we had done; but one point more we must glance upon. Mrs. Stowe, in spite of experience, in spite of science, determines that the negro is intellectually the white man's equal. She "has lived on the frontiers of a slave State <, for many years, on the frontier-line of slave states>," "she has [also] the testimony of missionaries," etc., and "her deductions, with regard to the capabilities of the race, are encouraging in the highest degree" [517]. Bravo! Mrs. Stowe! Your deductions are bold things, and override sense and reason with wonderful facility. Perhaps they would become a little more amenable to ordinary reasoning if, instead of living "on the frontiers of a slave State," you should see fit to carry your experience, not theoretically, but practically, into the heart of one; or still better, perhaps, avoiding the contaminating system, to explore at once the negro nature in its negro home, and behold in native majesty the *undegraded* negro nature. In native and in naked majesty, the lords of the wild might probably suggest more appreciable arguments, for difference of race, than any to which Mrs. Stowe has chosen to hearken. The negro alone has, of all races of men, remained entirely without all shadow of civilization.[30] It is a mere quibble to talk of his want of opportunities and instruction. Where were the white man's opportunities and instruction, when the power of mind guided him to the des-

---

30. We speak, of course, of the *real negro,* and not of the African. All Africans are no more negroes, than all fish are flying-fish. The real woolly-headed and thick-lipped negro is as distinct from many African races as he is from the Saxon. And when Mrs. Stowe tells us that Tom "looked respectable enough to be [a] Bishop of Carthage, as men of [his] color were, in other ages" [212], either she chooses to forget that all men of colour are not negroes, or she is lamentably ignorant of the facts to which she refers. [LSM]

tiny for which Heaven created him? when, by the sunlight of reason, he burst the bonds of ignorance, and, echoing the Almighty fiat, "let there be light," saw the day beam, which still to the negro was darkness? What guide had he? what opportunities? what instruction? further than the God-given intellect which nature has denied to his lowlier fellow? The white man needed no leading strings. God created him for the leader and the teacher. The mind of the white man sprang by its own power to that eminence which to the negro nature is unattainable.

Mrs. Stowe herself has, evidently most unintentionally, shown that, however her theories and her fanaticism may lead her opinions, instinct, even in her mind, is endeavouring to point her right. Every where in her book is the mulatto represented as the man superior to, and suffering in, his position. She has been obliged, wherever she has introduced her fugitives into the hearts of white families, and *fraternized* them with their white protectors, to represent these fugitives as white, with the slightest possible negro tint. Even she has not dared to represent the negro in those scenes where she has boldly introduced the mulatto. Even she would not have dared to paint a pretty little Quakeress liberator snatching up a negro bantling and covering it with kisses, and putting the mother into her own bed, and "snugly tucking her in," as she does by the white mulattoes whom she introduces [168]. Even in *her,* the instinct of race is too strong. She dares not so belie her nature. She takes the mulatto as an approach to the white man, gives scope enough to her fancy to make him a thorough white, and then goes ahead with her romance. The real unfortunate being throughout her work is the mulatto. The negro, except where her imagination has manufactured for him such brutes of masters as are difficult to conceive, seems well enough suited to his position. It is the mulatto whom she represents as homeless and hopeless; and we confess that, in fact, although far below her horrible imaginings, his position is a painful one. Nature, who has suited her every creation to its destined end, seems to disavow him as a monstrous formation which her hand disowns. Raised in intellect and capacity above the black, yet incapable of ranking with the white, he is of no class and no caste. His happiest position is probably in the slave States, where he quietly passes over a life which, we thank God, seems, like all other monstrous creations, not capable of continuous transmission. This mongrel breed is a most painful feature, arising from the juxtaposition of creatures so differing in nature as the white man and the negro; but it is a feature which, so far from being the result of slavery, is rather checked by it. The same unhappy being must occasionally exist wherever the two peoples are brought in contact, and much more frequently where abolition license prevails, than under the rules and restraints of slavery.

To conclude. We have undertaken the defence of slavery in no temporizing vein. We do *not* say it is a necessary evil. We do *not* allow that it is a temporary makeshift to choke the course of Providence for man's convenience. It is *not* "a sorrow and a wrong to be lived down." We proclaim it, on the contrary, a Godlike dispensation, a providential caring for the weak, and a refuge for the portionless. Nature's outcast, as for centuries he appeared to be, he—even from the dawning of tradition, the homeless, houseless, useless negro—suddenly assumes a place, suddenly becomes one of the great levers of civilization. At length the path marked out for him by Omniscience becomes plain. Unfit for all progress, so long as left to himself, the negro has hitherto appeared simply as a blot upon creation, and already the stronger races are, even in his own land, threatening him with extinction. Civilization must spread. Nature seems to require this, by a law as stringent as that through which water seeks its level. The poor negro, astounded by the torrent of progress which, bursting over the world, now hangs menacingly (for to the wild man is not civilization always menacing?) above him, would vainly follow with the stream, and is swept away in the current. Slavery, even in his own land, is his destiny and his refuge from extinction. Beautifully has the system begun to expand itself among us. Shorn of the barbarities with which a slavery established by conquest and maintained by brute force is always accompanied, we have begun to mingle with it the graces and amenities of the highest Christian civilization. Have begun, we say, for the work is but begun. The system is far from its perfection, and at every step of its progress is retarded by a meddling fanaticism, which has in it, to borrow a quotation from Mrs. Stowe herself, "a dread, unhallowed necromancy of evil, that turns things sweetest and holiest to phantoms of horror and affright" [434]. Our system of slavery, left to itself, would rapidly develop its higher features, softening at once to servant and to master. The satanic school of arguers are far too much inclined to make capital of man's original sin, and to build upon this foundation a perfect tower of iniquitous possibilities, frightful even to imagine. Men are by no means as hopelessly wicked as Mrs. Stowe and others of this school would argue; and these would do well to remember, that when God created man, "in the image of God created he him"; and though "sin came into the world and death by sin," yet is the glorious, though clouded, image still there, and erring man is still a man, and not a devil.[31]

We, too, could speculate upon the possibilities of this system, and present a picture in beautiful contrast with Mrs. Stowe's, as purely bright as hers is foully dark; but, as we remarked earlier in our argument, the fairest reason-

31. Gen. 1:27; Rom. 5:12.

ing is not from what a system might be, but from what it is. We grant that there is crime, there is sin, there is abuse of power under our laws; but let the abolitionist show us any rule where these are not. Utopias have been vainly dreamed. That system is the best which, not in theory, but in practice, brings the greatest sum of good to the greatest number. We challenge history, present and past, to show any system of government which, judged by this test, will be found superior to the one we defend.

"Oh liberté!" exclaimed Mme. Roland, when led to the scaffold, "que de crimes a-t-on commis en ton nom!"[32] *Theoretic* virtues are more dangerous than open vice. Cloaks for every crime, they are pushed boldly forward, stifling our natural sense of practical right, and blinding men with the appearance of a righteousness, which dazzles like the meteor, but warms not like the sun. Theoretic liberty and theoretic bread satisfy neither the hungry soul nor the hungry stomach, and many a poor fugitive to the land of freedom, sated full with both, has wept to return to the indulgent master and the well filled corncrib. The negro, left to himself, does not dream of liberty. He cannot indeed grasp a conception which belongs so naturally to the brain of the white man. In his natural condition, he is, by turns, tyrant and slave, but never the free man. You may talk to the blind man of light, until he fancies that he understands you, and begins to wish for that bright thing which you tell him he has not; but vainly he rolls his sightless orbs, unhappy that he cannot see the brightness of that beam whose warmth before sufficed to make him happy. Thus it is with the moral sunbeam of the poor negro. He cannot see nor conceive the "liberty" which you would thrust upon him, and it is a cruel task to disturb him in the enjoyment of that life to which God has destined him. He basks in his sunshine, and is happy. Christian slavery, in its full development, free from the fretting annoyance and galling bitterness of abolition interference, is the brightest sunbeam which Omniscience has destined for his existence.

32. "Oh liberty! what crimes have been committed in your name!" Jeanne-Marie Philipon Roland de La Platière (1754–93), French revolutionary; her husband was a Girondin leader, her salon a center of Girondin activity; guillotined with other Girondins.

6.

A Letter to the Duchess of Sutherland from a Lady of South Carolina

Messrs. Editors:

The letter, of which the following is a copy, has been sent by a lady of this State to the Duchess of Sutherland.[1] The original has the name and address of the writer, clearly given and in full, so that if the Duchess has the smallest desire to exercise her philanthropy, practically as well as theoretically, she will know where and to whom to address her answer. The writer has not chosen to put her name in print, as it can be a matter of no moment to the public. It is enough that a bona fide letter has been written, and a bona fide offer made from a respectable and responsible quarter. Let the Duchess, if her zeal be sincere and earnest, prove it now by action.

Yours, respectfully,

Charleston *Mercury*, Aug. 10, 1853 = *PSE*, pp. 350–60.

1. Harriet Elizabeth Georgiana (1806–68), third daughter of George Howard, sixth earl of Carlisle, by Georgiana Dorothy, daughter of William Cavendish, fifth duke of Devonshire; married in 1823 to George Granville Sutherland-Leveson-Gower, second duke of Sutherland; mistress of the robes to Queen Victoria. From Stafford House, the London residence of the duchess of Sutherland, was issued "The Affectionate and Christian Address of Many Thousands of the Women of England to Their Sisters, the Women of the United States of America" (also known as the Stafford House Address), which urged the abolition of slavery in the Southern states. For the text of the address, see *PSE*, pp. 477–78.

To her Grace, the Duchess of Sutherland: July 30, 1853

Madam and Dear Sister: The kind interest some time since manifested by your Grace, in common with the Countess of Shaftesbury,[2] and other noble ladies, in the cause of us women of America, whom you then condescendingly invited to your confidence in terms of christian sisterhood, induces me now to take the liberty of addressing you upon a subject near to every woman's heart, and more particularly near to every mother's.

As a woman, however exalted in rank above a large portion of your sex, your Grace still feels that woman instinct which unerringly assures you that the appeal of charity and christian love, however in individual and exceptional cases it may be spurned, can never be vainly made to the large woman-heart of any age or any country. Woman, as a body, has never sided, and never can side, with the oppressor. Man, burying duty beneath passion, may often deafen his conscience with the arguments of interest, and bustle it even quite from existence in the frantic struggles of ambition: but woman, in the subdued stillness of her usual life, in the quiet of her own self-searchings, finds that calm voice which is not in the storm, which is not in the whirlwind,[3] and which continually whispers to her the God inspired dictates of that all-enduring charity, that self-sacrificing love, of which by her nature she seems destined to be the constant prophet and exponent. If such be (as your Grace doubtless well knows that they are) the natural impulses of woman, how much are these enhanced by the mother's love, which, as she clasps to her breast her baby offspring, pours itself out to her God in the purest and most purifying prayers of which human lips and human hearts are capable; a mother's prayer for the offspring of her bosom! a mother's heavenward appeal for the child of her hope! Even the most erring of our sex, under the inspiration of this purifying, second existence, this being which must draw from us its good or its ill, have, for its sake, often turned from the evil of their ways, and hearkened to that lesson which bids them "go and sin no more."[4]

Your Grace, and the honorable Ladies acting with you, have then shown, in undertaking a great work, only a proper reliance upon your own sex in

---

2. Emily Caroline Catherine Frances (1810–72), first daughter of Peter Leopold Louis Francis Nassau Clavering-Cowper, fifth Earl Cowper, by Emily Mary, daughter of Peniston Lamb, first Viscount Melbourne; married in 1830 to Anthony Ashley Cooper (1801–85), seventh earl of Shaftesbury.

3. Nah. 1:3: "The Lord is slow to anger, and great in power, and will not at all acquit the wicked: the Lord hath his way in the whirlwind and in the storm, and the clouds are the dust of his feet." Cf. Job 38:1, 40:6.

4. John 8:11.

the appeal which you have addressed to the women and mothers of America. You rightly believe that we cannot coolly stand by, the witnesses and accomplices of those atrocities which you have heard depicted. I, Madam, a woman, and a mother, moved by your philanthropic appeal—not hastily but with mature deliberation, and after long reflection—(presuming, from the magnificent hospitality lately tendered by you to Mrs. Stowe, as the agent and representative of the woman move which it is your object to excite, that you are really desirous of forwarding, not by words only but by deeds, your charitable aims) now venture to address myself to you, as one who has both the means and the will to forward the herculean task which your Grace, in common with your most praiseworthy and noble sisters in the faith, has indicated a desire to undertake.[5]

I will not ask you, noble Madam, why America particularly has, of all countries of the earth, chanced first to attract your effort for the improvement of mankind. I will not ask you why slavery, which is in one form or another almost co-extensive and co-existent with society, should appear so peculiarly obnoxious among us. I will not ask why, when the great Empire of China, with its three hundred and fifty millions of souls, is systematically drugged under English legislative enactment, your Grace and the honorable sisterhood have not turned your sympathies towards its perishing millions.[6] I will not ask why, simply because these people are yellow and not black, they should so escape your Grace's sympathies that you calmly, and without remonstrance, see your own government almost force the poison down their throats, condemning millions to a mental and bodily prostration—to a lingering and brutish death, compared to which the ancient punishment of the hemlock bowl were a charity and a mercy. This entire oblivion of the woes and oppressions of other nations presents at first sight a strange contrast to the warm sympathies excited for America. But of this, it surely is not for us to complain. It is, as I interpret it, but a proof of the greater affection which you entertain towards us. As the parent chasteneth his child,[7] as the friend reproveth his friend, your anxieties are naturally most alive where your sym-

---

5. Harriet Beecher Stowe had departed for Europe on March 30, 1853. A high point of her tour was the levée held for her by the duchess of Sutherland at Stafford House (May 7), to which came a great part of fashionable and titled London.

6. The Chinese government had banned the opium trade in 1799, a ban ignored profitably but so blatantly that in March 1839 the impatient government sent an imperial commissioner to Canton, who confiscated and destroyed the opium stored by foreign merchants there. The Opium War between China and Britain followed (1839–42), concluded by the Treaty of Nanking, which opened Chinese ports to foreign trade and ceded Hong Kong to Britain.

7. Deut. 8:5: "As a man chasteneth his son, so the Lord thy God chasteneth thee."

pathies are strongest; and great indeed must be the affection which can make you thus turn your whole effort toward us, even to the detriment of the morals of your own beloved England. You leave her groaning under the shame of the Opium trade, until through your generous interference we shall be relieved of our sin and our sorrow. What I can, Madam, individually feel for such disinterested kindness, I am here most anxious to express, and this letter should be a proof to you at once of my confidence in your sincerity, and my firm reliance upon your christian sympathies and assistance.

My position is one of some difficulty, and your Grace will allow me, in the spirit of sisterly affection, to lay open to you its circumstances, that you may the better council and aid my decisions. I have not spoken hastily, but, on the contrary, have deliberated long, because I judged that time was necessary both to you and ourselves to think coolly and dispassionately upon this subject. I am, Madam, by birth, parentage, education, marriage, and residence, a South Carolinian. South Carolina, you are perhaps aware, is the heart and centre of the slaveholding States of this Union, and defends with peculiar warmth her rights and privileges upon the slave question. My ancestors became possessed, while under British rule, of certain lands and slaves which the then institutions of the country, enforced by British law, rendered the only form in which could be invested the little proceeds of their labor. The same land owned by those ancestors when they dared to raise the arm of resistance against the might and power of your noble Lion of England, the same slaves (or rather the descendants of the same slaves) who remained faithful to them through the prolonged and bloody struggle of a civil war, now, Madam, have descended to me by gift and inheritance, forming together the sole means of support for myself and children. So far, I have lived with my sable subjects, the busy but contented petty sovereign over a petty realm, believing that I was fulfilling my duty by staying at home, and devoting to their comfort and maintenance a large portion of my time as well as my moderate income. I have believed that God Almighty had seen fit, in his wisdom, to suit his creatures to the positions which they are intended to occupy. I have believed, dear Madam, that as he has formed you and me to be daughters, wives, and mothers, subject to woman's duties and unfit and unable to those of men, that He has equally formed divers men for divers positions in society, according to their powers of mind and body. And if ever God's seal was set upon the brow of any race with the stamp of inferiority, believe me, Madam, or rather believe the investigations of science and the experience of ages, it is upon that of the negro. Mark me, your Grace, I say not a curse. God creates not with a curse. Inferiority is by no means necessarily a curse. Genius, talent, and fortune, however they may ennoble, give no monopoly of happiness; and as some humble cotter, under your Grace's indulgent rule, may perchance lead an easier and a happier life than can your Grace's self under the accumulated cares, anxieties, and duties of your higher position, so many a woolly head lays itself quietly to sleep, while the aching brow of the master is burdened with watchfulness and care.

Mrs. Stowe has exhibited to you, ladies of England, her fancy picture of American negro slavery. Living in the midst of the institutions against which she has raised the now fashionable hue and cry, I can but smile at the clumsy daub which Europe has consented to receive as our portrait. But let this pass. Mrs. Stowe has luxuriated in the hallelujahs addressed to her, and, like many other false prophets, is rapidly passing to oblivion. The sensible, judicious, and womanly course which your Queen has pursued with regard to her, has done much towards placing this lady in her true position.[8] If you, noble ladies of England, have, in the pardonable excitement of a philanthropic zeal, allowed yourselves to be misled to the strange belief that the women of half a continent could forget their nature to revel in the grossest of imaginable crimes, and to educate their children to inevitable infamy, it is still a woman of England whose cooler judgment has set you right; and your Queen, in defending womankind by her practical condemnation of this slanderer of her sex and country, has vindicated her right to even a nobler title than that of Queen of an Empire upon whose dominions the sun never sets. She has proved herself a sound hearted woman. Although, however, Mrs. Stowe is disposed of, and her "tales of wonder" will probably take their place in future by those of Monk Lewis, the Brothers Grimm, or the yet more celebrated "Mother Goose," the question of our United States system of negro slavery is not so completely set to rest; and it is on this point that I now seek assistance from your sisterly sympathies.

It is not enough, we are told, that we make our negroes comfortable; we must make them free; and then follow dissertations numberless, on the inalienable rights of man, etc. Now, Madam, I have already suggested to you the idea in which I think you must concur, that the inalienable rights of men are very different, according to the character and capacity, mental and bodily, of the individual, kind, or race. Is it possible that your Grace, or myself, for instance, should have the rights of our husbands and brothers? Has the idiot the same rights as the sage? Does not the physical power in the first case, and the mental difference in the last, give inalienable rights and duties to the one side, which are withheld from, or not enjoined upon, the other? Does society, by placing the man and the woman, the sage and the

---

8. After a warning from the American minister, Queen Victoria was advised not to receive Harriet Beecher Stowe, lest doing so should seem to sanction the abolitionist movement.

idiot, in different positions, with differing privileges, and under differing restraints, commit a sin and an injustice? or is such action in accordance with the dictates of God's law, as exhibited in the varying nature of his creatures? What must become of our world if women would make themselves soldiers, and idiots be forced forward as lawyers? Surely you must acknowledge that these have their positions and inalienable rights of widely differing nature! What is good for the man is not always good for the woman; what is good for the sage is not always good for the idiot or the madman; man's right is surely not woman's right, nor can wisdom and folly claim the same privileges. Here then, Madam, in the case of the individual and the kind you cannot fail to perceive differing rights and differing necessities. Can you not also perceive it as possible, that differences of race may be at least as strongly distinctive?

I am but one of many, and mean to claim to myself no peculiar merit, when I say that I have studied this point deeply, conscientiously, and with the wish to fulfil my duties to God and the world; to my family, to my country, and to mankind. I believe that the negro holds with us the position for which his nature marks him, and that any serious attempt to change this position must result in the final extinction of his race in every country habitable and cultivable by the superior white man. In countries not habitable and cultivable by the white man, the negro may retain possession, but must fall back into his original barbarism. This position you, however, will deem subject to question, and the point stands in discussion. Now, Madam, it would certainly be impolitic in us, pending its at least doubtful decision, to act as though judgment were in favor of our opponents. Our negroes, in spite of Mrs. Stowe's assertions, present a body of the most comfortable peasantry and least corrupt lower class that the world knows. Shall we force them from this position to the fearful experiment of self-government? Or, rather, shall we turn them loose, not to self-government (for of this we believe them incapable), but to misrule? not to liberty, but to the wildest license? Shall we put weapons into the hand of the savage, solely that he may slaughter his civilized lord, without hope of bettering his own condition, but on the contrary with (we believe) the certainty of plunging him back to the lowest abyss of barbarism from which present institutions have raised him, to at least an imitative and semi-civilization?

From our opinions, dear Madam, as to the result of such an experiment, you differ. But is it not possible—nay, even probable—(high-born Duchess though you be), as knowledge comes not by intuition, nor can be made the monopolized prerogative of the rich and great, that you, who have certainly never in your life even looked through your *lorgnette* at a score of black faces, may be less likely to know the nature of this negro people than we, who, born and bred among them, have played with them and sorrowed with them, laughed with them and wept with them, even from our babyhood upward? With the grey hairs beginning to cluster around my brow, I am still cheerfully served by many of the same faithful negroes who watched with hope my tottering baby steps; their children labor for me, and their grand children are cherished and reared by me. Is it likely that you or I should feel the greatest affection for them, the warmest interest and closest sympathy? Allowing to both of us the ordinary feelings of women (I claim no more than the average share which is common and general to the rightminded of our sex), which of us is likeliest to judiciously consider, and to feelingly act for their weal? You are, I do not doubt it, actuated by a laudable spirit of philanthropy, and a general wish for the well-being of humanity. Allow the same to me; and am I not farther moved by the additional and closer feeling of interest in those who are near to me? Such a feeling there is, as may have existed in olden times between the Highland Chief and his kindred subjects; the feeling of protector and dependant; a something approaching the relation of parent and child.[9] Unless, then, I, and all Southern United States women situated like myself (and they are numerous, forming the majority of the female population of nearly half our nation) are utterly devoid of woman and human feelings, we sympathize with the negro more than can your Grace. On the same principle, though certainly more strongly indicated, your Grace, if you be a mother, must necessarily feel more for the son of your home and your bosom, than could I from any philanthropic impulses.

Such reasoning as this should, it might be supposed, be decisive in determining the world to leave to ourselves and our consciences the general management of affairs, and the internal police of our own country. But your Grace, and those cooperating with you, think differently; and I would, so far as my individual effort can, willingly satisfy you in all reasonable and practicable measures. I do not, of course, acknowledge the right of any foreign country, or of any number of the inhabitants of any foreign country, to interfere with our internal legislation. Such an assumption is, on the con-

---

9. "It might be reasonably supposed that the charitable Duchess might have some misgivings as to the suitableness of *her mission* to the African, if ever she should condescend to glance her eye over the once *clan* property of Sutherland, from which, in the years 1814 to 1820, fifteen thousand inhabitants were expelled, to transform a whole, once populous, district into sheep-walks." *PSE*, "Carey on the Slave Trade," pp. 415–16. In her *Sunny Memories of Foreign Lands* (London, 1854), Harriet Beecher Stowe praised the clearances of Sutherland—"an almost sublime instance of the benevolent employment of superior wealth and power in shortening the struggles of advancing civilization" (313)—and defended the conduct of the duchess against charges of cruelty and hypocrisy made both in Britain and in the United States.

trary, so preposterous, that were it not for the christian and sisterly spirit which mutually pervades our communications, believe me, dear Madam, such attempts would deserve the epithets of "impertinent interference," "impudent dictation," etc., which have been, I grieve to say it, rather hastily launched against that philanthropic move, headed by the Countess of Shaftesbury, to which your Grace, as mistress of Stafford House, stood, as it were, sponsor and godmother. The beautiful spirit of christian love which is at the foundation of, and pervades, your whole course of action in this affair, should have saved it from such reproach. Regretting that it should have been so misunderstood, and with a due appreciation on my part of its merits, in a similar spirit of affectionate charity is, dear Madam, dictated the proposition which I am presently about to make to you.

As you appear to regard it as an imperative duty of the civilized world to deliver this negro people from bondage, I presume you would deem it incumbent upon, or at least highly meritorious in, an individual situated as I am, to make a beginning, and set a beautiful example of disinterestedness and self-sacrifice by persuading my husband, or others upon whom I am, as a woman, according to the usages and decencies of society, to a certain degree dependant, to liberate and colonize, or to permit me to liberate and colonize, those whom we now hold in bondage. But here arise some difficulties. My ancestors, hard working colonists, were forced, as I have already said, by the laws of England, imposed by the nobles of your land (your ancestors, gentle lady) into the owning of this property. Shall their descendants (myself and children) go begging their bread in penance for the sin thus forced upon them, while the descendants of the very nobles thus forcing it yet revel in luxuries? If this system be a system of sin, you with me are at least equally guilty, and you with me should bear the expiation. I will not say but that, did I feel it a sin, I might and ought to cast it off without weighing the consequences. But even were I so disposed, the urgings to it, unaccompanied with some substantial sacrifice on your part, would come badly from you, who, with more than equal responsibility through your ancestors in the origin of the sin, should bear your full portion of weight in the removal of it.

Your Grace is willing to help with words and cheer us on. But words do little here. We want acts. Will your Grace, from your immense income, assist? I am quite willing to allow and to forward, for the improvement of these my black subjects, any experiments to which they shall not themselves object; but I believe that your plan is a wrong one. I believe that its end would be certain ruin to my negroes and myself. Would it not therefore be unjust both to them and myself that we should, unsecured of the results, be called upon to bear all the risks of such a venture, upon the simple speculation of those who, like your Grace, are little versed in the character and habits of this people? Believing, as I do, that I have pursued the best possible course for their interests, and having to the extent of my power, and according to the dictates of my conscience, fulfilled my duties towards them, I am not willing to run this risk, unless on the condition that your Grace shall bind yourself, out of the income of your immense property, to preserve from the abject want which is, in my opinion, likely to ensue from your experiment, these helpless creatures, whom I am (supposing always that they are consenting to the change) ready to transfer to you—and, further, on condition also that a certain sum shall be furnished to secure to my own family such maintenance as shall prevent their becoming outcasts from those habits of society to which by education and ancestry they are entitled. Your Grace has, I am informed, in conjunction with your noble husband, an income of some three hundred thousand pounds sterling per annum. One fifteenth part of this your annual income would suffice for the liberation of some one hundred and sixty negroes, who, as I have said, form, with the land which they cultivate (and which without them becomes valueless), my whole property. As your Grace, and the noble ladies who act with you, acknowledge your share in the common sin which we inherit from our ancestors in the establishment of slavery, we must, of course, understand that you are willing to furnish your mite to assist in throwing off the curse which, according to your belief, now sits like an incubus upon the civilized world, scowling vengeance upon the farthest descendant of those in any way (whether by act, complicity, or tacit non-opposition) concerned in so iniquitous a system. Anxious to contribute our share to the happiness of mankind, the women of America (not Mrs. Stowe and her compeers, the Abbe Kellys, Lucretia Motts, etc.,[10] but the true and sober women of our western world) will, I believe, be ready to give their aid in setting at rest, by any experiment, or series of experiments, which you may desire, the great question of negro capability, which seems now to be the all important one in your nobly charitable plans for the world's improvement; and what I can individually do, I am now, Madam, and dear sister, most willing and anxious to accomplish.

Here then stand, waiting your decision, one hundred and sixty souls, whom, as the first fruits of your efforts, you can easily free from all those evils, real or supposed, with which you understand them to be overwhelmed. One fifteenth part of one year's income will enable your Grace to do this. I am, as you may perceive, ready to make a very much larger sacrifice in proportion to my means, by the loss which I may suffer from the throwing

---

10. Abigail Kelley Foster (1810–87), born in Pelham, Mass.; abolitionist and woman's rights advocate. Lucretia Coffin Mott (1793–1880) organized with Elizabeth Cady Stanton the first Woman's Rights Convention, held at Seneca Falls, N.Y., on July 19–20, 1848.

out, as so much dead capital, of waste lands, which for want of negro labor must become comparatively valueless to me, and also by the inconveniences resulting from an entire and undesirable change of life and habits. This sacrifice I am, however, ready to make in consideration of the tender consciences of the Stafford House sisterhood, and to give you an opportunity first of personally experimenting upon the feasibility of your plans, and next of proving to the world the sincerity of your efforts in the cause which you undertake. I have, as a woman and a mother, been so startled by the curses, both loud and deep, lately showered upon our slave system, that I am anxious, for my own and my children's sake, that every opportunity should be given to the philanthropists of the day, to prove the truth or falsity of their position by any limited process of experiment which can satisfy them, without hazarding the ruin of nations for the verifying of an untried theory.

Try now, Madam, what can be done with these one hundred and sixty candidates for enlightenment. It will be the first step of real earnest endeavor which you will have made in the cause; and, if a wise one, it will assuredly be rapidly imitated. As I cannot doubt of your sincerity, I equally cannot doubt that you will be ready and anxious to accept my offer; and I shall expect soon to hear from you, by the transmission, in any manner or form that may be most convenient to you, of the (to you) almost insignificant sum which will make you absolute mistress to liberate, to colonize, to educate, and to bless, in all manner of conceivable ways, the one hundred and sixty souls whom I now offer to release to you; always with the proviso that you have their own consent to the change. It is probable, Madam, that after having done your best with these one hundred and sixty Uncle Toms and Topsys, you may have a truer appreciation of the negro character and capabilities for improvement than can be obtained from the perusal of Mrs. Stowe's romance, and may be able to guide your co-laborers and imitators, by some valuable hints, in the management of future and similar undertakings. Your Grace cannot, I presume, fail to perceive the merits of a plan which will thus enable you to exercise upon a small scale, and illustrate the merits of, your expansive system of philanthropy, thus setting to your friends and coadjutors an example of the only course which can prove to the world the sincerity of your professions, and to yourselves the truth or error of your opinions.

Should your Grace desire any further communication with me upon the subject for the completion or furtherance of your aims, I shall be happy to hear from yourself or any suitable agent. I have received from my husband full authority to act in this matter as may be most satisfactory to myself for the soothing of any such doubts or scruples of conscience, as might be awaked by the eloquent persuasion of your Stafford House appeal. Your

Grace, therefore, need fear no interruption or impediment in the prosecution of the well-intentioned and praiseworthy experiment which I propose for your consideration. Please address ———.[11]

Wishing your Grace all success and happiness in the new career which, with the most sincere feelings of kindness, I have suggested for your effort, and with the assurance that my one hundred and sixty black martyrs, big and little, shall on demand, and in consideration of the fulfilment of the above named reasonable terms, be promptly forthcoming, I am, Madam, with all respect and assurances of the highest consideration, your Grace's

                    Humble servant and sincere well wisher,
            ——— ———[12]

11. Her name and address are in the original given in full. [*Mercury*'s note]
12. Her name and address are in the original given in full. [*Mercury*'s note]

7.

Slavery and Political Economy

Political Economy, that science which has so successfully struggled against the prejudices of the dark ages of protective tariffs, duties, drawbacks, and the thousand and one shackles which corroded the limbs of fettered commerce—that noble science which, even in its almost infancy the foster mother of nations, extends their brotherhood from zone to zone and, opening to our view the panorama of future ages, shows us a world exulting in the noblest blessings of a christianized civilization—has yet pronounced no judgement upon the subject which now so intensely engrosses our attention. Our reviewer represents free-labor as the principle of this science;[1] but . . . this question is yet new to political economy. *Free-trade,* not *free-labor,* has been her aim (that these are things entirely distinct, the history of these States for the last quarter of a century fully exhibits); and it has needed all her energies to fight *that* battle through. Even now she stands with eagle-eye surveying the fields of conquest, breathless in victory, and yet on guard. Even now, as she surveys the rich products of a world daily more and more released from the blundering guidance of an ignorant and selfish policy, she

---

De Bow 21 (Oct. and Nov. 1856) = *PSE,* pp. 422–69; these excerpts at pp. 431–35, 437–46, 447–48, 451–53, 463. Publication reviewed: John Stuart Mill, *Principles of Political Economy, with Some of Their Applications to Social Philosophy,* 3d ed. rev. (London: John W. Parker, 1852).

1. [George Frederick Holmes], "Slavery and Freedom," *SQR,* n.s., 1 (April 1856): 62–95. George Frederick Holmes (1820–97) was a friend of David James McCord and LSM, having lived (1842–46) in Orangeburg, south of Fort Motte and Lang Syne, in pursuit of a legal career, in which he was disappointed; he later held a number of academic posts, ending at the University of Virginia.

watches for the renewal of attack. "A scotched snake is not killed."[2] The mischievous principle is checked but not extinct.

Slavery, an institution born with society, never attacked until the pseudo-philanthropy, rather than science, of recent years dragged it forward before the tribunal of a sickly new-light philosophy, has, half-stunned by such unexpected assault, hitherto scarcely muttered a word of defence. But this lethargy must be ours no longer. We must speak now, not in hasty declamation, but in logical defence. Slavery is truly and fairly a subject for the investigation of Political Economy. The wonderful development of this western continent, effected only through and by the means of slavery—her immense produce scattered over our globe, carrying food and clothing to the hungry and the destitute; her cotton and her sugar sustaining not only herself but the might of Europe's most powerful nations; her ever increasing expanse of new land, opening an asylum for Europe's starving millions, and staving off menaced revolutions—what are these but the glorious results of American negro slavery? a system which it is recently the fashion to contemn, but which must now come boldly forward to claim its true place in the world's development; and it is before the tribunal of Political Economy that it must claim this place, and prove the justice of its cause. Hitherto we have, as it were, played at shuttlecock with the assumed sin of the thing. England has thrown it upon America—America has cast it back upon England—Yankee-land has vociferated, "It is yours"; and the South echoes back indignantly, "Yours." But this is a paltry shuffling off of responsibility which suits not a great people. Where there is sin (with whomsoever originating), it soils the hands which cling to the ill-gotten spoil. We have been asleep, acting as though in a startled dream. Up! and away with it! sin there is none. Once and forever let us disclaim the blot. No sin! no sin! but laud and glory rather:[3] glory, not to man, the hitherto blind instrument, but to the great dispensing Providence, which shows us this light out of the seeming darkness. The pillar of fire is before us, and we acknowledge the hand that guides.[4]

Nothing is easier than a sneer.[5] Happily, however, a sneer is not an argument; neither can it profane that which is holy, nor change the just and the

---

2. *Macbeth* 3.2.13: "We have scorch'd the snake, not kill'd it." "Scotched" is a conjecture of the editor Lewis Theobald.

3. "The Communion: Proper Preface," *The Book of Common Prayer*, p. 255: "Therefore, with Angels and Archangels, and with all the company of heaven, we laud and magnify thy glorious Name."

4. Exod. 13:21–22.

5. Cf. "Who can refute a *sneer?*" in William Paley, *The Principles of Moral and Political Philosophy*, rev. ed. (London, 1821), p. 302, discussing Edward Gibbon's attitude toward Christianity. William Paley (1743–1805), English clergyman and theologian. LSM cites Paley's *Principles* below.

true into the false and unrighteous. It is the fashion with a certain modern school of philanthropists to sneer at Political Economy as the science of wealth; the science of pounds and pence; the spiritualized Shylock; the distilled essence of that spirit which, seeing only what is in the bond, insists always upon its pound of flesh.⁶ . . . These are of the sentimental school, extending from the Wilberforce and Clarkson brotherhood to Mrs. Stowe with her black, white, and yellow fraternity. It has been shrewdly remarked that there are two classes of philanthropists, the feelers and the thinkers.⁷ The first, showing its most perfect type in such characters as a Howard, a Mrs. Fry, or a Florence Nightengale (characters whose blessed influence far be it from us to underrate), descends in the mass to a set of sentimental Mrs. Jellaby's and Mr. Stiggins' getting up subscriptions to supply little negroes in the West Indies with flannel waistcoats and moral pocket handkerchiefs, and launching curses and anathemas against all who may venture to doubt the benefit of their procedures.⁸ These people never hesitate about the truth of the restless inspiration which pushes them on; they never listen to a suggestion that their new-light doctrines may perchance be not of God, but of the devil, and set up a howl of indignation over all who hint the possibility of their moral pocket handkerchiefs doing more harm than good. The thinkers, on the contrary, cool, quiet, calm, stoical perhaps in action, and little given to demonstrative sympathy, have on their side, doubtless, also their pretenders and their bigots; but, likewise, they have their good Samaritans. The first class have a salve ready for every sore, a bandage for every wound,

---

6. *Merchant of Venice* 4.1.253–58: "*Portia.* Have by some surgeon Shylock on your charge, / To stop his wounds, lest he do bleed to death. / *Shylock.* Is it so nominated in the bond? / *Portia.* It is not so express'd, but what of that? / 'Twere good you do so much for charity. / *Shylock.* I cannot find it, 'tis not in the bond."

7. [William Rathbone Greg], "English Socialism, and Communistic Associations," *Edinburgh Review* 93 (Jan. 1851): 1–33; 3–4; quoted at length by LSM in *PSE*, "Negro and White Slavery—Wherein Do They Differ?" pp. 187–88.

8. John Howard (1726–90), English reformer; promoted through Parliament bills improving prison conditions (1774); wrote *State of Prisons in England and Wales* (1777) and other books advocating prison reforms. Elizabeth Gurney Fry (1780–1845), English philanthropist; Quaker minister; active in reform of prisons, hospitals, madhouses. The indefatigable exploits of nurse Florence Nightingale (1820–1910) during the Crimean War (1854–56) had recently received much attention. In Charles Dickens' *Bleak House,* Mrs. Jellyby devotes herself so fervently to the cause of African emancipation that she neglects her husband and family (see also *PSE,* "Carey on the Slave Trade," pp. 415, 417). In chapter 27 of Dickens' *Pickwick Papers,* Mr. Stiggins, a reforming clergyman, deplores Toby Weller: "He has an obderrate bosom. . . . Who else could have resisted the pleading of sixteen of our fairest sisters, and withstood their exhortations to subscribe to our noble society for providing the infant negroes in the West Indies with flannel waistcoats and moral pocket handkerchiefs?" (*Pickwick Papers,* introd. Bernard Darwin [London, 1948], p. 368).

and rush with their ready remedies to staunch the blood wherever they perceive it to flow. The last, of more deliberate action, inspect the wound before they apply the remedy, painfully probe it, perhaps, or open the bleeding vein, and bid the sufferer often rather to bear the running sore than to heal it at the risk of his life.

With what propriety shall the first, however amiable, under its better developments, may be their ready impulse, exclaim against the last as butchers and miscreants—and yet such is the ground taken by modern philanthropists against Political Economy. Because Political Economy doubts the policy of their proposed expedients, they find no epithet too harsh for its expounders. Because Political Economy asks, doubts, studies, questions, and, seeing what appear hopeless ills, seeks to counteract rather than to cure them, searching for palliatives where it fails to find remedies, they pronounce it accursed—Anathema Maranatha.[9] . . . This science is not the Shylock it has been represented. It is not the science of dollars and cents. But, because it acknowledges wealth as its object, a sickly sentimentality takes fright at the word, connecting always by a strange perversion of ideas wealth with its abuses—as though to look at wine should nauseate with drunkenness, and the sight of food make one shudder at thought of a surfeit. Truly may all the gifts of life be put to an ill purpose; but not therefore shall we despise them all. And if, in spite of possible drunkenness and surfeit, we may still honestly eat bread and drink wine and not be defiled, even so may we righteously study wealth, i.e., the means of attaining and increasing our earthly comforts, and yet be guiltless of avarice, extortion, and all uncharitableness.[10] And if innocently we may thus seek our own enjoyment, is it not virtue, is it not christian charity, to seek the best means for the extension of these blessings to others? Is it a crime in us that we should endeavor to devise means whereby that bread and that wine may be shared with all? Is it a crime in us that we should ask how can this people, this nation, this world of nations, be made to enjoy the greatest possible proportion of these comforts of life that we call wealth? Surely this is christian charity, christian civilization! And this is the end and aim of Political Economy.

Political Economy professes to investigate (we take Mr. Mill's definition) "the nature of Wealth, and its laws of production <the laws of its production> and distribution: including, directly or remotely, the operation of all

---

9. 1 Cor. 16:22: "If any man love not the Lord Jesus Christ, let him be Anathema Maranatha."

10. Cf. "The Litany" in *The Book of Common Prayer*, p. 48: "From all blindness of heart; from pride, vain-glory, and hypocrisy; from envy, hatred, and malice, and all uncharitableness, good Lord, deliver us."

the causes by which the condition of mankind, or of any society of human beings, in respect to this universal object of human desire, is made prosperous or the reverse."[11] Surely here is space of almost boundless limit, and research of no belittling kind. The constant progress of man from barbarism to enlightenment, from brutality to civilization, from the crass ignorance of the savage, scratching with his nails roots from the earth, and with his teeth tearing the quivering flesh of his palpitating victims, to the highest improvement which science and philosophy have yet attained, all this and more, all progress, all possible worldly improvement, link themselves with this grand object of investigation. To own, to possess, to understand the *meum et tuum*,[12] is one of the first distinguishing characteristics of reason; and in proportion as man becomes enlightened on this point, he rises above the beast. He learns to own, and to permit others to own; he learns to give and to refrain from taking; he learns at once to be generous and just. Moral progress cannot advance but by improvement in physical condition. Improvement in physical condition can only be insured by accumulation of means of comfort—accumulation of means of comfort is wealth. These are truths so trite as scarcely to bear repetition, were it not that these are the axiomatic postull[at]a upon which Political Economy is based. Wealth is studied not to put self-interest above morals and religion, not to bid it clash with duty and charity, but to show how all work together in beautiful concord for man's improvement and progress. . . .

It is the poor and ignorant that Political Economy would assist and instruct. It is the masses that it would sustain against the oppression of the few. It is the wealth (i.e., the means of comfort) of all classes and all ranks, not of a few over-gorged capitalists pampered with Government protection, that she undertakes to defend. To naked and starving nations, blighted under the benighted policy of tyrannical governments, Political Economy came to feed and clothe them. If in so doing she could show, as she has shown, as she will yet in her future progress more clearly show, more beautifully develop (for the apostleship of Political Economy has but just begun), if, we say, she can prove that the good of all is irrevocably linked in the good of each; if she can prove (as she does prove) to the purse-proud capitalist that to preserve or increase his wealth his laborer must be fed, his country and his nation must thrive, or all his wealth, like fairy gifts,[13] turns in his hands to dry leaves

---

11. John Stuart Mill, *Principles of Political Economy, with Some of Their Applications to Social Philosophy*, ed. J. M. Robson (Toronto, 1965), p. 3.

12. "Mine and yours" (Latin).

13. Thomas Moore, "Believe Me, If All Those Endearing Young Charms," l. 4: "like fairy gifts fading away."

and trash; if she can prove (as she does prove) to the hungry laborer that his bread is none the dearer, his labor none the less in demand, because the rich man is accumulating his millions—that on the contrary even the most selfish hoarder hoards for the good of all; if she can prove (as she does prove) that labor and capital are not inimical but rather, working in unison, assistant handmaids each to the other; if she can prove (as she does prove) the truth of all these, at first sight, apparent paradoxes, and reconcile interests hitherto in unnatural and fraternal war, is she not indeed a prophet of peace, the beautiful development of christian civilization? Ever thus she comes before us, the teacher of that most beautiful of christian lessons, "Help ye one another."[14]

The great error of dabblers in Political Economy . . . is that they, by a strange misuse of terms, regard this science, which claims to investigate wealth and its causes, as the supporter of the wealthy and the oppressor of the poor, as though a wealthy nation should by necessity be composed of millionaires and beggars. Nothing is easier to demonstrate (did time and space allow) than that the wealth of the masses, and not the wealth of the few, makes a nation's wealth. Nothing is easier (and it would seem to us that even a word suggesting the idea should suffice) than to demonstrate that a nation of beggars, though mingled here and there with overgrown capitalists, is not a wealthy nation. Political Economy does constantly demonstrate this, and, aiming at the wealth of nations, seeks not to robe princes in velvet and jewels, but to give their people cheap bread and abundant clothing. But because it has shown that the same system which brings to the people cheap bread and clothing gives also to the prince his velvet and his jewels, because it has extended over these supposed opposing interests the wand of peace, those who half study its arguments strangely contend that, because it would better the rich, it must oppress the poor. Let them study it more deeply and they will find that Political Economy encourages, not the wealthy, but wealth, wars not against the poor, but against poverty; and surely no sane man will be found to contend that this is an unholy war; that the laborer can be too comfortably clothed, or his child too well fed; that the farmer's cottage is too snug, his cattle too fat, or his land too well tilled. Yet this is what Political Economy teaches us is a nation's wealth. This is what Political Economy teaches us is at once the wealth of the laborer and the wealth of his employer, the wealth of the prince and the wealth of his subject, the wealth of the individual and the wealth of the nation.

We have now to pass to the last branch of our subject, and to prove, or

---

14. The citation is not from the Bible; it seems to be an adaptation of such passages as John 13:34 and 15:12, 17; 1 Cor. 12:25; Gal. 5:13, 6:2.

at least suggest the grounds upon which it may be proved, that Political Economy will, when properly appealed to, bring the strongest possible arguments in favor of negro slavery. Political Economy, we have shown, is the science which considers wealth and its means of increase. Wealth is not money alone, but all desirable things which may be accumulated and exchanged, which may be lost by one individual or nation and gained by another individual or nation, passing from the possession of one into that of another. Thus individual or national wealth will be found to include all things desirable to a man or a nation which are extraneous from his or its individual or national existence, i.e., all things which he or it can possess, and transfer to another. A man's health, integrity, or industry cannot certainly be called his wealth, but they still fairly fall under the consideration of Political Economy because they are indisputably causes operating upon his condition in respect to wealth, and moreover may perhaps in themselves be considered as national wealth. They are certainly so in so far as the man himself may be considered as the property of the nation, to be lost or gained by one or another society, and capable of passing from the possession of one nation into that of another. Thus, then, Political Economy links itself with religion and ethics; for all that improves man, increasing his power and intelligence, makes him a more capable producer of wealth, makes him the better *wealth machine*. If this manner of enunciating our idea be objected to, as bringing man down to the brute and the steam-engine, let our antagonists remember that we do not degrade man to the machine, but bring every argument (this with the rest) to prove that no man can honestly benefit himself without tending also to benefit his fellows, and that even he of the most selfish and grovelling spirit is the better, morally and intellectually, for his honest efforts to improve his own condition. He is, to speak politico-economically, of higher value to his nation. There are wider and purer motives for action than simple self-interest; but simple self-interest (considering its universal prevalence) does more for the world's progress than any one human passion or desire. It exists in the bosom of every man, and he would be a monster in whom it should not be found. Mingling in some with the noblest virtues, in others with the lowest baseness, it still exists in all, and only is criminal when ministering to crime. It is not a virtue, but certainly not a vice. It is purely an instinct: the hunger of the spirit seeking always to gratify its longings, and exciting to crime or to virtuous effort according to the character and disposition of the individual in whom it exists, precisely as the honest man is pushed by hunger to labor for that bread which the thief in preference steals. But because the thief steals to satisfy his hunger, none surely will argue that hunger is therefore a sin. Political Economy sees in his hunger of the spirit a powerful motive for effort and a powerful incentive to good, except when combining with vice. Then only it becomes vicious, and then Political Economy, again siding with religion and morals, declares that vice and crime are injurious, and in their consequences both mediate and immediate degrading to man, incapacitating him as a producer of wealth, and in their nature tending to the disorganization of society.

Thus Political Economy never opposes but always strengthens the decisions of justice and morality. It does not, like good Paley, commit the terrible mistake, so degrading to humanity, of making self-interest the sole basis of virtue,[15] but it proves that self-interest is not a vice; that God, in giving man instinct and desires, made him not a creature of evil, but capable of both good and evil—that if our desires may be corrupted they may also be purified, and that in their purification consists not our spiritual but our worldly welfare. Religion teaches us submission to God and charity to men; ethics teach us justice to men; and Political Economy teaches us that charity and justice are prudence and wisdom. Thus all combine to the same great end, teaching that the good and the wise are one. The institution of slavery must, to prove its innocence, purge itself from sin before this three-fold tribunal.

The religious side of the question has already been so triumphantly argued, that no man taking the gospel for his guide needs to have it repeated. Accordingly, we find the most violent opponents of the system among the new-light and higher law men with whom any religion, further than the dictates of their own wild fancies, ceases to be even a pretext; and next to them the improved christianity mongers, whose creed is blood and murder, and the gospel according to Sharpe's rifles. In its ethical point of view, the defence of the system which has also been frequently, ably, and we think successfully undertaken, must be based upon the natural proprieties of the institution in particular cases, and upon the relative capacities, powers, and propensities of the men or nations concerned. To those who absolutely shut their eyes and ears to common sense, and insist upon a meaningless formula of words, in opposition to all truth and reason, nothing can be said, and they must go on forever, or until they see fit to turn from their folly, insisting, in the face of common sense, common law, and common practice, that all men are born free and equal. But to those who acknowledge a difference in men, different capacities, character, and tendencies, according to race,[16] and other inalienable natural distinctions; to those who recognize the almost axiomatic

15. Such is in truth the only interpretation which can be given to Paley's definition of virtue [in *Principles of Moral and Political Philosophy*, p. 27], viz, "Virtue is the doing good to mankind, in obedience to the will of God, and for the sake of everlasting happiness." [LSM]

16. We specially avoid here the question of unity or diversity of origin, which can make little difference in our argument. An existing difference in races, which centuries cannot eliminate, is equivalent in practice to perpetual difference. [LSM]

truth, that circumstances and varying degrees of development require difference of social position, the sometimes practice and even necessity of slavery can be indisputably proved. It is treading over oft trodden ground to endeavor to show that all men are not fit for all things, and that, wherever the Creator's will for his creature can be discovered in the tendencies and capacities of the creature, there can be no surer rule for man's guidance. The universal practice and judgment of the world have assigned to women and children a subordinate position to men. In the women's case this subordination is permanent, as are the constitutional characteristics which give rise to and justify it. In the child's it is temporary, as are also the peculiar characteristics in him causing its necessity. In either class the rule is general, in spite of exceptional powers existing in occasional individuals, and properly it is so. No general rule can be made to suit exceptional cases. Precisely similar are the causes and proofs of the justification and necessity of slavery in all its phases. The positions of women and children are in truth as essentially states of bondage as any other, the differences being in degree, not kind. They are states of subjection to the supremacy of others, and of greater or less deprivation of the rights of self government. This, the true definition of slavery, applies equally to the position of women in the most civilized and enlightened countries. That there are higher and lower degrees of subjection and deprivation makes no difference in the question of justice (if either is injustice both are injustice, as it is equally robbery whether I forcibly take from a man one dollar or a thousand), except in so far as it is necessary that these higher and lower degrees be in accordance with the peculiar characteristics and capabilities of the class thus held in greater or less subjection for their own benefit and that of society. The permanent natural characteristics, or the temporary condition, of certain classes of human beings indicate them as fitted for a certain position in the social scale and as unfitted for certain other positions, and their own as well as the general good of society requires that this fitness should be considered. The nearer the position of each class can be suited to its capacities, the nearer is the law of nature (that is of God) fulfilled, and the nearer is perfect justice attained. Perfect justice it is scarcely within man's capacities to attain, and all that can be done by the science of morals is to approach nearer and nearer (as does the mathematician in the squaring of the circle) to perfect truth. That system of government, then, and that amount of subjection which is needful to the highest development of the peculiar powers, and to the keeping in check the peculiar defects, of any class of men, is the most useful and the most just for that class.

The necessities of each class, race, or nation can only be calculated from its antecedent conditions and its actual developments. In the case of any society of men which have attained a certain degree of enlightenment, it is a just conclusion that themselves are the best judges of the proprieties and necessities of their case; but when a nation or society is in a condition unfit for self-government and inconsistent with its higher development, often the circumstance of contact with or subjection by more enlightened nations has been the means of transition to a higher development. When two nations, enlightened and unenlightened, are thus thrown in contact upon the same soil, nothing but slavery can prevent the destruction of the weaker race. In those phases of society where the developments of corporeal power are of more value, i.e., more useful to existing society, than mental (as in the first beginnings of society, where it is more important to men to know how to dig than to invent steam engines), the muscularly strong man becomes the master, the intelligent one the slave; and thus the functions of both are best fulfilled. Thus the weaker is protected (albeit often oppressed, for everything earthly is faulty), and the stronger aided in the point where he needs aid, i.e., mentally improved. In more advanced stages of society, where mind asserts its supremacy, intellect makes the master; intellect is the true strength, and mere muscular power needs not only the guidance, but the protection, of that mighty power which man's intellect teaches him to sway. The savage cowers before the builder of cities, or the inventor of steam-engines and magnetic telegraphs. The thought which commands the elements is stronger than muscle or fibre. Here, therefore, intellect (now become strength) protects, and muscle serves. In either case the weaker people perishes, but for the protection granted by the stronger, and, in return for that protection, serves. We do not say that this is done by regular compact. It is not so done; no society is formed by compact. Society is the result of instincts. Brutes and insects form societies as men; men, only by afterthought and progressive reasoning, think of compacts. The existence of society is an inherent necessity to man's existence; what therefore is needful to the existence of society cannot be unjust.

Thus, then, slavery is sometimes and to certain extents proved just. Political Economy may now be adduced as a powerful adjunct to define its limits, for we are far from granting that it would prove so frequent a remedy for the evils of society as our reviewer's argument appears to us to imply. And here Political Economy must also bring forward the test of utility. That position in which man is of the greatest utility and highest benefit to himself and to mankind—that position in which all his powers are exerted to the greatest advantage, his deficiencies kept in abeyance, and his faults under check— is by philosophical argument his legitimate duty, his highest interest, and in accordance with the eternal justice of things. The test of the right must be in its results, and surely the tree must be known by its fruits.[17] For although

17. Matt. 7:16–20.

it is very certain that every good deed does not, with the exact measurement of good boy story-books, bring its immediate reward, and every ill one its castigation, it is inconsistent at once with experience, and with every idea that man can form of the goodness of deity, that any regular system of evil can result in permanent and general good. The oppressor of the widow and the defrauder of the orphan may, in the inscrutable wisdom of Providence, be permitted to revel in his ill got gains; the murderer may hide his bloody hand, and unquestioned of justice pass through life high in the world's prosperity; but certain it is that, by the test of utility in result, the actions of such men are most injurious to society. A nation of defrauders and murderers could be nothing but a nation accursed, a people degraded to the lowest savagism, a robber band, in truth true Ishmaelites, whose hand should be against every man and every man's hand against them, "curtailed from all the fair proportions" of civilized society, and condemned to unprogressive barbarism.[18] And even in such condition, to prevent an entire obliteration of the species, some shadow of virtue, some good instinct must remain. At least there must linger that proverbial honor said to exist among thieves; there must survive some affection, some pity, some human passion, some virtue in short, or, worse than brutes, every man would be a Cain to his brother.

While, therefore, religion and morals say to us crime is wrong because it is crime, displeasing to God and hurtful to man, Political Economy confirms their decision on prudential motives. It teaches us that what is hurtful to man is impolitic, degrading him both individually and nationally, and checks progress because it destroys all security. Man is constantly aiming at advancement in his social condition, and in this constant individual effort to better himself, so long as honestly indulged, each pushes forward by his own fractional effort the great wheel of progress. Let crime or injustice intrude, and, precisely in proportion as these prevail, society is disorganized, men's rights become insecure, their energies flag, lethargy displaces effort, want displaces honest accumulation; man makes for himself a scourge equal to those which Heaven in its wrath has sometimes sent; and as, when pestilence or famine makes men insecure of everything but the life of today, they seek to enjoy that only, forgetting all else in a kind of reckless madness—"let us eat, drink, and be merry, for tomorrow we die"[19]—so with the prevalence of crime "all order dies."

> And one fierce spirit of the first-born Cain
> Reigns in all bosoms, that, each heart being set

---

18. Gen. 16:11–12; *Richard III* 1.1.18: "I, that am curtail'd of this fair proportion."
19. Eccl. 8:15; Isa. 22:13; Luke 12:19.

On bloody courses, the rude scene may end,
And darkness be the burier of the dead.[20]

All society in which crime is systematically encouraged must perforce rush more or less rapidly to destruction, and legalized injustice is national suicide.

Political Economy thus takes utility as the test of right. It does not set—this is the libel put upon it—utility above right. It does not say utility *is* right, but only brings utility to prove the right. The sense of right man receives from no argument or system of proof; it is instinctive with his nature. But in so far as it is susceptible of being clouded and misled, no test can be found other than God's approbation; and God's approbation, where man is not guided by special revelation, can only be read in results. All moralists agree, and all common sense confirms, that sound morality must always result in general good; and although we must do right for the love of right, and avoid wrong for the hatred of wrong, although the impulse of conscience is a guide to all men, not entirely extinguishable even in the most depraved, still general results must determine by the rule of cause and effect where and how man's instincts have gone astray. It is a common expression that the good man must act independently of consequences. But this abbreviation of speech, which is a truth only so far as it means that he must act independently of *personal consequences,* has led to many errors, and is, if taken literally, the grossest of fallacies. No sane man ever acts independently of consequences; no good man can for a moment deem it his duty so to do. There can be no virtuous action done without virtuous intent; and criminal intent makes the best action a crime. It is an innocent action to steep opium in alcohol. It is a right action to do this with the object of trade and to gain a livelihood. It is a virtuous action to do it with the intent of relieving the agony of a wounded or suffering creature. It is a criminal action to do it with the intent of poisoning a brother. The consequence aimed at makes the deed right or wrong. We do not contend that good intent always makes a good act, and that poisoning our brother with the good intention of sending him to heaven would be a virtuous action. But neither would it be a vicious, though a most lamentable and mischievous, one. It would be simply the action of a madman, of a being whose reasoning powers are ineffectual to his guidance and incapable of properly estimating consequences, and which would thus commit wrong ignorantly. The same man might possibly in another phase of his madness commit the murder without any calculation of consequences, or he might save the victim's life from some unexpected dan-

---

20. *2 Henry IV* 1.1.154, 157–60, reading: "Let order die! . . . But let one spirit of the first-born Cain / Reign. . . ."

ger, equally without consideration of consequences. In either case the madman is no more a responsible agent than are the inanimate means which he has used. In neither case is he either criminal or virtuous, precisely because he has not the power of calculating consequences or of estimating the importance of so doing. A sane man thus acting (if a sane man could thus act) would be guilty of criminal thoughtlessness; and on the other hand, however beneficial might be the result of his action, has no merit in it, because he has acted independently of consequences. Consequences (not personal but general) are the sanction or condemnation of God upon any course of action. Paley is to be condemned, not because he gives consequences as the aim of virtuous action, but personal consequences. To act from the hope of reward and fear of punishment (i.e., from consideration of personal consequences) is prudence, but certainly no higher virtue. To act with the hope and aim of doing all the good we can to our fellow men, considering and weighing consequences with the best judgment God has given us, is virtue, is the highest reach of morality; and, as we have already remarked, the result, or accomplished consequence, is the truest test we can have of the correctness or faultiness of our judgment. A man may be conscientiously right, and yet being of misguided judgment do what is in itself wrong and leading to evil—thus committing, not a sin, but an error, and being thus, although innocent in intention, the cause of ill. The only corrective of such misguided judgment (except in cases of distinct revelation) is the test of utility or ultimate good.

Herein, then, lies the great defence of American negro slavery which Political Economy (the science which considers the weal of nations) cannot on due investigation fail to pronounce. We do not say what has been done, but what inevitably must in the future be done. Men and prejudices have gone against us; but science cannot be swayed by prejudice or outcry; and however its advocates may, leaping to crude conclusions, often join in the chorused "hip hurrah" or the wild "halloo" of riot and fanaticism, at last she bears aloft the banner of truth, and points her worshippers to the rising sun of knowledge. All that is now needed for the defence of United States negro slavery and its entire exoneration from reproach, is a thorough investigation of fact, an investigation which will force sight into eyes that now will not see, and hearing into ears that now will not hear.[21] We want a broad exposition of fact! fact! fact!—fact without coloring and without distortion; fact whose simple truth shall put slander to the blush, paralyze the tongue of falsehood, and, taking the system and its results in their entire development, expose both in their fullest breadth and depth. So soon as our opponents can be

21. Jer. 5:21.

forced to look into the fact of this system, instead of taking it on hearsay from works of fiction and the mawkish sentiment of that class of "feelers" in philanthropy which we have endeavored in the earlier part of our article to depict, so soon as the public mind can be brought to a sufficiently sane condition on this subject to receive such testimony as would be decisive before any court of law or equity, our cause will be conclusively and triumphantly determined in our favor; and Political Economy (call it by what name we may, "social science," "national economy," "political science," what you will, still always the noble science, not, perhaps, too justly named Political Economy) will and must be our judge. Let hasty prejudice declaim as it may, that science, whose object is the weal of nations, itself the physician of social disease, must be called upon to pronounce our system (as we have endeavored to prove it) no disease, but the normal and healthy condition of a society formed of such mixed material as ours. . . .

Now we contend that the system of free labor is one of the necessarily recurring types of social organization, not *the* type, *but one of the types,* and the advocate of slavery who defends it to the exclusion of free labor, is as far wrong as he who defends free labor to the exclusion of slavery. Both are necessarily recurring types of social organization, and each suited to its peculiar phase of society. Free labor is a recent innovation, a social neoterism, says the reviewer [82]. Now, in spite of the imposing influence of a rather hard word, there is nothing so bad in a neoterism after all. It signifies only a thing of Northern growth; and such we grant the system of free labor to be. It is progress, an innovation if you will, but no more an innovation than commerce and navigation, than steamboats and railroads.

. . . Slavery was oftenest a rudimental condition, a state of progression wherein two or more unequally endowed peoples, existing on the same soil, could become, instead of clashing and destructive rivals, the assistants and protectors of each other. With the progress of society these separate peoples became oftenest so commingled in blood, interests, and capacities, that what had been distinct was no more. The serf, both in power of mind and body, was now the equal of his lord. The distinction, now become purely conventional, was no longer in the man, but only in the position of the man. Their relative positions (natural at first as those of child and parent) now became forced, and the inevitable progress of society was gradually, almost insensibly, to efface existing differences. That this progress should be constantly interrupted and impeded by man's passions and interests, proves nothing more than that (as we see with everything earthly) an inscrutable Providence sees fit to allow man's passions and interests to interfere with the natural course of events, the ill consequence of such interference only constantly proving itself by ill results. Still, with more or less impediment, such progress is and must be effected. The man who is by nature the equal of his brother cannot be his slave, except under exceptional circumstances, and no nation or race of men can ever, by any earthly power, be kept in subjection by another nation or race of men which is only its equal. There will need no foreign promptings, no excitements from abroad, such as abolition manufacture constantly circulates among our negroes, to show such a people its natural position. Man to man it will be felt, and man to man the true God-given power will assert its pre-eminence. So long as a people has not the impulse within itself, there is no surer sign of inferiority. We are not here contending for any utopian equality even in the most fully developed nations, nor do we believe in men being born free and equal under any system. We think it not unlikely that in the progress of time, with the fullest development of which man is susceptible, the higher and more perfectible races may attain under a constantly advancing civilization a nearer general equality than has yet been approached, and that, all classes of men being developed to their highest point of perfection, present differences of position may be diminished. A constant progression towards this the world has shown for centuries. But to this end bloodshed and violence alone can effect nothing. The man must be changed. Brute force may destroy, but can effect nothing. The lion may slaughter the man, but does not thereby make a man of himself. Brutal ignorance roused to resistance is brutal ignorance still, and the savage who is excited to murder his master can only be slaughtered or again enslaved, unless he be driven out from association with the civilized man.

Free labor, we contend, is as natural as slavery. Both are necessary institutions and neither universal. Both are sustained by the truest philosophy, and the "mendicancy, larceny, vice, crime, and pauperism" to which our reviewer alludes, "the destitution of the English labo[u]rer and the French proletaire, and the disintegration of European government and society" [84], are not the fruitage of the abolition of serfdom, but rather the result of its imperfect manner of abolition and the obstacles constantly opposed by the man in power to the natural advancement of his equal man. We are no upholders, under any system of society or in any condition of progress, of communism,[22] agrarianism, or any other artificial equalizer of men. Equality must, so far as equality is possible, be from the root in the nature of the man himself, and cannot be forced or coaxed by any hotbed culture. We defend

---

22. The only just and practicable communism which we can imagine, is the one exhibited by our own system of slavery, where the mass of inferior men is subjected to a ruler with whom the idea of competition is by nature impossible. Without such a head communism cannot exist. Louis Blanc and Co.'s communism was impracticable because naturally headless. [LSM]

a man's right to property in land with as much tenacity as any other possible right or possession. But it is not only the rights of property which the laws of Europe protect. Look for instance at the laws of England in favor of a privileged class. The laws of entail alone might suggest a more rational cause than free labor for the destitution of the English laborer. . . .

Free labor is indeed so new a thing that as yet it scarcely knows itself. Its trial is to come in revolutionized Europe. Great and fearful has been the struggle; great and fearful it may yet be. But one thing is certain. In proportion as the rising classes are fitted for the position which they claim, the horrors of the struggle, which exist only in their weakness, will be diminished. The firm demand which thoroughly knows its own limit, is irresistible and oftenest not resisted. An enlightened civilization is the only equalizer among men and, in as far as it is permitted to act without interference, acts always peacefully. We hope, we believe even, that the world has seen such horrors as no future circumstances can renew, and that the inevitable progress of the system of free labor will be peaceful and prosperous precisely in such proportion as the present and future man of Europe is and will be raised above the past. We speak here of the man of Europe, and only of Europe. For him of Asia little has been dreamed of liberty or free labor. His fate would seem to be bondage; and for him of Africa, savagism. As yet theory has interfered so little with these that in questions such as the one before us they are scarcely counted as of the world whose fate is in discussion. They have apparently accomplished that destiny of which they are capable; and tacitly they are left aside for future ages to determine whether such condition may be permitted to continue in a progressive world, or whether the irresistible impulse of a civilization which they are incapable of following must sweep them to extinction. When we speak of the world of men, Asia and Africa are for the most part forgotten. But the young giant, the offspring of Europe (for the man of America has already met that destiny which we anticipate as possible for him of Asia and Africa, and the transplanted energy of Europe has now become a new world), the young giant of America, shall it too follow in the wake of its parent, and show a unity in the form of modern civilization? Is the system of free labor also our destiny?

Most decidedly we answer: This is impossible, now and forever impossible, except by the total and entire eradication of a race which, transplanted at the same time with ourselves, has grown with us and become a dependent limb of our system, or rather a vital organ, to sever which is death. America has grown to her present point of maturity with the established system of negro slavery. The strong race and the weak, the civilized and the savage, him by nature ruler, protector, master, and him by nature subject, dependent, slave, are here not only cast together, but have been born together, grown together, lived together, worked together, each in his separate sphere, striving for the good of each, and together beautifully exemplifying the developed utility which earlier in our article we endeavored to indicate as the perfect condition of slavery—that condition which, fully exhibited, could not fail to elicit from Political Economy its sentence of approval, as the one in which these two races of men are mutually assistant to each other, and contributing, in the largest possible degree consistent with their mutual powers, to the good of each other and mankind. This system is in no way a laggard from that of Europe. It is a system quite as perfect in its kind, much more perfect in its development.

The results of the free labor system, so far as developed, truly do, as our reviewer has argued [65–69, 76–81, 85–86], teem with a wretchedness and misery, vice and crime, unknown to our quieter social condition. This is precisely because (as we have just remarked) our system, equal in kind, is more perfect in its development. Both are, with a progressive world, in a state of progress. Both are advancing to meet the highest tone of a fully developed christian civilization. Neither is, in itself, better or worse than the other. Each is proper, necessary, inevitable, in the phase of society which has called it forth. To force either into the place of the other is equal madness in either case, and in either case must lead to such fearful atrocities as must inevitably follow all human efforts to resist divine laws. The attempted enslavement of the English laborer would equal in folly (and nothing more) the attempted liberation of the American negro. Either, seriously undertaken, and with sufficient power to oppose the natural current of events, could but produce chaotic anarchy. Either would drown in blood the civilization of the continent wherein it might be attempted. Each of these systems works well its part; each has made noble progress; each is destined to further improvement, each to be perfected in its kind. Let but the unnatural animosity, whose source is ignorance, cease, and the social millennium will show that both are right, for both are in accordance with the laws of nature and necessity (which are the laws of God), and both must work together to the world's great progress. Both have indeed already done so. What century of man's world history developes such forward impulse as the last? And candid investigation must prove that, in this, a strong laborer has been the American negro slave. His labor has opened the new world of American agriculture with its great staples, cotton and sugar, which are the wealth not of his master only, not of one country only, but of the world. Even the lowest peasantry of Europe profits by them. Even benighted Asia, even savage Africa profits by them. Comfort and wealth, circulating through the arteries of commerce, extend from shore to shore; and every pulsation of the world's great heart sends further and further, with new comforts and new joys, the glad tidings of a constantly progressing improvement, of a world ever moving onward, ever happier, better, and more enlightened. These are the results of slavery, thus always blessing the slave even with the increasing abundance and comforts of which he is himself at once the producer and the recipient.

We have said that nothing but the extinction of the negro race in America can eradicate slavery. The negro can never be the white man's equal; and were slavery truly the evil, the moral sore, which our opponents suppose it, its cure could only be in the amputation of the limb. If the negro's fate be worthy of consideration, for his sake slavery should be maintained. But charity is an individual, not a national, virtue. Nations are not and cannot be good Samaritans. The only conceivable national charity is that wise policy which continually seeks the greatest good of the greatest number. The negro's cause then must be pleaded on the grounds of policy; and, as we have already repeated, Political Economy stands here to prove that christian charity is national policy. Slavery, which is the negro's protection, is the world's wealth. . . .

In our defense of Political Economy we must now only suggest to its opponents to remember, that no science is responsible for the natural tendencies which it studies and explains, but never produces; that Political Economy, in discovering the laws of society, in no wise creates them; and that it is no more than the ordinary physician responsible for the incurable ills of its patient. Let that impulsive kindness which condemns the coolness of its investigation pause at least to doubt if there be not oftenest truer charity in the action of the steady hand which guides the scalpel, separating vein from vein and nerve form nerve, even while the patient writhes under the infliction, than in the sentimental weakness which shudders and faints, daring not to look upon the anguish, and would, even at the expense of the sufferer's life, shading its eyes from his agony, hand the opiate which brings him at once relief and death.

Political Economy is the physician which the unthinking in his restlessness condemns. Look again, you who in earnest truth have thought him wrong, look again, and you may find a heart quite as warm as your own, a charity quite as true as your own, patiently striving to work out the problem which you have failed to read—to untie that Gordian knot which you have vainly thought to cut asunder. The true question is not, are the positions of Political Economy charitable or uncharitable? but, are they true or false? An inscrutable Providence has made an imperfect world, and, in the exercise of a wisdom incomprehensible to us, has created man a strange bundle of faults and virtues, passion and reason.[23] Governed alternately by truth and error, he

---

23. Cf. Alexander Pope, *An Essay on Man* 2.1–18.

gropes his way midst phantoms of darkness. Sophistry parades before him her twilight theories, strutting in the robes of wisdom. Folly peeps from behind her harlequin mask, while fanaticism stabs with a prayer, and hand in hand with hypocrisy dares call down Heaven's blessing upon deeds of Hell. Knee-deep in error, man works out the truth only by patient investigation and laborious research; and society must find its way to the goal of such perfection as earth permits only by the study of itself. Political Economy is this study.

8.

The Burning of Columbia

My name is Louisa S. McCord. I formerly lived in Columbia, South Carolina, owning the house in which I lived; I was living in Columbia in the early part of the year 1865, and was in the city at the time of its occupation by the United States forces. My house was in the lower part of the city, just opposite the South Carolina College grounds. I have read carefully the testimony offered for the defence in these cases. General Howard makes a mistake in saying in his deposition in these cases that his headquarters in Columbia were at the house of one of the professors of the University; his headquarters were at my house.[1] My family consisted at the time of four ladies; I was and am a widow.

The generals generally state that they knew of no pillaging. General Howard came to my house in broad day (about 2 or 3 o'clock P.M.), when it was actually under pillage of a very thorough kind. One of his officers entered

---

Mixed Commission on British and American Claims Established under Article XII of the Treaty of Washington, *British and American Claims. Appendix: Testimony* (Washington, D.C., 1873), vol. 23, "George Symmers *vs.* the United States and Frederick Ward *vs.* the United States, cases no. 228 and 294, depositions in rebutting for claimants," bk. 2, pp. 26–29 = *PDBL*, pp. 241–45. Two fragments are appended of a second account by LSM, preserved in James Parsons Carroll, *Report of the Committee Appointed to Collect Testimony in Relation to the Destruction of Columbia, S.C., on the 17th of February, 1865* (Columbia, S.C., 1893), pp. 10, 17.

1. Oliver Otis Howard (1830–1909), brigadier general commanding the Army of the Tennessee, was put in charge of Columbia after it had been surrendered to Federal forces in the morning of Feb. 17, 1865; Columbia was burned that night.

by my front door (which was unbolted in answer to his ring by some of the pillagers, with whom I was surrounded), and must have seen my house then crowded with them. General Howard, on horseback on my front pavement, must also have seen what was going on. I informed him also that I had but a few minutes before been throttled, and my watch was torn from me by a soldier in uniform, while others passed in and out with everything that could be taken in the way of plate, etc., while literally crowding on; the man who seized me was one in sergeant's uniform.[2]

2. "[The servants] brought us word that the Mayor of the city, Dr. [Thomas Jefferson] Goodwyn, had gone to surrender the city to Gen[eral] Sherman, but we still couldn't believe it. But we soon began to hear a distinct roar, a far off confusion which seemed to come nearer as we listened with our hearts in our mouths. Without any warning our back gate was burst violently open and in rushed pell mell, crowding, pushing, almost falling over each other, such a crowd of men as I never saw before or since. They seemed scarcely human in their fierce excitement—the excitement of greed and rapine. In one instant the large yard was full of them. . . . One horrible-looking man wore a coonskin cap with the tail hanging down behind, and the awful way in which that tail swung and jumped as he rushed about will always come to me as I think of that day. In less time than I have taken to write it, they had completed the ruin of all we had outside, and we saw a group of men headed by the coonskin cap coming toward the house. The doors were all locked, and we saw them looking at a large log lying in the yard, evidently suggesting its use as a battering ram—with that, fearing that violence would only excite to more violence, my mother told us girls to bolt the door after her as she went out, and that she would go down stairs and let the men in. Aunt Rache insisted on going with her; so the two went down and let in a perfect stream of thieves and robbers who, as before in the yard, simply spread themselves all over the house in one instant. There was a terrible system and skill about it all—the only confusion was caused by their anxiety to get ahead of each other, and the speed with which they dashed from side to side was wonderful. Again they smashed, tore, and pocketted every thing they could get at, Mamma and Aunt Rache only following them about trying to keep some sort of check on them, and above all to keep them from going up stairs, for the warnings and stories we had heard led us to expect no mercy from them. At last they turned toward the staircase, at the foot of which the two mothers were standing. The coonskin put his foot on the step, but Mamma slipped ahead of him and told him he couldn't go up. He tried to push past her, when she remembered the Masonic signal of distress, and made it, with the result that he struck her hand down, crying out, 'None of that!' He spied then what she thought safely hidden, a little leather thong to which was attached my brother's watch which had been her father's, and was last used by Willy Haskell and sent back to her, after his death at Gettysburg. This wretch caught her by the throat and jerked the watch out of her dress with such force that he broke the leather. Either he or one of the others—it must have been another one—had all of our knives gathered in sheaves in his hands, and shook them in her face. Poor Aunt Rache retreated, and no wonder. She rushed back up stairs to us—we heard her and let her in—and she almost fell into the room, white and faint, calling, 'Oh, girls, they are killing your mother.' It was a tragic moment, but the comic is always close at hand, and I remember the desperate convulsive laugh that went round when she suggested that we

General Howard "did not see anybody setting fires." If setting fires signifies an attempt to set fire, although not successful, General Howard has forgotten at least one incident of the night of the fire. The roof of my house having caught fire, I took my family down stairs to my sitting room (then occupied by General Howard and suite), stating that we would remain there either until the fire was extinguished or until it became so bad as to drive us into the streets. As we sat there, I was facing an open door giving laterally upon the entrance, and I saw a flake of burning cotton thrown into the entry from the front. It was thrown, not wafted or blown by the wind, but with the movement of a steady throw; it must have been matted by pressure of the hand or otherwise, and then lit; cotton which has been burning any length of time would be smouldering and black; there was no wind coming in by the door through which this cotton entered; the person throwing it must have been absolutely at the door, if not within it; it was a ground floor door, protected by a piazza and a very high and heavy hedge at least eighteen feet high. General Howard entering or coming forward from the back as the cotton fell, and not at the moment perceiving us, said, with some severity to his men, "This must stop; this was no accident, and it has happened several times before"; then looking up he saw my eye fixed upon him, and immediately he came toward me with the remark, "It is a singular thing that your men in leaving the town set fire to some cotton at the depot, which has been flying about ever since." I may say here, by the way, that, to the best of my recollection, there was no remarkable wind until the fire raised it.[3]

On the morning of the 18th February, 1865, a lady hearing that her house was intended to be burned that night, and after considerable waiting not being able to see General Howard, so urged me to report her case that I

---

must jump out of the window and slip down a big tree close to the house and so get away from the inferno down stairs. What might have happened I don't know, but just as the man was pushing past my mother, the door bell rang. She said the men stopped instantly, which she noticed; so when it rang again she said just on the chance, 'There are some of your officers, and you had better not let them find you here.' In one minute they were gone! Just like a flight of vultures. Sure enough it was an officer—Gen[eral] O. O. Howard, second in command I believe to Sherman, who had been asked by friends in Savannah to make his headquarters at our house as a protection." Smythe, pp. 61–62. After the fall of Savannah, Rachel Cheves (wife of LSM's brother John) and her daughter had come to Columbia to stay with LSM.

3. "Burning cotton was found in the most extraordinary places, and Gen[eral] Howard would say in his suave manner that it was remarkable how the cotton was blowing about. On one occasion when a ball of it was found burning in the back entry, my Mother answered him, 'Yes, General, very remarkable, through closed doors,' and he said no more." Smythe, pp. 63–64.

finally consented to do so. General Howard's answer was in a low, somewhat confidential voice, spoken while within three or four feet of General Sherman, who was also in the room when I entered.[4] He said, "The fact is, Mrs. McCord, our men got beyond us last night. We had to use severity; we shot some of them; some seventy of them were shot; but there will be nothing of the kind tonight. Rest assured there will be no fires tonight." And there were none.

Apropos of the discipline of the troops, I saw and heard from an enclosed piazza General Howard when a second time called from his sleep, my house having again caught fire. The fire light caused him to be plainly seen as he stood in my yard giving some orders to a sentinel; and in answer to some words spoken by the latter I heard him with raised voice and considerable severity say, "Now and until the fire is over." The sentinel again spoke, too low for me to hear, and again General Howard: "Till daylight then, and take care what you are about, sir." As he turned back into the house, the sentinel began a shuffling-down step to the tune and words, quite audibly sung, "We won't be back till morning, till daylight doth appear."[5]

It may be worth while mentioning, also, as indicating the pre-knowledge of the soldiers of the coming horrors of that night, that while the pillaging of my yards and buildings was beginning in the morning or early afternoon (owing to the seizure of my watch my idea of time through that day is very inaccurate), a slip of paper was secretly brought to me by a frightened servant girl; she said that a soldier had dropped it on the step and told her to bring it to me. It was a few words written in pencil and addressed to the "Ladies of Columbia," advising them to leave, if possible, for some place of safety; that a "terrible fate" awaited them, and adding that he wrote this because he had kind friends among us. This was signed by one giving his name and rank as second lieutenant in company and regiment, both of which he named. I believe this to have been sincerely and kindly intended; but it could do us no good, and might do the writer a great deal of harm. I doubted for one moment, and then destroyed the soiled scrap.

4. Major General William Tecumseh Sherman (1820–91) was in overall command of Federal forces operating in Georgia and the Carolinas. "Pamphlets, manuscripts, and every thing of the kind, formerly owned by me, were for the most part destroyed by our brutal invaders at the close of our Southern Struggle for Liberty. Whatever escaped *them,* was wantonly scattered by our ignorant negroes excited to join in their brutal Saturnalia. In our devastated homes little of value remained after the Vandal like progress of Sherman." LSM to Lyman C. Draper, June 3, 1870, in *PDBL,* p. 386.

5. "For He's a Jolly Good Fellow," st. 2: "We won't go home until morning, / We won't go home until morning, / We won't go home until morning, / Till daylight doth appear."

[FRAGMENTS]

1

One of my maids brought me a paper, left, she told me, by a Yankee soldier; it was an ill-spelled but kindly warning of the horrors to come, written upon a torn sheet of my dead son's note book, which, with private papers of every kind, now strewed my yard. It was signed by a Lieutenant—of what company and regiment, I did not take note. The writer said he had relatives and friends in the South, and that he felt for us; that his heart bled to think of what was threatening. "Ladies," he wrote, "I pity you. Leave this town—go anywheres to be safer than here." This was written in the morning; the fires were in the evening and night.

2[6]

I showed him the paper, which he glanced at, and then, in a somewhat subdued voice, but standing so near General Sherman that I think it impossible that the latter could help hearing him, he said: "You may rest satisfied, Mrs. McCord, that there will be nothing of the kind happening tonight. The truth is, our men last night got beyond our control; many of them were shot—many of them were killed; there will be no repetition of these things tonight. I assure you, there will be nothing of the kind; tonight will be perfectly quiet." And it *was* quiet—peaceful as the grave, the ghost of its predecessor.

---

6. This fragment is introduced in Carroll's *Report* (p. 17) thus: "On the following day, the 18th of February, . . . Mrs. L. S. McCord, at the request of a friend, having undertaken to present a paper to General Howard, sought an interview with that officer, second in command of the invading army, and found General Sherman with him. Her narrative of a part of the interview is as follows."

Louisa Susanna McCord. (*From the Collections of the Georgia Historical Society*)

Langdon Cheves, bust by Clark Mills, 1844. (*Courtesy of the South Carolina Historical Society*)

Mary Elizabeth Dulles, miniature by Edward Greene Malbone, c. 1806. (*Courtesy of Lenora Cheves Brockinton*)

David James McCord. (*From the Collections of the Georgia Historical Society*)

Langdon Cheves McCord. *(From the Collections of the Georgia Historical Society)*

Left to right: Louisa Rebecca Hayne McCord, Charlotte Reynolds, Hannah Cheves McCord, Elizabeth Horner Dulles, 1860. (*From the Collections of the Georgia Historical Society*)

Louisa Susanna McCord to Langdon Cheves, Jr., March 5 [1856]. (*Courtesy of the South Carolina Historical Society*)

Indian Rock, Narragansett, c. 1862/63, ink and wash over graphite on paper, by William Stanley Haseltine. (*Courtesy of the M. and M. Karolik Collection, Museum of Fine Arts, Boston*)

The British and North American Royal Mail Steamship *Persia*. (*Courtesy of the National Maritime Museum, Greenwich, London*)

The McCord house in Columbia. (*Courtesy of the South Carolina Historical Society*)

Gravestone of Louisa Susanna McCord, Magnolia Cemetery, Charleston.

Louisa Susanna McCord, bust by Hiram Powers, 1859. (*Courtesy of Lenora Cheves Brockinton*)

Part II

9.
Poems

To My Father

Oft in my bosom the self-flattering thought
Has roused itself—"I, too, may be a poet."
And again, o'ercome by my own weakness,
Have I shrunk before the blighting consciousness,
The damning fear, that I am built as one   5
Amidst the crowd: an atom in the sunbeam;[1]
Nothing more than all the triflers round me.
And yet there is a hope, it will not die;
If I would crush it, still it struggles here,
And in my heart it whispers, "Thou hast caught,   10
Perchance, one gleam of light from that sunbeam,
Which others may not see." I long to know
If there is in my soul one ray, one gleam,

"To My Father," "Poor Nannie," and "The Comet" were published in *My Dreams* (Philadelphia, 1848). "Guardian Angels" appeared in the *Southern Literary Gazette*, n.s, 2 (Nov. 13, 1852); "Woman's Progress" in the *Southern Literary Messenger* 19 (Nov. 1853); "Thy Will Be Done" in Epes Sargent, ed., *Harper's Cyclopaedia of British and American Poetry* (New York, 1881). See *PDBL*, pp. 41–43, 72–78, 112–13, 149, 150–54, 157.

1. Geoffrey Chaucer, *Canterbury Tales*, "The Wife of Bath's Prologue and Tale," ll. 866–68: "limitours and othere holy freres, / That serchen every lond and every streem, / As thikke as motes in the sonne-beem."

Of true poetic fervour. I have seen
Thee, with a kind indulgence, read my lines, 15
Penned with a trembling hand, a tearful eye,
And I have drunk thy hope-inspiring praise,
And hugged myself therein. But out, alas!
On my ill-founded hopes! Too partial judge,
Thou can'st not say if 'twere the man's, 20
Or but the parent's, heart which felt and throbbed
Its answers back to *my* heart's throbbing struggles.
Wise in all other points, thou might'st forget
Thy wisdom in the follies of thy child.
Doubting and trembling still, I cast my lines, 25
Then, here, before the world; and it must judge
'Twixt me, and my own struggling thoughts, which rise,
Now in Hope's wild commotion, and now sink
Back, back, upon myself and nothingness.

Poor Nannie

Late was the hour, and dark the night;
    Sharply and chill the cold winds blew;
And gathering clouds bedimmed the light
    Which some faint stars still struggling threw.

And still as each a cloud o'ercasts, 5
    And murkier grows the gloomy night,
Howling their rage upon the wastes,
    December's blasts are in their might.

Nature in terror seems to moan;
    The tardy labourer seeks his home, 10
And shudders, as he hastens on,
    That some through such a night must roam.

And now upon the blast there seems
    To rise a soft, a plaintive tone.
He stops, and listening turns, but deems 15
    'Twas but the wind, and hastens on.

Again upon his ear it falls,
    Again its soft tone makes him start;
It seems a woman's voice that calls
    For pity from the gentle heart.   20

He turns, resolved to face the blast,
    That in its fury threatens death;
He shrinks not from the dreary waste:
    A woman's dying near his path!

And as he turns, the thrilling tones   25
    Again sweep by upon the air.
He pauses, though a woman moans!
    'Tis not the tempest bids him fear:

No; he has courage which would meet
    The warring elements in arms;   30
Nor would the sturdy woodman's feet
    Turn back from any mortal harms.

But he has heard a whispered tale
    Of evil Spirits in the gloom;
Which says that, when they weep and wail   35
    Through midnight storms, 'tis o'er a tomb:

An empty tomb, which, ere the morn,
    They seek to fill with human corse;
And weep, that wanderers forlorn
    May yield them to their hellish force: 40

Then, wandering through the dreary waste,
    They meet their dreary unwept doom,
And hear, borne on the wintry blast,
    The dirge which fiends howl o'er their tomb.

'Tis this he dreads; and, as the sad   45
    And plaintive sound once more he hears,
He turns away his hurried tread,
    And e'en to listen now he fears.

And hastening on, in whistling winds
    He fancies still the ghostly wail;
Trembling, at last, his cottage finds,
    And shuddering tells the fearful tale.

And was it then some demon foul
    Which sought to mock the wanderer's ear?
Or yet, some evil damnèd soul,
    Thirsting his dying groans to hear?

Oh no! that sound was what it seemed,
    A feeble woman's plaintive moan.
Nor evil demon, sprite, nor fiend,
    But a poor mortal's dying groan.

For on that bare and trackless field,
    There lay a being, fair, but frail;
Whose bosom once with pride had swelled
    At what her tears did now bewail.

Alas! her fatal beauty led
    To shame, and houseless misery;
And now, the earth her dying bed,
    She mourned her hapless destiny.

And, as far o'er the gloom she sees
    A twinkling taper's feeble light,
"Alas!" she sighs, "what happy days
    My folly, in their bloom, could blight!

"Where burns that feeble taper's blaze,
    I, with my aged father, dwelt;
And happy was I with his praise,
    The greatest pleasure that I felt.

"When, with a parent's joy, he'd gaze
    Upon the daughter of his love,
And then his trembling hands would raise,
    To call a blessing from above;

"And then would press me to his heart,
    Call me his own, his dearest one,
And then tears to his eyes would start,
    As he'd pray God for me alone.

"But then came one, whose flattering tongue, 85
    To win me from my father, strove.
Alas! I listened, and e'er long
    He made me fly a father's love.

"And when I wept my home to leave,
    And fear and doubt were on my brow, 90
He whispered that I must not grieve—
    Said I should be *his* Nannie, now.

"I trusted. And could I forget
    The love my father bore his child?
I only was his all, and yet 95
    I fled, by treachery beguiled.

"I fled, and left him here alone,
    His gray hairs sinking to the grave;
I fled, and left him here to mourn
    That daughter, whom his love forgave. 100

"Yes; for they tell me, when he should
    Have called down curses on my head,
Low in the dust, to heaven he bowed,
    And still for his poor Nannie prayed.

"And now I hear that he is sick, 105
    That age and wo his life-blood numb;
That grief his worn-out heart must break,
    And sorrow drive him to the tomb.

"And vainly have I sought the way,
    To soothe one pang, to dry one tear; 110
That I might kneel to him and say,
    'Father, your wandering Nannie's here.'"

She hushed, and the loud raging storm
    Howled louder as it swept along,
And seemed to mock the fragile form, 115
    Whose fate upon its fury hung.

Far roars the blast, the forests groan;
    Ruin all nature doth survey,
And seems to claim it as its own;
    All nature bows, and owns its sway. 120

*   *   *   *   *

But hushed at last, the storm is done;
    Calmly the wrecks of nature lie;
And brightly now, the rising sun
    Smiles from the clear, unclouded sky.

But where is she, who late bewailed 125
    The cruel wind's relentless rage?
Was it her sad complaints prevailed,
    That Ruin ceased his war to wage?

And did she reach her father's home?
    And may she close his dying eye? 130
And may she, though with sorrow dumb,
    Show him his Nannie, ere he die?

The old man lay upon his bed;
    Alone he wept his daughter's fate;
Near him he hears a stranger's tread; 135
    He turns—her corpse is at his feet.

Calmly he looks; one word, one sigh
    Escape not from his agèd lips;
He looks on that dull, clouded eye,
    And from its lids the cold frost wipes. 140

He seeks to dry the frozen tears
    Which glisten on those pallid cheeks;
His weak hand drops; and all his cares
    Death's touch, at once, now kindly checks.

And low in one cold grave they lie, 145
    To dust by stranger hands conveyed;
No stone to draw the pitying eye
    Is o'er their earthy mansion laid.

And winter's blast, and summer's sun,
    Have passed upon this silent spot, 150
And gloomy autumn hastens on,
    And none have come to mourn their lot.

Yet there is one who should have wept
    His ruined Nannie's hapless doom,
That one who like a serpent crept, 155
    And stole her from her father's home.

*   *   *   *   *

And now by the receding light
    Of the bright sun that sinks to rest,
Behold a stranger gaily dight,
    To yon lone cottage rides in haste. 160

And when he sees its ruined walls,
    The still grave, now the only home
Of those whose semblance memory calls,
    The living image, from the tomb;

And when he hears the mournful tale, 165
    Which those can tell who laid them there,
Sighs bid at length his bosom swell,
    And in his eye glistens a tear.

Dashing his hand across his brow,
    Plunging his rowels in his steed, 170
He hurries on, and seeks to throw
    Off memory with his courser's speed.

But still, as hastening on he'd hide
    The woful scene of misery,
He fancies Nannie by his side, 175
    Th' upbraider of his treachery.

And, borne upon the gentle breeze,
    A murmuring sigh sounds in his ear,
And a low whispering voice, which says,
    "What, has poor Nannie not one tear?" 180

Ah! few the sighs her misery
    From that light, thoughtless heart can draw,
And seldom on her memory
    He deigns a backward glance to throw.

In the gay world he drowns the wo 185
    Which for one moment swelled his breast;
Grown cold as is the frozen snow,
    His heart grief seldom can molest.

And now he haunts its dazzling glare,
    And laughs, and there his smiles are many; 190
But few the thoughts he gives that tear,
    Which once he shed for his poor Nannie.

The Comet

Hast thou no resting-place, thou wandering thing?
Art thou an emblem of the soul, which roams
Eternally, and seeks a home and rest?
What art thou, that thou flashest o'er us thus
In course eccentric?[2] Lo! as some wanderer 5
Thou passest, a lone stranger through the sky,
And every star peeps forth, as if to watch
Thy meteor course, and, as thou passest, pales
Its timid ray, and seems to whispering say,
"We know thee not, strange thing, thou'rt not of us." 10
And, in calm brightness, the pale moon looks down,
And thou, as 'twere a troubled spirit, shrink'st
From her soft light, while with her gentle smile

---

2. Perhaps a reference to the Great Comet of 1843, the brightness of which, and its tail nearly two hundred million miles long, caused a sensation. Also, Halley's comet appeared to the earth in 1835–36; and in 1846 Biela's comet, as it passed the sun, broke in two.

She seems to say, "Wanderer, thou'rt not of us."
And the earth answers her, from rustling leaves, 15
And wave, and murmuring stream, "Thou'rt not of us."
'Tis echoed through the universe. And thou,
Outcast from Heaven and Earth, whence art thou?—Say,
Is thy wild light some evil thing which spreads,
As has been deemed, sickness and desolation? 20
And dost thou bear with thee the curse of worlds,
Grim Famine, hungry War, thy satellites?
Or art thou but some wandering discontent?
Some thought, which may not find a resting-place,
Fixed to one constant round of endless change, 25
For ever wandering, and for ever doomed
To wander on alone; teaching itself
To suffer; gnawing itself, and bringing home
Its direst misery? a misery
Of loneliness unshared, which nought can know 30
And nought can pity? And (for thou art alone)
Men curse thee; and they point as 'twere a scourge,
Precursor of strange ills; and trembling watch
Thy beaming course, which should be beautiful
But that they deem some new strange ill must follow. 35
Hast thou a thought to know thyself accursed,
And feel that all things hate thee? An' thou hast,
E'en in thy lofty state, I pity thee,
Bright, lonely one: methinks to find a home
Thou'dst hide thy rays, and sink to loneliness, 40
And shrink into the bosom of some cloud,
Or drop into the ocean's billowy bed,
That all no more might shrink from thee, and say,
"Strange thing, whence art thou?—thou art not of us."
  Lo! thou art gone, perchance to seek for rest; 45
And the sky, which but now cast back thy beam,
Has lost thee, and with open smile it seems
As 'twould rejoice to find itself again
Free from thy fearful light. I pity thee,
That all things shun thee thus. E'en tho' thou wert 50
As foul as thought can paint, or fancy dream,
Some demon spirit, bent on ill and wo,
Still I must pity thee: for thou'rt *alone*,
And *loneliness*, methinks—is *misery*.

Guardian Angels

Echoing from yon rose-tree's branches,
    Laughter pealing long and gay,
Merriest tones mirth heavenward launches—
    There my children are at play.

Honey-suckle tendrils twining,
    Grasping catch their wavy hair;
While their mirthful eyes peep shining
    As though stars were glimmering there,

In and out, 'midst flowers gleaming
    Glistening now, and now withdrawn,
As 't were heaven-sent sun-rays beaming
    Light from angel-watchers down.

And are not these angels?—watching
    Every step and look?
Beam these eyes not near us, snatching
    Young ideas from thoughts unspoke?

Yes; untaught they learn to know them;
    From my heart each thought they win.
Can I dare that heart to show them
    Torn with passion, smirched with sin?

No, my babies! Echoing round me,
    When I hear your voices thus,
Heavenly links I feel have bound me,
    Which I may not, dare not, loose.

Ye my guardian angels linger,
    Bidding me each thought review;
And I feel that Heaven's finger
    Points me to the right through you.

Woman's Progress

And is this progress? Are these noisy tongues—
In fierce contention raised and angry war—

Fit boast for womanhood? Yon shrewish things,
In wordy boisterous debate—are these
Perfected woman's exponents to show
Her model virtues to a later age?
And shall our daughters cast their woman robes,
A useless cumbrance, aside, to seize
Some freer imitation of the man,
Whose lordly strut and dashing stride attract
Their envious love for notoriety?
Shall they, with flashing eye and clanging tongue,
Mount in the rostrum, lecture in the streets,
And, in the arena of election strife,
Claim with shrill voice, and rude dishevelled locks,
"Your votes! your votes!" ye loud-mouthed populace!
Nay. Should that peach-like cheek but feel the breath
Of yonder foul-mouthed crowd, methinks its bloom
Should wither in the contact. God hath made
A woman-nature holier than the man's—
Purer of impulse, and of gentler mould—
Let her not stain it in the angry strife
Which these, our modern female Reverends,
Learnèd M.D.'s, and lecturing damsels, seek
To feed their hungry vanity, and bring
Unnoticed charms before the gaping crowd.
'Tis surely not for this that God hath given
That soothing voice, so sweetly taught to whisper
Pity, and hope, and sympathy, and love,
And every holier thought, whose gospel tongue
Can preach its comfort to grief's riven heart!
Here, in the crowd, 'tis harsh and dissonant;
Its softer notes must struggle to a scream
Of impotently shrill, unmeaning effort.
'Tis surely not for this that God hath given
The soft light hand, whose velvet touch can soothe
The achings often both of head and heart.
Here, it would illy stand her in the strife;
And doubled fist, and tiny foot advanced
In attitude of combat, were a mock—
And oh! alas! how foul a mimicry!—
Of man's contemptuous life. 'Tis not for this,
Sweet Sisters! not for this! that God hath given

That purer soul, whose impulse (like the flower
Instinct with life that ever seeks the sun 45
And in his rays doth live) turns to the truth
And loves, and hopes, and doth expand itself
Only to nobler instincts! Stronger to hope,
Loftier to bear than man's; yet meeker too
To patiently endure—this soul, methinks, 50
To strife of grosser passions God formed not.
The fallen woman is the viler man,
Even as her fall is greater. From the height
Of her own nature's lofty pedestal,
She flings herself with grovelling pride, as though 55
The nightingale should cease its chaunt, and turn
The aspiring wing, which nature taught to rise,
Earthward again, stooping its course to spar
And jangle with some harsh, unnatural note,
In emulation of yon dunghill cock. 60
Sweet Sister! stoop not thou to be a man!
Man has his place as woman hers; and she,
As made to comfort, minister, and help,
Moulded for gentler duties, ill fulfils
His jarring destinies. Her mission is 65
To labour and to pray; to help, to heal,
To soothe, to bear; patient, with smiles, to suffer;
And with self-abnegation nobly lose
Her private interest in the dearer weal
Of those she loves and lives for. Call not this 70
(The all-fulfilling of her destiny,
She the world's soothing mother), call it not,
With scorn and mocking sneer, a drudgery.
The ribald tongue profanes Heaven's holiest things,
But holy still they are. The lowliest tasks 75
Are sanctified in nobly acting them.
Christ washed the apostles' feet, nor thus cast shame
Upon the God-like in him. Woman lives
Man's constant prophet. If her life be true
And based upon the instincts of her being, 80
She is a living sermon of that truth,
Which ever through her gentle actions speaks,
That life is given to labour and to love.
Through this rough world her angel ministry,

Like sweetest water bubbling through the sands 85
Of arid desert, cheers the weary heart,
And leads the restless soul which cursed its fate
To pause, to think, and learn to love that God
Who, midst the parching waste of suffering,
Has dropped this comfort like a boon from Heaven 90
To bid him drink and live.
       Sweet Sisters! thus
God wills that we should be; and who profanes
This, the last formed, so the most perfect, work
Of His creative will—this woman nature—
Who seeks to drag it down, to smirch and blot 95
Its purer being with the tainting blight
Of passion's license, doth profane the hope
Of God's creation; doth blot out the light;
Sully the purest beam of reasoning life,
And cast man's nature back upon the beast 100
To strive and grovel in the lowest lusts
Of passion's vile excess. As God is love,
So reasoning nature lives in him through love;
And Woman in the trueness of her being
Is still the never-ceasing minister 105
Of love which wearies not, which toils and bears,
And, sorrowing for the loved ones, doth forget
Her own life's anguish, soothing others' woes.
Then let our holy task be still to cleanse,
But not to change, our natures. Let us strive 110
To be *more* woman—never to be man.
These reverend Misses, doctors in mob caps,
And petticoated lecturers, are things
Which make us loathe, like strange unnatural births,
Nature's disordered works. Yon chirping thing 115
That with cracked voice, and mincing manners, prates
Of rights and duties, lecturing to the crowd,
And in strange nondescript of dress arrays
Unfettered limbs that modesty should hide;
Thus raising, as it were, rebellion's flag 120
Against her being's nature—call it not,
Sweet Sisters, call not that unsexèd thing
By the pure name of Woman. Let us strive
With silent effort in the Woman's cause,

Perfecting, in its destinies, our sex, 125
And cast aside this foul attempt which clings
To degradation as it were our pride.
Oh! let us be the woman of God's make;
No Mrs. Bloomer, Abby Kelly thing
Aping man's vices, while our weaker frame 130
Knows not his harsher virtues. Let us be
Strong—but as Woman; resolute in right—
All woman—perfect woman—no false ape—
No monster birth—no female Caliban,
Mocking our nature with unnatural shades 135
Of strange and foul resemblance.[3] Gentle, pure,
Kind, loving Woman never can degrade
Her own God-given nature. Only then
When she distorts it to unnatural ends
Doth she degrade her being. Man may rail, 140
Or mock, or pity her; with tyrant strength
May trample on her weakness, or may sneer
As though his being were of higher mould;
But not for this is she degraded; rather
Ennobled, in the gently bearing it. 145
There is no degradation which springs not
From our own inmost being. Noble things
Are never trampled into meanness. Low
May be their uses, but vile purposes
Soil not the diamond's hue. Our inmost worth, 150
At our own heart's tribunal, rights itself,
And e'en midst persecution calmly rests
On its proud consciousness. A noble thing
Is Woman's undistorted nature. Let
No taunt, nor jeer, sweet Sisters, shame us from it. 155
Woman, true Woman, is of larger worth
Than rank or power can fashion. Far above
All that the loud reformer ever dreamed,
Her virtues are no wordy theories,
But sky-born instincts touching on our earth 160
Still in full flower from Heaven.

---

3. *Othello* 1.3.401–2: "Hell and night / Must bring this monstrous birth to the world's light"; *Hamlet* 1.5.27–28: "Murder most foul, as in the best it is, / But this most foul, strange and unnatural." The use of "resemblance" is Miltonic: *Paradise Lost* 4.363–64, 6.114–15, 9.538.

Thy Will Be Done

Thy will be done! Almighty God,
Our weakness knows no other prayer
    But this: "God's will be done!"
We cannot shape our future good;
To mark thy mercy's bounds we fear:
    Father! thy will be done!

Still to our weakness clinging fast,
With naught to point or guide our way,
    We cry, "God's will be done!"
And 'mid the storm of life, the blast
Of warring tempest, still we say,
    "Father! thy will be done!"

And this the surest charm to lull
The tempest in its raging might,
    Great God! thy will be done!
Should universal nature fall
To wreck and ruin, 'mid its Night,
    Father! thy will be done!

We know that Thou canst guide us best;
And if we live, or if we die,
    Thy will, oh God! be done!
Our weakness seeks on thee to rest;
It loves to cling to thee and cry,
    "Father! thy will be done!"

10.

Caius Gracchus
A Tragedy in Five Acts

> The seeming truth which cunning times put on
> To entrap the wisest.
>
> *Merchant of Venice*[1]

To My Son

Too young thou art to read a Mother's heart;
Too young to guess that quenchless fount of love
Which ever gushes forth in joy and woe,
Limitless, always. If careworn and sad,
By want or sickness bowed almost to earth—   5
Or yet if triumphing in life's success,
Flattered, beloved, admired—the Mother finds
(Be she true woman with a woman's heart)
No moment when that heart can idly rest
From the long love which ever fetters it   10
In bondage to her child. My boy, thine eye
Some day perchance may fall upon these lines;

Caius Gracchus: A Tragedy in Five Acts (New York: H. Kernot, 1851) = *PDBL*, pp. 161–232. LSM's source for the outline of the plot, and for much of its detail, is *Gaius Gracchus* by the Greek biographer Plutarch (c. A.D. 46–after 120). In the notes below to the play, all dates are B.C. Gracchus' *praenomen* is more accurately spelled "Gaius" (abbreviation "C."), and thus it is given in the notes when referring to the historical Gracchus; when to LSM's character, "Caius" is retained.

   1. *Merchant of Venice* 3.2.97–101: "Thus ornament is but the guiled shore / To a most dangerous sea: the beauteous scarf / Veiling an Indian beauty; in a word, / The seeming truth which cunning times put on / To entrap the wisest."

And, catching here the shadow of my love,
Thy soul may guess its fullness, and may feel,
Through every struggle in this changing life,   15
That, like a guardian angel hovering round,
To comfort, check—to pity, or to blame—
To chide, to hope, to pray—it watching stands,
But never to condemn. A Mother's heart
Might throb itself away in patient woe—   20
Might break to end its pang—but never, never
Could deem her child a thing of vice or shame.
God bless thee, boy! and make thee stainless, pure,
Upright and true, e'en as my thought doth paint thee.

DRAMATIS PERSONAE[2]

CAIUS GRACCHUS.

OPIMIUS, } Roman Senators.
LUCULLUS, }

POMPONIUS, } Friends of Gracchus.
LICINIUS, }

FULVIUS, *Factious Citizen.*

SEPTIMULEIUS, *Citizen.*

LIVIUS DRUSUS, *Tribune.*

PHILOCRATES, *Slave of Gracchus.*

CORNELIA, *Mother of the Gracchi.*

LICINIA, *Wife of Caius Gracchus.*

Senators, Citizens, Tribune, Child, etc.

SCENE: *Rome; Carthage.*[3]

---

2. Designated "Characters," and preceding "To My Son," in 1851 ed.
3. "The Scene is at Rome. First Scene of Fourth Act, in Carthage" (1851 ed.).

ACT I.

SCENE I. *A Street of Rome.*

POMPONIUS[4] *and Citizens.*

Pomp. Orestes stays to keep his quaestor with him.[5]
First Cit. And will he bear it, think you?
Pomp.   Will who bear it?
First Cit. Why, Caius Gracchus.
Pomp.   Truly, I think not.
    He's not the man I deem him, if he bear
    Outrage so foul and grossly palpable.   5
    No longer mince these senators their doings,
    But boldly now (enough that Gracchus did them)
    His noblest acts they read in backward sense.
    With juggler's slight the cheated eye to trick,
    They show black, white; white, black; and merit trip   10
    From virtue into fault.
Second Cit.   We've heard the talk
    How, when the Senate could not manage it,
    He from the cities for our troops procured
    Their needed clothing; and how fumed the Senate
    Because, forsooth, 'twould make the people love him.   15
Pomp. Yes, but ye have not heard how, few days since,
    Micipsa sent ambassadors to say
    That, through regard to Caius Gracchus, he
    To our Sardinian troops would furnish corn—
    And wot ye, how the Senate sent their thanks?[6]   20
First Cit. Well, what said they?
Pomp.   They said—but mark me well;
    Note what paternal love they guard us with—

---

4. Marcus Pomponius (Rufus?) and Licinius are recorded as the *hetairoi* (comrades) of Gaius Gracchus (Plutarch *Gaius Gracchus* 16.4–17.1). Velleius Paterculus (2.6.6) adds that Pomponius was an *eques* (knight) and compares him in his death to Horatius Cocles, who "kept the bridge" against King Porsenna. See also Valerius Maximus 4.7.2.

5. Lucius Aurelius Orestes as consul in 126 went to Sardinia to suppress an insurrection there and remained as proconsul until 122, when he came back to Rome to celebrate a triumph. Gaius Gracchus was a member of his staff as quaestor but in 124 returned to Rome without his commander's permission.

6. Micipsa (misspelled "Micipia" in 1851 ed.) was, from 148 to 118, king of Numidia, in northern Africa, south and west of Carthage.

They said they would not take one grain of the corn;
Our troops might starve, ere they should live from aid
That through the means of Caius Gracchus came. 25
First Cit. Fie! Fie! you joke with us! Did they say that?
Pomp. Ay, and the ambassadors, with loud insult thrust
Forth from the Senate-house, were bid begone,
To tell Micipsa that his proffered aid
Rome needed not; that we were rich in corn; 30
That Caius Gracchus had no other end,
Only his name to wind to Rome, by sending
These hired flatterers of his proud ambition.
Such words, and other oft, as rough repeated,
They were bid take with them, and pushed away 35
From our proud Senate-halls. And now our troops
May starve, forsooth, or steal, or eat their bucklers.
Ye know, ye Roman citizens, how full
Our granaries are! What though we die like rats,
And through our sewers if dead corpses sweep 40
Foully putrescent? Our patricians bear
Musk to their noses, scented vinegar,
Snuffing of spices; swear these corpses have
A stench plebeian, most unfit and vexing
To their patrician, nice olfactories! 45
We die! What then? The Senate is content,
So we live not through Caius Gracchus' means!
First Cit. These are our rich!
Pomp. Ay; and the sequel now
We find of this, his crime unpardonable,
That Caius still must in Sardinia drag 50
A longer life of exile.
Third Cit. Of our Senate
This then is the decree?
Pomp. Ay; doff your caps!
Be humbly thankful; bow to it, my brothers;
This the decree of our patrician fathers! *Clamors and hissing.*

Enter OPIMIUS *and* LUCULLUS.[7]

---

7. Lucius Opimius as praetor in 125 suppressed the revolt of Fregellae; as consul in 121, his colleague being absent in Gaul, he was instructed by a senatorial *consultum ultimum* (final decree) to deal with Gaius Gracchus and his followers, killing or condemning to death by trial some three thousand citizens; restored and dedicated the temple of Concord; found

Opim. What noisy riot's here? What have ye, thus
    Gathering in crowds, to plot and murmur at?
First Cit. We would have Gracchus back.
Opim.   Have Gracchus back!
    Gracchus is at his post; what would ye more?
    He's honored in his office, and remains
    Selected to it, by the Consul's will.
Third Cit. Ay; long enough you've honored him. We'd like
    To see him back, and hear his own account
    Of matters in Sardinia.
Opim.   Wranglers ever!
    Thus are ye always, restless, discontent,
    And gaping with large mouths, at what, ye know not.
    Leave Gracchus to his duties, and the Senate
    Will give to the country's servants honor due.
    Off to your work! The days are turning long,
    That ye find time in the streets to linger thus,
    So many hours of your nothings talking.
First Cit. We talk of Caius Gracchus.
Opim.   Insolent!
    Who heeds of what ye talk! Off! off! I say.
    Are ye not satisfied your share to leave
    To your own tribunes, of the government?
    You'd all be lords, forsooth, and make your laws
    The hungry appetite to suit of each
    New, squalling brat, who comes into the world
    To help eat out our city dry, and then
    Put finger in his eye, and pule and whine,
    To catch his neighbor's dinner. Off! begone!
    Away to your work; and meddle not, nor make;
    For ye might chance to break, where ye would mend.
First Cit. [*Aside.*] Thus they out-talk us. We had best away,

---

guilty in 109 of corruption and accepting bribes when supervising the partition of Numidia after the death of Micipsa, he went into exile. The identity of LSM's Lucullus is not certain. A Lucius Licinius Lucullus was praetor by 154, consul in 151; another Lucius Licinius Lucullus, praetor in 104; a Publius Licinius Lucullus, tribune of the plebs in 110. None is plausible; it is likely that LSM created a necessary confidant to Opimius, borrowing for her fictional character the name of the most famous Lucullus, general and aesthete of the first century B.C., whose biography was written by Plutarch. No Lucullus appears as a character in Marie-Joseph Chénier's *Caius Gracchus* (1792), Vincenzo Monti's *Caio Gracco* (1800), or James Sheridan Knowles' *Caius Gracchus* (1815, 1823).

But let us give one cheer before we go.
[*Aloud.*] Huzza for Caius Gracchus!
Citizens. Huzza! huzza! 85
Exeunt Citizens, with Pomponius.
Luc. Do you note that?
Opim. Ay, damn him! Note it well!
He'll be the incubus will ride us yet;
And faith, he'll spare no spurring when he mounts.
His flashing eye has that within it speaks
A daring spirit, near which, did he live, 90
Tiberius now would seem to us mild and humble.[8]
His voice has tones which strike into the heart.
I late was in Sardinia, and I heard
When he addressed the troops. There was a thrill
Upon each noted wording of his tongue 95
That made me shiver. Terror was upon me,
And why I knew not. While I hated him,
And could have plunged a dagger to his heart,
Tears crept into mine eyes, and I must weep
When he upbraided them their want of duty. 100
I felt as if myself had sinned, and been
The recreant soldier whom his tongue disdained.
And when he spurred them to a nobler course,
My bounding heart burst forth its loud huzza;
Spite of myself, it worshipped Caius Gracchus. 105
And yet I hate him. If his burning words
Can stamp them so, upon a heart like mine,
Which nature, circumstance, and every tie
Point him its bitter, great antagonist,
What wonder if the people hail him home, 110

---

8. Tiberius Sempronius Gracchus, elder (by nine years) brother of Gaius, as tribune of the plebs in 133 proposed agrarian legislation intended to reform the use of Roman public land, now in the hands of the wealthy, by redistributing it among poorer citizens. Despite the support of many aristocrats, the Senate was able to oppose the legislation; thereupon Tiberius took his laws directly to the people's assemblies, an act legal but against custom, where the laws were passed and a commission, of which Tiberius and his brother were members, set up to carry out the laws' provisions. When Tiberius announced his intention to run for the office of tribune the following year, he and some of his supporters were surprised on the Capitol by a mob of senators and their clients, led by the Pontifex Maximus, Scipio Nasica, and murdered. Scipio Nasica and his victim Tiberius Gracchus were first cousins, their mothers being sisters.

Not with applause, but wild and frantic transport!
Luc.   He must not come; for the ripe city waits,
   Like willing damsel, wanton at his wish,
   To fall into his arms.
Opim.   He must not come,
   If art or fraud can hinder. I have feared him   115
   Since first (how well I note the day) he stood,
   Forgetting all the sham of modesty
   That he had nursed to cheat our foresight off,
   And in the rostra boldly dared to stand
   In loud defence of Vettius.[9] How he threw   120
   From his bared shoulder the discarded gown!
   And stamped, and strutted, in fierce passion casting
   His fluent words in eloquent appeal
   Forth to the trancèd people, who screamed out,
   Maddened almost for joy, their raptured triumph,   125
   In hailing their plebeian orator.
   I hate the villain, from my heart's deep core,
   And I would scant at nothing which could cast
   The people from their love and worship of him.
   Pshaw! here comes trooping back the noisy crowd;   130
   I have no stomach for their prate today—
   Let us pass on.   *Exeunt.*

SCENE II. *The same.*

Enter Citizens, with POMPONIUS *and* FULVIUS.[10]

First Cit.   Huzza for Caius Gracchus! Coming back!
   Huzza! Huzza!
Second Cit.   Huzza for Fulvius too!
   Come, three times three! Huzza! huzza! huzza!
Third Cit.   But tell me first, what mean you? that he'll come
   Spite of the Senate's orders?
Ful.   Bah! unlearn,   5
   If ye are Romans, that poor starling note,

---

9. This speech is mentioned by Plutarch (*Gaius Gracchus* 1.3); Gaius Gracchus enjoyed a very high reputation as an orator, as such praised by Cicero, although disliking Gracchus' politics (e.g., *Brutus* 125–26). Nothing is known of Vettius or the charge against him.

10. Marcus Fulvius Flaccus, a supporter of Tiberius Gracchus, was elected a member of Tiberius' agrarian commission (which survived its founder) in 130, consul in 125, and tribune of the plebs in 122; his two sons were killed with him in 121.

> Ever the same of "*orders*," "*Senate's orders*"!
> Are ye not men to feel when ye are trampled?
> Are ye not men to turn, if ye be struck?
> Or will ye bide the *Senate's orders* still,   10
> And fight, and work, and pine, and starve, and die,
> By senatorial, august decree!

Third Cit.   But still it is unheard of that a quaestor,
> Abandoning his post, should suddenly,
> Thus unattended, leave his general.   15
> It is a knotty question, and I'll ask
> Our tribune Livius Drusus, who comes yonder,
> What is the law of right, in such a case.[11]

Pomp.   Ask Livius Drusus! He's but half a tribune;
> For with his conscience while the Senate tampers,   20
> He dallies with their gold, and fingers it
> Until truth finds no color in his eyes,
> But only yellow gilded. Let him pass.

Second Cit.   Nay, let him speak; he is our tribune still,
> And slander may mis-speak him.

Enter DRUSUS.

>   You have heard   25
> Some talk perhaps of Gracchus' coming home,
> And that he's looked for presently. We're puzzled
> To know what we should think of the affair.

Dru.   Think of it, as all quiet citizens
> Should think of mutiny against the laws   30
> Of our paternal Senate. Think of it
> As of a bad example, to be shunned,
> And meet him with your frowns.

Ful.   Ah! who is this?
> My once-time friend! Why Livius Drusus, you,
> When last I quitted Rome ('tis, let me see,   35
> Some three, four years ago) were then, me-seems,
> A noble-minded Roman, who cringed not
> Flattering the mighty rich. 'Tis true, this gown

---

11. Marcus Livius Drusus, tribune of the plebs in 122, opposed Gaius Gracchus and his adherents; consul in 112; celebrated a triumph after his proconsulship in Macedonia (110); censor in 109. LSM's harsh view of his character is not shared by her source, Plutarch (*Gaius Gracchus* 8.4–10.2).

           Was of a coarser texture; Livius showed
           Less exquisite in dress. I'm from the camp, 40
           And have forgot how city manners change;
           This butterfly, fresh from the chrysalis,
           Must read my lesson to me. When he crawled
           In caterpillar form, I can remember
           That Caius Gracchus was to him a God, 45
           To whom he could not low enough demean
           And bow himself to the earth; but now his wings,
           Belike, being spread, he'd soar a higher flight.
           I crave your pardon, Drusus; you would take
           Your place in the Senate; or, at least, have lands 50
           And monies to re-gild those gaudy wings.
           True! true! all this must be; and then, of course,
           When, in the palm of every Senator
           Who meets you bowing, glittering silver lies,
           And with his "Good-day, Drusus," he doth slip 55
           The bait into your sleeve, how can it be
           That Gracchus should be other than a scoundrel!
           Faugh! Let us go! His cant doth sicken me!
           Paternal Senate, says he? Ha! ha! ha!
           Paternal humbug! Curse it! Let me pass. 60
                                                      Exit with Pomponius.
Dru.   Hear, citizens! This is your Gracchus' friend!
       Note how he taunts your tribune, and judge then
       What to expect from him who taught the lesson.
       This forwardness it is for you to check.
       When Gracchus comes, be shy of him, and cold; 65
       With distant look as of inquiry stand,
       Staring as though his features were forgot,
       And you would try to think if you had seen
       The stamp of them before; then shake your heads
       And turn away indifferent. Hark ye farther, 70
       Let's have no palming with him. Mark ye well?
Second Cit.   Ay, ay; let us alone. We'll make him know
       How to respect our honorable Senate.
Dru.   Well then, remember.   *Exit Drusus.*
First Cit.   That's our tribune, is it?
       And you will mind him! Curse you for a fool 75
       And scurvy knave! This Drusus is not worth
       One little finger of our Caius Gracchus,

    And yet you stand there, staring while he talks
    As though his words were oracles.
Second Cit.   Be still;
    Let me alone and mind your own affairs.   80
    See how your Gracchus will work out of this!   *Exeunt.*

      SCENE III. *Room in* Cornelia's *house.*

       Cornelia[12] *and* Licinia.[13]

Cor. Nay, stay within doors, daughter; 'tis the place
   Most meet and fitting woman. In a crowd
   Showing like this the angry feelings, jarring
   And froth of human passion, if you track
   In loneliness your unprotected way,   5
   You chance to meet rough words and harsh misuse.
Lic. But only some few yards! Pray let me go!
   I'll wrap my mantle well, so none shall know me.
Cor. And should you chance to meet your husband thus,
   What would you gain? With that wild crowd around you, 10
   You would not dare to greet him to his home:
   A quiet comeliness there is, becomes
   A woman's greeting; and believe me, dear,
   However daring bold himself may be,
   Man never loves, within a woman's eye,   15
   To see the mimic of his conduct glassed.
   'Tis meek endurance, quiet fortitude,
   That make her life and beauty. We may rear
   Heroes, whose dauntless will shall shake the world,
   Or like a moral Atlas, bear its burden,   20

---

12. Cornelia was the daughter of Publius Cornelius Scipio Africanus, the conqueror of Hannibal. Her maternal grandfather, Lucius Aemilius Paullus, was one of the consuls commanding the Roman army at the battle of Cannae in 216, in which he was killed (see chap. 2 above, "Separate Secession," p. 40). Her husband, Tiberius Sempronius Gracchus, was twice consul (177 and 163), celebrated two triumphs, and was censor (169). Her learning and cultivation were renowned; her letters, of which some disputed fragments survive, were commended by Cicero (*Brutus* 211) and Quintilian (1.1.6).

13. Licinia was the daughter of Publius Licinius Crassus Dives Mucianus, who replaced Tiberius Gracchus on the agrarian commission; succeeded Scipio Nasica as Pontifex Maximus in 132; was consul in 131; proconsul of Asia in 130, he was captured by rebels against Rome and put to death. Forbidden, like the wife of Fulvius, to go into mourning for her dead husband, Licinia was also deprived of her dowry (Plutarch *Gaius Gracchus* 17.5). There seems to have been one daughter of the marriage; no son is known.

	A universe of care, upon their shoulders.	
	But in our bosoms if too fierce the flame	
	That feeds such spirit-struggles, we must check,	
	Or drive it back, at least, to seeming quiet.	
	If hard the effort, it is woman's task.	25
	Her passions, if not smothered, must be hid,	
	Till, in their faintly-beating pulse, herself	
	Will scarcely know her blood the same which bounds	
	Through manlier veins unchecked.	
Lic.	But mother, you	
	Methinks are hardly glad to know he's coming.	30
	Your cheek has found no flush of expectation,	
	Your eye no glance of triumph. There you sit	
	And argue calmly with me, while I'm mad	
	To strain him to my heart.	
Cor.	Your love, my child,	
	Is wild with youth. Mine, sobered with life's age,	35
	By thought and sorrow tamed to curb itself,	
	Is therefore not less true, and might perchance	
	Die for the loved one, full as soon as yours.	
Lic.	But tell me, mother, when you heard it said	
	Your son was coming home, why did a tear	40
	Start to your eye? And while my poor heart beat	
	And fluttered with the wildness of its hope,	
	Why did you simply wipe that tear away,	
	Nor ever even say, "I'm glad to know it"?	
	Surely you love him, mother!	
Cor.	Surely, yes.	45
	But see, the loved one here!	

Enter GRACCHUS.[14]

---

14. Gaius Sempronius Gracchus adopted, and expanded, the policy of his brother Tiberius, whom he also desired to avenge. As tribune of the plebs in 123, and again in 122, he secured the passage of a large body of legislation which, among other things, assured wheat to the Roman plebs at a subsidized price, founded colonies to relieve overpopulation in Italy (including one at the site of Carthage, destroyed in 146, the founding of which Gracchus supervised in person), and transferred the courts trying senatorial extortion from the senators to the equestrian order. But his legislation extending Roman citizenship to Rome's Latin allies and Latin status to other Italians was opposed by Livius Drusus and others, who sought to detach the plebs from Gracchus by surpassing Gracchus' own laws in the plebs' favor, and by taking advantage of the plebs' reluctance that their own privileges should be extended.

Grac.   Ah! my sweet bird,
Who watchest for thy mate, now tune thy song
To welcome home the wanderer. Mother, here
I bring you home the heart whose thought hath been
Ever for you, this dear one, and for Rome.   50
Cor.   Welcome to Rome, my boy.
Lic.   But thou art strange!
Why truly, mother, thou didst promise right
That I had lost my love. This is not he!
This bearded soldier, seamed and browned in the wars!
Grac.   What, saucy one! Would'st thou disown thy lord?   55
Nay, I am used to keep a stricter rule,
And will allow no mutiny in the camp.
So rebel, come, that I may punish thee
With this, and this—and thus with kisses plague thee!
Lic.   Nay; get thee gone. I must perforce admit,   60
By these rough ways, thou'rt still the feather-head
Who left me here, some many years agone.
I thought thou hadst grown wiser.
Grac.   How's this, mother?
You have not been half strict enough, I fear,
In the training of this sauce-box. But, your pardon,   65
I am a fool; for I stand trifling here,
While your grave look has some big import in it.
What is it, mother? Speak. I too have learned
To wrap me much in deeper thoughts of late.
Lic.   Nay, Gracchus—prithee, love! nay, not that look!   70
Thou mak'st me thus already weep to think
That thou art come again to this stern Rome.
Grac.   What, have you not grown older? Still the same
My little pet must pout its rosy lip,
And sulk at business, when it rivals love!   75
Smooth down thy ruffled feathers, pretty one;
For surely not my wish, but need, doth force
My thought aside so soon, to wander from thee.
Mother, your anxious look should find its words.
Cor.   Unwillingly, with harshness thus to break   80

Gracchus and his ally Fulvius, when they were not reelected to the tribunate for 121, were faced with the dismantling of much of their work; riots broke out (on whose responsibility, is not clear); and Gracchus, along with Fulvius and many others of their supporters, was killed.

  Upon our happy meeting; but I fear
  Each moment lost is so much life-blood drawn,
  Weakening your cause, to make it hang its head
  As evil-conscienced, or as sick at heart.
  Rome's all afire; and your best lovers now   85
  Half-turned against you, pondering, shake their heads
  As doubtful of your course.
Grac.   What! would they wish
  To see me drag out life the Senate's drudge?
  To rot away my soul, like worthless carcass
  In the highway cast, for daws and crows to pick at!   90
  Toil down my spirit to old age's weakness!
  All for the profit of the proud usurpers,
  Who from between our teeth the hard-earned bread
  Snatch wantonly, to make them luxuries
  At which the starving people stare, and wonder   95
  What are their uses and their purposes!
Cor. Be cool! be cool! and heed that you do not,
  In blaming one extreme, to the other rush.
  But for the present, think first of yourself,
  And purge yourself from rashness. Claim your right,   100
  Making appeal to the censors of your cause.[15]
  Where you are slandered, charge the slander back,
  And cleanse the name that envy seeks to blot.
Grac. Mother, you're right. I loiter here too long.
  Farewell, Licinia, I'll be quickly back.   105
  Send your best wishes with me and cheer up.   *Exeunt.*

SCENE IV. *Street of Rome.*

SEPTIMULEIUS[16] *and several Citizens.*

Sept. Now is the time for Gracchus' friends to rise;
  And I may count, I'm sure, as one of them.

---

15. Two censors were elected at Rome to conduct the census, or enrollment, of the citizen population every five years; they also had responsibility for public morals, leasing public lands and buildings, and examining the rolls of senators and knights, any one of whom the censors could eject for offenses falling under their jurisdiction; they served for eighteen months. Gracchus appeared before the censors of 125–24, Gnaeus Servilius Caepio and Lucius Cassius Longinus Ravilla.

16. Septimuleius (misspelled "Septimulieus" in 1851 ed.) is mentioned by Plutarch as an enterprising friend of Opimius: having stolen the head of Gracchus from those who had

        He knows what he's about, and he has forced
        The censors to a hearing. He's an eye
        Into the marrow of a thing that looks
        As deep as any man's—
First Cit.   And you, who watch
        Ever the veering wind, make up your mind
        That now into his sails it fairly blows,
        And trim accordingly. I hope indeed
        Your judgment may, for his sake, be a true one.
Sept.   'Tis time we should of the event hear news.
        Ah! here it comes! Licinius and Pomponius;
        They'll tell us all about it.

                Enter LICINIUS *and* POMPONIUS

            Good-day! Good-day!
        My hearty greetings do attend ye both.
        Good luck to you, and all of Gracchus' friends!
Pomp.   You love him well.
Sept.   Ay; and I hope not low
        He counts in his esteem my humble service.
        Now pray ye, let us hear how goes the trial!
Pomp.   Fully the censors have acquitted him.
        How could they less, when truths showered on them so?
        He showed how he his duty had surpassed,
        And served for years, more than the law obliged;
        How he had gone forth rich, and come back poor,
        While others piled their wealth of hoarded gains,
        Stolen treasures, griped from conquered provinces
        And towns 'neath taxes groaning. When they dared
        Implied conspiracy to charge him with,
        His flashing indignation struck all dumb
        The cowardly accusers, flinching, who
        Did eat the words which scarce had passed their lips;
        Their strangled statements shuffling, turning o'er,
        Backward their import, to excuse it, working.
Sept.   Of what conspiracy could they accuse him?
Pomp.   Of favoring commotions 'mong the allies,

---

killed him—Opimius had promised an equal weight in gold for it—Septimuleius enlarged his reward by scooping the brain out of the skull and replacing it with molten lead (*Gaius Gracchus* 17.3–4).

   And waking up revolt throughout the states 35
   Of conquered Italy.
Licinius.   Ah! there peeps out
   The stumbling block, that lies in Caius' path.
   But we'll pass on. Good-day to you, citizens.
   Will you walk with us, Septimuleius?
Sept.   No,
   I have much pressing business on my hands. 40
   Wish you good-day, and much prosperity,
   To you and all of Gracchus' friends. Their merits,
   Weighed truly, are enough for them. Farewell. *Exit with Citizens.*
Pomp. Fair words and soft, but, like the babbling brook,
   Not over deep, methinks.
Licinius.   He is of those 45
   Who follow with the stream, and guides his course
   By the full current's veering; a light thing,
   Whose talk is worth the noting, as it shows
   Only—true weathercock—the changing wind.
   But not so Fulvius, whom just now we named; 50
   He in his character, I fear, is fixed,
   And that none of the wisest; while so far
   He has besotted the great mind of Gracchus
   To think too kindly of him, that it thus
   Doth much out-calculate his true desert. 55
   'Tis oft a lofty spirit shows in this
   The weakness of its temper, taking up,
   Through love of one of a far meaner soul,
   Some high conception, which doth catch the stamp
   And likeness of its own excelling virtues. 60
   Of noble natures 'tis the practised fault,
   Thus to mislead their judgments to the thinking
   Those whom they love as noble as themselves.
   And thus his soul in keeping Caius gives
   To Fulvius, who by noisy blustering drags— 65
   And by his plottings and dissentious riot—
   Unkind suspicion on the name of Gracchus.
Pomp. But you're too hard on Fulvius. There's no proof
   That he has tampered with the states, nor been
   The cause of this disturbance.
Licinius.   No—no proof; 70
   But there's suspicion rank; and his demeanor,

With loud and quarrelsome debate, doth give
Much strength to rumor. Were't not for the love
That Gracchus bears him, there had been a search
Of close inspection, when great Scipio died, 75
And all men whispered "poison."[17] Many then
On Fulvius cast suspicion's clouded eye;
But he was Gracchus' friend. This was the claim
That made his evil sacred. The great love
That from the city's heart flowed out on Gracchus 80
Hushed up the loud-mouthed vengeance. But there was,
In this heart-homage even, a dark taint
Upon the name of Gracchus, which was joined
With that of Fulvius, while men whispered low—
Casting uneasy glances, as though thought, 85
Fearing to speak, yet could not hush itself—
Longed to find words, yet doubting trembled still
To think those words o'erheard. While no man dared
To boldly name a guilt, yet all seemed stunned,
As wildered by some dark imagining. 90
O'er Gracchus fell the shadow of a shame,
Whilst he, for love of Fulvius, dared not stand
To boldly face inquiry, and cast off
The sickly taint of that day's damnèd work.
Pomp. Would it had never been! For Drusus now, 95
The Senate's tool and their most vigilant spy,
Makes this the point, whence all his venom casts
Its evil spite on Gracchus. 'Tis a lever,
Which, though it lies all rusted by disuse,
From its forgotten corner now he drags, 100
To work his mischief. Still I have a kindness
That clings to Fulvius. Had you heard him lash
This very Drusus, when he wagged his tongue
In evil words to raise the citizens

---

17. Publius Cornelius Scipio Aemilianus, twice consul (in 147 and 134), elected censor in 142, the destroyer of Carthage in the Third Punic War (149–46), was by birth the grandson of Lucius Aemilius Paullus who died at Cannae, and thus Cornelia's first cousin; he was adopted by the childless son of Cornelia's father, Scipio Africanus; he married (the marriage was unhappy and childless) Sempronia, Cornelia's daughter and the sister of Tiberius and Gaius Gracchus. Gaius Gracchus served under him at the siege and capture of Numantia in Spain (134–33). Despite these connections, however, Scipio Aemilianus was opposed to the policies of his brothers-in-law. His sudden death in 129 was attended with rumors of murder.

                    'Gainst the return of Gracchus, you'd have felt,   105
                    With all his noisy faults, he has a heart,
                    And that belongs to Gracchus.
Licinius.   I yet doubt it.   [[*Exeunt.*]]

ACT II.

SCENE I. *Street of Rome.*

SEPTIMULEIUS *and crowd of Citizens.*

Sept. I knew it! bless the Gods! We're almost now
         Upon the ladder's top. The people's voice
         Will hoist up Gracchus! Then, good luck, his friends!
First Cit.   Spite of the Senate they will make him tribune.
Sept. Ay; to be sure they will! and he will make   5
         A glorious tribune too! Pray ye, remember
         I've always been his friend. No shuffler, I,
         To catch the passing time. I've ever kept
         My service in his cause, and I know, too,
         He notes my merits kindly.

                    Enter FULVIUS.

Ful.   Huzza, boys!   10
         The votes are counted. Gracchus is our tribune!
         Huzza for Caius Gracchus!
Citizens.   Huzza! huzza!
Sept. I told you so! I'm one of his best friends!
         Huzza for Caius Gracchus!
First Cit.   Now we've got
         A tribune who, as cunningly as need be,   15
         May pose the law against your Livius Drusus.
Ful.   Ay, let our lordly rulers champ the bit
         And fret their hearts out; 'tis not like that Gracchus
         Will abdicate the tribuneship to please them.
         He's fairly mounted and he'll ride them down.   20
         'Twill do me good to see the proud patrician
         Bending beneath the spur, plunging and foaming,
         Like high-bred courser vaulting from the will
         Of who would ride him; forced again to crouch,
         Groaning in mingled rage and agony,   25

        Till whip and spur at last have done their work,
        And the proud blood is tamed to bow its neck,
        Offering its head to meet the ready rein
        Which leads him to his task.
First Cit.   Bravely we did
        Our duty, did we not, in the election?
Ful.   Bravely you did, and well. Before your might,
        Like a scared thing, the startled Senate shrank.
Second Cit.   Now let's away to drink our tribune's health.
First Cit.   No, no. You know that Gracchus said we should
        Be orderly, and that the people showed—
        These were his words—"most nobly when they spoke
        With calm decision and with majesty
        The nation's voice; and that each citizen
        Should as a fraction of the breathing whole
        Maintain in him his country's dignity."
        So let us all go home, and have no noise.
Ful.   Pooh! pooh! 'Twas for the Senate Gracchus spoke.
Second Cit.   He said the people, though.
Ful.   Well, I know that.
        But, simpleton, his words were meant to move
        The Senate's ears, not yours. 'Twas but a flourish.
First Cit.   And yet, I thought the words were from his heart;
        And more than that, I found a judgment in them.
        We citizens are too much given, in truth,
        To drunkenness and riot.
Ful.   Bah! good sheep!
        Would you too turn philosopher? Be off!
        And if you like, get drunk. Why should he curb
        (Gracchus is far too wise a man for that)
        Of their poor pleasures, the vexed citizens?
Third Cit.   Come; Fulvius ought to know; he's Gracchus' friend,
        And has a heart too, for the people's cause.
        He knows the right, I'm sure, better than we.   *Exeunt.*

SCENE II. *House of* CORNELIA.

LICINIA, CORNELIA, *and* LICINIUS.

Lic.   Come, tell us all about it. Pray, Licinius,
        Be not so chary of your words. My mother,
        Though she says little, loves as well as I

        To hear you talk of Gracchus. 'Twas, they say,
        The greatest crowd that ever was in Rome;
        And we know well, that all the Senate's power
        Was listed to oppose him.
Licinius.   Lady, yes.
        But 'gainst their combined force, backed as it was
        By most obsequious bribery and corruption,
        The stream of life came pouring into Rome,
        As though, the being of the state in danger,
        Its life-blood all came rushing to the heart
        To keep existence in. And boldly did
        The general pulse beat forth new-given life.
        'Twas a new Rome, as through its crowded ways
        The swaying populace, bent on its course,
        And o'er the Campus Martius sweeping, showed,
        In its flood-tide, a human ocean rising,
        The murmuring of whose restless waves spoke out
        Oppression's death. Your husband, noble lady,
        And your proud son, Cornelia, through its midst
        Passed stately on; the people's voices claiming
        Not as a favor done him, but a due
        Owed to themselves and Rome. And boldly they
        To the call responded. From their bending rafters
        The house-tops even, straining 'neath the weight
        Of gathered thousands, echoed back the name
        As spoke the people's voice, "Gracchus for Tribune."
Cor.   Then it was nobly done! No need was there
        To cringing beg a flattered people's voice.
Licinius.   No; rather even then, when he did ask
        Their voices from them, firmest he rebuked.
        But gently 'twas, with nobleness, as would
        The follies of his child a parent check.
        And still, meseemed, at each rebuke, they thronged
        More loving close around him.
Cor.   Gods! I thank ye,
        For that his spirit lags not in the race
        Of its youth's glorious promise. Here he comes.
        We'll go and greet our tribune to his home.   *Exeunt.*

SCENE III. *Street of Rome.*

OPIMIUS, LUCULLUS, *another Senator, and* LIVIUS DRUSUS.

Luc. We're beaten to our trenches, and we fight
Now for existence.
Sen. We must back a step.
Luc. Give back and we are lost. Our enemy
Will scarce with one step only let us pause;
But back, and back, and back, will hustle us, 5
Till his position he at will may choose.
Opim. He's like to choose it, act howe'er we may;
And yet with you I say, we must not back;
'Tis certain ruin. You must help us, Drusus.
Dru. Nay, I have tried my best. The people's will 10
Outdoes your plottings. I'm almost ashamed
That with them I too am not striving.
Opim. Pshaw!
Where's your ambition which would crush down Gracchus
And make yourself (what you to aspire have right
At least as full as he) Rome's one great man! 15
Have you so soon renounced the noble task,
That you already shirk its burden off?
And more, do you forget the benefit
That, in this duty's exercise, accrues
To your own person and your properties? 20
Your fortune will be made, e'en with the blow
That drives away these hungry blood-suckers.
Monies and lands a grateful Senate gives
To who thus nobly props his country's cause.
Dru. In truth the Senate doth with liberal hand 25
Dispense its favors; and, although the mob
Doth cavil at the freedom of the gifts
Its generosity dispenses to me,
My conscience clears me; and I must confess
Too hungry grasping is this eager mob; 30
An humbler deportment it should bear;
And, while I love the people, I must side
Thus far with noble Senators. I'll do
What in me lies, to crush the spirit out
From this proud faction. Honesty doth point 35
As well as interest to the quelling it.

Opim.   Most certainly; and common sense doth prove
　　　There's honesty in interest. Shall I starve
　　　Or live a beggar because chance hath put
　　　What should be mine in food and property　　　　　　40
　　　Into another's hand? Most surely not;
　　　For thus defrauding self and wife and children,
　　　Is it not greater sin, than if I drain
　　　The stranger's surplus off? I much misdoubt
　　　This ever-prosing honesty that leaves　　　　　　45
　　　On homely pulse its advocate to starve,
　　　To rear in rags his children up, while thrusting
　　　By way of comfort down their hungry throats
　　　Old saws and adages, importing still
　　　That honesty is the best policy.　　　　　　50
　　　'Tis a fine lesson for who'll act it out;
　　　Though, truth to say, I've found it ever was
　　　A glorious virtue to grow lean upon,
　　　And apt excuse for lazy ne'er-do-wells
　　　To trap their misery in—　　　　　　*Noise without.*
　　　　　　What tumult's this?　　　　　　55
Sen.   It is the crowd whom Fulvius feeds with drink
　　　And tops them to the height of all their whims.
　　　I have a hope to see this Fulvius prove
　　　The doubtful spoke, where Gracchus' wheel shall crack;
　　　A rotten prop at heart, which must give way　　　　　　60
　　　When most the pressure of the time shall need it.
　　　Hark! How they join his name with that of Gracchus,
　　　Twin-brothers in their hearts.

　　　　　　Noise approaches, with cries of "Gracchus," "Fulvius," etc.

Dru.　　　　　　They come this way;
　　　'Twere best I should pass on. 'Tis fault to them
　　　That I too much frequent the company　　　　　　65
　　　Of honorable Senators. I'll go.
　　　Though pure my purposes, most prudent 'twere
　　　I should not meet them here.　　　　　　*Exit Drusus.*
Opim.　　　　　　Ay; go thy ways
　　　To salve thy conscience for the job on hand,
　　　And into love with meanness cheat thy thought.　　　　　　70
　　　Bah! It is rank, and his offence's foulness
　　　Doth cast its filth upon ourselves who use it.

Would we were rid of the necessity!
The rotten thing doth haunt me with its stench.
But what means this?

Enter Citizens, riotously and drunken.

How now! What would ye here? 75
And whence this loud uncivil conduct? Come ye
By Gracchus sent, to edify the town
With beastly scenes of drunken merriment?
First Cit. [*drunk*] Please your honorable senatorships, we would—
Opim. Ye would—vile things! What care we what ye would! 80
Ye refuse of the city, foul excrescence
Upon a sickly growth! Is it for ye
We are so bandied by this Gracchus? Off!
If ye will play the beast, go shut ye up
In your own houses, tumble as ye will; 85
Get drunk and beat your wives; be hogs at home,
Ye drudges, it is all that ye are fit for!
But if your sovereign majesties would spare
Such exhibitions in the public streets,
Meseems to hide them were some point of wisdom. 90
Second Cit. Will't please your lordships hear us?
Opim. Hear ye! No.
But rid the soilèd streets of your foul tread,
And for the purer air you'd leave, we'll thank you.
Third Cit. Would you the right of citizens deny us?
Opim. Ye citizens, in troth!—Be off, vile spawn! 95
Ye refuse scum of a licentious city!
Your breaths do load the air. Be off! I say.
First Cit. We'd better go. They have small patience with us.
And truth to say, our addled brains are fit
But poorly for encounter with their wits. *Exeunt.* 100

SCENE IV. *Another part of Rome.*

Enter GRACCHUS, FULVIUS, *and* LICINIUS.

Grac. But you are too unruly. You have schooled
The citizens to riot. When they should
By hardy temperance, steady perseverance,
Push on to their great end, you rouse them idly
To drinking and excess. Those powers of mind 5

	Which to a resolute effort should be turned	
	You make them drown in license and debauch.	
Ful.	Why, one would think, you had not yet unlearned	
	Your school-boy lesson; that you truly deemed	
	The popular majesty an enthroned thought,	10
	And not a joke to gull the dirty crowd	
	And coax the votes from its high mightiness.	
Grac.	You word it well; an enthroned thought it is!	
	The might of mind, whose myriad streamlets meet,	
	One gathered flood of condensed light to form.	15
	Each dirty rivulet its ripple brings,	
	Which, in the sweeping current mingling, drops	
	Its dust and dross. Its purer part goes on,	
	And on, and on—until at last the whole,	
	By the great alchemy of reason, flows	20
	Pure as it must be, from its origin.	
	Thought sprang from God; and all bestained with earth,	
	Struggling and creeping still, at last the truth	
	Is forced upon the day. The world's great mind,	
	Though stumbling oft in error, must at last	25
	Work out its vexèd problem, and perfection,	
	Wrought from reflected deity in man,	
	Burst sun-like from the mist of error forth.	
Ful.	Strange pantheon this our mottled world, in sooth,	
	Of embryo deities? At a cheap rate	30
	You make your Gods, and their divinityships	
	Do trick themselves as easily in wisdom	
	Picked up, 'twould seem, in filth and public gutters.	
	Yon drunken blackguard, rolling in the dust,	
	And yonder snub-nosed, wide-mouthed, gaping crowd,	35
	With their shag-heads, and vacant staring eyes,	
	Are these the exponents of your godlike thought?	
Grac.	These, even these, are men; and I could weep	
	To see their nobler natures thus debased.	
	It is the sin of those who, better knowing,	40
	Do dam the stream, instead of cutting out	
	A clearer course to give its current way.	
	If yours the better mind, its effort turn	
	To raise, not crush them lower in their mire.	
Ful.	I must be off, or you till midnight preach,	45
	And their divinityships, the citizens	

	Whom you today address, will take it ill,	
	If you are hoarse, and thence not eloquent.	
	Farewell! may all the Gods shower blessings on you.	*Exit Fulvius.*
Licinius.	You waste your teaching on a heart like that.	50
Grac.	The heart is good. The head, in truth, sometimes,	
	For want of thought to steady it, doth wander	
	On bootless errands. 'Twill correct itself.	
Licinius.	The heart is sapless, rotten at the core;	
	And the head weakened by its selfishness.	55
	From head and heart alike, great thoughts are born;	
	The truly noble cannot sever them.	
	I'd shun the man who at his nature scoffs	
	And, trampling on his own divinity,	
	Feels not the *consciousness* of human greatness.	60
	Forgive me, that, but dealing in few words,	
	In honest sooth I'd warn you: shun this Fulvius.	
Grac.	He is my friend. I'll hear no ill of him.	
Licinius.	Gracchus, it cannot be, a mind like yours	
	Should fail to fathom such a shallow thing	65
	As this same Fulvius. Pray you—	
Grac.	Pray you, cease,	
	Nor stun me with unwelcome counsellings.	
Licinius.	But one word, only!	
Grac.	What! You'd quarrel, would you?	
	Who underrates my friend, doth carp at me.	
Licinius.	Would it were only at yourself I carped,	70
	For then you'd listen patiently; but here—	
	Well, well; I've done. Your frown speaks stinted patience,	
	And anger listens to no argument.	*Exeunt.*

SCENE V. *House of* CORNELIA.

CORNELIA *and* LICINIA.

Lic.	Mother, I'm sick with fear, and mad to see	
	Your brow so calm, while every heart-throb bursts	
	My breast with expectation. There are plots	
	And underhanded councillings; glances dark	
	And sidelong whispers, of I know not what.	5
	I fear me much, there's something wrong of late.	
	Caius seems wrapt and moody in his thought;	

      And, when I question him, he answers short
      With matters of no moment; how he hears
      This neighbor's bitch has puppied; or belike
      This other's cow has sickened in her horn;
      And how the corn hath musted in the ear,
      And harvest should be coming. These are not
      The thoughts which wrench his anxious heart in twain,
      And rob me of its larger moiety.
Cor. Poor child! You have not hardness for the time,
      And run to meet your sorrows—hugging them
      Like cherished visitors. I know not what
      The unquiet face of Rome doth indicate.
      We can but watch the struggle.
Lic.   Mother, no;
      We can do more; much more. Remember, mother,
      How you have lost one son. You've often wept
      And told the story to me of his fate.
      Oh mother! save this last one! Keep him close
      As jewel on your heart. Watch over him
      Like unweaned infant nestling at your breast!
Cor. Daughter, we can but wait until we find
      What darkens in the cloud which overhangs us.
      We know not if ambition stocks it full
      Big with black mischief, or if nobler worth
      But works its virtuous ends through shaded ways.
Lic. We know there's risk in it. This is enough.
      Then, mother, stop your son! Oh! hold him back!
      By all the throes that brought him into being,
      By all the hopes and fears that watched his growth,
      By all the pangs that even now I know
      Must rend your mother-heart to think of him,
      Oh! save him to that heart! Save him to me!
Cor. Daughter, to guide his course is not for me;
      Complete he stands, and in full manhood strong.
      No more my task his pliant youth to mould;
      Himself the drama of his life must make.
      But of his course, believe me, dear, could I,
      By the deep aspirations of my heart,
      Its unsketched outlines fix—the struggle come
      'Twixt life and honor—I would bid him die.

| | What though the effort burst my mother-heart!
| | When virtue's weighed 'gainst vice, good men must die
| | To throw their lives in the balance.
| Lic. | Mother! mother!

     You fright me with this passion! Not for nothing   50
     Did Etna late her baleful fires cast
     Ominous of evil. Trembling Sicily,
     To her foundations shaken, saw huge flames
     Burst from the bosom even of the sea;
     While the big waters swallowed up her coast   55
     In hungry menace of some coming ill,
     And subterranean mutterings spoke of woes
     Unmeasured and unknown! They come, and dark
     Their scowling shadows fright me.

Cor.   But why thus
     Trick out imagined ills in giant form,   60
     And ghastly robe with terrors! Thus we act
     Like foolish children, whispering goblin tales
     Until on end their bristled hair stands up;
     And, in the unnatural sound of their cramped breaths,
     They fancy whispering spirits at their backs,   65
     Strange steps in the loud beating of their hearts,
     And in their garments rustling some wild blast
     Of unimagined horror! Come, my girl,
     Cheer up, and be to Caius, if you can,
     A friend who loves his life less truly far   70
     Than his unsmerchèd honor.

Lic.   I will try;
     But mother, 'tis a lesson sad to con,
     And young am I to learn it.

                    Enter GRACCHUS.

                         Gracchus! Ah!
     My heart's best life!

Grac.   What! weeping, sweet one? fie!
     Your eyes are full of tears; you have not wrung   75
     The baby yet from out their stainèd lids.

Lic. Treat me then as a woman, and I'll try
     To hush the baby in me. Tell me what
     Works in your mind to make you almost shun me?
     And why I see you ever with such look   80

>   Of grave abstraction? Why you whispering start
>   When suddenly I meet you with your friends,
>   As though my presence jarred you? And that Fulvius
>   Who haunts your company, I love him not;
>   What have you still to do, whispering with Fulvius?   85
> *Grac.*   Pooh! pooh! a jealousy you have of Fulvius;
>   Some grudge of the young bride, yet unforgiven.
>   He made me frolic once too late of night,
>   When you, the pretty tyrant of my house,
>   A new-made wife (some se'nnight old) sat watching   90
>   And deemed my duty cold. Forgive him, love!
>   We'll lecture him to greater gravity.
> *Lic.*   It is not *that* which frets me, and you know it.
>   There's mischief in the wind. What is it, Gracchus?
> *Grac.*   A mischief, say you? Ah! belike the storm   95
>   Has scattered mother Tyra's brood of chicks.
>   Poor soul, I passed her at her post this morning,
>   Cluck, clucking on, as she herself had been
>   The very hen that hatched them.
> *Lic.*   Gracchus! Gracchus!
>   You'll break my heart, and yet I needs must laugh   100
>   To hear your folly.
> *Grac.*   Laugh then, sweet; 'tis best.
>   That rainbow face is pretty. Is't not, mother?
>   Forgive me, though, I am in haste; pray, mother,
>   The gown you fitted for me yesterday;
>   I must be off again.   *Exeunt.*   105

SCENE VI. *Public Square.*

Crowd of noisy Citizens.

> *First Cit.*   He must come presently. Would I could meet him
>   With clearer conscience. On last night's misdeeds
>   My aching head an ugly sermon preaches.
>   Of Fulvius I scarce know what we should think.
>   They say he's Gracchus' friend, but certainly   5
>   Their lessons oft run counter.
> *Second Cit.*   Truly, he helps
>   To make sad fools of us. Here Gracchus comes.
> *First Cit.*   I wish yon drunken crowd would hush its riot.

Enter GRACCHUS.
Great cheering and much drunken noise among Citizens.

Grac. Be still and hear me. You who've drugged your brains
       Until their surfeit doth of mind and thought   10
       Exclude the entrance quite: get home, sleep off
       This self-taught idiocy. Be men again
       Before ye come to prate of governing
       A people's councils. Your own vices lash,
       Lay bare your consciences—starve them to reason,   15
       And then you may be heard. Your voices now
       Are but the idiot's babbling, madman's yell!
       Ay, cower—shrink away; ye are no things
       To keep men company. Yourselves have cast
       In wantonness your noble birthrights from ye!   20
                              Many citizens steal away.
       Friends, brothers, Roman citizens, I come[18]
       As ye have willed it, that I may explain
       And speak to you concerning your own rights.
       Man has, in every station, rights his due.
       Our slaves look to their masters for support.   25
       The very claims we hold upon their labor
       Make us a rule to tender them again
       What comforts we can furnish to their lot.
       If placed by circumstance, necessity,
       Beneath our rule, protection thence we owe: 30
       And he evading basely these, degrades
       Himself below the thus defrauded slave.
       You, Romans, have a sterner government;
       For our rich nobles, who do make themselves
       Perforce the country's purse-holders, forget   35
       To leave some portion of your gains for you
       Whose toil and heart-ache won them. Are ye poor?
       Why do your starving infants beg in vain
       A hard, dry crust? Why are their shivering limbs
       Wrapt but in rags, as they cower tearful round   40
       The dying embers of your empty hearths?
       Are there no vacant lands, the people's due?
       Where are the rich fields that your fathers conquered?

---

18. This speech invokes the precedent, by echoing the first lines, of Antony's speech over the corpse of Julius Caesar (*Julius Caesar* 3.2.75–109).

And where the exuberant harvests that yourselves
Have made Rome's property? What justice gave them   45
New riches to the rich? The proud patrician
Who toiled not, bled not, in the gaining them;
Who sat at home by the fire and warmed himself
By talking over battles that *you* fought;
He waited for no law to make them his;   50
But by the strong hand of oppression seizes
The bread which should have fed your hungry babes.
Is there no corn in the market? You will find
A large abundance. There have lately been
New importations from the provinces.   55
Why do you starve, then? Why do you not buy?
You smile as though the bare idea were strange.
You cannot buy. You have no monies. Rich,
Usurious, speculates the plunderer
On your starvation. Beggars which you are   60
His robberies make you, and he taunts you then,
Mocking your poverty by this display,
Showing how rich the country is in grain,
While he, from hunger-clenchèd fingers, screws
To pay for a mere handful, your last doit!   65
With poverty your chilling bed-fellow,
And hugged by hunger, while ye thus are driven
To wrap ye in your rags and wait for death,
Who are those laborers, well-dressed, happy, sleek,
Tilling the fields which, citizens, are yours?   70
From the depopulated country fly
The shepherd and the husbandman, to make
Room for the rich man's slave. Beasts have their dens,
They hide them in their caves, and there may rest;
But you, who in the cause of Italy   75
Your heart's-blood spill, ye Roman citizens—
To you she gives no home! She leaves you nought
Save only God's light and the air you breathe!
The poor man has no home; he claims no shed
'Neath which his huddling brats may gather them.   80
From place to place the forlorn things he drags
And with their mother lays them on the earth
There, where the soldier sleeps. What mockery, then,
To call on such, ye generals of Rome,

And bid them fight for their domestic Gods, 85
Their homes and sepulchres! *Their* sepulchres!
Their fathers' bones are scattered to the winds,
And the patrician ploughs them through his fields,
Nor heeds plebeian graves! And yet they fight;
Plebeians fight and die. The Roman blood 90
Boils up in the combat and the victory's won,
For what? That these proud rich may sit and revel
In some new luxury, some dear-bought pleasure,
While you, ye so-called masters of the world,
In your possession hold no foot of ground! 95
To your assistance you have summoned me;
And, where the anxious thought you dared not word,
Your walls speak to me. Public monuments
In blotted and scrawled sentences implore
Succor to Rome. Dare ye then help yourselves? 100
On you I call, to make your effort too.
What can my single power? The slough is deep;
We must, if we would pass, unite our strength;
With shoulder to the wheel, and a great heart
Of resolute effort, we must bring the force 105
Of a whole people's thought, a nation's might.
And, when a nation acts, if 'twould not end
Its struggling cause in anarchy and license,
With calm endurance every citizen
Should feel the weight of the whole cause is his. 110
Rise to your task! Upon your souls let in
The light of reason. From the agglomerate crowd
Spring forth to life as individual men,
Conquering the world within yourselves, ere grasping
To rule the external. Be self-conscious, bold, 115
But never violent; though firm, yet curbing
Your passion's fierceness to due energy.
Your cause is just, and in its justice strong.
Make it not weak by tumult, angry riot,
Obstreperous threat, and vulgar, wordy menace. 120
Let reason, based on conscious truth, be backed
By resolution firm, and stubborn will,
With all its nerves strong knitted to endure.
If these the temper of your striving souls,
Then let us on. The trial lies before us. 125

But much I fear that ye will flinch the struggle.
There was a noble heart which throbbed to free
This trampled people to its natural rights;
And how were its bold efforts seconded?
Ye called on him for succor, as ye now   130
Call for my feebler help. Ye called, implored,
Entreated him—and then, and then—your blushes
May speak the tragedy, whose damning stain
Doth stamp upon your annals its dark blot!
What need I name that name, whose syllables   135
Each, in its separate wording, should call forth
A newer vengeance on the coward hearts
That shrank in danger from him! Ye know well
I speak to you of Tiberius. He who strove
With you, and for you, in the noble cause   140
Of his true heart's devotion. Are ye, Romans,
The sons of those who starting flew to arms
When, from a wanton insult to their tribune,
They by a foreign war wiped off the stain
Thus cast upon the country's majesty?[19]   145
They thought the doom of death fit punishment,
When, failing in respect, Veturius stood
Heedless, nor making way before their tribune
Who in the Forum passed him.[20] But *ye* saw,
In your most awful consecrated temple—   150
The holy capitol of Rome—the blood
Of your own sacred magistrate defile
Its violated walls; ye saw, nor shuddered;
Or, if ye shuddered at the sacrilege,
Ye stood and let his bloody corse be dragged   155
Like refuse carrion, through your city's streets.
Ye saw him, like a dead dog, tost in the waves
Of Tiber, which reluctant shrank, as fearing
To sanction crimes so horrible. 'Tis said
The naiads of the river rose that night,   160

---

19. The tribune, one Genucius, should perhaps be assigned to the year 241, when Rome went to war with Falerii; but Plutarch's reference is otherwise unattested (*Gaius Gracchus* 3.3).

20. Plutarch *Gaius Gracchus* 3.3. This Gaius Veturius, together with the date and details of the incident, is otherwise unknown.

             And terrible forebodings mourning shrieked
             Of misery to Rome, for such a deed.
             Ye Gods avert the omen, and accept,
             Ye angered deities, the sacrifice,
             Which here I vow to make you, of my life,   165
             In the great cause for which my brother bled:
             The cause of Rome, of liberty, and man!
First Cit.   Let us go home.
Second Cit.   Shall we not cheer him?
First Cit.   No.
             Let us go home and con his lessons well;
             Tears and obedience are his homage due;   170
             Cheers are too boisterous.   *Exeunt.*

ACT III

SCENE I. *House of* Cornelia.

Cornelia *and* Gracchus.

Grac.   Wolves breed not lambs, nor can the lioness
       Rear fawns among her litter. You but chide
       The spirit, mother, which is born from you.[21]
Cor.   Curb it, my son; and watch against ambition!
       Half demon and half god, she oft misleads   5
       With a bold face of virtue. I know well
       The breath of discontent is loud in Rome;
       And a hoarse murmuring vengeance smoulders there
       Against the tyrannous rule which, iron shod,
       Doth trample out man's life. The crisis comes;   10
       But oh! beware, my son, how you shall force it!
Grac.   Nay, let it come, that dreaded day of doom,
       When, by the audit of his cruel wrongs
       Heaped by the rich oppressor on the crowd
       Of struggling victims, he must stand condemned   15
       To vomit forth the ill-got gains which gorge
       His luxury to repletion. Let it come!

---

   21. *Coriolanus* 3.2.125–30 (Volumnia to her son Coriolanus): "let / Thy mother rather feel thy pride than fear / Thy dangerous stoutness, for I mock at death / With as big heart as thou. Do as thou list. / Thy valiantness was mine, thou suck'st it from me, / But owe thy pride thyself."

	The world can sleep no longer. Reason wakes	
	To know man's rights, and forward progress points.	
Cor.	By reason led, and peaceful wisdom nursed,	20
	All progress is for good. But the deep curse	
	Of bleeding nations follows in the track	
	Of mad ambition, which doth cheat itself	
	To find a glory in its lust of rule;	
	Which, piling private ill on public wrong,	25
	Beneath the garb of patriotism hides	
	Its large-mawed cravings; and would thoughtless plunge	
	To every change, however riot waits,	
	With feud intestine, by mad uproar driven,	
	And red-eyed murder, to reproach the deed.	30
	Death in its direst forms doth wait on such.	
Grac.	Man lives to die, and there's no better way	
	To let the shackled spirit find its freedom	
	Than in a glorious combat 'gainst oppression.	
	I would not grudge the breath lost in the struggle.	35
Cor.	Nor I, when duty calls. I am content,	
	May but my son prove worthy of the crisis:	
	Not shrinking from the trial, nor yet leaping	
	Beyond the marked outline of licensed right;	
	Curbing his passions to his duty's rule;	40
	Giving his country all—life, fortune, fame—	
	And only clutching back, with miser's care,	
	His all untainted honor. But take heed!	
	The world doth set itself on stilts, to wear	
	The countenance of some higher, better thing.	45
	'Tis well to seek this wisely; but with haste	
	Grasping too high, like child beyond its reach	
	It trips in the aspiring, and thus falls	
	To lowlier condition. Rashness drags	
	Remorse and darkest evil in her train.	50
	Pause, ere the cry of suffering pleads to Heaven	
	Against this fearful mockery of right:	
	This license wild, which smothers liberty	
	While feigning to embrace it.	
Grac.	Thought fantastic	
	Doth drapery evil thus with unsketched ills.	55
	No heart-sick maid, nor dream-struck boy am I	
	To scare myself with these. There's that in man	

         Doth long to rise by nature. Ever he
         Crouching in lethargy, doth wrong himself.
Cor.   Most true and more. I reverence human mind;   60
         And with a mingled love and pride I kneel
         To nature's inborn majesty in man.
         But as I reverence, therefore would I lend
         My feeble aid, this mighty power to lead
         To its true aim and end. Most often 'tis   65
         When crowds do wander wide of right, and fall
         To foul misuse of highest purposes,
         The madness of their leaders drags them on.
         I would not check aspiring, justly poised;
         But rather bid you "On!"—where light is clear   70
         And your track plainly marked. I scorn the slang
         Of "greedy populace," and "dirty crowd,"
         Nor slander thus the nature which I bear.
         Men in the aggregate not therefore cease
         Still to be men; and where untaught they fall,   75
         It is a noble duty, to awake
         The heart of truth, that slumbers in them still.
         It is a glorious right to rouse the soul,
         The reasoning heart that in a nation sleeps!
         And Wisdom is a laggard at her task   80
         When, but in closet speculations toiling,
         She doth forget to share her thought abroad
         And make mankind her heir.[22]
Grac. [*Looking towards the street.*] Ah! Fulvius comes.
Cor.   Your evil ghost doth haunt you in the form
         Of this same factious citizen, who errs   85
         From no bold error which outstrips the right
         (And thus misleads oft by exaggerate good),
         But, selfish to the core, he counts the worth
         E'en of his madness.
Grac.   Mother, you are harsh.
         But I've no time to battle in his cause.   90

---

22. The preceding passage (3.1.1–83) was chosen to represent *Caius Gracchus* in Duyckinck, *Cyclopaedia of American Literature* 2:252–53; the same excerpt was repeated in Forrest, *Women of the South Distinguished in Literature,* pp. 482–84; and J. W. Davidson, *Living Writers of the South,* pp. 354–57.

SCENE II] *Caius Gracchus* / 215

    Forgive my haste. I've business which must make
    My best excuse for lack of courtesy.   *Exeunt.*

SCENE II. *House of* OPIMIUS.

OPIMIUS *and* DRUSUS.

Opim.   Enough, I say, of this vile, canting folly!
    From its endurance out beyond the verge
    You push my fretted patience. Leap at once!
    Into it, man! Speak out: what is your price?
    We'll pay you what you will, so you will rid us   5
    Of this bold demagogue. Speak, hungry leech!
    Come, we are private. Something chokes you. Gulp it.
    Your honesty I'll not betray, nor tell
    The secret to your compeers, by what star
    You trace your windings. But one thing you see—   10
    I know you; so leave off your shuffling; speak,
    And speak out boldly. What's your will? your price?
Dru.   But you, too quick, at nothing fire up.
    I tried to think, if it were best for Rome—
Opim.   Pshaw! pshaw! man! Let Rome be. We'll talk of her   15
    When you'll have settled all your own affairs.
    What think you of the fine Sardinian fields,
    Or Agathyrnum[23] garden? Lycia has
    Groves too, luxuriant, where her saffron grows.
    Come, courage, man! plunge to the crumb o' the loaf,   20
    Nor stand like hungry mouse, nibbling his crust
    The while he eyes some well-stocked larder's store
    Where longing dares not enter. What's your will?
Dru.   Nay, if your generous liberality
    My honest zeal sees fit to compensate,   25
    With thanks I'll take the rich Sardinian field
    And Agathyrnum garden.
Opim.   What—*both,* man?
    Thy maw is large—the swallowing chokes thee not.
    But we've no time to chaffer. Mind our bargain!
    Gracchus to Carthage—or the fields of Drusus   30
    Must seek some other tenant.

---

23. Town on the north coast of Sicily, between Tyndaris and Calacte.

Enter Lucullus.

Ha! Lucullus,
Well met. Our wise good friend—our honest Drusus—
This worthy benefactor of his country,
Agrees with us, that for the destined plan
Of colonizing Carthage, there is none 35
So fit as Caius Gracchus, and doth promise
To so bestir himself that he will make
The post fall to his lot. Good man! he sees
(Moved by considerations of much weight)
How hangs the city's weal upon our plans. [*To Drusus*] 40
Good-day, my worthy friend; I see you're off. *Exit Drusus.*

Luc.   It would have saved us many an aching head
Of wearing thought, and anxious watchfulness,
If we a nest had sooner found to lodge him.
To think is fearful, over all the laws 45
With which his influence has already checked
And bounded in the Senate's shackled power.
In every thing he does, the people praise him;
And, truth to say, were it not Caius Gracchus,
My thought would fix him honest. He so strongly 50
Doth dwell upon the majesty of Rome,
Whate'er the under-current of his feeling,
It shows most fairly. Where he even finds
His bitterest foes, within the Senate's heart,
He to a noble line of duty works them. 55
It was a wise and moderate decree
That he, for instance, argued them to pass
About the corn that our propraetor Fabius
Sent us from Spain.[24] Most needed too it was,
As antidote to angered feelings roused 60
By Fabius' tyranny throughout the province.
I wish the thought had come from any man
Sooner than Caius Gracchus. 'Tis a stamp
Of new-coined honor to him—a fresh feather
To deck his plumèd cap. But what's the good 65

24. In 123 Gracchus persuaded the Senate to pass a decree ordering that the grain which the governor of Spain, Quintus Fabius Maximus, had compelled the Spanish cities to send to Rome should be sold, and the money returned to the cities (Plutarch *Gaius Gracchus* 6.2). Fabius was Opimius' colleague in the consulship of 121.

	From this short banishment we can expect?
Opim.	Drusus is schooled and ready (curse the fate
	That needs me tamper with so foul a thing!)
	To make the most of his absence. He'll propose
	Some petted laws, the people's love to coax. 70
	Or rather (for they have no thought to love)
	To catch the popular voice which drowns itself
	With its own echoes often. Thus we'll soothe
	And, flattering, choke with their own wish the crowd,
	The turbulent throat of its loud worship hushing 75
	That ever follows Gracchus; and the idol
	Thus undermining from his pedestal,
	The fickle homage of the people bring
	To this our man of wax—nice-moulded thing—
	That we must prop on Gracchus' vacant stool. 80
Luc.	He has a law, they say, that strikes us home
	Closer than any yet, and in the Forum
	He will propose it presently.
Opim.	I've heard
	Much talk of it; and we I fear must stand
	To witness one more triumph. May it be 85
	At least his last. [[*Exeunt.*]]

SCENE III. *Street of Rome near Forum.*

Enter POMPONIUS *and* LICINIUS.

Pomp. On! We've no time to lose. I fear already
We've lost the argument. In all due form
Before I left was every right discharged.
By the presiding tribune prayer was said,
The business noted, and the herald read 5
The law which was proposed. A noble one!
Associate with the Senate it would give us
Three hundred knights to share the authority
Of our judicial courts. Quick, let us in.   [[*Exeunt.*]]

SCENE IV. Forum.

Assembled People, Licinius, [Opimius,] Lucullus, Pomponius, *etc.*
Gracchus *is addressing the Assembly.*

Grac.   You've heard the law proposed. You've heard my colleague[25]
       Declaim against it in no measured terms.
       Branded you've heard it by our noble consul[26]
       As most licentious, revolutionary.
       Citizens, to you I turn.   *Turns his face towards the Forum.*
Opim.   [*Aside to Lucullus.*] Do you mark that?   5
Luc.   'Tis clap-trap cunning, which will take the people.
Grac.   To you I speak, the country's pulse and life;
       Ye are Rome's masters—her true governors
       At once, and truest servants. 'Neath those shreds
       The ragged emblems of your poverty,   10
       And parti-colored badges of your rank,
       Beats the great heart of Rome. This law is made
       Not for convenience to the cradled rich,
       Who, wrapped luxurious in the dainty folds
       Of purple robes, and on their downy cushions   15
       By sweetest music lulled, now frighted start
       At the harsh tones I utter; it is made
       For your necessities, ye struggling poor;
       Judge *ye* then, of its merits: If it be,
       As says our consul, revolutionary,   20
       I do deny that it can be licentious.
       Your courts of law I would not make less strict,
       Nor from the doom inherited by vice
       One hair's weight would I take. I would but give ye
       Judges who in their duty read their law.   25
       I would, at least in part, snatch frighted Justice
       From bold Corruption's lucre-stainèd hand.
       Who[m] have ye now for judges? Who[m] but those

---

25. Livius Drusus.

26. Gaius Fannius, consul in 122, in charge of Rome while his colleague Gnaeus Domitius Ahenobarbus was commanding Roman forces in southern Gaul. With the support of Gracchus, Fannius had been elected over Opimius (who had to wait until the following year) but had turned against his ally after entering office. When a great concourse of Italians was expected to flood into Rome in aid of Gracchus' legislation (including, presumably, the law extending Roman citizenship), Fannius pronounced an edict barring from the city during the voting period all who were not Romans; see below, 4.3.4–11.

The enthroned rich? Of all our natural rights
The bitterest foes! The Senate is your judge: 30
At once aggressor proud, and vengeful tyrant.
Where then is your appeal? Your refuge, where?
Romans, the fathers of this Senate were
Rome's noblest citizens; the country's prop,
And every way her boast. They won them rights, 35
From which, with all their vices, still their sons
Ought not to be cast down. Leave them the dues
Their Fathers' virtues won. Revere in them
The noble legacy of by-gone deeds;
But rouse ye 'neath oppression! See ye not 40
How with slow step and guarded look she comes;
Oft pausing; watching opportunities;
Doubtful advancing; seizing timidly
Some right disputed; till, now bolder grown,
With fearless stride, and open face of guilt, 45
She grasps at what she wills, nor feigns to hide
Her bold aggressions beneath justice' sham;
Corruption seizes with her myrmidons,
And every avenue to justice blocks.
   I have proposed, that with our Senators 50
An equal number of associate knights
Should now be added in authority
To judge all causes. Why the loud outcry
Indignant raised against me? 'Tis that thus
Our Senate feels the people has some voice, 55
Dictating its own councils; that the law,
Half wrested from that class which has no heart,
Nor with you, nor yet for you, may be spoken
Thus, through another court. Decide ye now;
To you, from that high Senate, I appeal: 60
Ye poor—ye suffering—ye sorrow-taught—
Ye crowd of trampled men, with souls as high,
And blood as red, as those who trample ye!
Because ye are plebeians, nor can boast
The blood of twenty fathers, have ye less 65
The rights of Romans and of citizens?
Plebeians have done noble acts in Rome,
And stamped in lines of blood some glorious deeds
Upon our country's annals. Have ye heard,

Or has the Senate bade ye blot it out 70
From Roman memories? Have ye forgot
That once, twice, thrice, Rome saw her battles turned,
Appeased her angry Gods, and victory snatched
From enemies already triumphing?
Three generations to the Decii owed 75
Their rescued safety.[27] Curius, from our coasts
Who drove the Epyran Pyrrhus—and, to tempt him,
When, from his earthen pot and frugal meal
Of garden vegetables, he was offered
The gold and luxuries of conquered Samnites, 80
Turned smiling from them, telling them to learn
That but an added lustre was the stamp
Of poverty, to who by virtue governed—
Was not *his,* too, this scorned plebeian blood?[28]
I will not shame you, by recounting farther 85
The noble deeds that every child should know;
Your hearts will count them for me. But one more,
And that my noble brother, I will name.
I thank my mother that she gave me not
For father, an Egyptian Ptolemy; 90
But, from the offers of a kingdom turning,
Gave heart and hand to a plebeian Roman,
And son and brother to a Gracchus made me.[29]
    Are there of us, Plebeians, those whose gains,
By honest hoarding, prosperous adventure, 95
Among the richer class give them a place,
And who would spurn the poor, to rank themselves
By flattering adulation of the great?
Oh! learn ye that there is no higher place
Than that from which the self-ennobled turns 100

---

27. Three Roman consuls named Publius Decius Mus—father, son, and grandson—became types of unselfish dedication to the Republic, having each died in battle (340, 295, and 279) to secure Roman victory.

28. Manius Curius Dentatus, consul four times, censor in 272, conqueror of Samnites, Sabines, Senones, Lucani, and King Pyrrhus of Epirus (in 275), was the hero of many stories illustrating his humble birth and incorruptibility.

29. Gracchus (or LSM) alters chronology for the point of the argument: Cornelia received a proposal of marriage from a King Ptolemy of Egypt (probably Ptolemy VIII Physcon) after the death of her husband, Gaius' father (Plutarch *Tiberius Gracchus* 1.4).

A helping hand to lend to who would rise,
Like him, from abjectness.
      Are there would sell,
For dirty gold and for patrician hire,
The city's rights? Shame them, if such there be,
Ye nobler hearts, in your coarse woven gowns;   105
E'en midst their ill-got luxuries, and their robes
Of showier texture, shame them with the sight
Of poverty, which is too proud to take
The price of virtue!
      Romans, I leave you now
To answer for yourselves, and by your voices   110
Decide your fate. Speak out: Freemen, or Slaves?
Ay, more, ay, worse than slaves: outcasts and beggared,
The crouching suppliants to a lawless rule.
 One word to you, ye noble Senators;
Though ye misdoubt me, as a friend I speak,   115
Of Rome and of no party. Conscript fathers,
I plead to you, with filial duty bending,
As son to a harsh parent. Let us end
This so unnatural struggle. Be but just,
We ask no more. This quarrel once removed,   120
Our rights acknowledged, and our privileges
Laid open fairly, to the strengthening 'tis
At once of you and us. Some ill-got gains,
Some power unjustly grasped, once given o'er,
Proud in your aristocracy ye stand,   125
And to Rome sacred. Strong in property,
Strong in construction of our laws ye stand,
Strong in the people's love, and in opinion;
Strong in the association of great deeds;
Strong in the immortal memory of the past.   130
Rome's history is yours, and is your fathers'!
The people love you for the names that grace
The glorious annals of our brightest years.
Oh! cast not from you all the homage due,
Which now a nation stands prepared to pay!   135
 I've done, and leave the question to the vote
Of you, our here assembled centuries.

Presiding Magistrate. [*Rising.*] According to your judgments, speak, Quirites.

*The people commence separating into centuries preparatory
to giving their votes.* [[*Exeunt.*]]

SCENE V. *House of* CORNELIA.

CORNELIA *and* LICINIA.

Cor. Well, who comes now, Licinia, that your eye
    So often plays the truant to your work?
Lic. 'Tis Fulvius with Licinius; I will beckon,
    That they may tell us how the day has turned.
Cor. Do so. 'Tis like enough they have the news.   5

Enter FULVIUS *and* LICINIUS.

Ful. Hurrah! Let's have a bout! But pray ye pardon;
    I had forgot myself, most gentle ladies.
    And yet I wot, your best wine were poor pay
    To greet such news as mine.
Cor.   Well, give the news,
    And you shall have the wine; right good, forsooth;   10
    A true old bottle of the finest stamp.   *Servants bring wine, etc.*
    How goes the day?
Ful.   A glorious victory!
    The law is carried, and three hundred knights
    Hold judgment now, as with the Senate equal.
    A glass for that; my news is thirsty, ladies,   15
    And I must wash my throat, ere I go further.
Lic. Nay, give the rest; and you shall have full time
    To drink your wine at leisure. Say, what next?
Ful. What next? Why next, the glorious people voted
    That Caius should, from the equestrian class,   20
    Himself make the selection, to fill up
    This most important post. What think you, lady?
    A kiss of thanks from those same rosy lips
    Would scarce be more than, by their great deserts,
    The greasy rascals have a right to claim   25
    Their honest guerdon. But again I see,
    Lady, I'm trespassing. You blush reproof
    Stronger than words can speak it. Pray forgive.
Cor. You're too rough, Fulvius. In your news I know not
    If good or evil lurks.
Ful.   Good! *Glorious,* call it!   30

	Gracchus, supreme in power, may govern Rome.
	What shall we make of him? We need but choose.
	Consul? Dictator? Say, what shall it be?
Cor.	Nothing but Caius Gracchus and the friend
	Of Rome, and of no party.
Ful.	You are humble!
Cor.	Humble? My pride ne'er found a higher flight!
	To see my son the greatest man in Rome
	And wish him virtue to maintain his place!
	Call you this humble? 'Twere a grievous fall,
	To have him barter, for a foolish rank,
	The glorious title of his country's friend!
	But here he comes.

Enter GRACCHUS.

Lic.	Ah! Gracchus, my heart's throne!
Grac.	My pretty bird, and my home's blessing, thou!
	Mother, you've got the news. Fulvius, I know,
	Lags never, in the telling of what's strange.
Licinius.	And yet he has not told them what's more strange
	Perhaps than all the rest. They have not heard
	How you from the Comitium[30] turned away
	And from the Senate-house, to which their looks
	Our orators in reverence always fix,
	And to plebeian Rome dared word your speech;
	While frowning muttered the incensed patricians
	Their unheard words of anger. 'Twas an act
	Which must have weight, all simple though it seemed,
	Through all Rome's history. The turning point
	Betwixt patrician crushing tyranny,
	And true plebeian freedom.
Cor.	May it prove
	But freedom, and not license!
Grac.	Nay, good mother,
	What means your ominous word, chilling our hope?
Cor.	I tremble at the spirit you have raised,
	And anxious watch its full development.

30. A broad rectangle of ground, in front of the Curia Hostilia (the Senate House) and between it and the Roman Forum; for what Gracchus' innovation in oratorical posture implied, see Plutarch *Gaius Gracchus* 5.3.

>   Perchance a thing of light, Minerva armed,
>   Sprung from the teeming brow of deity;
>   Perchance a demon foul to blast our eyes,
>   With fiendish horrors, and mad revelling, 65
>   Frighting off hope, to wither up our hearts.
> Grac.   But mother, thus you'd fright off effort too,
>   And weaken thought with gazing on itself.
>   No victory is gained but meeting risk;
>   And no abuse, however wild the rage 70
>   To which may run unlicensed tyranny,
>   But should be better than the stagnant pool
>   Of abject brutishness, and cringing fear,
>   Misery unstruggling, and imbècile woe,
>   To which, 'neath the dominion, Rome drives fast, 75
>   Of lawless aristocracy's abuse.
>   The madness into nature may be tamed;
>   The spring, too strong at first, be tempered right,
>   The exigencies of its need to suit;
>   But crouching idiocy, that, 'neath the stripes 80
>   Of unchecked power, doth drivel out its last
>   Of crushed humanity, can only rise,
>   As doth the monster, beastlike from its lair,
>   To fury roused at last, but not to reason.
> Cor.   You argue well. And yet in purposes 85
>   Well reasoned even, oft to evil leads
>   Too rash precipitance. As half-spent torch,
>   From a child's hand, the mighty forest fires,
>   Thus human passions, easily aroused,
>   Storm forth their angry blaze. The frighted thing 90
>   That waked the crashing storm, bewildered shrinks
>   From fierce destruction, in its raging might,
>   Which, hissing, roars alternate; and doth gaze,
>   In terror stupified, at its own work.
>   You drop the spark, but can you rule the flame 95
>   Of unchained passion's might?
> Grac.   I know not, mother.
>   But 'tis a thing to try.
> Cor.   Step coolly, then;
>   With well directed foot of prudent caution.
>   Haste trips us in the race.

Grac.   My foot is in,
    And I have boldly met the threatened risk.   100
Ful.   Ay, more than boldly; nobly! Rome must make
    New words to praise you.
Grac.   Pray you, praise me not.
    I'd rather see my mother's clouded brow
    In complacent approval smooth itself,
    Than catch the flattery of crowds like you.   105
    When the whole soul of energy is bent
    To work some object that it needs must win,
    Or find itself undone, no will it has
    Of words to catch the windy flattery;
    But, in its conscious effort wrapped, it finds,   110
    So greedy for success, no thought nor taste
    To greet a smaller praise.
                      I had forgot
    To tell you, mother, what annoys me much.
    It seems, determined by some adverse luck,
    I must be off to Carthage.
Cor.   Ha! indeed!   115
    Thus evil chance doth work; and yet, perhaps,
    'Tis better thus. We'll talk of it again.   [[*Exeunt.*]]

ACT IV.

SCENE I. *Carthage.*

Workmen occupied in building.

First Work.   This Caius has a resolute heart, methinks,
    Or from the start he would have given up.
    With my good will, I'd not have struck one stroke
    After the breaking of our standard staff.
    It was an evil omen.
Second Work.   And—far worse—   5
    When by the winds our solemn sacrifice
    Beyond the marks laid for the city's bounds
    Was scattered borne; and when the howling wolves
    With deafening clamor came, and carried off
    The very marks themselves. It was a daring,   10

          Most manifest of outraged Heaven's will
          To persevere against such fearful omens.
First Work.   And yet we have succeeded. It would seem
          Some other way the Gods their warning meant.
Third Work.   For Gracchus' self, some say, it was intended.   15
First Work.   And that is what I fear. I love so well
          His noble heart—almost, to ease him of it,
          On my own shoulders I'd take all the risk.
Second Work.   Hush! do not be so foolhardy, to dare
          The judgment of the Gods! I shudder thus   20
          To hear you speak. Do you not see, there's that
          Doth mark out Gracchus as one made for sorrow?
          He is of those who bear upon their brow
          The stamp of some sad doom.
First Work.   And yet methinks
          A noble brow it is.
Second Work.   Ay, oftenest thus   25
          The noblest do the Gods mark out to bear
          The sorrows of the world.
Third Work.   Stop! Here he comes.

          Enter Gracchus *and Messenger.*

Grac.   An information, say you, against Fulvius?
Mes.   Yes, sundry charges—and, in truth, no light ones.
          'Tis likely to go hard with him, for Drusus   30
          Gains ground in every way, and bears his power
          In its full strength against him: while Opimius
          Pampers at wish the now o'ergorgèd crowd,
          Till, with indulgence cloyed, the multitude,
          Drunk with the surfeit of its palled desires,   35
          Doth, as the boon of so much license, promise
          The consulship in guerdon.
Grac.   Ha! Opimius!
          This doth need looking after. We will sail
          With the first favouring wind. My duties here
          Have prospered so, that they my present eye   40
          No longer need. An hour or two, and then,
          Some few directions to my workmen given,
          I will be with you.   *Exeunt.*

SCENE II. *Street of Rome.*

SEPTIMULEIUS *and Citizens.*

Sept. I do not like at all the looks of things.
 This information against Fulvius bodes
 No good to Gracchus. It is certain, too,
 That from the tribuneship he'll be turned out.
First Cit. The people may find means to hinder that.
Sept. They can't! They can't! Opimius is a man
 Will have his way. He's a great man; and I
 Begin to think, an undue noise we've made
 And pother for this Gracchus.
First Cit.   Ha! I thought
 You were no timeserver; his best of friends!
Sept. Timeserver! surely not. But if a man
 Is thick with faults, I've got an eye to see them.
First Cit. And his bad luck doth make each fault a twin,
 To who rates merit only by its gains.
Sept. Pshaw! you're a crabbèd fellow! I care not
 For further talk with you. But mark my words,
 Gracchus has seen his last of the tribuneship. [[*Exeunt.*]]

SCENE III. *Another part of Rome.*

Enter GRACCHUS *and* LICINIUS.

Grac. Scarce have I set my foot in Rome, returned
 From an accomplished business, which they hoped
 Would keep me for a lifetime from her walls,
 Than boldly shows their game. When was the time
 That ever Roman consul dared to issue
 Such proclamation as the Senate now
 Has coaxed from Fannius?[31] Citizens of Rome
 Not born within her limits, must forthwith
 The city's precincts leave! Chased like mad dogs!
 Deprived at once of citizenship, forsooth!
 Because the Senate cannot buy their votes.

Enter DRUSUS *and another Tribune.*

---

31. See above, 3.4.3–4 and note.

Dru.	Gracchus, good-day. Would I could hail you still	
	Colleague, and brother tribune. With regret	
	We lose your valued service.	
Grac.	[*turning from Drusus, speaks to Licinius*] Bah! 'tis foul!	
	Would you believe it: these two worthy tribunes,	15
	These noble, true, and honorable men,	
	Who, for the disappointment I have met,	
	Now speak their sorrows—would you think that these,	
	These very two, with simpering look, and lip	
	Of flattering condolence, were the men	20
	Who at the election counted up the votes,	
	And thus procured by fraudulent return	
	That I, a tribune fair elected, stand	
	Here officeless? Faugh! Let's away! This meanness	
	That crawls and licks the dust, it sickens me.	25
	I'd sooner meet Opimius, or such villain,	
	Who, what he does, does boldly. There's a show	
	Almost of honor in his dashing crime.	
	But this mean, crouching shame, that blushless seeks	
	Its smerchèd visage with the soilèd cloak	30
	Of honesty to wrap! Faugh! 'tis the taint	
	Of carrion—dead game. True hound will shun it.	
	They are not worth the running down. Let's off.	
Dru.	This 'tis to serve one's country! Taunted thus,	
	My conscience stands me true.	
Grac.	Conscience, quoth he!	35
	Where picked he up the word? Conscience! ha! ha!	
	I had a parrot once, could talk and prate	
	And chatter words in its sharp querulous tone,	
	As though it knew their sense. Conscience, forsooth!	
Dru.	To rail abusive is the loser's wont.	40
	Upon the gainer's side the laugh doth rest.	
Grac.	Call you it gaining, winning as you do?	
	Truly you've gained what you can never lose:	
	A stamp of vice, a never changing shame	
	That haunts you to your grave. Did you but know it,	45
	You've gained a loss, which makes you as a stench	
	In every true man's nostrils! Come, Licinius.	
	Exeunt Gracchus and Licinius.	
Dru.	I would arrest him in the people's name	
	For disrespect to their tribunes, but that—that—	
Trib.	But that we are ashamed. Drusus, he speaks	50

	Such bitter truths as we deserve to hear.	
	Would I had never joined the dirty game!	
	His words cling to me as a nauseous soil,	
	And my whole soul, meseems, doth stink of it!	
	We've played our honor and our souls of men	55
	Against the Senate's monies and their lands;	
	And, as he tells us, we have gained a loss	
	That damns us in the filth of our own acts.	
Dru.	Why, man! what means this puling face of grief?	
	Doff it; or you'll betray to peering eyes	60
	The mysteries of our nice diplomacy.	
Trib.	Time has been—ere I let the Senate's gold	
	Filthy my itching fingers—I could stand,	
	Bare my clean bosom to the crowd, and feel	
	Lighthearted by inspection.	
Dru.	Pshaw! Cheer up,	65
	And don't give way to whimsies such as this.	
	It was to serve the country that we labored,	
	And slightly doubtful means are often fit	
	To work an end of certain benefit.	*Exeunt.*

SCENE IV. *Street of Rome.*

FULVIUS *and* GRACCHUS.

Ful.	Pluto and the infernal Gods! Give up?	
	What, man! Back out before this rascal consul?	
	This proud Opimius? Why, ere this I thought	
	His lawless rule, and grinding usurpation,	
	Had purged your halting conscience of its doubts.	5
Grac.	Fulvius, my soul hath fire enough, nor needs	
	Your flashing speech, of flint to tinder words,	
	To rouse it into action. Of my breast	
	The tight-drawn cord, vibrating with the touch,	
	Like high-tuned instrument rings back your words	10
	In tones of passion, till almost it bursts.	
	What unskilled tuner are you, thus to screw	
	And tighten up a string already wound	
	Above its pitch of tone?	
Ful.	But what's the matter,	
	That we must tamely stand, to bide this insult?	15
	What's this Opimius? Is he god, or ghost,	
	Or fiend, or devil, that we shrink, and shrink,	

And cower before him thus? A consul he
Of yesterday's election! Hardly more—
And yet already he hath lessoned us 20
To due humility, 'twould seem: for ever
"*Give way*" 's the word! Give way! give way! forsooth!
And in the Furies' name, I would know, why?
I'll not give way. No! Let him fight it out,
I'll meet him where he dares. For you, how meekly 25
You stand to see your labor's fruit laid waste!
Your life's work thrown aside! These he prepares
All to undo. Your laws he will repeal.
The colonizing Carthage, which himself
So lately thought—and the assembled Senate— 30
Then all important, now he will annul.
The faintest trace which of your name is left
Upon the country's acts, he'll foul, and blot,
And from the city's memory trample out.
Why such unheard of course? Hardly in power, 35
The rein he strains of his authority
Almost to bursting. Cramped and fettered laws
Are dragged and fretted to find out some term,
That to your injury may be worded thus;
The import of their execution ever 40
Being still the same and one, to lash at Gracchus.

Grac.   Curse on his heart, 'tis true! Find but the means—
I tell you, find the means!—nor ever ring
The changes thus of his accursèd wrongs
On my impatient ear! Find but the means: 45
This doublehearted traitor I will meet,
Nor shrink the struggle, be it to the death!

Ful.   Come with me to my house; you'll meet some friends
Who wait to talk upon this matter there.   *Exeunt.*

SCENE V. Cornelia's *House.*

Gracchus *and* Cornelia.

Cor.   All wrong! all wrong! What mean, thronging our streets,
These hired bands? No Roman faces these!
Strangers who skulk at noon-day, 'neath the garb
And roughness feigned of country reapers hiding

	Some ill intent. I like it not; it smacks
	Of evil purpose.
Grac.	Nay; to be trampled on!
	Forever driven to the wall by fraud
	From these our task-masters, yet be reproached
	When in their own base coin we pay them home
	Some trifling arrears! Curse them, I'll strike,
	And with their own unholy weapons maim them!
Cor.	This is a mistimed anger, and I grieve
	That you to beard Opimius have resolved.
	His aim is your imprudence; and you thus,
	By this hotheaded Fulvius spurred, now cast
	Your every point into his ready hand.
	'Tis the calm right that you should seek to win,
	Nor cheat your heart, while nursing its revenge,
	To think that duty works it. Call you this,
	This rampant hate, and angry violence,
	Which drives a thoughtless people to the verge
	Of lawless anarchy, which grasps at fraud
	To work its selfish ways, and makes success,
	Not right, its rule of action—call you this,
	Because you link with it some real wrong
	Inflicted on a thoughtless populace—
	Call you this patriotism? Search your heart
	And read its motives clearer.
Grac.	You much wrong me,
	And travesty my truest feelings, mother,
	In most unworthy garb.
Cor.	Would it were so!
	Most willingly I'd take the wrong myself,
	To know your object pure. But you have let
	Your passion much mislead you. You have been
	So erring in your selfish thought, to lose
	The higher point of action. May you find
	Occasion fitting to retrace your steps!
	The time's unripe, and you would force it on,
	Not by a gentle teaching to the truth,
	But gag it to your own ideas of right,
	And force mankind to gulp your system down.
	Oh! check this energy, whose mistimed warmth
	Has in the crowd a storm of passion roused

>   Of inauspicious aspect. Con again
>   The lessons you yourself had taught, ere letting
>   Our moneyed landholders' oppressive frauds   45
>   Opposing frauds within your bosom wake,
>   Driving the noblest feelings to that verge
>   Where virtue becomes rashness, and ambition
>   Outtracks the path of right. If yet 'tis time,
>   Unspeak your spell. The angry turmoil sooth[e]   50
>   Of differing tempers, which now clashing rage
>   Like the wild waves of some tumultuous sea,
>   Each lashing each to anger.
> Grac.   Can it be
>   That I in passion thus have drowned the right?
>   There is a half contrition in my heart   55
>   That speaks your judgment true. Your calmer thought
>   Doth damp the fierceness of my anger's hate;
>   And, with cooled passion, my big faults do rise
>   To taunt me with their folly. I will try;
>   Trust me, I'll do my best; and now farewell.   60
>   Licinia need not know all that is passing.
>   She has, you know, not half your courage, mother;
>   Let her be quiet; if the storm must burst,
>   She'll learn it time enough.   [[*Exeunt.*]]

SCENE VI. *Capitol.*

> OPIMIUS, *Lictors, friends of Opimius, Senators, etc.*
> GRACCHUS, FULVIUS, *and friends of Gracchus.*
> OPIMIUS *standing by the altar, robed in white, and crowned
> with cypress.*

> *Opim.*   Thou, Jupiter Capitoline, to whom
>   Acceptable thus far our offerings seem,
>   Watch over us and Rome!
>   Lictors, remove,
>   And let these entrails by the aruspices[32]
>   Be in accordance with all form examined.   5
> *Lict.* [*Passing with the entrails strikes against Fulvius and exclaims.*]

---

32. "Auruspices" in 1851 ed. The (h)aruspices were diviners imported from Etruria, who predicted events by inspecting the entrails of sacrificed animals.

Stand off, ye crew of traitors, and make way,
That honest men may pass.
Ful.   Traitor to me!   *Strikes him.*
Take that to mend your manners, ribald tongue!
First Cit.   And that!

    Citizens rush with daggers upon the Lictor, who falls.

Second Cit.   And that!
Grac. [*Rushing forward.*]   Fulvius, you ruin all!
What means this mistimed brawl, unmannerly?   10
Ful.   I've been insulted, and have not the temper
To suck up harsh words, fattening on abuse,
And nurse its quiet with the promised dream
Of what some "by-and-by" may bring to pass.
I've been insulted; and, if corpses speak,   15
Quintus Antyllius there may calculate
What strength my passion casts into a blow.
Grac.   Too much, alas! and not, I fear, to end
With this, of a poor lictor the one death;
For many, noble are the heads whose doom   20
Is in that one impatient blow entailed.
Opim. [*Advancing.*] Tremble, ye Roman people! Citizens,
No more I bid you now be bold—but rather,
In the amazement of my terror, warn ye
Before offended Deity to crouch.   25
Ye have full cause for fear! Our sacrifice
Profaned by blood in passion shed, unholy—
Accursèd on our heads our prayers cast back,
Heap vengeance from the gods: for murder soils
With bloody sacrilege our holiest rites.   30
Here at the altar of our angered god,
Let us now seek to humbly expiate
This impious deed.   *Turns and kneels at the altar.*
         Great Jove! hear us and pity!
Promiscuous let thy thunders strike us not.
In wisdom judge thou, and in justice doom!   35

    Corpse of Antyllius is brought forward on a bier.

The innocent victim which to thee we bring,
Receive in expiation of this deed
Ill-omened and unrighteous. Of our hearts

                See every spouting wound interpreter,
                In blood speak forth our will to right the insult   40
                Of thy profanèd temple; from its walls
                Polluted, to wash out the bloody stain,
                And make revenge co-equal with the crime.
                                Rises and turns towards attendants.
                Now through the Forum, by our weeping Senate
                All in its bleeding livery escorted,   45
                The consecrated victim bear, and rouse
                The frightened people to revenge their god.
                            Exit OPIMIUS *with attendants, bearing the body and
                            followed by Senators, making loud acclamations of
                            grief and indignation.*
Ful.   A fig for all their weeping! What have they
        To whine and wail, like over-pampered child,
        Because a noisy lictor meets his death?   50
Grac.   They weep for joy that in that same dead corse
        A weapon you have given, which they will wield
        With deadly import. Curse your reckless passion!
        That in a moment's space has done more harm
        Than years of sober council can unmake.   55
Ful.   Pshaw! You'll turn orator, and make a speech
        In honor of this beggar's funeral!
        With care and watching your mind wearied out
        Doth, thus enfeebled, turn to start at shadows.
Grac.   Would it were so! But from this hasty deed   60
        Doth spring a progeny of thick-coming ills,
        That but to gaze at chills me. Come, Licinius,
        And you, Pomponius, I would speak with you.
                                Exit with Licinius and Pomponius.
Ful.   It is a noble heart, though somewhat slow
        To meet the exigencies of the time.   65
First Cit. I would we had not killed this lictor, though.
        Slowness sometimes is virtue. It were well
        If we had been less sudden.
Ful.   Well, I wish
        As prompt an arm there was for every one
        Of these our Senators who weeping stand   70
        Around a paltry lictor's bier to wail.
        Who would believe that this same capitol,
        Which now so loudly they proclaim profaned,

　　　　　Shows yet upon its walls the scattered stains
　　　　　Tiberius Gracchus' blood had sprinkled there?　　　　75
　　　　　Him they cast forth, the refuse of their hate
　　　　　(Rome's tribune by her Senate done to death);
　　　　　No funerals were granted to our prayers:
　　　　　He was the people's friend—what needed he
　　　　　Of sanctifying forms and ceremonies?　　　　　　　80
　　　　　But now, behold! in this unrighteous farce,
　　　　　About a hireling's corse Rome's nobles stand,
　　　　　In feignèd penitence to bow their heads;
　　　　　And, in their weeping expiation, seek
　　　　　To magnify a fault, whose heightened crime　　　　85
　　　　　Upon the people's head their hate would pile.

　　　　　　　　　Enter Messenger.

Mes.　Sent by your friends, I come to tell you, Fulvius,
　　　　That, with pretence to save the commonwealth,
　　　　Opimius, sanctioned by the Senate, issues,
　　　　To the patricians and the knights, an order　　　　　90
　　　　That they shall all, well armed and well escorted,
　　　　Attend him in the morning; and 'tis said
　　　　A price is set on your and Gracchus' head.
Ful.　Hear you this, citizens? Who stands by me?
Citizens.　I—I—and I—and I—and all of us!　　　　　　95
Ful.　I thank you all. Come with me, and we'll hold
　　　　All things in readiness to meet the morning.
　　　　Huzza for Rome! but down with our proud Senate!
　　　　We will pronounce them traitors to the people,
　　　　And set a price upon their heads. Let's vote it.　　100
　　　　Who will say "ay"?
Citizens.　　　　　　Ay, ay.
Ful.　　　　　　　　　　　It is pronounced.
　　　　We do decree these reverend Senators
　　　　Shall lose their heads whenever we can catch them;
　　　　And that their weight in gold shall be the prize
　　　　Of every man who can pick up so much　　　　　　105
　　　　By pillaging the overflowing hoards
　　　　Of these our sacred rats: time-worshipped scourges,
　　　　Deities to whom, not hoping good we've prayed,
　　　　But rather for the ill we sought to shun.
　　　　Huzza then for the people! For the Senate,　　　　110

Down with them! Hang the Senate!
Citizens.   Huzza! Huzza!
Down with the Senate.   *Exeunt, riotously.*

SCENE VII. *Street near the Statue of the Father of Gracchus.*

Enter Gracchus, Pomponius, *and* Licinius. *Citizens passing and following.*

Grac.   All then seems vain. Our every scheme is nought.
Each, as it nears us, in the light of hope
All radiant glitters, as, in early beam
Of morning's sun, the dew besprinkled web.
But stretch the eager hand to seize it—lo!   5
Our lightest touch its nothingness but proves;
And, with the broken fragment of its thread
All shattered in our grasp, forlorn we stand,
Orphaned of hope, and our own fancy's fool!
Oh! had I steeled my heart against ambition,   10
And in its unity but held the hope
That worked me first to action—seeking to bring
The people to that perfectness which nature
Makes their inherent right—I had not been
Thus in the web of mine own faults entangled!   15
My soilèd hands, ungrateful to the Gods,
In impure sacrifice have lost their strength.
The workman is not equal to his task.
Pomp.   Rather the task is one impracticable,
From nature doomed to failure. For who talks   20
Of the crowd's fickleness, talks nothing new.
How oft tomorrow finds, where now they fawn,
Their bitter mockery, or their loudest hate!
And today's idol is the cast off thing
Which yesterday they trampled under foot!   25
Blame not the weakness of your hand, but rather
The rotten stuff you work on.
Grac.   Yet, I feel
There dwells in them a self-redeeming power.
They must by nature's instinct have the sense
That I have sought to rouse. But I, unskilful,   30
Play not upon their hearts. Some loftier mind
Must wake the spirit that to me is dead:

Rousing the human soul that in them sleeps,
To its high note of harmony and truth.

As they pass the statue of his father, GRACCHUS *pausing
stands for some time earnestly gazing at it.*

Pomp. Let us pass on.
Licinius.   He heeds us not. He's wrapped 35
  In contemplation of some distant thought
  That finds no home with us.
Pomp.   'Twere best to leave him.
  We but upon his privacy intrude.
  He seems as he, by gazing, hoped to drag
  A spirit from his father's statue forth, 40
  And would hold converse with him. Let us on,
  And leave him to himself.
Licinius.   Nay. Rather we
  Should closely watch him; for in times like these
  He needs his every friend. We intrude not;
  He heeds us not, nor longer knows our presence. 45
  Following the heaving sigh, see that slow tear!
  In mute communion spring they from his bosom,
  All anguished with the throes of some big thought
  That seeks to force its being into life,
  Then struggles back into his panting breast, 50
  Which hugs the living torture to itself.
Pomp. It is a fearful struggle—but he wakes.
Grac. Let us go home. My mother watches for me;
  While my young wife, novice in sorrow, wraps
  Close to her beating heart my baby boy, 55
  And wonders why its father stays so long.

Exit with Pomponius and Licinius.

First Cit. Would I could right him, were it with my life!
  At least let's follow and keep watch for him.
Second Cit. Yes—we will cheer him up; huzza about him,
  As does the crowd round Fulvius.
First Cit.   And get drunk, 60
  Go mad as they do? No, no. In the face
  Of Gracchus look, and learn there to be sober.
Third Cit. Truly it is a face that doth draw tears!
  I never thought so great a man, and wise,
  Could need the pity of poor folks like us. 65

But now to look at him, 'twould seem indeed
That his tried heart doth throb and ache, all one
As 'twere my own poor son's! [[*Exeunt.*]]

ACT V.

SCENE I. *Street near* Gracchus' *house.*

Enter Cornelia *and* Licinia, *with Child.*

Lic. I will watch here. He needs must pass this way,
 And I will see him.
Child. Mother, are you cold?
Lic. No, child.
Child. What ails your hand to shake so, then?
Cor. Come hither, little one. Your mother's sad;
 Her head aches; she's not over well today. 5
 Let her be quiet. She'll be better soon.
Child. If she's not well, why does she stand in the street,
 And gazing round to see who passes by?
Cor. Hush! hush! you should be with your nurse at home,
 Instead of coming to ask idle questions 10
 Thus at street corners.
Child. Nay then, what have you,
 And what has mother either, got to do
 Thus at street corners? I have heard you say
 Often, that women should not run the street.
Lic. Peace, malapert! Your nurse is watching for you. 15
 Run to her and she'll take you home.
Child. I will not.
Lic. You will not? What!
Child. I am not naughty, mother!
 I only wish you'd let me stay with you.
 You look so sad and grave, as father did
 This morning when he kissed me.
Lic. Chatterbox! 20
 You were asleep until your father went;
 And 'twas in dressing you, I left him time
 To give me thus the slip.
Child. I did not sleep;
 I only held my eyes close shut, because——

Lic. Because? Say on.
Child. Because you talked so sad 25
It made me cry to hear you, and you know
Father laughs at me when I cry, and says
I'll never make a soldier. So I kept
My eyes close shut, and then he could not see
And thought I was asleep. It was no harm; 30
Don't look so sorry, mother; was it wrong?
I did not think there had been harm in it.
Cor. Poor baby! get thee home. 'Tis a sad thing
To tutor thee thus early to thy griefs.
Go home! go home!
Child. Do let me stay. I'm good. 35
Cor. No, no; go home, and we'll come presently;
And look you on my table, you will find
A pretty toy, with the new whip you wished for
To drive your wooden horse. Run home now; quick!
Or you'll not find them there.
Child. [*Kissing her.*] Dear Grandmama! 40
Mama, do kiss me too. I'd rather stay;
But I'll be good, and you'll come quicker home,
And then I'll show you how my horse will trot.
Perhaps he'll canter too, with his new whip. *Exit Child with Nurse.*
Lic. Sorrow! thou earnest teacher! to whom life 45
Is but a school wherein man's heart is curbed
To do thee homage—lay thy heavy hand,
Gently as sorrow may, on that young head.
Let the deep anguish of my burdened heart
Work out the task at once, for him and me! 50
And for myself, I only pray that I
May be so tough of heart, it shall not break
Until my double duty is performed.
Cor. Hush! Here are steps.
Lic. 'Tis Caius comes. I knew
He could not else, but he must pass this way. 55
Cor. It is not Caius. Here are rapid steps,
And noisy words, and clashing arms, with sounds
Of boisterous brawling, and of drunken mirth. *Noise without.*
Lic. Mother, I am afraid! Where shall we go?
Cor. Be still and stand aside. They will not hurt you. 60
I see now: it is Fulvius with his friends.

Oh Rome! how art thou sunk, when such as these
May claim the name of patriots!

Enter FULVIUS *and noisy crowd of Citizens, armed.*

Cit.   Which way now?
Ful.   On to the Aventine hill! Seize it, and make
      These proud patricians learn to know their masters!   65
Citizens.   On to the Aventine hill! Death and revenge!
      Hurra! down with the Senate! Hurra! on!
      Death to the proud patricians! Death and sorrow,
      Hunger and cold, as they have brought on us!
      Starvation seize them! Let them rot in gutters   70
      And gasp their lives out, sprawling on the ground
      As they have bade us do. On! on! to crush them!   *Exeunt with Fulvius.*
Lic.   'Tis fearful, mother! Surely these are not
      The men who call themselves the friends of Gracchus!
Cor.   I would they did not. 'Tis the festered limb   75
      That makes his cause to halt, and there's no surgeon
      So skilful he can lop the gangrene off.
      I fear me, the whole body dies of it.
Lic.   I would I were a man, with a man's soul,
      And not the coward nature modelled me!   80
Cor.   What would you, fair face, if you were a man?
Lic.   I know not what I would, but I would try
      To stand by Caius as another self.
      I would have cast myself before that crowd,
      Instead of shrinking from its noisy riot;   85
      And would have frowned on them, as Caius might,
      Borrowing the solemn thunder of his voice,
      And, with his quiet majesty of mien,
      Bid them go home, and hush their savage tumult.
      I am a coward—ay—a very hare   90
      For panting fearfulness, and yet, methinks,
      I could for Gracchus cast my life away,
      E'en as a worthless straw! I heard last night,
      When he believed me sleeping, sighs burst forth,
      With groans of bitter anguish, as his heart   95
      Would burst itself in the uttering. On his brow
      I laid my soothing hand. Big sweat-drops there
      Stood, as when, labor-worn, the workman tired
      Doth resting pant, from overstrainèd toil.

SCENE I]   *Caius Gracchus* / 241

	I rose and pressed my lips to his, which burned	100
	With a hot fever; quivering, too, they seemed	
	All tremulous, as nerved with agony.	
	Clinging, I hoped to cool them with my breath;	
	But tear-drops then came coursing from his eyes	
	Slowly, as thunder-drops before the storm;	105
	And then, from head to foot a shivering came!	
	Oh mother! It was fearful thus to see	
	The strong man in his agony!	
Cor.	My child,	
	E'en in my breaking heart, which overcharged	
	With its own miseries bursts, I feel there's room	110
	Still left to pity thee. But helpless all,	
	While pity grasps the burden, until reason	
	Doth totter 'neath the load, yet fails she still	
	To ease thee of one fraction of its weight.	
	Let us go home. You can do no good here.	115
Lic.	No, I must stay. Gracchus went out unarmed,	
	As though on simple business to the Forum,	
	And I have brought him this. [*Shows a dagger.*]	
Cor.	'Tis a small help.	
	But here he comes.	
Lic.	Dear heaven! I give you thanks	
	For this one comfort, in so many sorrows!	120

Enter GRACCHUS *and friends.*

Grac.	Mother! Licinia! What do you here?	
Lic.	We watch for you. I pray you, Caius, come,	
	Come with me home! You shake your head; well, then—	
	Come with me anywhere! In other worlds	
	We'll make a home elsewhere.[33] Nay, smile not thus,	125
	As though in mockery of my simple suit!	
	What's Rome to you that you should die for her,	
	And leave your wife and boy?[34] Come, dearest—do!	
	Come, drown ambition, drinking deep of love!	
Grac.	Licinia, would you save your husband thus?	130

---

33. *Coriolanus* 3.3.133–35: "Despising / For you the city, thus I turn my back. / There is a world elsewhere!" The speaker is Coriolanus.

34. *Hamlet* 2.2.553–54: "What's Hecuba to him, or he to her, / That he should weep for her?"

                    If I have erred ambitiously—at least,
                    Not by a foul desertion bid me swell
                    My much repented fault. Should I a traitor—
                    Recreant—turn cowardly, to shun my friends,
                    Would you, love, longer own my tarnished name,   135
                    Or rather weep for Gracchus as one dead,
                    With horror shrinking from the counterfeit,
                    Whose shame could blight his honor! E'en yourself,
                    With all your gentle cowardice, would shun
                    And blush to name the father of your boy.   140
                    Entreat me not, then, with an early shame
                    To blot his fair young brow; but rather let
                    A father's blessing guard his orphaned pillow.
                    Bear him my parting kiss, and now, *farewell.*
Lic.   [*Falling on her knees catches his robe.*]
                    No, no! Come home with me! I'd love you still,   145
                    Though you of the world's shame were made the butt;
                    I'd love you in my heart's world, and forget
                    Men's flouts and hisses, as the howling cry
                    Of savage beasts that roam in unseen wilds.
                    Men's voices hurt us not; we'll let them pass,   150
                    And think that they are spirits, gibbering ghosts,
                    That wander in some stranger world to ours.
                    The wind doth blow and hiss us every day,
                    And howls and whistles in its mocking rage,
                    And yet we heed it not. The forest trees   155
                    Do constant whisper 'mong their summer leaves,
                    And yet we never fret to learn their secrets!
                    Men's talk, as innocent, would hurt us not,
                    Would we but doom them exiles from our world
                    And live in our own hearts!
Grac.   Dearest, you'd spurn—   160
                    None sooner than yourself—this foolish dream,
                    Did once your better reason find its sway.
Lic.   Speak to him, mother! Bid him stay with us.
                    What is the world to him? Its thought wounds not.
                    He would not bleed because it frowned! Speak, mother!   165
Cor.   Alas! I cannot in your cause, my child.
                    Our life is for the world. Man doth forget
                    His every highest purpose, scorning it;
                    And from the level of his high intent

	Doth thus degrade himself.	
Lic.	Oh! I am mad!	170

      I cannot reason; I but pray: "Come home."
      You do not leave me now as formerly,
      Tribune or lawgiver, from the rostra speaking;
      Nor yet a glorious war doth summon you,
      Where, should death be your lot, at least I'd see   175
      Your corse brought home for noble funerals.
      Meek victim of an angered foe, you go—
      Oh Gods! for what? I had forgot—take this.   *Gives the dagger.*

Grac.   As a last gift I take it. But I go
      Unarmed, as he should do whose mind is fixed   180
      To suffer violence, rather than commit it.

Lic.   You go before the murderers of Tiberius
      To throw your life away! And I must soon
      A weeping suppliant to the river stand
      To beg the corpse of Gracchus! Mother, kneel!   185
      Do you not love your son? Does your heart beat?
      He is your all on earth! Kneel with me, mother;

                                    Draws Cornelia to her knees.

      Pray to him here, as though he were some god!
      He will not dare refuse you! 'Twere a shame
      To see him spurn his mother! I am mad;   190
      I cannot pray. Pray *you* as though great Jove
      Were looking down upon us! Mother, pray!

Grac.   Mother, have pity! Rise. Remember, now,
      Your oft-spoke lesson. Death is nothing, standing
      Close elbowed by dishonour. Kneel not to me.   195

Cor.   I do not kneel to you. Hear me, ye Gods!
      My supplications are to you for this
      My last, best hope in life; my *only one!*
      I pray ye now to give him strength to bear
      This heavy trial; parting, worse than death,   200
      From the heart-stricken loved ones! Go, my son.
      I have no word to stop you. If your life
      Without dishonour can be saved, remember
      You owe it to your wife, and to your boy.
      Farewell! The gods protect you!

Grac.   Noble mother!   205
      Forgive me that I have so often spurned
      Your wiser councils. Now the ghosts of them,

While your reproach is mute, look mournful back
To show me all my folly, and my sin.
Farewell! *Disengages himself gently from Licinia,*
who falls fainting into Cornelia's
arms.
                      And for this poor heart-broken thing,   210
Receive her, mother, as the legacy
Of all the love I bear you. *Exit, with friends.*

Cor.   He is gone!
What mean my niggard eyes that they do leave
Their fount for sorrow dry! Let madness come!
Or drivelling idiocy, that droops its life   215
In moping corners! It were peaceful rest! *Pauses thoughtfully.*
But this is weakness. Thus Heaven wills it not.
My laggard spirit faints before its time;
My task is not yet done. Up! up! and work!
Life yet has duties, and my comfort is   220
Yet to fulfil them. Daughter! Daughter! wake!
We must go seek our boy, who waits us still,
To show us how his wooden horse can trot!
Oh! what a motley is this struggling world! *[[Exeunt.]]*

SCENE II. *Aventine Hill.*

GRACCHUS *and* FULVIUS.
Crowds of Citizens in the distance.

Ful.   I'll bear no further cringing.
Grac.   I ask none.
But rather that you'd meet a noble risk
To save our friends by what perchance may prove
Our proper immolation. Come with me
To plead before the Senate.
Ful.   I am tired.   5
You have my son; do with him what you list.
He's soft enough to coax and wheedle for you!
His mother's readiness of tears he has,
And blushing face, and gently cringing voice.
No gift have I of words, nor will I crouch   10
The Senate from its crabbèd whim to move.
I come here armed for fight.
Grac.   And will, I fear,

                Make sooner than not meet the war you seek.

                            Enter Messenger.

                What news? Your eager look seems full of speech.
Mes.   The Senate mock your offers, and have seized   15
                Young Fulvius prisoner. Criminals, they say,
                Before they plead for mercy, should surrender.
Ful.   They say we plead for mercy! Hear you that?
Mes.   Opimius, eager for hostilities,
                Advances with a corps of infantry,   20
                Backed by a company of Cretan archers.
Ful.   Hurra! I will prepare for them. Ho! friends,
                Come up! we've work on hand.   *Exit.*
Grac.   And I, alas!
                Have nearly done that share which falls to me.   [[*Exeunt.*]]

                    SCENE III. *Streets of Rome.*

                *Confusion of fighting. Citizens and troops
                passing to and fro. Then enter two Citizens, wounded.*

First Cit.   I pray you bind my arm. Nay, not so tight!
                Your whole of fear was cast into that jerk.
                Be easy; of too little moment are we
                For them to follow us. Beneath their thoughts
                Are we to feed or kill. As we may starve   5
                Until our bodies trip them in the streets,
                So may we live, if from their dignity
                We of our lubbard carcass keep the sight,
                Nor shock them with the thought that we are men
                Who breathe Heaven's air like them.
Second Cit.   Well, I'll take heed   10
                To keep me from their track. That rascal Fulvius
                Will scarce again tempt me to meet them.
First Cit.   Hang him!
                It was most foul to run and leave us there,
                All weltering too, in wounds and broken bones!
                And then of men to see the difference!   15
                How Gracchus stood, and with his cry of "*Peace!*"
                Did check Opimius (who strewed corpses round),
                And cried, "*Shame on you, Consul! Spare your people!*"
                And would not leave the ground, though all unarmed,

                    Until he was dragged off, and crying still:
                    "Consul, you break the pith of your own strength!
                    The people is the sinew of the country.
                    In mercy spare your slaughter!"
Second Cit.   Here are troops!
                    Help us, great Jupiter! Troops! troops! Let's run.   *Exeunt.*

SCENE IV. *Temple of Diana.*

Gracchus, Licinius, Philocrates.
Enter Pomponius.

Pomp.   Fulvius, unsaved by his ignoble flight,
          Is seized and slain. Our victors lap up gore
          Like thirsty hound, and livid death now sits
          The close familiar of our firesides.
          Mothers, who but just now sent forth their sons
          With life all blooming, hug a bloody corpse;
          While widows weep, bewildered children stare
          On stiffening limbs which but this morning's sun
          Might see them frolic with. One slaughter-house,
          Rome suicidal dies 'neath her own blows.
          The dastard crowd, all frightened, crouching shrink
          From the red death that tracks them, and, in hopes
          To win impunity, now crack their throats
          With loud huzzas, and adulation forced
          Of these their task-masters. With bended brows,
          Heads leaning towards each other, then they name
          What price your head doth in the Senate bear;
          While their slow fingers, as an itching seized them,
          Do round their weapons' handles rub themselves.
          I would not trust their love.
Grac.   Slight cause have they
          Longer to couple love and Gracchus' name.
          Oh! I have sinned most heavily to drag them
          Like sheep thus to the slaughter. There's an instinct
          That makes man bold in right, but coward stamps him
          Defending wrong. This holy weapon I
          Struck from the people's grasp, and blunted it
          With bold injustice. By aggression roused,
          I answered with aggression. Wrong met wrong.
          Blood followed; and, upon its smoking tracks,

How with fierce joy the Senate raised its cry, 30
Hallooing to the vengeance, while, unnerved,
All paralyzed of strength, the people's arm
Fell lifeless in its effort! Vice met vice.
When moral virtue fled, Reason abashed
Shrank timid from her post, and Justice threw 35
The tangled reins of the State to open license.
Might reared her haughty head, and frowned down Right.

Enter CORNELIA *hastily.*

Cor. My son, seek surer refuge. In this shrine
But slender trust is left.
Grac. You, mother—here!
Follow not thus this shattered wreck, but think 40
Your son is dead already.
Cor. Slander not
The uninjured shapings of your body's strength,
Nor shame your mother, calling thus her son
Some weak and shattered thing.
Grac. 'Tis not indeed
The body fails me, but my heart is sick. 45
I'm wearied in the struggle and would die!
Death frights the happy; but the sorrow-worn
Springs to its rest, all hopeful as the school-boy
Rejoicing in his promised holiday.
Cor. Man has no right to name his hour of rest. 50
Up and be doing! 'Tis our being's law,
Till heaven shall give release. Life's duties swarm;
Each moment, with its task, marks lethargy
The heaviest sin of man. Up! up! and work!
How should we dare to make a whim our guide, 55
When obligations crowd us with their claims?
Fulfil the uncanceled bonds! Let reckoned dues
Prove life by right is idle, then might man,
Manumised at will, his fettered being shift.
But you, high duty's bondsman, would defraud— 60
Shunning its task—the world of what you owe!
Grac. I've striven till my heart with hoping faints.
All wearied shrink I from the thought of life,
Whose fear doth fright me like the hideous dream
Of some strange midnight horror.

Cor.   Rouse! For shame!   65
    Wake up your flagging energies; be bold
    To probe beneath these flutterings; you will find
    Your courage sound beneath them. For the right,
    Man even in despair should ever strive.
    The very effort, howsoever vain,   70
    Is always something gained. To the great work
    It warms the blood of the world, which wrestles on
    Still against failure, like the strong man struggling,
    Until the end of truth at last is reached.
    We are the thews and sinews of the world,   75
    And in our efforts there is nothing lost;
    All work to good or ill. Go with these friends;
    For life and duty strive; nor be the coward
    Who, shrinking, dreads on his own heart to look,
    And dies, to shun responsibility.   80
    My son, I know, can never thus be brought
    By fear to shirk his manhood.
Grac.   Mother, I go.
    May heaven so bless you, as your son shall strive
    To prove the honor and the love he bears you,
    By working out the noble thoughts you teach.   85
Cor.   Then once again farewell! These bursting tears
    Now come to show the woman's heart, whose boldness,
    Your sickly resolution to upbraid,
    Usurped the man. Oh! were they tears of blood,
    Feebly they'd speak my anguish.   *Exit Cornelia.*
Grac.   Come, Pomponius,   90
    Lead on. I'll follow you. Philocrates,
    You've ever been a true friend to your master;
    Take with my thanks this trifling boon as token
    Of gratitude and love. Be to my son [*Offers a ring*]
    What you have been to me.
Philo.   Have I offended,   95
    That, sharing with you thus far all your fortunes,
    I now should from your danger be thrust off?
    I will not leave you.
Grac.   True heart! Then, come on.   *Exeunt.*

SCENE V. *Bridge near Rome.*

Enter GRACCHUS, POMPONIUS, LICINIUS, PHILOCRATES.

Pomp. We've reached our point. You, Gracchus, hasten on.
   Philocrates, 'twere best to follow him.
   Methinks, Licinius, you and I, at bay,
   With the vantage of this bridge, should hold awhile
   Some scores of our pursuing enemy.   5
   Our farewells, Gracchus, have no time for words.
Grac. True deeds live not in words. 'Twould pain me more
   To leave you to the death you rush to seek,
   But that I feel, though striving still to keep it,
   My life is forfeit to this day's disasters.   10
Philo. The enemy is on us. Master, fly!
Grac. Come then, good friend; and you brave hearts, farewell.
                                        Exit Gracchus with Philocrates.
Licinius. Now at their highest let us stake our lives;
   A bloody ransom for the life of Gracchus.

               Enter OPIMIUS *with troops.*

Opim. Off, traitors! Clear the way!
Pomp.   Stand back! we carry   15
   Deaths for some score of you.
Opim.   Out, villains! Back!
   Charge them, my men! This mockery of fight
   Doth shame your manhood. What, ye coward rabble!
   Shrink ye before two men? Get on, ye scum!
   You rate your lives too high! They are not worth   20
   Such doubt and higgling for. On! There you go!
   Cut down the rascals.   *They fight; several are slain. Opimius strikes at*
                              and wounds Licinius.
                Ha! You got it then.
Licinius. A scratch! I'd stand my ground with fifty such.
   Come on; we're only warming to the fight.
                                        They fight again and Licinius falls.
   I've done my last, Pomponius. Make the most   25
   Of your unaided strength. Each moment brings
   Perhaps a life to Gracchus.   *Dies.*
Pomp.   Noble friend,
   I have no time to weep. Your merits speak
   Full as the hundred mouths whose gashes pour

  Your flooding lifeblood out.   *Soldiers attack him again.*
         No breathing time!   30
         They fight. Several of the enemy fall,
         and at last Pomponius.

Opim. You're done with now.
Pomp.   Curses on this weak arm
  That could not stay you longer.   *Dies.*
Opim.   Fellows, on!
  We've lost here too much time. Its weight in gold,
  Remember, is the price of Gracchus' head.
        Soldiers rush over the bridge, trampling
        on bodies, and exeunt.

SCENE VI. *Public Road.*

Several Citizens.

First Cit. May the Gods guard him. 'Tis a hard run chase.
Second Cit. And he'll be beaten in it. Here he comes.

     Enter GRACCHUS *and* PHILOCRATES.

First Cit. How the sweat stands in big drops on his brow!
  He's quite outworn with running.
Third Cit.   Here, on horseback
  Comes Septimuleius, who so often boasts   5
  The warmness of his friendship. He'll be like
  To lend the beast to save his periled life.

   Enter SEPTIMULEIUS *and another Citizen on horseback.*

Grac. Prythee, your horse, my friend. I have no strength
  To course it farther thus.
Sept.   I've hurt my foot;
  I cannot run, and would not dare stand here   10
  To let Opimius see me give you aid.
  Make your best speed; I can do nothing for you.
Grac. [*To other Citizen*] And you, are you too, friend, hurt in the foot?
Cit. No; but you'd best pass on. I cannot lend
  Nor care to risk my horse.
Philo.   Come, master, on!   15
  They have no help for us. Their hearts are dead
  For very fright within them, and are numbed
  To the forgetfulness of friendship. Fear

                Doth from the coward's choked up bosom chase
                All feeling else. The enemy is here.   20
                                        Exeunt Gracchus and Philocrates.
First Cit.   You might have lent your horse, if for the sake
                Only of bygone kindness.
Sept.   Hold your tongue,
                Or I for treason 'gainst the state impeach you.
                Huzza! I say, for Rome and for Opimius!

                            Enter OPIMIUS, *etc.*

Opim.   Which way went Gracchus?   *Septimuleius points.*
                            Thanks, good fellow! Come,   25
                There's gold, you know, for him who wins this game.
                                Exit Opimius, followed by Septimuleius, etc.
First Cit.   That fellow owes to Gracchus his son's life;
                And more than that, saving his family
                From beggary and ruin. Gracchus lent him
                Four thousand sesterces to aid him once   30
                When troubles thronged him, and I know right well
                These never were repaid.
Second Cit.   Let's follow on
                To watch what's doing.   *Exeunt.*

                    SCENE VII. *Grove of the Furies.*

                Enter hastily GRACCHUS *and* PHILOCRATES.

Grac.   Here must I stop. Exhaustion seizes me.
                Ye Goddesses, grim tenants of this grove,
                Sprung up in vengeance from the angry blood
                Of Coelus, shed by his exasperate son,
                Receive me, a self-offered sacrifice   5
                To ward your vengeance from unhappy Rome.
                Let my spilt blood, that soon will sprinkle round,
                Upon your dark-leaved cedars' roots, its life,
                Smooth down those jealousies, and heal dissensions
                Whose earthquake troubles in their tremblings rock   10
                The fated city to its threatened fall.
                Methinks ye heed my prayer. I see ye now.
                Your blood-shot eyes gaze on me with a look
                Inexorable and yet half in pity.
                Your serpent hair towards me hissing seems   15

As 'twould th' expiatory victim seize!
Officiating priest, my brow I bind
With cedar wreaths, for my own sacrifice,
And wait the blow that to your vengeance gives me.
Philocrates, there yet is time. Escape.   20

Philo.   Never.

Enter Opimius *with troops,* Lucullus, Septimuleius, *etc.*

Opim.   There stands the traitor. Down with him!
Ye pause, ye rabble crew, as though ye saw
    Some god to wonder at.
Soldier.   Methinks it is.
    I would not dare to touch him for my life.
Second Sol.   Nor I. The thought would haunt me to my grave.   25

They throw down their arms, and
Lucullus rushes to strike Gracchus.

Luc.   Then take thy death from me.   *Philocrates throws himself in the way,*
receives the blow, and at the same
time strikes Lucullus. Both fall.

                    Base slave! Stand off!
He's killed me. Oh! to die by a slave's hand!
Grac. [*looking at Philocrates*]   And thou art gone, my last true friend, before
    me.   *Septimuleius creeps behind Gracchus*
                            and stabs him.

    'Tis done! I thank ye, Gods!   *Dies.*
Sept.   The gold is mine!
    Consul, the gold is mine!
Opim.   Villain! it is.   [[*Exeunt.*]]   30

Part III

11.

Letters

To Sophia Cheves Haskell

Dear Sophy   St. Matthews April 8th [1836]

It was all over sooner than I expected; I wrote to you Monday, poor Mother's troubles finished the next day; she died Tuesday afternoon; quietly, satisfied, quite conscious of her state, and talking to us all, until about ¾ of an hour before her last breath; she spoke of you all often wished she could have seen you but seemed to try to let that and every thing else trouble her as little as possible. She was buried in our little burying ground on Wednesday afternoon; it could not be delayed longer owing to the nature of her Malady;——She died without inflamation which made her sufferings, although great[,] less than they might have been. I feel as I wander about the house and have to take her place in a thousand things as if I were doing wrong all the time;—Anna has to be prepared to start for the North in a few days and I have to turn over every work trunk and closet, it absolutely makes me sick to meddle with all her little arrangements, her patterns, clothes cut out for the children etc.

Father seems to feel it very much; so did Anna for the first day or two; the children as usual care for nothing;—poor little things I am almost inclined to punish them, to make them look dull. I must stop. John is starting in half an hour, ~~sudde~~ unexpectedly for Columbia to see about the means of getting Anna and Grandmother to Charleston on their way to the North. God bless you all.

Your affectionate Sister
Louisa Cheves.

To Langdon Cheves, Jr.

Dear Lang,   Portman Shoals Oct[ober] 7, 1839

I do beleive I have not written to you once this summer, and I do beleive I need not make many apologies on the ~~subject~~ occasion, for I do beleive *votre Seignorie* will forgive the sin, sooner than you would the infliction of a page of excuses on the subject.

We have been at home just one week; and I have surmounted a summer at the Springs, which thank Heaven *est finie* and I am again released f[ro]m playing belle which, nolens volens, seems some how or other to be my destiny when I go into company. Next time I go to matronise Miss Anna in the gay world, I vow it shall be in a cap, or some such distinguishing mark of old age; folks shall not think that my venerable self, stepping close on nine and twenty, has any ambition to pass as young Lady, any more. I'll pin a piece of paper with, "*aged twenty-nine*," on my shoulder, and if that don't scare off the young seventeen-year olders who come to flirt with me, the dear knows what will. I am tired to death with rivalling Nan in their good graces. But I am talking of by gone ills which really seem now like the confused bustle of a dream;—we have been going thro' such very different scenes of late that the contrast seems unreal. On our way home we met Gen[eral] Hayne ill at Ashville; Father of course delayed his journey;—we staid to see him die, and then brought on his widow and two sons here.[1] Poor Mrs Hayne,—the shock has been a fearfully sad one to her. She is in dreadful spirits and not very good health, so I am obliged to be pretty constantly in attendance on her;—and I confess the 24 hours I spent over Gen: Hayne's death-bed with my subsequent attention to my poor friend, have not at all contributed to raise the bustle of the Springs in my estimation; perhaps I might have judged their fooleries more indulgently a few weeks ago, tho' at best, *vraiment,* they

---

1. Robert Young Hayne (1791–1839), law student and close friend of Langdon Cheves, who turned over to him his prosperous law practice; attorney general of South Carolina (1818–22); U.S. senator (1822–32); prominent nullifier; argued states' rights against Daniel Webster (1830); governor of South Carolina (1832–34). LSM's youngest brother (born April 9, 1829) was named for Hayne; her second daughter, Louisa Rebecca Hayne McCord, was named both for LSM and for Hayne's second wife, whom he had married in 1820, Rebecca Alston Hayne.

don't suit my fancy.——Talking of the Haynes, puts me in mind of my baby (what used to be, that's to say) Hayney. He managed to break his arm some time ago[;] how, I know not; I never received Charley's letter informing me of the accident, only his subsequent notices of its recovery. I suppose the youngster would be almost willing to break his other arm now that the first one is well, as it resulted in his being sent to Philadelphia and getting a month's petting f[ro]m Grandmother. I received a letter f[ro]m Charlotte a few days since, it distresses me to hear of her being sick so often.[2] I wish she could manage to get well and keep so. I presume the cares and anxieties of the summer, have affected her health injuriously, and hope therefore that with their passing away and the return of cool weather, she will be better. I was very glad to hear that her Father's health was improving, I had heard a few days before a report of its being very bad. She tells me you won't grow fat;——however as you have got thro' the summer without melting away altogether, I begin to have some hopes of you.——I hear you are living close in your office still. At least so was reported to me by Mr. Beaufort Watts whom I had the felicity to light upon at Greenville;[3] ——He called to see me and bounced in with a most exhilirating "how do you do Miss Cheves?" which ought in Charity to have made me answer with as good-natured a "quite well I thank you," but I was thinking of some thing for Mrs. Hayne at the moment and I was bothered, and my wits, if they were any where had gone a gadding out of my own head, and so I stared at him with that vacant look which says so distinctly "who in the name of wonder can *you* be?" until the poor man had to go thro' the very awkward ceremony of introducing himself. I'm scrawling in a tremendous fashion; I don't think you can make it all out; but I beleive I am, or ought to be in a great hurry, so I can't help it. We leave here the 20th of this month probably, which will take us to Columbia about the 25th. I do not know if we will stop any time;——We go down with Mrs. Hayne and it will depend some what upon her wishes. She leaves her sons in Columbia and f[ro]m there Father purposes taking her to Charleston leaving Anna and myself at St. Matthews.

I beleive I may as well say good-night, for there's the clock striking twelve, and there's the cat mewing at the entry door; for all the world, *jist* like a ghost. Give my love to Charlotte.

Your affectionate Sister
Louisa Cheves.

---

2. Charlotte McCord, eldest daughter of David James McCord, married Langdon Cheves, Jr., on Dec. 24, 1839. Her mother had died in early August.

3. Beaufort Taylor Watts (d. c. 1869), secretary of legation in Colombia and Russia; secretary to many governors of South Carolina.

To William Porcher Miles

Dear Sir[4]　　　　　　　　　　　　　　　　Lang Syne May 2d, 1848

As you alone among my friends, have had the kindness to hint to me some of the many defects of the little volume which I was bold enough to offer for criticism,[5] although I fear you treated me much too gently, I now venture, emboldened by your friendly comments, to take the very great liberty of begging for your opinion of the accompanying manuscript. I am conscious that I am asking what I have no right to do, and intruding upon some leisure hour which you could employ much more profitably and pleasantly,—but still I venture to ask the favour.

It is to me more than an amusement,—it is an absolute comfort, an almost necessity, to put my fancies upon paper, and I have a strong desire to find out whether or not they are worth the putting down. I have no unprejudiced friend near me to whose judgment I can appeal. May I, as the greatest possible favour, beg you to pull to pieces, to be as ill-natured as you can, with the productions which I trouble you with? If they are *abominable trash*, I will really thank you sincerely if you will tell me so, without any sugaring. I do not wish to extract compliments from you;—I would not give a pin for them. I am begging for what would be of real use to me;—for a true and honest opinion, from a person, capable as you are, of giving one. The more fault-finding, the greater will be my debt of gratitude. My wish is, if possible, without making a fool of myself, to dis-cover whether I can do something, or nothing,—and I take the liberty of throwing myself for this once upon your charity, promising never to repeat the infliction, and hoping that you will without disguising or softening in any way, give me your opinion. I assure you that were you to tell me I had sent you the most nonsensical stuff that ever was penned, I should thank you for your sincerity and endeavour to profit by your judgment.

---

4. William Porcher Miles (1822–99), professor of mathematics at the College of Charleston; member of the U.S. House of Representatives (1857–60); as mayor of Charleston, received the funeral cortege of Langdon Cheves; represented Charleston to the Confederate Congress, where he served as chairman of the Committee on Military Affairs. Miles was a cousin of David James McCord.

5. *My Dreams* (Philadelphia, 1848). "Mrs. McCord thanks you very much for your candid and friendly opinion and criticisms on her Poems. She says she values them more because you have been candid enough to blame, where you thought it deserved, and that she is satisfied that you are right, and hopes that your advice will be of service to her. She would be glad to have your further counsel." David James McCord to William Porcher Miles, March 17, 1848, William Porcher Miles Papers, SHC.

If I impose too troublesome a task upon you, pray refuse without hesitation my request. If you find it convenient to oblige me, let me beg you to do so *entirely at your leisure*. I merely take this opportunity of sending to you as I happen to have a servant going to town on other business.

I regretted much that your indisposition prevented us from seeing you when in town. Hoping that you have long before this entirely recovered and with kind regards to your Mother and Sister, beleive me dear Sir

with much respect
Your's etc.
Louisa S. McCord.

To William Porcher Miles

Dear Sir,   Pendleton June 12th, 1848

Having left home on the 29th, I failed to receive before my departure, your's of 28th ~~inst~~ ulto which has followed me hither. I am most sincerely obliged to you for your kind criticisms, and so far from thinking them harsh or in any degree "*hypercritical*," am only most agreeably surprised that you have found in my manuscripts so much to approve of. Although I feel that you have said all the good you can of them, and noted their faults most gently, I still am confident that after the appeal I made to your *charity*, you would not willingly mislead me, and I am much gratified to find, that you think there is in my productions, the proof of *some power*. Although I have been pushed back in every possible way, and have myself endeavoured for many a long year to crush my own propensities, there has been a struggling consciousness of something which has goaded me on to my recent experiments, and one word of sincere and well-judged approbation, though it were mixed with a bushel of fault-finding, would be enough to cheer me on. I only fear your judgment as being too indulgent;—if you had struck harder, I would feel more certain of my footing. My misfortune is, that I am most wofully ignorant, and not knowing even *where* to look for the information that I want, find it now, rather late in the day, to begin my groping in the dark. It is however a comfort even to try,—and try I will. An effortless life, is, to a restless mind, a weary fate to be doomed to; and as no other door is open to me, I may as well push on at this. Should I fail, the very effort will have given an object to many an otherwise dissatisfied hour, and although I shall have gazed at the sun in vain, it will at least have been a comfort to dream that I could reach him. (Don't say "bottled sunbeams,"—please,—

though I believe my simile deserves it.)⁶ ——Of the faults you have pointed out, some I was before conscious of and deemed irremediable;—others, if I had the manuscript at hand, I would set about trying to doctor at once. C. Gracchus at least. The other⁷ I do not hope to be able to do any thing with; it was written some dozen years ago, and the spirit of it has passed away from me. I am most annoyed at the idea of my halting lines and defective measure, but must try and hunt up the culprits for correction. You show me some historical blunders which I have fallen into. Livius Drusus for instance I might just as well have made a young man, as an old one, but was really ignorant enough not to know anything about him. I must stand up though for the Gracchi. They are among my *bona fide* heroes. Plutarch from whom I have pilfered largely, gives them I think a high position;—and does not Niebuhr (I ask, for truly I am lamentably difficient in information and have forgotten what little I have known about it) consider them as having nobly acted in a good cause?⁸ I confess to being a thorough upholder of the people's rights and in present scenes, although I cannot quite go with Louis Blanc and M. Albert,⁹ much less can I sympathise with fallen dynasties, however much I may deem beggar-kings an object of pity.¹⁰—— As to my productions being *closet dramas,* what else can a Woman write? The *world of action* must to her be almost entirely a closed book. I am extremely obliged to you for your kind offer to give me the *benefit* (for truly it is a *real benefit*) of your advice, and if I shall in future be able to do any thing, will venture again to appeal to your judgment for assistance. As regards my M.S.S. I am here, too far away, for you to get them sent to me. Pray let them occupy an empty corner of some drawer, until I get home again, and perhaps next winter I may be able to g do something with them. I shall keep your letter as a commentary upon their defects, and will try to dragg, coax, or push them, into perhaps a somewhat better shape.

---

6. In bk. 3, chap. 5 of *Gulliver's Travels,* Gulliver describes a scientist at the Grand Academy of Lagado, who "had been Eight Years upon a Project for extracting Sun-Beams out of Cucumbers, which were to be put into Vials hermetically sealed, and let out to warm the Air in raw inclement Summers." Jonathan Swift, *Prose Writings,* ed. Herbert Davis (Oxford, 1965), 11:179.

7. Not identified.

8. The account of the Gracchi in the *Römische Geschichte* (1811–32) of the German historian Barthold Georg Niebuhr (1776–1831) is an encomium going beyond even what LSM claims of it.

9. Albert-Alexandre Martin, called Albert l'Ouvrier (1815–95), French revolutionary politician; member of the Provisional Government, then of the National Assembly (1848); imprisoned (1848–59) for his part in uprisings of May and June 1848.

10. King Louis Philippe of France had abdicated on Feb. 24, 1848, and gone into exile in England.

Allow me to reiterate my sincere thanks for the trouble you have taken in compliance with my request. Pray remember me most kindly to your Mother, Aunt and Sister. Tell your Aunt that I am such a shabby letter-writer, and was so busy physicking little negroes and packing up etc. before leaving home that I did not find time to thank her for her kind note and acceptable etc.[']s sent up by my servant Betsy; but in spite of my neglect did not feel the less kindly her attentions.

Mr. McCord joins in kind remembrance to all. We will be very glad to see any of you if you can be tempted to visit these regions.

Believe me dear Sir

very truly and respectfully your's
Louisa S. McCord—

To Mary Cheves Dulles

Dear Mary   Columbia Oct[ober] 9th, 1852

I will not write you a letter, but one line to thank you for the little box sent by Mrs. Lieber. The girls would have answered your kind epistle to them, but I have been too busy to rule paper etc. for the poor little things who have been rather neglected by me, owing to my having my hands full with Mr. McCord who has been seriously sick ever since I wrote to you. I do not know what is has been the matter with him. He has been bothered and plagued by numbers of things and people of late and all sorts of disagreeable affairs (I don't mean anything of our own at home) and in truth I believe it just broke him down. He is doing better now; indeed has improved very much in the last 36 hours and I believe is going to get pretty well again. He is a regular spoiled one though and wants a deal of nursing.

If Hayney comes to Philadelphia, do give my love to him. Tell him he ought to have written to me. I have not known his direction all the Summer. I guess he is glad to escape the persecution of my epistles.

I think I may as well stop; my head is splitting with pain. I have slept very irregularly for the last fortnight, and to cap the climax of unrest, last night when every thing else got quiet, one of my carriage horses began to kick in the stable. Ben goes off every night and there was nobody to quiet it, and so it kicked away to its heart's content and I lay awake to listen to it, and this morning I feel pretty much as if I had got all the kicks on my head instead of only in my ears.

Please any time, if not too troublesome, get me some gloves a size larger for the girls. Those sent are very pretty but rather tight. 2 pair each will do, and 2 or 3 pair more for *me* will last for six months. I am a terrible glove-consumer.

Goodbye—Love to all—Write to me soon.

Your's affectionately
Louisa S. McCord—

Oh! Mrs. Stowe! One word of that abominable woman's abominable book,—I have read it lately and am quite shocked at *you*, my dear Cousin, Miss Mary C. Dulles, for thinking it as if I remember right, you said you did, a strong exposition against slavery. It is one mass of fanatical bitterness and foul misrepresentation wrapped in the garb of Christian Charity. She quotes the Scriptures only to curse by them. Why! have not you been at the South enough to know, that ~~men~~ our gentlemen dont keep mulatto wives, nor whip negroes to death ~~and~~ nor commit all the various other enormities that she describes? She does not know what a gentleman or a lady is, at least according to our Southern notions[,] ~~no~~ any more than I do a Laplander. Just look at her real benevolent gentleman (as she means him to be) her Mr. St. Clare, or her sensible woman Mrs. Shelby and ~~too~~ two more distressing fools and hypocrites I never met with. The woman (Mrs. Stowe I mean) has certainly never been in any Southern State further than across the Kentucky line at most, and there in very doubtful society. All her Southern ladies and gentlemen talk coarse Yankee. But I must stop. The thought of Mrs. Stowe doubles my infliction of horses heels. Read the book over again my dear child and you will wonder that you ever took it for anything but what it is, i.e. as malicious and gross an abolitionist production (though I confess a cunning one) as ever dis-graced the press. Encore adieu—

Yours always
L. S. Mc———

To Henry Charles Carey

Dear Sir Lang Syne Fort Motte, So[uth] C[arolin]a
Jan[uar]y 18th, 1854

I was pained to see from your kind letter to Mr. McCord, that you considered my article for the "Southern Quarterly" as having been written consequent upon the reception of the copy of the "Slave Trade" etc., which you were so polite as to send me last summer.[11] The truth is, that having pur-

---

11. See *PSE*, "Carey on the Slave Trade," reviewing Henry C. Carey, *The Slave Trade, Domestic and Foreign: Why It Exists, and How It May Be Extinguished* (Philadelphia, 1853; rpt. New

chased a copy of the work some time before receiving the one sent by you, my article was written before the arrival of the latter,—upon seeing which, for fear of apparent dis-courtesy, I was much inclined to suppress what I had written; but, in sober earnest, your book is, in my opinion, (I am sure not intentionally on your part) of so mis-chievous a tendency upon a subject of vital importance to us of the South, that I felt it even a duty to dispute its accuracy. It is,—excuse my saying so,—of a class of works which do us more harm than the most violent abolitionist attacks; assuming the ground of a wrong where wrong does not exist, and with laboured argument upon false grounds, forcing to fearfully practical conclusions. This too upon a subject which we have studied deeply and believe that we understand well; while every line which you write, shows that our system is to you an unstudied one, which you condemn from theory, not insight.——You believe the negro to be an oppressed race, while we believe him to be a protected one. You assume the ground that we are committing a constant injustice towards him, while we are convinced that we are his only safeguard from extermination, at least in this country. We believe that and living as we do, surrounded by, governing, and fostering this people,—we have a right to believe, that we know more of negro-nature, and certainly more of our own treatment of them and of their condition among us, than can the Duchess of Sutherland who understands as little of negroes as of cotton-planting; and yet you have praised her mis-chievous interference in a subject of which she is as profoundly ignorant, as, in all probability she is of Greek and Hebrew.

When you remember that this subject is one with which, nationally, as well as individually, our every interest,—life, fortune, and fame,—is inseperably linked, you will scarcely be surprised that we should be sensitive upon the subject, and intreat our friends to open their eyes before they determine whether or not it is indeed midnight with us.——My blow was aimed at a mis-chievous theory, and, permit me to assure you, without any feeling of personal disrespect.

You refer me to Bastiat's "*Harmonies*". I have read them attentively before this, as well as the correspondence in the "Journal des Economistes." I regret that Bastiat should have agreed with you, to at least a considerable extent, (his premature death prevented his fully developping how far) in what I can-

---

York, 1967); also William Gilmore Simms to Henry Carey Baird, Dec. 17, 1853, in Mary C. Simms Oliphant et al., eds., *The Letters of William Gilmore Simms,* 6 vols. (Columbia, S.C., 1952–82), 3:267. Henry Charles Carey (1793–1879), publisher and political economist, born in Philadelphia. His praise of the abolitionist duchess of Sutherland, which is mentioned below, is reproved at *PSE*, pp. 414–17.

not but believe a mistaken and I fear a harmful theory.[12] It is a subject which I have been studying lately, with much interest, and the more I look into it, the further I am, I must say, from agreeing with you. I shall continue however my endeavours to enlighten myself upon the subject, and am much obliged to you for the little volume forwarded to me.

Believe me, Dear Sir, in spite of these widely differing opinions

Very respectfully etc. etc.
Louisa S. McCord—

To Langdon Cheves, Jr.

My Dear Brother   Columbia January 16th, 1856

I only write a line to tell you that Father was moved in to my house the day before yesterday. He has never assented to the idea of change, but seems constantly to think himself on a journey and in a boarding house; refers now to the Sandhills as his home and frequently asks when we will get back. He seems anxious indeed to get back, says he was comfortable there etc. It is very painful and makes me feel like a jailer, but perhaps he may get better accustomed to the change. He is altogether much as when you left him. If there is any change either for the better or worse I will let you know.——— I hear by a letter from Mr. Huger to Anna that you left Charleston as you expected with Charlotte.[13] I hope that she and baby are well, and that you left the girls happy at their school.

I enclose an acc[oun]t sent to Father for foreign reviews. I suppose you had better pay it and if you see fit stop them.———Father of course makes no use of them and I take them myself———Anna is still here but leaves I believe in a few days———Hoping that you are none the worse of your journeyings in such uncomfortable weather and with love to Charlotte and Baby, believe me my dear Brother, always

Most affectionately Your Sister
Louisa S. McCord

12. "We are happy to remark . . . the first number, from the pen of Mr. Bastiat, of what he apparently intends as a series of papers, under the title of 'Harmonies économiques' (Concordances of Political Economy). Not only from this gentleman's well known power as a writer, but also from the striking views here presented, in his usual terse and concise diction, we anticipate a treat of instruction in what is to follow." *PSE,* "The Right to Labor," p. 98. Claude-Frédéric Bastiat died on Dec. 24, 1850, at the age of forty-nine; the series of papers, left incomplete at his death, was published posthumously as *Harmonies économiques.*

13. LSM's sister Anna was married in 1841 to Thomas Pinckney Huger (d. 1875), planter, engineer, railroad executive.

To Langdon Cheves, Jr.

My dear Brother   Columbia Jan[uar]y 25th, 1856

   I wrote you two days since that Father was doing much better. Yesterday he was again worse (in wandering of mind, and *excitement*) than I have ever seen him. The Doctor has been with him for hours, and has made him consent *temporarily,* to stay where he is.[14] But it will not last. He is resolute (and will I am certain recur to it,) to go as soon as possible, and he fixed upon the Sandhills because when he speaks of it people have to tell him that it belongs to him. I do not think it will be possible to keep him here, unless he could get the impression that this house belongs to him. Would it not be possible to make him go through the form of a purchase? I think if you could come up it could be managed. He might appear to buy this and sell the other. So long as he has the impression of owning that place, so long as he thinks this is not, and that is, his home, these attacks will constantly bring on the same results. Yesterday he was much excited and with an unusual persistance of determination, while wandering in his mind worse than I have ever seen him and with much more excitement. I do not know what to do, I am giving up every moment of my time, neglecting business, children and every thing else, but without success. I do not know what to do. I know my dear Brother that it is difficult, very difficult for you to leave home and yet I fear I can do nothing without some assistance from you. Father seems stronger, better; but in proportion as he is stronger and better it is more difficult to controul him, and in truth my dear brother with his mind in its present condition, he *needs controul.* I think if you could come up and speak to him decidedly which you could do, even though his mind is wandering (which I believe it *always* is, more or less) you might be able to do something. He would submit to your advice, (being under some restraint with ~~him~~ you, as with a stranger) in cases where I could do nothing with him. I think with judicious persuasion, the influence of the doctor, and you at hand to appear to make payments and manage money matters, that such an apparent transfer might be made of this place, as would incline him to believe us when we might say "it is yours," and he would at least submit to what everybody would tell him; as he did at the Sandhills even though not in his own mind conscious of the truth of the fact. Could such a state of affairs be brought about I think he would stay in one place just as soon as another for he is now entirely without

---

   14. LSM's physician in Columbia, John W. Powell was thirty-five years old in 1860, according to the U.S. Census, Richland District. In 1858 he accompanied the McCord family to Europe, until called back by illness in his family. During the war he served as surgeon to the First Regiment, South Carolina Volunteers.

any ideas of localities, though clinging most tenaciously to those of property. Could not some arrangement of the kind be made, and the Sandhill establishment broken up? I think it could if you could be here for a few days, perhaps for a single day—I think I now understand the state of his mind much better than I did before he came to my house and I think there is no possible way of controuling him without giving up in this one point. He must own property, he must be told "this is yours," wherever he stays; and in the midst of all his confusion of mind it is useless to tell him so now. Some form, some apparent transfer must be gone through, before he will submit to be so told. He now gets angry ~~if I say so~~ or at least displeased if I say so, and seems the more resolute to go away. I am almost *certain,* that a feigned purchase, if you could only be here to act as his agent and appear to arrange matters for him, might be effected and then I think the difficulty would be at an end.——I am sorry to trouble you my dear brother. Like myself you have heart and hands[,] both, fuller than you know how to bear with. But I know not what to do. I think you could help Father now as no one else can do, because you can assume a kind of authority as manager of his business. I do assume a great deal in other points, but the moment business of any kind is spoken of, Father immediately speaks of you and says it will be arranged when he sees you, which he seems to expect to do almost daily. He seems to have forgotten your last visit. When you come up again, *speak to him sick or well, about business.* It will do good. If he cannot transact business, we can at least deceive him into the belief that he is doing so. This *must* be done my dear Brother, for his own sake as well as ours. If he leaves me here, as he *will* do under present circumstances, it will be a wretchedness and a shame to us all. People will not understand that we have done our best and it will seem that the old man who has been what he has, and who has made us all, is turned out to pine and to suffer. Besides he *will* suffer. I find ~~the~~ since he has been here that June has recurred to his old habits, and although[,] under my eye, I can trust him, ~~I~~ it would be madness to do so were he alone.[15]——

As yet I hear nothing from my poor Hayney.[16] Do you think there can be

---

15. "I see I never told you about the beginnings of Marianne. Her father was a very valuable servant of my grandfather's, named June. He was a mulatto, wonderfully clever, but a hard drinker and very bad-tempered. . . . As she grew older she became my mother's personal attendant and remained faithful to her through all the vicissitudes of war, freedom, and everything else." Smythe, p. 8.

16. "Our poor Hayne . . . received his death blow in Florence. He was attacked with a dreadful haemorrage of the lungs, which threatened him with immediate death on the 10th of Dec[ember] last; but he partially recovered, and lingered on till the 14th of August last. . . . We had been kept in the dark as to poor Hayne's state by the loss of important letters in the Pacific, that was lost; which told us his case was hopeless; the next only said

hope? I send twice every day to the office in hopes of hearing something, but it is the same blank suspense continually, continually.——If you have rec[eive]d the letter young Heyward is said to have written you, let me see it my dear brother, no matter what it is.[17] Let it be the worst, it cannot kill my hope for I have no hope to kill. But I want to know about my poor boy. He belonged to me so young and so long, I cannot but feel that it is my child.

Dear Langdon, believe me

Your affectionate Sister
Louisa S. McCord

To Langdon Cheves, Jr.

My Dear Brother   Columbia March 1st, 1856

It distresses me to have to trouble you so often; but it cannot be helped. Father is at this time in a more excited condition than I have ever seen him. He takes positions in which it is impossible not to oppose him and, as you know, all opposition irritates. For instance, his besetting idea is now that *he is ruined*. If I assent or dissent the consequence is a storm of indignation in either case. I send for the Doctor[;] it does little or no good. The Doctor has combined he supposes with me to deceive him. June he accuses of officious impertinence and intermeddling. In short all have combined against him and he is most unhappy. I try to stay away from him as you advise; but he sends for me constantly and constantly the same scene follows. If I tell him he is not ruined, he says I do not know what I am talking off and that he is tired of being dictated to and does not want to be advised. If I assent either by word or silence that he *is* ruined, he then insists upon my accounting to him for all the missing funds and accuses me of having managed things for my own benefit and made him a beggar. I tell you all this, not to complain and not that I expect much help (for I know it cannot be given) but only that you may not think me unreasonable in annoying you so often with my letters.——At present I write to you by his particular and urgent order, that

---

he was better, and able to sit up, and ride out if the weather became milder; and he wrote quite cheerfully himself; so that we began to think he would come back to us." Sophia Cheves Haskell to Eleuthera Du Pont, Nov. 11, 1856, Langdon Cheves III Papers, SCHS. The Collins Line steamer *Pacific,* having departed from Liverpool for New York on Jan. 23, 1856, was never seen again.

17. Joseph Manigault Heyward (1830–62), son of Charles Heyward, a planter on the Combahee River, and Emma Barnwell Heyward; died of exposure in Virginia.

you may answer immediately and let him know the state of his affairs. This he urges you to do by the most solemn and even pitiable appeals. What you can say my dear Brother, I do not know, but perhaps it would be well for you to write something, more or less accurate as you please.———Excuse me if I suggest; but suppose for instance you make a rough statement of ____ thousand p[ai]d for old acc[oun]ts; ____ thousand plantation expenses; ____ thousand remaining in factor's hands. Close accuracy would be a matter of small moment. He wishes to know too whether *this house* is paid for. If you see fit you can set down $2000 which he has stumbled upon lately as its value. He insists that he is in debt for it to somebody he does not know who; that the debt will accumulate and ruin him and all his family and he wishes to know that it is settled. Sometimes he seems to think I must stay with him and then again tells me he can never consent to my living in the same house with him. I sometimes think it will be best actually to take the $2000 and put up buildings on a part of my lot as I suggested to you in my letter of yesterday, where I can take refuge and send my children as may be found needful. I *must* have a hiding place for them, if this state of affairs is to continue long. For weeks, for months it may be resisted, but to go on and on and on with not a corner of the house sometimes where I can sit with them quietly as a mother with her children, with nothing to soothe and everything to excite them, must affect their young minds dangerously and is enough to turn them all into maniacs. My own head reels under it.———My idea is to put up a house with about four rooms where my children could be sent (calling it their homes) or where I could myself go whenever it should be thought best that the house should seem clear of them; or where in fact we could stay in case of necessity. Father would then be convinced that this house is his own, while I could manage and do with every thing precisely as I do now staying here except when necessary to leave temporarily. I think it likely that we would thus do better. If you say so, I will engage workmen at once. If I could even tell him that I am building a house, that I had some place independant of him, I think he would be less suspicious of me. He thinks I am here with a kind of vulture wish to devour his substance and complete the ruin which he believes that I have been largely inculpated in bringing upon him.

Will you write? Do, please! It is useless to bother you to write to Father; only in answering me, slip in something in the shape of an account, stating roughly if you think fit, as I suggest above; and if you think right you may if you choose give me credit for the $2000, and I believe I will build something at once. I told you yesterday that I have already engaged some servants houses to be built with all speed. My yard is too much crowded to be safe for warmer weather, and only two days since I had to turn 3 servants out of their bedroom, to turn the little apartment into a wine room. Besides Cilla must have accomodation.[18]

Believe me my dear Brother it distresses me to trouble you about all this; but I cannot act without your authority, and although it may be all useless, it seems to me the best chance for getting on. Besides, Father is at once violently peremptory and pleadingly urgent in his desire to know from you, as soon as possible, whether he has the means of subsistance.———

I hope you have had no measles beyond the first case. It would indeed be sad for you to be troubled now with such a disease among your people. Indeed my dear Brother in the midst of all my own difficulties and troubles I do not forget how much you have to bear and to do, and it is with shrinking and pain that I feel myself obliged to write to you on these annoying subjects. Is your own health quite good now? Take care of it, for all our sakes. With love to Charlotte and Baby, believe me my dear Brother, always

earnestly and affectionately y[ou]rs
Louisa S. McCord

To Langdon Cheves, Jr.

[Columbia] March 5th [1856] Tuesday night[19]

I send the above[20] my dear Brother, as an excuse for what I fear you will consider my persecution of you. It is an attempt of our dear old Father to write something; I believe a letter to you. He is very anxious to hear from you and evidently much irritated with *me* because he does not do so. He seems to think it is *my fault.* I offered to write for him but he would not allow me to do so, and says[,] when he found he could not write, that he will send down June with a message. Indeed he wished to send him today, and with difficulty has been prevented. He is much irritated, much displeased, and is altogether in a far more painful condition than when you saw him. Could you not my dear brother, write or even cause Charlotte to write, if it be but 2 lines, say every week? It would I think assist in soothing Father. My position is here so intensely distressing that you must excuse me if I press upon you more urgently than you think right. I know you have troubles, I know you

---

18. "I find to my dismay that Father's woman is in such health as requires accomodation out of the house, (she has h is now occupying my down stairs chamber to be near him) as she is *enceinte*, needs rest etc. she says, and will need nursing etc. in 2 or 3 months." LSM to Langdon Cheves, Jr., Feb. 29, 1856, in *PDBL*, p. 313.

19. March 5, 1856, was a Wednesday.

20. Two lines of a tiny scrawl, wavering across the head of the first page of this letter; scarcely recognizable as handwriting; see illus.

have cares; perhaps even, you are not well yourself, perhaps I am goading you beyond endurance; but God help me what can I do? Do write, my own dear Brother; write, just a few lines and if you think no harm of it, remember my suggestion in my last letter. Father is alternately moody and violent on the subject of his affairs; now urgently pleading that you will send him a statement of them, and again angrily insisting upon it. I tried to deceive him, to make him believe that I had heard from you, and gave at a guess the amount which I supposed might be in the factors hands as if stated by you; but he asked to see your letter, and when I had to say I had mislaid it, you may imagine what he thinks of me. Can you not make a rough guess or calculation of the state of things? A thousand or two here or there, would make little difference. All that is needed is the appearance of giving an account, for he has little or no idea of numbers. He told me yesterday that he had *150 thousand dollars* in his factors hands, and then talked of it as only *15 hundred*. Just give a statement of some balance and it will be right. I am sure I need not say any more. You will write. I only fear that I cannot keep him quiet until you will have time to receive and answer this; and that he will send June down; which I wish very much to avoid, ~~and~~ as June is his only efficient attendant, and I should fear his getting into trouble if he is sent off alone, after all the excitement and worry he is going through. You will write I am sure and immediately.

As regards the question of building some small house to call mine, and pretend at least to live in, and to hide out of the way in if needful, I more and more fear that it is indispensable. Indeed if Father lives for many months as he is (getting indeed as he has done constantly worse) I see no possibility of doing without it; He will become frantic if he believes that I am fixed on him here with no other home; and I have determined if I can possibly get any thing done *immediately,* to undertake it on my own responsibility. The only question is whether the carpenter can get lumber etc. which it seems is difficult to obtain, in time for my purposes. I have spoken to a carpenter and find that I can probably get what is needful for $1500 or not much more, including the servants houses already ~~building~~ ordered, and I believe in the act of framing. This is much less than I thought would be required, and if you think yourself not authorized to meet the expense on Father's acc[oun]t I will not push you further. I would not my dear Brother make you do anything that would embarrass you or that you think doubtfully right, only as I happen to be scant of funds, if you think it wrong to advance to me, say so; that I may borrow in time for the payment of this sum. I am sure if you think it wrong to ~~do~~ advance it, it *is* wrong. You know much more of business than I do and if you tell me that you ought not to give it, I shall not misunderstand you, and have no doubt that you will do what is right. Please however whether you give it or not, *pretend* to have paid $2000 for this house. Father will never be satisfied, I think, until he has been told that this sum is paid. I told him that it was paid, but he says he wants *you* to tell him so. He is constantly confused about localities, thinks he is constantly moving etc., but still always refers to his $2000 house, and his uneasiness about the non-payment of the debt which he insists is owing without any fixed idea as to whom owing. If *you* tell him it is done, I think he will perhaps be satisfied on that point.

I hope you have had no more measles and that things are well with you. I have received but one letter from you since you were here. I say this not complainingly but only pleadingly. I am sure you will write to me soon.——— I trust that your little boy has escaped the measles. Anna writes me that your girls both look remarkably well. I wish my poor little things were with them; but they are nearly two years younger than yours; too young to send from home. With love as usual, I am my dear Brother always

Y[ou]r affectionate Sister
Louisa S. McCord

Perhaps before getting this you will have written in answer to my last. If so; so much the better, and this may go for nothing.

Dear Lang   Wednesday morning
I have opened my letter to tell you that Father seems much weaker this morning, having taken a little walk out and had to be brought home—lifted in a chair. He will probably now[,] as always when weak, be quieter for a while; but even now asks anxiously if I have heard from you and seems very uneasy at not doing so. He cannot calculate that you have not had time to answer since my letter of last Saturday and is very unhappy at not hearing from you. I will do the best I can in every thing. Always my dear Brother

Y[ou]rs affectionately
Louisa S. McCord

To Langdon Cheves, Jr.

Dear Langdon   Columbia April 13th, 1856
Although I wrote to you yesterday, I must, to satisfy Father, do so again today; merely to make a statement to you upon which he insists. I did not mention yesterday, because I hoped then to avoid bothering you with it, that one particular fancy by which Father is constantly beset, is a determination to free June, Cilla, and any child or children they may have. This is a constant, daily, sometimes hourly, subject of discussion with them, and I am

called in to promise etc., which I have been obliged to do over and over 50 times, in the most solemn manner, to the servants themselves as well as to Father. I hoped this would satisfy him, but he now insists upon calling in a lawyer to draw up papers etc., and has even named that drunken creature Treadwell whose name he has got from the servants.[21] Of course if he insists upon seeing a lawyer, I must have DeSaussure;[22] but I am anxious to prevent the unpleasant discussion and exposure consequent upon anything of the kind, and have promised him to write to you, and you must give your promise, as I have given mine, that if surviving him the required arrangement shall be made. At present June belongs to me by deed of gift, given some 10 or 12 years since, and Cilla, as you know, is willed to me.[23] They will be perfectly worthless after all that has passed and I would ask nothing better for my own comfort than to let them go if they choose it. This, Father cannot however be made to understand, and he insists that you are to *promise compensation to me from the estate and* to *assistance to me in insuring to these servants their promised freedom.* All I wish you to do is to say that you make this promise which will be only so far binding, that in case of my death before Father, you will remember that the promise to the negroes is a *bona fide* one, if they choose to leave the State at his death. This promise I have been obliged seriously to make them, in order, if possible, to prevent their tampering with and exciting Father, which I sometimes (perhaps unjustly) fear they do. The compensation part may be forgotten, except to satisfy *him,* for they will really be worthless after all this. I am not even certain that they will be willing to release *me* from the ownership; but Father will not listen to such a suggestion, and I think it best not to carry the discussion of the subject with them, further than it is forced on by Father himself. All I want you to do then is to say that you will see his wishes attended to.

    This is all that I now have to trouble you with. Father is, as usual, wandering extremely, but fortunately now entirely satisfied about his house. The building of the little establishment which I am getting on with rapidly, has already done much good. He watches its progress, and seems now thor-

    21. LSM's Treadwell is apparently James D. Tradewell, graduated (although involved in a near-dueling escapade in 1828) from South Carolina College in 1830, admitted to the bar in Columbia in 1832, and "dreadfully drunk" in Mary Chesnut (p. 356).

    22. William Ford DeSaussure (1792–1870), prosperous Columbia attorney, judge, politician, U.S. senator (1852–53), and delegate to the secession convention in December 1860.

    23. "I give to my daughter Louisa, my house servant Priscilla, also, my house and the land whereon it stands in the Sand-Hills near Columbia, with my Library, Carriage and Horses, and the Household and Kitchen furniture." Langdon Cheves, "Last Will and Testament," Nov. 6, 1854, printed copy, Langdon Cheves I Papers, SCHS.

oughly satisfied, not only that *this* is *his,* but that it is my intention some day to leave it; and in proportion as he is convinced that I really intend to go away, he becomes anxious that I should remain. He wants me, but cannot bear that he should be *obliged* to keep me; and thus the sight of a house in which he thinks I can live, keeps things right. His greatest annoyance now, besides the June and Cilla emancipation question, is a habit of imagining that there are two of sundry persons habitually about him, and particularly myself. I have a double, whom as I cannot give a name for, he constantly calls the "nameless one" and "the lonely one", and whom he thinks I have displaced in his house and in the Lang Syne property. Indeed it is with this "lonely and nameless one", rather than with myself, that he desires the arrangement about June and Cilla to be made. He considers them to belong to her and not to me, and because he cannot see her, wishes you to be a surety for the promises made. He is constantly annoyed with the fear that I am doing her some injustice and says he is sure I must have some dispute with her; otherwise he would see us together or at least I could tell him where she is. In all this you can do nothing except to say that you will see his wishes concerning the negroes in question fulfilled. It will be better if you can write it, but if you do not do so in a few days, I must only do my best to make Father believe that you have done so.

He sends you many messages about coming up etc. which can only be painful to give and receive, and so I leave them. I know you could not come now, unless under urgent necessity, and I do not think any such now exists.

Give my love to Charlotte and kind remembrance to Mrs. Lieber if she be still with you, though I think she was to leave about this time. I am anxious to hear how you have got on with y[ou]r plantation troubles.

I am, dear Brother,

Y[ou]r affectionate Sister
Louisa S. McCord

To Langdon Cheves, Jr.

Dear Brother   Columbia Dec[ember] 18th [1856]

I wrote to you yesterday about June—I find there are obstacles preventing his remaining in the Guard House, as I wrote you that he would, and I send him down by this even[in]g's cars to Charleston, to be placed in the Work House in care of Messrs. Capers and Heyward to whom I have written desiring them to *keep him for ten days subject to your order,* and at the end of that time, (failing to receive instructions from you) to sell him to *leave the State* and in such manner as to prevent his return.[24]——

This is a painful business to me, but my life ~~and~~ or that of my children may depend upon proper action and I cannot hesitate.

Always, dear Langdon

                                       Your affectionate Sister
                                       Louisa S. McCord

Should it be desired that June's wife (who I think he cares nothing about) and child should go with him, only write me at once, and I will send them down.

To Langdon Cheves, Jr.

Dear Brother   Columbia Dec[ember] 20th, 1856

You have doubtless before this rec[eive]d my two letters concerning June. I beg you to do in ~~it wh~~ the business what you think best. I have no wish to receive one cent for him;—Only I must never see him again. His wife and child are with me and subject to your orders, should you deem it desirable to send them with him. It is absolutely necessary for me to go to my pla~~c~~entation early next week. Should you wish therefore to give any immediate order concerning the woman *write to Mr. Boyd*. I have not spoken to her to know whether she has any wish on the subject. She is behaving quietly.—— I wrote you that I directed Capers and Heyward to hold June subject to y[ou]r order for ten days. This gives you time to direct any thing or to prolong the time indefinitely as you may desire. I want to put the thing off my mind; it makes me sick.——I will not write about it again unless in answer to anything from you.——

Father is perfectly quiet and composed. Boyd shaves him, drives him, assists in dressing him and not the slightest objection is made. This confirms my previous suspicion that for some reason June kept up the excitement of his mind in order to have his own way with him. Perhaps I am wrong, but unless accounted for in some such way, the change is singularly sudden.——Father is evidently and constantly failing gradually. This cold weather would be against him, but *four* large fires constantly kept up in his house keep it comfortable even for him.——

I must go to my plantation on Tuesday if possible, and if possible remain there for 2 or 3 weeks. Father is doing so well with Boyd that I will leave

---

24. Capers and Heyward was an auction house and commission merchant firm located on the south side of Adger's Wharf, Charleston; owned by Thomas Farr Capers and Thomas Savage Heyward.

him more willingly than I could ~~have done under any~~ have done under any other circumstances.

I will need more money. What I draw f[ro]m Frazer and Co. is by no means sufficient.[25] I have to draw more largely than I can afford on my own factor, but I will not bother you with this now. I will write again if I do not see you by some time in January. I know of no immediate necessity for y[ou]r coming up, only if you should come before I leave Lang Syne I would come to meet you. But there is really no need for you to come——
      Affect[ionate]ly L. S. McCord——

To Langdon Cheves, Jr.

Dear Langdon   Lang Syne Fort Motte January 7th, 1857

Your's of 23d Ult. was forwarded to me here. I cannot regret my dismissal of June. It pains me to think of on *his* account, but I had no alternative. He had become really dangerous for me and mine. My man Ben is still much the worse of the treatment rec[eive]d f[ro]m him and indeed will I presume always be the worse for it.——As regards Father, there is nothing to regret. I enclose you two letters from Boyd which will shew you that he is doing better than he did with June.——I will return to Columbia in a week. I ~~will~~ have got a new Overseer who seems to "take hold" well and I must hope to get on tolerably. The last year has been a most disastrous one to me in every way.

I hope y[ou]r thrashing machine and all else is doing well with you. With love to all y[ou]r family I am dear Brother, always
      and most affectionately y[ou]rs
      Louisa S. McCord

To Hiram Powers

Dear Sir,[26]   Columbia July 29th, 1860

Your kind letter of April 18th was received so long ago that I have no excuse for not having answered it sooner. Frequent indisposition, and an

---

25. Located at North Central Wharf in Charleston, the factor and shipping firm of John Fraser and Company was founded by John Fraser (c. 1777–1854), an immigrant from Scotland who set up business about 1803. The company was very prosperous and played an important role in Confederate trade with Europe during the war.

26. Hiram Powers (1805–73), sculptor; born in Woodstock, Vt.; established a studio in Florence in 1837.

intensely hot summer will, I hope, go some way to excuse me. I had hoped too, that I might hear from you again, on the subject of the little design for my Father's monument which you promised me. I know however that you are a busy man, and I wait your liesure. My own bust too, you said you would soon ship, and give me notice of. All this has made me delay from day to day, and week to week, thinking I might hear from you; until more time has past than I thought. We grow old so fast without knowing it!

I shall still hope to hear from you soon with the promised design, and also when you send my own bust,—which I shall value, not only as your work, but as a remembrancer of a friendly acquaintance with you, which I hope some day to renew in our own land.——Pray do not imagine that the nation which has given birth to a Powers, is so little appreciative of the Sculptors art as to regard Mills as a sculptor. I don't know how it happens, while every body knows that he is a humbug,—a mere plaster-dauber, too ignorant even to be called an imposter, he yet is called to what ought to be great works.[27] The truth I fear is, that we are a bragging rather than an earnest people; and our wise legislators, in their eager scramble for power and place, deem such subjects I presume scarce worth consideration. They had to spend some hundred thousands of the people's money; it did not take 5 cents from their individual pockets. What cared they for the result? They had to canvass for the next Presidency, or to send comfort to John Brown, or to preach a tirade against Southern slave-holders, and so they snapped their fingers at Art. (Art! Half of them don't know what the word means.) But the business was to be done some how or other. Mills was near, (If it had been the hod-carrier who brings his plaster, it would have done as well.) he, or somebody for him, had the impudence to ask for the *job,* (yes,—*the job!* For I don't believe the question of art was considered half so much as it would have been, had there been question of building a brick wall) and so they gave it to him.——My dear Sir, have you lived so much in your Studio, that you have not learned that in this world, and most particularly I fear, in these United States, "he that asketh receiveth;"[28] and the more impudently he asks the better[?] Verily we are a great nation for go-aheadativeness. But when people go ahead so dreadfully fast, they are like the saucy chick running about with the egg-shell on its head, apt to tumble into dirty places. For my part I despair of any good result from such legislation, and as our rulers are, generally speaking, almost as well fitted to their places as Mr.

---

27. Clark Mills (1815–83), sculptor and bronze founder; born in Onondaga County, N.Y.; commissioned to make equestrian statues of Andrew Jackson and George Washington, the latter work being dedicated on Feb. 22, 1860. Mills made a bust of Langdon Cheves in 1844.

28. Matt. 7:8; Luke 11:10.

Mills to his, I look forward to a general "*smash up*" as the only regenerating hope of our country. You perceive I am a thorough disunionist:—and so ends my discourse of which Mr. Mills has been the text.

You have doubtless heard of the death of our old friend Wm. Preston.[29] I found him, on my return, much enfeebled in body and mind. He continued gradually to sink through the winter until his death, which came in good time to prevent his feeling too acutely his worn-out condition.

I shall hope to hear from you again before very long. You must excuse me, my dear Sir, if I again put you in mind that I have forgotten your banker, and am ignorant of how a remittance should be made to you. You will I am sure have the kindness to inform me on this subject whenever you write giving notice of the shipment of my bust. Possibly in these times of Italian commotion there may be a difficulty of communication;—I do not know;—I am happy to believe however that in Florence you enjoy comparative quiet.

With kind regards to your wife and daughters and from my young people, believe me always Dear Sir

With sincere respect
and very truly, yours
Louisa S. McCord

To Hiram Powers

Columbia, So. Carolina

Dear Mr. Powers   Dec[ember] 24th, 1860

Your kind letter of 16th Sept[ember] has remained too long unacknowledged. It found me in the wild mountains of North Carolina (where I had taken my young people for a few weeks recreation) nursing two daughters, desperately ill of Typhoid fever. With happier result than was anticipated, both are, after three months struggle against the malady, convalescent.—— But now, we are in the midst of a revolution. Our spirited little State has declared its independence. On the 20th Inst. she threw down the gauntlet by an ordinance of secession from the United States government, and now waits the result. A bloodless revolution (an unheard of event in history) can scarcely be expected; and yet some of us hope that such may be. Our example will, we firmly believe[,] be in a few weeks followed by Florida, Geor-

---

29. William Campbell Preston, born in Philadelphia in 1794; resident of Columbia from 1822, when he became a law partner of David James McCord; elected U.S. senator as a nullifier in 1833, as a Whig in 1837; resigned in 1842; president of South Carolina College (1846–51). Preston died in Columbia on May 22, 1860.

gia, Alabama and Mississippi. Other States we hope will (although not yet so fully compromised to action) soon fall in with us, and a Southern Confederacy be constructed.——You have been so long away from America that you will probably know little of the cause of complaint and sympathize not greatly with the throbbing spirit of our now fully roused country. Besides, we of the Southern U[nited] States, have been constantly so misrepresented,—loud mouthed fanaticism has so cried down our institutions, and pretended philanthropy so covered us with slander and falsehood, that it would be asking too much of a far-off spectator to understand and appreciate our action. I wish I could show you how right we are; but it would require a perfect volume of a letter, to give the history of almost half a century of slowly encroaching injustice. I have no right to trouble you with all this, and can only say that slandered as we have been before the world, we yet have courage to "bide our time", and the day will yet come when the recollection of the honors bestowed on such foul-mouthed railers as a Sumner, or a Mrs. Stowe, will bring a blush to the cheeks of those who have been guilty of them.[30] I must trouble you no more about our politics; though I am sure if this little sheet had room enough for all I want to say, I could make a good South Carolinian of you. I see it in your eye. This much I have said, only to excuse my apparent neglect of your kind letter. My Brother to whom I forwarded the designs enclosed has been, head and heart, occupied in our struggle—Called from a quiet agricultural life, he is a member of the Convention which has just cast the die of action for us. I saw him for an hour lately; the Convention having been summoned to meet in Columbia, whence an alarm of Small-Pox caused its adjournment to Charleston. With the adjournment, he of course left, and had only time to tell me that, thanking you for sending the designs, he will[,] with your permission, perhaps use one of them, with slight modification[,] for a construction of South Carolina granite, which he deems better suited to our time and present action, than marble would be. If this is permitted, he would of course desire to make to Prof[esso]r Fantarchiotti such compensation as is proper for the trouble he has taken and will be glad to do so when we shall communicate with you in the same way.[31]

Will you remember that I have begged you to make me a duplicate (only

---

30. Charles Sumner (1811–74), U.S. senator from Massachusetts (from 1851) and antislavery advocate, was celebrated for his invectives against the South. On the phrase "bide our time" see chap. 2 above, "Separate Secession," p. 38 and note.

31. Odoardo Fantacchiotti (1809–77)—LSM's misspelling is owed to Powers' unclear handwriting—was employed briefly by Powers as a finisher before opening his own studio as a sculptor, and also as a forger of Italian Renaissance pieces; Powers passed along to him many commissions.

life size) of my Father's bust? I shall hope that our political disturbances will not interfere with the safe arrival of the busts both of my Father and myself, when you find opportunity to send them. Whatever be the condition of our country, your New-York agent (Mr. Dehon) will doubtless be able to arrange to send them safely to Charleston.[32] I anticipate indeed that we will ere long be better friends with our Northern neighbours than (writhing under the oppression of an unjust government) we have hitherto consented to be.

You perceive that we are in full condition to sympathize with your Italian struggles.[33] In the surging waves of national struggle against oppression nations fraternize in heart. Garibaldi's is truly a splendid character. Can it be that he is destined to receive only the reward of his own conscious power and rectitude and that after Europe has, as you well remark[,] "become hoarse with shouting his name," he is to be past over and forgotten by those into whose hands he has placed the results of his efforts! His reward has perhaps been great enough in the resounding cry which passing through Europe has been again echoed back from our Western shores giving him a world fame above that of monarchs; but yet it is a sad comment upon worldly justice, if such be the end of the Strong Man.———

Excuse my long letter, but even a Woman has the right to wake up when revolution is afoot, and when our Sons (even boys) throw aside their Greek, Latin and mathematics to practice rifles and study military tactics.

Remember me kindly to Mrs. Powers and your daughters. Tell the fair haired one, that I saw only yesterday a rose bud that she gave my little girl, pressed into a bouquet with one which you gave me, and kept as a memorial of Florence and your household—

Believe me dear Sir

Most truly and respectfully yours
Louisa S. McCord—

---

32. Theodore Dehon (d. 1861) was the banking partner of Sidney Brooks, Hiram Powers' close friend and adviser since 1843. "The next morning [after the departure of the Federal army from Columbia on Feb. 19, 1865] we went home greatly relieved to find the house still standing, but what a scene of desolation it all was. Every out-building had its door burst open—fences were thrown down—the garden trampled, furniture broken, books torn up and thrown about, pictures smashed and cut out of their frames and everything small carried away. As we reduced chaos to order we found of course that many things were still left—the oil paintings for instance that were afterwards burned in Henry Cheves' house and my mother's bust—but the first look was of utter sweeping destruction." Smythe, pp. 69–70.

33. Italian revolutionary leader Giuseppe Garibaldi (1807–82) expelled King Francis of the Two Sicilies from his own capital of Naples on Sept. 7, 1860.

To Langdon Cheves, Jr.

Dear Brother   Columbia April 20th, 1861

I just missed meeting you and the girls, a few days since, in Charleston. You left, I was told, on Friday and I got in on Saturday just as the white flag was raised on Fort Sumter. I went down to see where the company with which Cheves is, was likely to be located. They are now on the outskirts of Charleston, near the Ashley River bridge, and, as (for the present I suppose) all is quiet, I came back to my girls.——This has been a glorious affair of Fort Sumter, and truly it would seem to have set old Lincoln crazy. Did ever any stupid animal ever so set fire to its own nest! He has given us Virginia already, and how much else will follow?

In the midst of affairs so all absorbing you must excuse my troubling you with a few words of business. My Factor's books show my funds run dry, and I find it needful to consider coming demands. Being most anxious for you to do just as you please, I only need to know whether or not you *desire* to make any payments to me this year. Please do exactly what you wish. There is no inconvenience to me, except to know what to anticipate. It is very probable that the times will make you willing to let alone all payments for this year. Pray do so if it suits you; only dear Brother you will let me know (will you not?) what you wish.——

I hope Charlotte keeps well. With kind love to her and all at home with you, believe me dear brother, always

and most affectionately y[ou]rs
Louisa S. McCord—

To Augustine Thomas Smythe

My dear young Friend   Columbia April 28th, 1863

Since the terrible calamity which has stricken down the hope and the joy of my house, I hardly know how to write. The "vacant chair,"[34] and desolate hearth are too constantly before me, to let me think of much else. Still I must send a few words to thank you for your remembrance of us in our sorrow. My heart, springs forward to every touch or sign of affection from

---

34. Longfellow, "Resignation," st. 1: "There is no flock, however watched and tended, / But one dead lamb is there! / There is no fireside, howso'er defended, / But has one vacant chair!"

those who have known and loved *him*. Many letters I have received, but yours is the first word that comes to me from any of those whom I have known principally as his college companions. If it wakes afresh the sources of my grief,—believe me, there is still a mournful pleasure in feeling that the link is not quite broken. It brings sadly before me (and yet I love to remember them) the bright young faces of a year or two back. How changed now could the remnants of that little circle be collected![35] We have gone through a lifetime of struggle and of sorrow in the interval. May God grant to all (to those who like my own One have gone from us, as to those who remain) that this terrible war may have worked out its purifying blessings; and that in the sudden wrench which has thus cast so many forth from boyhood to manhood's fiercest struggles, the saddening influence may have left its ennobling result. My all is gone; but I cannot cease to watch with loving interest those (his friends) who have yet to work through the struggle in which he has fallen. God bless you! I can write and think of nothing but as connected with him. It is as well to stop. This is enough to say (and you will believe me) that thinking of you with affectionate kindness I shall always be pleased to hear from, or to see you.

My Daughters remember you always with kind regard. They have not been well; but I hope are improving. This War is a fearful trial to all who think;[36] and its shock falls sharply upon the young.

Again I pray may God bless and guide you.

Always and most truly
Your friend
Louisa S. McCord

To Sophia Cheves Haskell

My dear Sister,   Columbia July 16th, 1863

Until your letter, (received last evening,) I had heard nothing of our latest sorrow. *Our* sorrow I say, for I claim to halve it with you. Willy and Aleck, since my great agony, have seemed half to belong to me. They could not fill the place of my own lost darling,—but they were so kind and so linked with

---

35. "We start and look around / On all for which we've toil'd. Alas! how changed!" LSM, "The Village Churchyard," ll. 247–48 (*PDBL,* p. 143), adapting Alexander Pope, *Eloisa to Abelard,* ll. 99–100; cf. John Milton, *Paradise Lost* 1.84–87; Byron, *Childe Harold's Pilgrimage* 2.711. All are ultimately derived from Vergil *Aeneid* 2.274–76.

36. "I have often said, this world is a comedy to those that think, a tragedy to those that feel." Horace Walpole to the Countess of Upper Ossory, Aug. 16, 1776, in W. S. Lewis et al., eds., *Horace Walpole's Correspondence,* 48 vols. (New Haven, 1937–83), 32:315.

him in my thoughts, that I took them into my heart as some thing left of him. Do not think me selfish that I thus put my sorrow side by side with yours for the loss of one of these. I rather think to give you such sad comfort as we find in the recollection of what was loveable in our lost ones; and Willy was not only brave, but very kind, and gentle, and good. It is a great comfort to think, (as I said of Charley) that nothing can be more painless, than a prompt death on the battle field. Not death, indeed, should it be called;—for death is the struggle, the doubt, the anguish of parting, while the weakened mind dreads the transit which in its strength it could face calmly. Here, in its full strength, it finds an easy passage from *life to life*.[37] Death has no time to startle even with the shadow of its terrors. To us alone (lingerers by the wayside) is left the sorrow and the loss.

Falling as he has done, so far away from us, there will perhaps no relic of dear Willy come home to you; and you will, I think, like to know that I have in my possession the sword which he carried through 12 battles. It was brought to me by one Col. McCready (sent by Willy) only a few weeks since, for me to take care of.[38] I wrote him word that nobody should touch it till he came for it himself. But to you and his Father it now[,] of right, belongs. Should it chance that a watch be sent to you, do not think it a mistake. I lent him the last one used by Cheves, begging him to wear it in the fight and bring it home to me.——I would come and see you but would do you harm. I need to be alone a great deal, and cannot always command myself as I should. With any change I would likely be ill and a burden to you. My girls seem to feel as if their brother was lost a second time. Poor children, these shocks are very trying to them. This fearful war brings to our daughters a sadder fate than to their slaughtered brothers.——Once more dear Sister you know my sympathies are with you all. Would to God, I had anything else to give—

Truly yours
and most affectionately
Louisa S. McCord

37. 2 Cor. 2:15–16: "For we are unto God a sweet savour of Christ, in them that are saved, and in them that perish: To the one we are the savour of death unto death; and to the other the savour of life unto life."

38. Lawyer and historian Edward McCrady, Jr. (1833–1903), was a lieutenant colonel in Brig. Gen. Maxcy Gregg's First Regiment, South Carolina Volunteers, in which William Haskell also served.

To Thomas Smyth

Dear Sir[39]   Columbia August 15th, 1865

Highly flattered, as I am by the compliment paid me in your requesting my opinion of your argument on the currency question, I must, at the risk of appearing ungracious in return, dissent entirely from your views.[40]——— There is no form in which we can ask payment of our debt from Yankee rule, which would not be considered by our enemies (such I still cannot but feel them to be,) as a begging of Charity; and moreover it will be a charity as certainly refused as asked. I would therefore quietly keep my poverty, content to save my honest pride, where I cannot my purse.[41]———The *State* is too poor to do anything; and her rising money-makers will never consent to be heavily taxed for their own, their children's, their grandchildren's, even to five generations of life-times, to save those who are already conveniently disposed of, on the list of the ruined. Indeed, crushed and driven, as we are[,] to the wall, by a power which has now no law but its own mandates, it would be suicidal, in whatever is left to call itself "the State", to assume such a debt.———

Excuse me for so entirely differing from you, and believe me with none the less high respect and cordial regard

Very truly yours
Louisa S. McCord—

To Hiram Powers

Charleston, South Carolina

Dear Mr. Powers,   March 20th, 1870

Remembering your kindness of eleven years back,—subdued by troubles,—and led by that clinging which draws us towards scenes and persons

---

39. In *PSE*, "Diversity of the Races," p. 163, LSM had noticed the anthropological work of Thomas Smyth (1808–73), Irish-born pastor of the Second Presbyterian Church of Charleston. On June 27, 1865, his son Augustine married LSM's daughter Louisa.

40. "It is difficult for those who are away to understand the utter pecuniary prostration in which the war has left this section of the country. . . . It is as if at a single word and in a single moment the issues of every state and national bank and of the government should prove without value or effect, and the people, instead of currency, should find that they had, as representative of toil and years of labor and hard-earned competency, pieces of waste paper." Charleston *Daily Courier*, July 7, 1865. How to counter this obliteration by the war of most of South Carolina's wealth was much discussed.

41. Byron, *Don Juan*, canto 1, st. 220, ll. 7–8: "So thank your stars that matters are no worse / And read your Bible, sir, and mind your purse."

connected with the calmer or brighter spots of past life, I would almost venture to address you as "my friend." More than you said or did when I was with you there was that in your look which made me think that you could appreciate the courage of enduring suffering, and that your sympathies would be with the oppressed. I have been wishing,—almost intending,—daily, for three years to write to you. But the laying bare of bleeding wounds is an agony, and I have shrunk from it. My want of health for some time made me scarcely able to bear it,—and even now I feel myself a coward in the effort.

Besides I have been told, but I will not believe it, that Hiram Powers has warmly expressed his sympathies against the heroic struggles of our recent lost but glorious cause. I *cannot* believe it. As I remember your calm, but penetrating eye, looking as it were, into the thought of your sitter for his likeness; I think that I too caught the idea of *your mental* likeness, and I will not believe that you can now say "well done" to the destroyers of a noble people. But we *are* destroyed, and I fear as a people past from life forever. The true-hearted among our survivors have to look with pride, only upon our sufferings, and upon the graves of our dead. We fought for our rights and our liberties. Our very boys were heroes in endurance, and in death. But now, ground down, and writhing beneath the heel of a brutal conqueror, none can even live, without giving up something of the purity of his feelings by submission to the unblushing and utterly lawless tyranny of a brutal rule; and the wreck of as noble a people as ever trod *God*'s earth, must, I fear, inevitably fall away from its higher characteristics. *God* only knows how much a wearied Soul can bear, and still live on uncontaminated! Alas! too often those whom we thought strong, bend under the load; and the proud heart bows, when, failing the power to resist, it ought to break. I thank *God* that I am of those whose age gives hope of a release before the complete moral extinction of my people shall be effected. The open endeavour, the shameless boast of our conquerors is, to displace the high-toned Southerner, by the vilest of Yankee white and brutal negro. Is it unchristian or unphilosophical, that I find a comfort,—at least a small hope, in the fact that the lawlessness of the so-called general government is fast dragging it to its destruction? That already open bribery governs every thing from the president down;—That already actions worthy only of a common swindler are considered no shame, scarcely glossed over, in the highest places. And for our down-trodden state, is it not enough to say that the Bench of its supreme Court is filled by a renegade jew, a low Yankee lawyer, and a Yankee negro?[42]

---

42. Franklin J. [Israel] Moses, Sr. (1804–77), chief justice; Amiel J. Willard (1822–1900), emigrated from New York; Jonathan Jasper Wright (1840–85), born and admitted to the bar in Pennsylvania.

That the congressional member from South Carolina (a wandering Yankee preacher, and even in his own home, an acknowledged imposter) has just been expelled because he was a little too barefaced in the *selling* of U.S. Cadet Commissions, and has come back to be probably returned again by negro votes.[43] Our State, so-called, Legislature——But why go on with details that sicken in the recital? You know what such a rule must bring.

For myself only, and to excuse my hitherto not writing to you, I would say, that the last I heard from you was late in 1860 or early '61. I cannot say which, as the wanton destruction in Columbia (where I was during the Vandal-like performances of Sherman) of all papers etc. deprive[s] me of data. About that time a letter from you informed me that your bust of my Father, Langdon Cheves, was completed and would very shortly be shipped from Genoa—Further I know nothing from you. Then came our struggle for all that was dear to us,—and with it a seclusion from the outer world, preventing any communication. Then followed the sweep of our dearest and noblest; and all whom I then had to depend upon, now lye under the soil they fought to defend. Left a son-less widow, with two daughters, and an infant grand daughter (born after her Father's death from the field of Manassas) I am now, ruined in property, and a partial dependent upon a son-in-law; (the husband of the little girl I had with me in Europe) a young man struggling for the support of his family. My Brother under whose suggestions I was acting when seeking to procure from you my Father's bust, died from the first shell cast at Morris Island.

I ought to have written to you immediately after our war came to its sad termination;—but I *could not*. Neither have I at any time been able to command the sum necessary to meet the expense of getting the bust, if it be still in existence. Hoping however that at no distant period, I may effect this object, I have tried, but vainly, to dis-cover any thing about it. I was told that your agent, Mr. Theodore Dehon, died during our war;—and I do not know who may now act for you. I write therefore to yourself, that you may at least not deem me forgetful of the proper respect due to you,—as well as to the memory of my Father,—by what may seem to you a strange neglect of the commonest proprieties of life. But truly it has seemed to me often, that I belonged to life no longer, and could you know one half of the troubles I have gone through, I would need to make no apologies to gain your forgiveness.

Can you tell me anything of the Bust? Do you know if it was ever shipped,

---

43. Benjamin Franklin Whittemore (1824–94), born in Massachusetts, a minister of the Methodist Episcopal church, resigned as a member of Congress on Feb. 24, 1870, preventing by one day his expulsion for accepting bribes in return for assisting appointments to the military and naval academies; as LSM predicted, he was reelected; but, Congress declining to reseat him, he accepted election instead to the South Carolina Senate (1870–77).

or anything of its further fate? If it came to America, is it likely that I can do anything to find it? Excuse me if these questions may seem out of place but possibly Mr. Dehon, unable to communicate with us here, may have mentioned the difficulty, and told you what disposition was made of the bust.[44]

And if you will write to me, will you not tell me that you have been slandered, when they said that you could cast an unkind thought or word, upon as noble a cause, and as heroic a people as ever the great *God* in his mysterious wisdom, has permitted to be crushed!

If you will write to me, direct to Mrs. McCord, care of Augustine T. Smythe, Charleston, South Carolina.

If after this tardy explanation, anything in my conduct toward you may still appear remiss, remember how hard it must be to rake up the ashes of the past from the most painful scenes of a life which shows me now everywhere little but graves, and you will excuse, in whatever I may still seem to fall short.

With kindest regards to your wife and daughters if they still remember be {me}, I am, Dear Sir always with the greatest respect and regard

Yours very truly
Louisa S. McCord

To the Board of Managers of the South Carolina Monument Association

Copy
Ladies   Charleston June 17th, 1870

Permit me to tender you my resignation as president of your association. Much as my heart has been with you in our work, I know not now, how to continue it. A powerful faction in our State, which seeks for her the degradation of negro equality, is forcing itself fearfully forward; and from such, I neither wish nor could ask help. Their abandonment of principle, throwing a shame hitherto unknown, on the once honored name of South Carolina[,] is too odious for me to be willing to come in contact with it.

I have been asked what need of ineffective opposition to no effect? and why can I not work on quietly?

---

44. "You are in error in regard to my letter saying that the bust of your dear father had already been done. I would not have so informed you, for it has not been executed. The war commenced before I could begin it and I found it difficult to pay expenses during the war. I could proceed only with those few commissions which commanded ready money." Hiram Powers to LSM, April 12, 1870, Hiram Powers and Powers Family Papers, Archives of American Art, Smithsonian Institution, Washington, D.C.

Because I could not ask help from negro-fraternizers. Because to our beloved dead, principles are a nobler monument than marble. Because three generations of honored graves that for me, South Carolina bears upon her breast, would become to me a constantly haunting reproach, could I link hands, even in the performance of a good act, with the murderers of her fair fame. South Carolina is fast becoming to me, but as one great grave of the great past;—One proud memory which must pass away before the sweeping tide of corruption. The deed of 16th June has taken the lead in the cutting away of the dike which might have saved her from destruction.[45]——May *God* grant that some great head and heart shall yet arise to the rescue! But I see them no where.

Accept with my resignation my heartfelt regrets for its necessity.

I am

very respectfully yours
Louisa S. McCord

To Augustine Thomas Smythe

My dear Son,   Charlottesville Nov[ember] 14th [1871]

I see that the papers announce Charleston as having been freed by frost from the fever. If this is, as I hope[,] true, Lou will soon be with you to prepare for her approaching sickness.[46] I have, in truth, been very uneasy about her; there having been so much to add to the usual nervous excitement naturally attendant upon her condition. There has been no object nearer my heart than to help her, and yet I have been utterly powerless to do any thing; and now I do not know whether I may do the more mischief, trying to do, or not to do. I need scarcely say to *you,* that were I to follow my impulse, my place would be, where it has always been in her suffering or sorrow, with my hand on hers. I know, although she will try not to show it, that the tension of feeling excited by her condition in recent surrounding circumstances must be severe; and in any hitherto period of her life, I would weeks since have written to her, that I would be with her in the time of trial. But truly

---

45. On June 15, 1870, a convention of what came to be called the Union Reform party (among whom were, it was announced, from twenty to thirty black delegates) met in Columbia in preparation for the state elections to be held in October. The following day, it adopted a platform (reported in the Charleston newspapers of June 17) declaring support of the Fifteenth Amendment as fundamental law and affirming that the changes effected as results of the war should be "regarded as verities having the force and obligation of law" (Charleston *Daily Courier,* June 17, 1870).

46. Augustine Thomas Smythe, Jr., was born on Dec. 21, 1871.

(and not doubting her affection and your kindness) I fear that my doing so would in the end bring more pain than comfort. I therefore write to you, rather than to her, to advise me what you would wish me to do. Seeing her, after she will have become settled in the return, to what I must call her home, will better enable you to judge if there is anything sufficiently urgent to change the plan which I had thought most prudent—i.e. to stay away. I want you to answer me, as sincerely as I write, and quite independantly of all consideration of my supposed feelings. One honest, kind, and truthful word, is more grateful to me, than all the made up apologies and courtesies ever spoken. I have loved, and I do love you because I think you truer with me than other people are.——You know my difficulties. They are in no wise lessened. In Charleston I can never be quiet, even in appearance, except permitted to remain in such seclusion as I require. I want no civilities from any body; but only to be permitted to come and go, as coldly and as quietly as I please, and having nothing to do with visits. I am so tired, I do not want to argue or dispute to no good purpose, and if I see people, they talk and goad me on to impatience and hard words; and then comes mischief and sorrow to Lou, whom I am trying to help. Now would my presence under these circumstances tend most to irritate or to soothe?——Neither am I sure that Lou is not going to be confined at your Mother's house. I do not know whence I have this indistinct impression.——Again, this KuKlux inquisition despotism—will it not probably stretch its arms through the State?[47] In truth Charleston deserves no exemption from it. Through her, from the egg of Reform was hatched out the ugly abortion styled "Tax payers Convention,"—which, laugh at it as you may, had none the less a telling effect; and the cowardly notice which this meeting saw fit to take of the KuKlux, did, I believe, largely help to call down recent reckless attacks.[48] Now, might not the presence of an offensive and discontented individual like myself, even though only an old woman, help to draw disagreeable attention. Do not laugh, as though thinking that I make myself of much impor-

47. Because of Ku Klux Klan activities in South Carolina, on Oct. 17, 1871, President Ulysses S. Grant suspended habeas corpus in nine upstate counties. Federal forces arrested several hundred persons and tried them in federal courts, with eighty-two convictions secured through November 1872.

48. The Taxpayers' Convention met in Columbia May 9–12, 1871, called, amid clamorous charges of mismanagement and theft of public funds, to investigate the government's accounts. Responding to a motion by Attorney General Daniel Henry Chamberlain, James Chesnut, as chairman of the convention's executive committee, agreed in deploring the "prevailing violences" but blamed them on the climate created by "bad government, corruption in high places," which "set the example of moral decadence and disregard of law." *United States Congressional Serial Set, House Reports*, 42d Cong., 2d sess., ser. 1531, v. 2, pt. 3, n. 22, pt. 3, pp. 494–95.

tance. Men have quarelled and shot each other, for a dog—for a shadow;—and I have heard it stated, right or wrong, that women have been threatened and watched, in the dragonade district. I might be, under some circumstances[,] a dangerous inmate, and it would be too late to move out of the way when the lash would be raised, not over me personally but over my nearest and dearest.

All these things considered, had I not better stay away? Tell me the truth;—and only don't let Loulou think that I am unkind or unloving. I am more anxious for her than ever,— even because I cannot tell her so.——

Answer me entirely at your liesure. If you say "Come on" I will do so towards middle December, (D.V.)[49] for some weeks only. But it will be a sin and a wrong in you, to say so, if you think that I had better not. Defer answering as long as you please. Twenty-four hours would be enough to fix me either way. I enclose a slip from yesterday's paper showing that the Habeas Corpus is, to use the slang of the day, being "played out" all over these so called U[nited] States.——

Excuse my long letter——I know you don't approve of such. I congratulate you, on escaping better than you deserve, the risks of fever; (Lou writes me that you keep well) and am always

Your affectionate Mother
Louisa S. McCord

I just see by an old Charleston paper lent me, resolutions debated by the Survivor's Association in Columbia against *the KuKlux*!!![50] And these were So[uth] C[arolin]a generals, soldiers etc. "Knock him again——He has no friends."[51]
Could they not at least say *nothing*? Must they get on their knees to lick the boots of Grant's drunken soldiery! The whole country has stood aghast at Grant's lawless proceedures and now and now those who should be S[outh] C[arolina] gentlemen, would appear to endorse them! They will get their pay in kind if they do not take care, the next time votes are called for.

---

49. *Deo volente* (Lat. "God willing").

50. The Charleston *Daily Courier* of Nov. 13, 1871, reported a meeting of the statewide Survivors' Association, held in Columbia the day before. The meeting unanimously adopted a resolution, called "the KKK resolution" by the reporter, that "at no time has this Association given countenance or encouragement to any organizations or combinations for the purpose of violating the established law of the land, or the rights of any persons thereunder, and hereby earnestly and solemnly declare their disapproval of all such organizations, if any there be, existing in this State."

51. *The Oxford Dictionary of English Proverbs*, 3d ed. (Oxford, 1970), p. 374, cites Dinah Maria Mulock (1826–87), *Woman's Thoughts* (1850), p. 156, for "the familiar tragio-comic

To Louisa McCord Smythe

Dear Daughter   Drummondville Feb[ruar]y 8 [1874]

Thanks for your letter of 30th. I was glad to get all your details of the little ones. There is no want of news or matter of interest to me, when you talk of yourselves. Gussy must be a funny little fellow. I am glad that my dear little Loula is looking better again. I suppose you are doing her education very gently. If she grows fast, *raison de plus* for so doing. Sweeping, and digging and playing, and a very little lessons is wisest.——I am sorry Dr. Reynolds is so much afloat.[52] It is very hard;—but I wish they would quit hanging on to the Leitch's.——I fear Lottie is not the better for or rather I should say, I fear she is the worse for their indecision. She does not seem to have been very well lately. I wish Dr. R. would go to Virginia and set up a little boys school, or anything for a decent maintenance, and be satisfied with that if nothing else comes.

I am glad to hear that Mary-Anne etc. have gone to Zimmerman's.[53] They will probably be able to make themselves useful enough to secure a tolerably comfortable home, so long as things do not blow up. If it would be useful to them, I should be glad that Gus should help them from me a little, to any amount not exceeding $20 p[e]r annum, and put to my debit. He will be the better judge though, if it would do more harm or good. Too much help might make them slack in their own efforts and Mr. Z. slack in assisting them, as their service might entitle them to be assisted.——

I have already written that the money business (last check) was all right with me at last. I am getting on quietly here. Took a sleigh-drive a few days since to the Falls. The ice from the River was scattered a few weeks since by a wind storm, and the water is of a dirty brown. The surrounding woods were beautifully laden with snow and ice, which would have glittered magnificently if the sun had shone;—but the sun just would not. Today the Sun is brilliant for the first time lately, and I see quite a number of sleighs flying about. It is Sunday though and I cannot venture—being a stranger here. I do not want to get myself talked about as a dissipated old character. I went

---

saying: 'Hit him hard; he's got no friends!'" *Punch* 23 (Dec. 18, 1852): 261, has a cartoon with the caption, "'Hit him again! He has no friends.'—Old Saying."

52. On Oct. 7, 1873, Henry Elliott Hayne, secretary of state and black, entered South Carolina College as a student. The resulting tumult included the resignation and dismissal of the faculty, among them James L. Reynolds (father of LSM's daughter-in-law Charlotte), who secured a position at Furman University in Greenville, S.C.

53. "Mary-Anne" is probably LSM's former servant, daughter of Langdon Cheves' servant June (see LSM to Langdon Cheves, Jr., Jan. 25, 1856, and note). Daniel Alexander Zimmerman purchased Lang Syne plantation on Dec. 1, 1870 (see *PSE*, pp. 492–93).

to church this morning. Unfortunately met with the misfortune of losing my neutral tint spectacles the other day. Hope in a week or so to get a pair (by order of a storekeeper here) from Montreal. Have got a very abominable pair of blue ones now, that hurt almost as much as they help. My bad writing is not all from my faulty eyes—I have got my pen in an abominable condition.

Long ago I got letters from you that I could not answer then wherein you seemed to distress y[ou]rself much about "Aunt Anna." It is useless and wrong for you to do so. She has the misfortune to be very effortless and has been kept entirely in the dark about her own affairs. Pinckney has been always a very bad manager and doubtless there is a pretty bad muddle in their affairs. But Mr. C. Huger will get himself fairly compensated for board etc.[54]—and as Anna's Trustee, he ought to try and manage something for her, if Pinckney continues, as he doubtless will do, incapable. They still have a part of the Ogeechee Plantation and the Altamaha Place. The first I told you, Sophia wrote me that Paul had rented.[55] Does Nan still keep her servant[?] I fear so. She ought to do without her. If she has Cara, it costs ~~her enough~~ to keep her, as much as would maintain herself. In such troubles as we go through, we must all make efforts or suffer. I have been displeased at the evident efforts of the Hugers to draw us into the net of their own folly. I did not at all like a letter I rec[eive]d some time since from my old friend Miss E. P. Huger.[56] Poor old Soul she has suffered too—but I have enough to do with my own. If Nan and her Husband need help, it should come from his relatives who have helped to squander her property. Only do not let yourself be made unhappy about it. Dear love to all.

To Augustine Thomas Smythe

My Dear Son
Drummondville, Ontario, Canada
March 29th, 1874

Thanks for y[ou]r letter of 23d rec[eive]d last evening. The enclosure was yet not needed; and yet I am glad it has come. I have a restless feeling (I do not believe in presentiments) that I must go somewhere or do something soon,—and keep most of my funds in nasty green backs ready. It is, I know, only the anxious habit of a mind, used to trouble and going ahead to meet

---

54. Probably Cleland Kinloch Huger (d. 1892), Thomas Pinckney Huger's younger brother.

55. Sophia Cheves Haskell's youngest son, Paul Thomson Haskell.

56. Elizabeth Pinckney Huger (d. Jan. 4, 1882, aged 78), Thomas Pinckney Huger's eldest sister.

it. But I feel safer with $50 or $100 in my trunk. I wrote you more than a week ago a letter that I hope did not worry you,—but I could not help it. I took into my head (I hope I was all mistaken) that Lou's letters indicated etc. etc. I won't talk about it again. Only let me trust you to tell me honestly and sincerely if anything is wrong with her.

I have been not a little anxious too about Lottie. She is a sacred charge to me, (none can be more so—) and I am very anxious to know if and how I can be of use to her. I do not see that you can help me though. But if anything should occur to you, I think you will say it.——If remaining where I am, (and I will not move unless for causes above suggested) I can scarcely need further funds (still retaining as I wish to do $50 always on hand) until about first ~~May~~ June[.] But do not trouble y[ou]rself to remember. I will write a fortnight before needing it. I am at present abundantly supplied for all contingencies. Forgive me for troubling you so much. An old Lady here of 85 deliberately pitched herself headforemost into a well the other day. If I were not as firm to my principles, as you sometimes want to quarrel with me for being, I would feel some days mightily inclined to follow her example. *A propos* of principles or the want of them,—I hear that Semmes(!) has gone over to glorifying the Union, and wanting place![57]——

I will write tomorrow morning (i.e. per same mail as this) to Lottie, so you *need not tell them* of my obnoxious letters—Only remember, it is my right to know if I am *wanted* at any time.——Forgive me and believe me

most affectionately
Y[ou]r Mother
L. S. McC——

To Langdon Cheves III

Charlotte, No[rth] C[arolin]a
Dear Langdon[58]　　　　　　　　　　　　　July 11th [1876]

I have been intending[,] and intending, to answer your letter of 14th Ulto. But in truth, I have been so utterly demoralized by all that has been going on through our (?) State,—Lou's continued sickness exciting personal anxieties; and then the jollification, and fraternizing, and gush of loyalty and

---

57. Probably Raphael Semmes (1808–77), Confederate naval commander, most famously of CSS *Alabama*; arrested and imprisoned after the war (Dec. 1865–April 1866); lawyer in Mobile.

58. Langdon Cheves III, son of LSM's brother Charles and Isabella Middleton Cheves, was engaged in genealogical research into the Cheves family.

love;—and the burying of hatchets; and dancing in chains;[59]—that, as I could not kneel down and shout "glory! glory!,"[60]—nor find my way to the "love, peace, and charity" frame of mind,—I have been trying to keep very quiet and very stupid, hemning, in good-woman style, pocket handkerchiefs, and so forth. I left Cleveland Spr[ing]s (because it was hot, and because I could better find here the pocket h[an]dk[erchief]s etc. to hemn) nearly two weeks since. But here,—hot, is hotter, and hottest!! People say, unprecedented weather. Here, however, I am trying to stay until Augustine Smythe can get away from the law, and start with Lou etc., for V[irgini]a—whither I shall, with all speed, join them *en route*.

I presume the ladies of your family are all off long before this for Flat Rock; and, I hope, escaping such heat, as (judging from what is experienced here) Charleston, I fear, must have. Are you and Henry[61] such thorough men of business, that you do not intend to indulge yourselves in your usual recreation of a mountain holliday? This is a hot season in which to begin with such a change.——I hope Rice crops get on safely, and suppose if Tilden is elected, there will no longer be fear of Hawaiian treaties etc.[62]——I have of course written,—and can write,—nothing of my Father in my present restless state of mind. If I live to get back to Charleston next winter, it will depend, I suppose[,] upon the turn of things, whether I can again gather up my scraps of recollection to write more. I wish you had thought of asking it of me a half dozen years ago. By-the-way, my Fathers monument is I hear at last raised. The blessed S[outh] C[arolina] Centennial blotted it out as much as possible. It is eight months after date of contract. I hope the inscriptions will be satisfactory to you. I would have consulted you about them; but they were all done before I knew you. For in truth, only since our short correspondence, have I known you as Langdon Cheves. My heart warms to the name, and to my nephew, who is, I believe[,] worthy of it.

You ask in your letter whether I can tell anything of the farm in V[irgini]a left to my Father by his grandfather. I cannot. I only remember to have heard,

---

59. LSM appears to refer to celebrations of the Centennial on July 4, 1876.

60. Perhaps alluding to "Glory, glory, hallelujah" in the chorus of "The Battle Hymn of the Republic" (publ. February 1862) by abolitionist and feminist Julia Ward Howe (1819–1910).

61. Langdon Cheves III's brother, Henry Charles Cheves.

62. Samuel Jones Tilden (1814–86) was Democratic candidate for president in 1876. A reciprocity treaty between the United States and Hawaii, signed in January 1875 to take effect eighteen months later, would open American markets to Hawaiian exports and therefore provoked opposition from American producers, such as the growers of rice and sugar in the Southern states.

in my childhood[,] that Father made ~~en~~ research for, and I believe found it. That it had been taken possession of, and passed to other claiments whom it would have been difficult to dispossess—my Father probably possessing no papers or titles securing it. I do not know whether it was a farm or a house in the town or village of Woodstock.

As for the lot in Abbeville, on which my Grandmothers grave is now covered and enclosed—Your Aunt Sophia writes me that I have proved to be right in the reasoning which led me to the conclusion that it belonged to Alexander Cheves, and was the home of the young Mother, destined never to know her son. Old Mr. Perrin knows all about it and says that titles and papers were burned with Village C[ourt] House.[63]——The Langdon arms were given to Father, by Mrs. Elwyn (Langdon-Elwyn the family were called) originally Miss Langdon daughter or descendant of Gov[ernor] Langdon of I think Massachusetts but of V[irgini]a stock, and when we knew them hailing from New Orleans.[64]

I hope that Harrie is better of the tendency to "not very well" which was hanging about her when you wrote and that she and others are all comfortable at Flat Rock.[65] To yourself if in Charleston, I must only I suppose wish you such patience under heat as I cannot practice myself, and am

Affectionately y[ou]r Aunt
Louisa S McCord

To Preston Powers

Dear Sir[66]   [Charleston May 29th, 1878]

I ~~have~~ rec[eive]d, yesterday, ~~recd~~ your letter of 8th Inst. ~~I today~~ and today enclose such likenesses as I can procure of my Father ~~wh but but~~ and which

---

63. Thomas Chiles Perrin (1805–78), Abbeville lawyer, planter, politician, and railroad executive.

64. Elizabeth Langdon Elwyn, wife of Thomas Elwyn and mother of Philadelphia physician and philanthropist Alfred Langdon Elwyn (1804–84), was daughter of John Langdon (1741–1819), born Portsmouth, N.H., and governor of New Hampshire 1805–9 and 1810–12. John Langdon's mother was a descendant of Governor Thomas Dudley (1576–1653) of Massachusetts Bay Colony, of whom LSM may be thinking when she makes John Langdon governor of Massachusetts. The Langdons being settled in Portsmouth, N.H., since the mid-seventeenth century, it is not clear how LSM ascribes to them "Virginia stock," unless she assumed this from the residence in Virginia of her great-grandfather Thomas Langdon before his emigration to South Carolina.

65. Langdon Cheves III's sister, Harriott Cheves.

66. Third son of Hiram Powers, Preston Powers (1843–1931) took charge of his deceased father's studio in September 1874; he was named after William Campbell Preston. This letter survives in draft.

are I regret to say exceedingly faulty. I cannot understand why these photographs taken from paintings seems to distort the face,—The mouths in both being ~~abominable~~ quite crooked—The ~~better likeness of the two~~ roughest looking of the two (taken f[ro]m a ~~pa~~ very inferior painting ~~of~~ by Morse, since of telegraphick ~~fame~~ celebrity, but beginning his career as a portrait painter)[67] ~~conveys (rough as it is) more idea of the expression of face of forehead face though the mouth is fearfully distorted than the smoothly finished one. The profile likeness is essentially correct—The Morse picture~~ conveys (rough as it is) more idea of the expression of ~~face~~ face forehead and eye—~~(the mouth is quite fearfully distorted)~~ than the smoother one. The profile likeness is ~~probably~~ an essentially correct profile outline. None of them can give ~~even the~~ [two? illegible words] shadow of the man—~~the greatest~~ who although now almost forgotten in the scramble which follows our noble but disastrous war ~~almost forgotten~~, was the greatest ~~that our State ever gave to the country~~ in self poised character and massive intellect that our State has ~~produced~~ ever given to the country—

To describe his appearance I can only give my own recollection, of impressive and commanding ~~appearance~~—"King-like" ~~as a~~ [two or three illegible letters canceled] to use a common ~~rather than correct~~ rather than correct ~~expression~~ comparison [which?] was by the masses frequently applied to him [line missing from torn page]—and no personal ambition beforehand. he looked born to command ~~penetrating eye chest thick formed~~ —penetrating eye—chest well formed with square and broad shoulders.

To further illustrate character I copy a part of the engraving upon his ~~tomb~~ monument which is usually ~~granted to be~~ considered to correctly designate the man—

viz—"Langdon Cheves"

"so wise,—so pure,—so strong,—his country needed,—but Death had called him."

Again

"Massiveness of intellect,—purity of purpose,—wisdom of judgement,—and indomitable energy of execution,—combined to make the patriot statesman and the model man."[68]

~~Now I can do nothing more and Now I have only further to repeat that I can do nothing more to help you.~~ I think I can say or do nothing more to

---

67. Samuel Finley Breese Morse (1791–1872), whose career as a painter culminated in his establishment of the National Academy of Design, of which he was first president, had a studio in Charleston during the winters from 1818 to 1821.

68. For the complete text of LSM's epitaph for her father, inscribed on the base of the obelisk raised at the Cheves tomb in Magnolia Cemetery, Charleston, see PDBL, "Memoir of Langdon Cheves," p. 262.

help you and must now put my trust in your artist skill ~~to help me to a good likeness~~ ~~to the bust which I ask~~ wish for —I am ~~however~~ in no ~~w~~haste ~~whatever~~ and ~~should~~ would prefer that you should take your time and suit yourself to your own spirit of inspiration for the working impulse.

Would ~~it be~~ you object as the man is now 21 years in his grave and in such a country as ours now is, that is enough to stamp into oblivion every thing worth remembering— ~~would~~ would you object to engrave upon the base of the bust the name "*Langdon Cheves*["] and below it "*Clarum et venerabile nomen*"[69]—

[*word missing from torn page*] ~~the statue of Calhoun and~~

Regarding the replacing of the statue of Calhoun I would be most happy to do any thing useful or agreeable to you;[70] but I not only have ~~of later~~ for years shrunk too much from the world to ~~be kn~~ have influence with anybody, but I know little of what is going on— and have not ~~the smallest~~ connection or acquaintance with ~~the~~ any of the town council nor with those moving in the matter. My world is dead and in the past. ~~In fact~~ My ~~own~~ private impression however is that the town council has not the slightest idea of doing anything in the ~~matter~~ business and that ~~the town is too poor~~ whatever may be talked about in that line, the citizens ~~have~~ will save their ~~surplus~~ funds to ~~pay~~ pay the onerous taxes laid upon them,— ~~and consuming~~ Our corner of the world does not prosper, and if the Calhoun monument or Calhoun statue shall ever be raised, it ~~will~~ must be without help of mine.

In a day or two the Bill of Exchange on London for £50 will be forwarded to you. The person upon whom I depend for ~~its execution~~ arranging it for me is for a ~~day or two out of~~ short time absent f[ro]m the town.[71]

69. "Illustrious and venerable name," Lucan *De bello civili* (*The Civil War*) 9.202; also inscribed on the Cheves obelisk in Magnolia Cemetery. The words are part of Cato the Younger's eulogy on Pompey the Great, Julius Caesar's adversary in civil war, who was murdered when he sought refuge in Egypt (48 B.C.).

70. Shipped in April 1850, Hiram Powers' statue of John C. Calhoun went down with the *Elizabeth* off Fire Island, N.Y., on July 19. Salvaged and repaired, the statue was placed in the Charleston City Hall until, for fear of Federal bombardment during the war, it was sent to Columbia, where it was destroyed in the burning of the city during Sherman's occupation.

71. The completed bust of Langdon Cheves, which arrived in Charleston in January 1880, is reproduced and discussed in Wunder, *Hiram Powers* 2:29–30.

Bibliography

Barnwell, John. *Love of Order: South Carolina's First Secession Crisis.* Chapel Hill, N.C., 1982.

Bennett, Susan Smythe, comp. "The Cheves Family of South Carolina." *South Carolina Historical Magazine* 35 (1934): 79–95, 130–52.

———, comp. "The McCords of McCords' Ferry, South Carolina." *South Carolina Historical Magazine* 34 (1933): 177–93.

Burke, Edmund. *Letter to a Noble Lord.* In *The Writings and Speeches of Edmund Burke.* Vol. 9, pt. 1, *The Revolutionary War, 1794–1797,* and pt. 2, *Ireland,* ed. R. B. McDowell, pp. 145–87. Oxford, 1991.

Conrad, Susan Phinney. *Perish the Thought: Intellectual Women in Romantic America, 1830–1860.* New York, 1976.

Davidson, Chalmers Gaston. *The Last Foray: The South Carolina Planters of 1860, a Sociological Study.* Columbia, S.C., 1971.

Davidson, James Wood. *The Living Writers of the South.* New York, 1869.

Duyckinck, Evert A., and George L. Duyckinck. *Cyclopaedia of American Literature.* 2 vols. New York, 1856.

Eacker, Susan A. "'A Dangerous Inmate' of the South: Louisa McCord on Gender and Slavery." In *Southern Writers and Their Worlds,* ed. Christopher Morris and Steven G. Reinhardt, pp. 27–40. College Station, Tex., 1996.

Forrest, Mary [Julia D. Freeman]. *Women of the South Distinguished in Literature.* New York, 1861.

Fox-Genovese, Elizabeth. *Within the Plantation Household: Black and White Women of the Old South.* Chapel Hill, N.C., 1988.

Fraser, Jessie Melville. "Louisa C. McCord." M.A. thesis, University of South Carolina, 1919.

Genovese, Eugene D., and Elizabeth Fox-Genovese. "Slavery, Economic Development, and the Law: The Dilemma of the Southern Political Economists, 1800–1860." *Washington and Lee Law Review* 41, no. 1 (Winter 1984): 1–29.

Gillespie, Neal C. *The Collapse of Orthodoxy: The Intellectual Ordeal of George Frederick Holmes.* Charlottesville, Va., 1972.

Huff, Archie Vernon, Jr. *Langdon Cheves of South Carolina.* Columbia, S.C., 1977.

Jones, Norrece T., Jr. *Born a Child of Freedom, Yet a Slave: Mechanisms of Control and Strategies of Resistance in Antebellum South Carolina.* Hanover, N. H., and London, 1990.

Kelley, Mary. "Designing a Past for the Present: Women Writing Women's History in

Nineteenth-Century America." *Proceedings of the American Antiquarian Society* 105 (1995): 315–46.

Lounsbury, Richard C., ed. *Louisa S. McCord: Poems, Drama, Biography, Letters.* Publications of the Southern Texts Society. Charlottesville, Va., 1996.

———, ed. *Louisa S. McCord: Political and Social Essays.* Publications of the Southern Texts Society. Charlottesville, Va., 1995.

———. "*Ludibria Rerum Mortalium:* Charlestonian Intellectuals and Their Classics." In *Intellectual Life in Antebellum Charleston,* ed. Michael O'Brien and David Moltke-Hansen, pp. 325–69. Knoxville, Tenn., 1986.

McCurry, Stephanie. "The Two Faces of Republicanism: Gender and Proslavery Politics in Antebellum South Carolina." *Journal of American History* 78 (1992): 1245–64.

Manly, Louise. *Southern Literature from 1579–1895: A Comprehensive Review, with Copious Extracts and Criticisms.* Richmond, 1895.

May, Caroline. *The American Female Poets, with Biographical and Critical Notices.* Philadelphia, 1848.

O'Brien, Michael, ed. *All Clever Men, Who Make Their Way: Critical Discourse in the Old South.* Fayetteville, Ark., 1982; 2d ed., Athens, Ga., 1992.

Pease, William H., and Jane H. Pease. *James Louis Petigru: Southern Conservative, Southern Dissenter.* Athens, Ga., 1995.

Rable, George C. *Civil Wars: Women and the Crisis of Southern Nationalism.* Urbana, Ill., 1989.

Read, Thomas Buchanan, ed. *The Female Poets of America.* Philadelphia, 1849.

Smythe, Louisa McCord. *For Old Lang Syne: Collected for My Children.* Charleston, S.C., 1900.

———. "Recollections of Louisa Rebecca Hayne McCord (Mrs. Augustine T. Smythe)" (typescript). South Caroliniana Library, University of South Carolina. Columbia.

Stockton, David. *The Gracchi.* Oxford, 1979.

[Tardy, Mary T., ed.] *The Living Female Writers of the South.* 1872. Rpt. Detroit, 1978.

Thorp, Margaret Farrand. *Female Persuasion: Six Strong-Minded Women.* 1949. Rpt. n.p., 1971.

Wauchope, George Armstrong, ed. *The Writers of South Carolina.* Columbia, S.C., 1910.

Woodward, C. Vann, ed. *Mary Chesnut's Civil War.* New Haven, 1981.

———, and Elizabeth Muhlenfeld, eds. *The Private Mary Chesnut: The Unpublished Civil War Diaries.* New York, 1984.

Wunder, Richard P. *Hiram Powers: Vermont Sculptor, 1805–1873.* 2 vols. Newark, N.J., 1991.

Index

A. NAMES

When a name is followed by more than one page reference, annotation is signified by boldface type. Authors being reviewed by LSM are excluded, apart from the page number where annotation can be found. Fictional persons named in her review of Uncle Tom's Cabin *and speaking characters in* Caius Gracchus *are indexed only when annotated or when mentioned elsewhere.*

Adams family, 4
Aemilius Paullus, Lucius, **40**, 190n, 196n
Agassiz, Louis, 73n
Agathyrnum, 215
Albert, Prince, 100
Albert l'Ouvrier (Albert-Alexandre Martin), 260
Amazons, 71
Angell, James Burrill, 4
Antony, Mark, 208n
Antyllius, Quintus, 233
Apis, 62, 63

Balaam, 87, 88
Barnburners, 62
Barnwell, Robert Woodward, **33**, 40, 46
Bastiat, Frédéric, 11; *Harmonies économiques* of, 263–64; LSM's translation of *Sophismes économiques* of, 11, 17
Baxter, Sally, 4–5
Ben (McCord servant), 261, 275
Bess. *See* Elizabeth I of England
Betsy (McCord servant), 261
Blanc, Louis, **57**, 144n, 260
Bloomer, Amelia Jenks, 178; item of apparel named for, **65**, 69, 70
Bobadill, Captain, 35
Boyd, Mr. (Cheves nurse), 274, 275
Brisbane, Albert, 27
Brooks, Sidney, 279n
Brown, John, 7, 276

Buchanan, James, 33n
Bulwer-Lytton, Rosina Doyle Wheeler, 59
Burke, Edmund: his *Letter to a Noble Lord*, 13
Burke, William, 90
Butler, Andrew Pickens, **32**, 33, 40, 46

Cabet, Etienne, 24
Caesar, Gaius Julius, 208n, 296n
Cain, 140, 141n
Caius Gracchus, 5, 13–14, 17; excerpted in anthologies, 214n; LSM on writing of, 260; review of, 1, 14. *See also* Plutarch; Shakespeare, William
Calhoun, John C., 42–45; statue of, by Hiram Powers, 296; letter of, to Henry Stuart Foote, 43–44
Caliban, **88**–89, 112, 178
Caligula, Gaius, 44
Cannae, battle of, 40, 190n, 196n
Capers and Heyward, 273–74
Cara (Huger servant), 291
Carey, Henry Charles, 13; LSM's letter to, **262**–64
Carlyle, Thomas, 24–25
Carthage, 115n, 183n, 196n; Gaius Gracchus founds colony at, 191n, 216, 225, 230
Cassandra, 33
Cassius Longinus Ravilla, Lucius, 193n
Cato the Younger, Marcus Porcius, 296n
Centennial of 1876, 292–93
Chamberlain, Daniel Henry, 288n

Charleston: fire of 1861, 8
Chénier, Marie-Joseph: *Caius Gracchus* of, 184n
Chesnut, James, 288n
Chesnut, Mary Boykin, 8, 14
Cheves, Alexander (grandfather), 1–2, 294
Cheves, Alexander (brother), 3n, 16
Cheves, Anna Maria. *See* Huger, Anna Cheves
Cheves, Charles Manly (brother), 2, 257, 292n; death of, 6, 17
Cheves, Charlotte McCord (sister-in-law), 3, 5, 257, 264, 269, 273, 280
Cheves, Harriott (niece), 294
Cheves, Henry Charles (nephew), 279n, 293
Cheves, Isabella Middleton (sister-in-law), 292n
Cheves, John Richardson (brother), 8, 150n, 255; part in dispute over father's will, 12
Cheves, Langdon (father), 1, 2, 3, 10, 11, 16, 17, 256, 258n, 276, 290n, 293–94; bust of, by Preston Powers, 9–10, 294–96; *clarum et venerabile nomen*, 296; dispute over will of, 6, 12, 17; epitaph of, 295; last illness, 6, 264–75; LSM defends, 18, 37n; LSM's devotion to, 6; LSM's memoir of, 6, 9, 293; and McCord children, 268; *My Dreams* dedicated to, 165–66; regal bearing of, 295; and secession crisis of 1851–52, 29n, 33, 34n, 37, 40, 42, 44, 46; watch belonging to, 150n; and wife's death, 255; will of, cited, 272n. *See also* Powers, Hiram
Cheves, Langdon, Jr. (brother), 3, 7; delegate to secession convention, 278; killed at Battery Wagner on Morris Island, 18, 285; LSM's letters to, 256–57, 264–75, 280; LSM's letters to, cited, 6–7, 7, 12, 42n, 269n, 290n
Cheves, Langdon, III (nephew), 9; LSM's letter to, **292–94**; LSM's letter to, cited, 6
Cheves, Mary Elizabeth Dulles (mother), 2, 16; death of, 3, 16, 255; letter of, to Alexander Cheves, 2–3
Cheves, Mary Langdon (grandmother), 1, 294
Cheves, Rachel Susan Bee (sister-in-law), 150n
Cheves, Robert Hayne (brother), 6, 17, 256n, 257, 261; last illness and death, 17, 266–67
Cheves, Sophia Lovell. *See* Haskell, Sophia Cheves

Cheves family: tomb of, in Magnolia Cemetery, Charleston, 9, 10, 293, 295, 296n
Christianity: abolitionism a perversion of, 48–49, 137; charity of, 52, 62, 91; as civilizing influence, 26; LSM praises, 12; political economy and, 130, 133, 134–35, 147; and Southern slaveholders, 102–3; Southern slavery as ornament of, 117–18, 146; as veil for Harriet Beecher Stowe's "malignant bitterness," 84, 262; woman as upholder of, 76–77, 120
Cilla. *See* Priscilla
Clarkson, Thomas, **48**, 132
Columbia, S.C.: Federal occupation of, 9, 18, 149–53, 279n, 285, 296n
Comet of 1843, Great, 172n
Comitium, 223
Confederacy, the, 258n, 275n, 278, 292n; gunboat of, 8; LSM's dedication to, 8, 10
Coriolanus, Gnaeus Marcius, 212n, 241n
Cornelia, 14, **190**, 196n, 220n; "mother of the Gracchi," 182
Couthon, Georges, 31
Curius Dentatus, Manius, 220
Curtius, Marcus, 36
Cytherea maccordia, 3

Danton, Georges-Jacques, **31**, 33n
De Bow's Review, 10, 17
Decatur, Stephen, 40n
Decii, 220
Dehon, Theodore, **279**, 285, 286
DeSaussure, William Ford, 272
Desmoulins, Camille, 33
Domitius Ahenobarbus, Gnaeus, 218n
Don Quixote, 86
Draco, 62
Draper, Lyman Copeland: LSM's letter to, cited, 152n
Dulles, Joseph Heatly (uncle), 3n
Dulles, Mary Cheves: LSM's letter to, 261–62; LSM's letters to, cited, 5, 6, 13
Dulles, Sophia Heatly (grandmother), 2, 256, 257; letter of, to Joseph Heatly Dulles, 2
Dumas, Alexandre, the elder and the younger, **60**, 85

Elizabeth I of England, 69, 70, 71, 80
Elwyn, Elizabeth Langdon, 294
England: and abolitionism, 131–32; condition

England (cont.)
of laboring classes of, 13; laws of, 145;
and opium trade, 121–22
Eve, 65, 73

Fabius Maximus, Quintus, 216
Fannius, Gaius, **218**, 227
Fantacchiotti, Odoardo, 278
First Regiment, South Carolina Volunteers,
265n, 282n
Foote, Henry Stuart, 43, **44n**
Fort Sumter, 1, 8, 280
Fourier, Charles: and Fourierist phalanx,
27n, **68**
France, 17; revolution and despotism in, 11,
22–23, 30, 31, 33, 41, 91–92, 260
Francis of the Two Sicilies, King, 279n
Frankenstein, 90
Franklin, Sir John, 55
Fraser and Company, John, 275
Fry, Elizabeth Gurney, 132
Fulvius Flaccus, Marcus, **187**, 190n, 191n

Garibaldi, Giuseppe, 279
Garnett, Miss, 8
Genucius, 211
Giant Despair, 87
Gibbon, Edward, 131n
Giddings, Joshua Reed, 91
Goodwyn, Thomas Jefferson, 150n
Gracchi, the, 260. *See also* Cornelia
Gracchus, Gaius Sempronius, 181n, 183nn,
184n, 186n, 188n, 190n, **191**, 193nn,
196n, 216n, 218n, 220n, 223n; eloquence of, 187n
Gracchus, Tiberius Sempronius (cos. 177,
163 B.C.), **190n**, 220; statue of, 236–37
Gracchus, Tiberius Sempronius (tr. pl. 133
B.C.), **186**, 187n, 190n, 191n, 196n,
211, 212, 220, 235, 243
Grant, Ulysses S., 288n, 289
Gratiot, Amédée, 27
Greeley, Horace, **27**, 52n
Gregg, Maxcy, 282n
Grimm, Jacob Ludwig Carl and Wilhelm
Carl, 123
Griswold, Rufus W., 89n

Haiti, 48, 90n, 109
Hamilton, James, Jr., 42
Hampton, Ann Fitzsimons, 8
Hannibal, 190n
Haskell, Alexander (nephew), 9, 281

Haskell, Charles (nephew), 18, 282
Haskell, Charles Thomson (brother-in-law),
16, 282
Haskell, Mehitable, 56–57
Haskell, Paul Thomson (nephew), 291
Haskell, Sophia Cheves (sister), 2, 10n, 16,
291, 294; letters of, to Eleuthera Du
Pont, 7, 266n; LSM's letters to, 255–
56, 281–82
Haskell, William (nephew), 18, 150n,
281–82
Hawaiian Treaty, 293
Hayne, Henry Elliott, 290n
Hayne, Rebecca Alston, 256, 257
Hayne, Robert Young, 42, **256**
Hercules, 21, 38
Heyward, Joseph Manigault, 267
Holmes, George Frederick, 130
Horatius Cocles, 183n
Howard, John, 132
Howard, Oliver Otis, **149**–53
Huger, Anna Cheves (sister), 2, 16, 255,
257, 264, 271; as belle, 256; financial
troubles of, 291; letter of, to Anna Dulles, 3
Huger, Cleland Kinloch, 291
Huger, Elizabeth Pinckney, 291
Huger, Thomas Pinckney (brother-in-law),
264; incapacity of, 291

Isocrates, 37n
Israel, 38

Jackson, Andrew, 276n
Jellyby, Mrs., 132
Jesus Christ, 72n, 176, 282n
Jonson, Ben, 35n
Journal des économistes, 11, 263
Judas, 37
June (Cheves servant), **266**, 267, 269, 270,
290n; arrested and to be sold, 273–75;
and emancipation, 271–73

Kelley Foster, Abigail, **127**, 178
Kennedy, John Pendleton, 5
Kingsley, Charles, 13
Knowles, James Sheridan: *Caius Gracchus* of,
184n
Ku Klux Klan, 288, 289

Lamartine, Alphonse-Marie-Louis de Prat de,
26–27
Lang Syne (plantation), 6, 8, 130n, 273, 274,

Lang Syne (plantation) (*cont.*)
275; library of, 4–5; LSM receives, 3, 16–17; sacked by Federal forces, 18; sold, 9, 18, 290n; visitors to, 3–4
Langdon, Thomas, 294n
Langdon family, 293–94
Lenclos, Ninon de, 60
Lewis, Matthew Gregory, **109**, 123
Licinia, 190
Licinius, 183n
Licinius Crassus Dives Mucianus, Publius, 190n
Lieber, Francis, 11, **48**
Lieber, Matilda, 261, 273
Lilliput, 36
Lincoln, Abraham, 1, 280
Livius Drusus, Marcus, **188**, 191n; LSM on, 260
Louis Philippe of France, 25n, 27n, 260n
Lucullus, 184

McCord, Charlotte Reynolds (daughter-in-law), 8, 18, 290, 292
McCord, David James (husband), 1, 3, 10, 11, 16, 130n, 258, 261, 262, 277n; death of, 6, 17; ill health of, 5, 257, 261; predicts civil war, 5; letter of, to William Porcher Miles, 258n
McCord, Hannah Cheves. *See* Rhett, Hannah Cheves McCord
McCord, Langdon Cheves (son), 7, 14, 16, 17, 280; death of, 8–9, 18, 280–82, 285; *Caius Gracchus* dedicated to, 181–82; ill health of, 5; notebook of, 153; troubled eyesight of, 6–7; watch belonging to, 150n, 282
McCord, Langdon Cheves (granddaughter), 18, 285
McCord, Louisa Rebecca Hayne. *See* Smythe, Louisa Rebecca Hayne McCord
McCord children: LSM's poem on, 174
McCrady, Edward, Jr., 282
Magdalene, Mary, 82
Manassas, Va.: second battle of, 8, 14, 18, 285
Mann, Horace, **88**, 91
Martineau, Harriet, 59
Mary-Anne (or Marianne; McCord servant), 266n, 290
Micipsa of Numidia, King, **183**, 184
Miles, William Porcher, 9, 9n, 14; LSM's letters to, **258**–61
Mills, Clark, 276–77

Minerva, 70, 224
Monroe, James, 2
Monti, Vincenzo: *Caio Gracco* of, 184n
Morse, Samuel Finley Breese, 295
Moses, Franklin J. [Israel], Sr., 284
Mother Goose, 123
Mott, Lucretia Coffin, 12, **127**
My Dreams, 13, 17, 258

Narragansett Bay, R.I., 4, 5, 17
Nashville Convention, **29n**, 33, 36–37, 42
Newton, Sir Isaac, 152
New York *Knickerbocker*, 14n
New York *Observer*, 68n
New York *Tribune*, 27n, 52n
Niebuhr, Barthold Georg, 260
Nightingale, Florence, 132
North, Jane Caroline, 5–6
North British Review, 13
Noyes, John Humphrey, 68n

Oneida Community, 68
Opimius, Lucius, **184**, 193n, 216n, 218n
Opium War, 121n
Orestes, Lucius Aurelius, 183
Ottoman sultan, 67
Owen, Robert: and Owenism, 24

Pacific (Collins Line steamer), 266n
Paley, William, **131n**, 137, 142
Parkman, George, 90
Penates, 77, 79
Perrin, Thomas Chiles, 294
Perry, Benjamin Franklin, 6
Persia, British and North American Royal Mail Steamship, 17
Petigru, James Louis, 6
Phaethon, 54
Pilate, Pontius, 72n, 103
Plautus, Titus Maccius, 46n
Plutarch, 184n; main source for *Caius Gracchus*, **181n**, 260
Poe, Edgar Allan, 89n
Pompadour, Jeanne-Antoinette Poisson, marquise de, 60
Pompey the Great, 296n
Pomponius Rufus, Marcus, 183
Porsenna, King, 183n
Portia, 70, 132n
Powell, John W., 265, 267
Powers, Hiram, 7, 17, 294n; bust of LSM by, 7, 276, 277, 279; planned bust of Langdon Cheves, 9–10, 18, 278–79,

Powers, Hiram (cont.)
    285–86; letter of, to LSM, 286n; LSM's letters to, **275**–79, 283–86. *See also* Calhoun, John C.
Powers, Preston, 9; LSM's letter to, **294**–96; LSM's letter to, cited, 9–10
Preston, Caroline Martha Hampton, 8
Preston, William Campbell, **277**, 294n
Priscilla (Cheves and McCord servant), 271–73, 274; pregnant, 269
Prospero, 88n
Proudhon, Pierre-Joseph, **24**, 26
Ptolemy VIII Physcon, 220
Pyrrhus of Epirus, King, 220

Reynolds, Charlotte. *See* McCord, Charlotte Reynolds
Reynolds, James Lawrence, 290
Rhett, Hannah Cheves McCord (daughter), 8, 17, 18; ill with typhoid fever, 277
Rhett, John Taylor (son-in-law), 18
Robespierre, Maximilien de, **31**, 68
Roland de La Platière, Jeanne-Marie Philipon, 118
Rome, 44, 183n, 190n; courage at, 38–39; office of censor in, 193n; war with Falerii, 211
Rubicon river, 41
Ruffin, Edmund, 1, 3
Ruth, 35

St. Clare, Augustine, 262
San Marino, 36
Sand, George, **26**, 59, 60
Sardinia: Gaius Gracchus serves in, 183n, 184, 185, 186
Scipio Aemilianus, Publius Cornelius, 196
Scipio Africanus, Publius Cornelius, 190n, 196n
Scipio Nasica Serapio, Publius Cornelius, 186n, 190n
secession, 33n, 272n, 278; Ordinance of, 277; separate, in South Carolina, 28–46
Semmes, Raphael, 292
Sempronia, 196n
Septimuleius, 193
Servilius Caepio, Gnaeus, 193n
Shaftesbury, Anthony Ashley Cooper, seventh earl of, 13, 120n
Shaftesbury, Emily Caroline Catherine Frances Cooper, countess of, **120**, 126
Shakespeare, William: *Coriolanus* a model for *Caius Gracchus*, 13, 212, 241; female characters of, 70; "a woman Shakespeare," 59n; "that great master of the human mind," 88–89
Shelby, Mrs., 262
Sherman, William Tecumseh, 150n, **152**, 153, 285, 296n
Shylock, 132, 133
Simms, William Gilmore, 13; letter of, to Henry Carey Baird, 262n
Sisyphus, **83**, 84
Smith, Elizabeth Oakes Prince, 52n
Smith, Gerritt, 12
Smyth, Thomas: LSM's letter to, 283
Smythe, Augustine Thomas (son-in-law), 9, 18, 283n, 286, 290, 293; LSM's letters to, 280–81, 287–89, 291–92
Smythe, Augustine Thomas, Jr. (grandson), 287n, 290
Smythe, Louisa Cheves (granddaughter), 290
Smythe, Louisa Rebecca Hayne McCord (daughter), 7, 9, 17, 18, 283n, 292, 293; how named, 256n; ill with typhoid fever, 277; pregnant, 287–89; letters of: to Sophia Cheves Haskell, 10, to William Porcher Miles, 9; LSM's letter to, 290–91
Solomon, 79
South Carolina: Centennial of, 293; conservative principles of, threatened, 11; financial collapse of, 283; as LSM's home, 122; under Reconstruction, 9, 284–85, 286, 287, 288–89; Survivors' Association of, 289. *See also* secession
South Carolina College, 5, 11, 18, 33n, 48n, 149, 272n, 277n, 290n; hospital in, 8
South Carolina Monument Association, 18; LSM's letter to the Board of Managers of, 286–87
Southern Literary Gazette, 17
Southern Literary Messenger, 17
Southern Quarterly Review, 10, 13, 17, 30n, 262
Sparta: women in, 61
Stanton, Elizabeth Cady, 127n
Stiggins, Mr., 132
Stowe, Harriet Beecher, 12, 124, 125n, 127, 128, 132; and the duchess of Sutherland, 121; LSM reviews *Uncle Tom's Cabin* of, 4–5, 13, 83–118; malignant influence of, 262, 278. *See also* Victoria, Queen
Sue, Eugène, **60**, 85
Sumner, Charles, 278

Sutherland, Harriet Elizabeth Georgiana Leveson-Gower, duchess of, 13, 262n, 263; LSM's letter to, **119**–29

Symmers, George, v. the United States, 149n

Taxpayers' Convention, 288
Tilden, Samuel Jones, 293
Tradewell (or Treadwell), James D., 272

Varro, Gaius Terentius, 40
Vettius, 187
Veturius, Gaius, 211
Victoria, Queen, 100, 119n; character and abilities of, 70–71; and Harriet Beecher Stowe, 123; income of, from slave labor, 103
Volumnia, 212n

Walpole, Horace: letter of, to the countess of Upper Ossory, 281n

Walsh, Robert Moylan, 90n
Ward, Frederick, v. the United States, 149n
Washington, George, 276n
Washington, Treaty of, 9, 149n
Watts, Beaufort Taylor, 257
Webster, Daniel, 90n, 256n
Webster, John White, 90n
Webster, Noah, 87
Whittemore, Benjamin Franklin, 285
Wilberforce, William, **48**, 132
Willard, Amiel J., 284
Worthington, Edward Dagge, 3–4
Wright, Jonathan Jasper, 284

Young, Brigham, 66

Zimmerman, Daniel Alexander, 290
Zschokke, Johann Heinrich Daniel, 24

B. AUTHORS

Not included below are citations from books and articles being reviewed by LSM.

"The Affectionate and Christian Address of Many Thousands of the Women of England," 13, 119

The Bible
  Genesis, 71 (1:27), 117 (1:27), 140 (16:11–12)
  Exodus, 63 (16:3, 14–35, 32:4–6), 131 (13:21–22)
  Numbers, 87 (22–24)
  Deuteronomy, 121 (8:5)
  Joshua, 28 (9:23)
  Ruth, 35 (1:14)
  1 Samuel, 38 (4:21–22)
  1 Kings, 107 (18:27)
  Job, 45 (16:21), 109 (38:11), 120 (38:1, 40:6)
  Psalms, 85 (115:5–6)
  Proverbs, 69 (16:18)
  Ecclesiastes, 140 (8:15)
  Isaiah, 140 (22:13)
  Jeremiah, 85 (5:21), 142 (5:21)
  Ezekiel, 49 (16:23), 103 (16:23)
  Nahum, 120 (1:3)
  Matthew, 26 (5:42), 37 (25:21), 49 (12:31), 81 (26:39), 91 (12:33), 103 (27:24), 107 (7:3), 139 (7:16–20), 276 (7:8)
  Mark, 23 (5:9), 26 (12:17), 77 (4:39)
  Luke, 51 (10:37), 107 (18:11), 140 (12:19), 276 (11:10)
  John, 26 (13:34, 15:12, 17), 82 (8:7, 8:11), 120 (8:11), 135 (13:34, 15:12, 17)
  Acts, 72 (3:13–17)
  Romans, 117 (5:12)
  1 Corinthians, 48 (13:4), 133 (16:22), 135 (12:25)
  2 Corinthians, 282 (2:15–16)
  Galatians, 135 (5:13, 6:2)
  Revelation, 31 (6:8), 37 (22:6), 48 (13:5–7)

The Book of Common Prayer
  "The Communion: Proper Preface," 131
  "Forms of Prayer to Be Used at Sea," 10
  "The Litany," 133

Bunyan, John, *Pilgrim's Progress*, 87
Butler, Samuel, *Hudibras*, 33 (3.2.677–82)
Byron, George Gordon Noel, Lord
  Childe Harold's Pilgrimage, 54 (3.301–4), 281 (2.711)
  Don Juan, 283 (canto 1, st. 220, ll. 7–8)
  Heaven and Earth, 67 (1.3.272–73)

Carlyle, Thomas
  "Four Fables," 25

"The Gifted," 25
"Model Prisons," 50
"Occasional Discourse on the Negro Question," 48
Sartor Resartus, 24
Carroll, James Parsons, *Report of the Committee Appointed to Collect Testimony in Relation to the Destruction of Columbia*, 149, 153
Charleston *Courier*, 283, 287, 289
Charleston *Mercury*, 32, 33, 34, 44
Charleston *News and Courier*, 10
Chaucer, Geoffrey, *Canterbury Tales*, "The Wife of Bath's Prologue and Tale", 165 (ll. 866–68)
Cheves, Langdon
  Letter to John Taylor et al., *Niles' Register*, 42
  Speech of the Hon. Langdon Cheves in the Southern Convention at Nashville, 42, 44
Cicero, Marcus Tullius *Brutus*, 187 (125–26)
Croly, George, "The Woe upon Israel," 38 (ll. 35–40), 278 (ll. 35–40)

Davidson, James Wood, *The Living Writers of the South*, 14, 214
De Bow's Review, "Mrs. M'Cord's Caius Gracchus," 1, 14
Dickens, Charles
  Bleak House, 132
  Pickwick Papers, 132
Duyckinck, Evert A., and George L. Duyckinck, *Cyclopaedia of American Literature*, 214

"For He's a Jolly Good Fellow," 152 (st. 2)
Forrest, Mary, *Women of the South Distinguished in Literature*, 214

Goldsmith, Oliver
  The Deserted Village, 97 (l. 164)
  She Stoops to Conquer, 61
Grayson, William J., *The Hireling and the Slave, Chicora, and Other Poems*, 13
Greg, William Rathbone, "English Socialism, and Communistic Associations," 132
Guizot, François, *Democracy in France*, 25

Hale, Sarah Josepha, *Woman's Record*, 10, 13
Hart, John Seely, *The Female Prose Writers of America*, 10
Howe, Julia Ward, "The Battle Hymn of the Republic," 293

Journal des économistes
  "Bibliographie," 27
  "Chronique," 26, 27

Lieber, Francis, *The Necessity of Continued Self-Education*, 48
Livy *Ab urbe condita* 36 (7.6.1–5), 40 (22.45–49)
Longfellow, Henry Wadsworth
  Evangeline, 64 (2.59)
  "Excelsior!" 67
  "Footsteps of Angels," 64 (st. 4)
  "Resignation," 280 (st. 1)
Lucan *De bello civili*, 296 (9.202)

McCord, David James, "Life of a Negro Slave," 92
McCord, Louisa S.
  "British Philanthropy and American Slavery," 12, 13, 75, 90
  Caius Gracchus, 51 (2.4.22–28), 214 (3.1.1–83)
  "Carey on the Slave Trade," 12, 90, 125, 132, 262
  "Diversity of the Races," 12, 73, 283
  "Enfranchisement of Woman," 13, 55, 56, 59
  "Justice and Fraternity," 10, 11, 12
  "Langdon Cheves: Review of 'Reminiscences of Public Men,'" 37
  "Last Will and Testament," 9
  "A Letter to the Duchess of Sutherland from a Lady of South Carolina," 13
  "Memoir of Langdon Cheves," 6, 295
  "Negro and White Slavery," 132
  Poems: "The Comet," 172–73; "Guardian Angels," 174; "Poor Nannie," 13, 166–72; "Thy Will Be Done," 179; "To My Father," 165–66; "The Village Churchyard," 281 (ll. 247–48); "Woman's Progress," 13, 174–78
  "The Right to Labor," 10, 11, 264
  "Separate Secession," 11, 190, 278
  "Slavery and Political Economy," 11
  Sophisms of the Protective Policy, 11
  "*Uncle Tom's Cabin*," 2, 60
  "Woman and Her Needs," 13
Mackay, Charles, "The Good Time Coming," 62 (st. 1)
Mathew, William M., ed., *Agriculture, Geology, and Society in Antebellum South Carolina: The Private Diary of Edmund Ruffin, 1843*, 3

Mill, John Stuart, and Harriet Taylor Mill, "Enfranchisement of Women," 55, 58
Milton, John
  Paradise Lost, 50 (4.800–802, 808), 65 (4.799–809), 73 (4.34–35), 106 (4.201–4); 178 (4.363–64, 6.114–15, 9.538), 281 (1.84–87)
  Il Penseroso, 33 (ll. 173–74)
  "Sonnet X: To the Lady Margaret Ley," 37 (ll. 6–8)
  "Sonnet 18: On the Late Massacre in Piedmont," 35 (l. 10)
Moore, Thomas, "Believe Me, If All Those Endearing Young Charms," 134 (l. 4)
Mulock, Dinah Maria, Woman's Thoughts, 289

New Orleans Delta, 43–44

O'Brien, Michael, ed., An Evening When Alone: Four Journals of Single Women in the South, 1827–67, 5

Paley, William, The Principles of Moral and Political Philosophy, 131, 137
Pliny Natural History, 54 (35.85)
Plutarch
  Fabius Maximus, 40 (14–16)
  Gaius Gracchus, 183 (16.4–17.1), 187 (1.3), 188 (8.4–10.2), 190 (17.5), 193 (17.3–4), 211 (3.3), 216 (6.2), 223 (5.3)
  Tiberius Gracchus, 220 (1.4)
Pope, Alexander
  Eloisa to Abelard, 281 (ll. 99–100)
  An Essay on Man, 147 (2.1–18)
Proceedings of the Woman's Rights Convention, 56, 58
Punch, 289

Quintilian Institutio oratoria, 190 (1.1.6)

Ruffin, Edmund, Report of the Commencement and Progress of the Agricultural Survey of South Carolina, for 1843, 3

Scott, Sir Walter, "Fording the River," 65 (l. 1)
Seneca Epistulae morales, 31 (35.1)
Shakespeare, William
  Coriolanus, 85 (5.3.64–67), 212 (3.2.125–30), 241 (3.3.133–35)
  Hamlet, 39 (1.5.98–99, 102–4), 65 (4.5.180–81), 73 (1.2.139–42), 85 (3.2.237–38), 178 (1.5.27–28), 241 (2.2.553–54)
  2 Henry IV, 23 (1.1.9–11), 140–41 (1.1.154, 157–60)
  Julius Caesar, 208 (3.2.75–109)
  Macbeth, 32 (2.3.109), 38 (1.7.60–62), 43 (1.7.25–28), 131 (3.2.13)
  Merchant of Venice, 65 (1.3.44; 5.1.1), 132 (4.1.253–58), 181 (3.2.97–101)
  Midsummer Night's Dream, 38 (1.2.36–37)
  Othello, 107 (3.3.93), 178 (1.3.401–2)
  Richard II, 23 (2.4.11)
  Richard III, 140 (1.1.18)
  The Tempest, 88
  Venus and Adonis, 107 (l. 1020)
Smith, William Henry, "Miss Mitford's Recollections," 56
Smythe, Louisa McCord, "Recollections," 7, 8–9, 150, 151, 266, 279
Stowe, Harriet Beecher, Sunny Memories of Foreign Lands, 125
Suetonius Gaius Caligula, 44 (55.3)
Swift, Jonathan, Gulliver's Travels, 259

Tennyson, Alfred Lord, "Locksley Hall," 51 (ll. 175–78)

United States Congressional Serials Set, 288

Valerius Maximus Facta et dicta memorabilia, 183 (4.7.2)
Velleius Paterculus Historiae Romanae, 183 (2.6.6)
Vergil Aeneid, 281 (2.274–76)

Woodward, C. Vann, ed., Mary Chesnut's Civil War, 8, 14, 272
Wunder, Richard P., Hiram Powers, 296

THE PUBLICATIONS OF THE

SOUTHERN TEXTS SOCIETY

An Evening When Alone:
Four Journals of Single Women in the South, 1827–67
Edited by Michael O'Brien

Louisa S. McCord: Political and Social Essays
Edited by Richard C. Lounsbury

Civilization and Black Progress:
Selected Writings of Alexander Crummell on the South
Edited by J. R. Oldfield

Louisa S. McCord: Poems, Drama, Biography, Letters
Edited by Richard C. Lounsbury

Soldier and Scholar: Basil Lanneau Gildersleeve and the Civil War
Edited by Ward W. Briggs Jr.

Louisa S. McCord: Selected Writings
Edited by Richard C. Lounsbury